SCOTLAND
WHERE TO STAY

BED & BREAKFAST

D0544648

INSIDE BACK FLAP: KEY TO SYMBOLS AND PAGE MARKER

Published by the Scottish Tourist Board
P.O. Box 705, Edinburgh EH4 3EU

Cover: A Highly Commended Bed and Breakfast in Blairgowrie.

ABOUT THIS BOOK

For more than thirty years, **Where to Stay** has been the Scottish Tourist Board's official guide to holiday accommodation in Scotland. Bed and Breakfast in Scotland is one of the cheapest and most convenient forms of holiday accommodation and is excellent value for money.

Bed and Breakfast places and university accommodation in all parts of Scotland are listed here in alphabetical order by place-name, or, in the case of isolated countryside locations, under the nearest town or village.

If you are looking for accommodation in a particular area, the map section on pages xxvii to xxxii will enable you to identify locations.

Telephone numbers. The telephone number, exchange name and dialling code (in brackets) are given immediately below the address. The dialling code applies to calls made anywhere in the UK except for local calls. If in doubt, call the operator by dialling 100.

Map References. These are given against each place name listed in the guide. The first figure refers to the map number, the latter two figures give the grid reference.

DISABLED VISITORS

Many places listed in this book welcome disabled visitors. Those which have been inspected under the Scottish Tourist Board's Classification and Grading Scheme have their access facilities shown thus:

  Access for wheelchair users without assistance

  A Access for wheelchair users with assistance

  P Access for ambulant disabled

It is always advisable to telephone the establishment in advance for further information.

Details of the criteria used for these symbols are shown on page 219. Further details from STB.

The undernoted organisations are also able to provide further information and advice:—

Scottish Council on Disability
Information Dept
Princes House
5 Shandwick Place
EDINBURGH EH2 4RG
Tel: 031-229 8632

Holiday Care Service
2 Old Bank Chambers
Station Road
HORLEY
Surrey RH6 9HW
Tel: Horley (02934) 74535

BOOKING

It is always advisable to book accommodation in advance. This applies particularly during Easter and July and August.

Your travel agent will always be delighted to help you and to take care of your travel arrangements.

For those who have not booked in advance the accommodation booking services are very useful. More details on page xxvi.

There are about 160 Tourist Information Centres in Scotland, a list of which is given on pages xix to xxvi. Not all operate the Book a Bed Ahead scheme; but whether they do or not, they are always glad to help with accommodation problems.

RESERVATIONS

Whilst the Scottish Tourist Board can give advice and information about any aspect of holidays in Scotland, it is **not** in a position to arrange accommodation or to make reservations; this should be done through a travel agent, a Tourist Information Centre which provides this service or directly to the hotel.

When you accept offered accommodation, on the telephone, or in writing, you are entering into a legally binding contract with the proprietor of the establishment. This means that if you cancel a reservation or fail to take up the accommodation (regardless of the reasons), or leave early, the proprietor will be entitled to compensation if it cannot be relet for all or a good part of the booked period. If a deposit has been paid it is likely to be forfeited and an additional payment may be required.

COMPLAINTS

Any complaints or criticisms about individual hotels or guest houses should where possible be taken up immediately with the management. In most cases the problems can be dealt with satisfactorily, thus avoiding any prolonged unhappiness during your stay.

If this procedure fails to remedy the grievance to your satisfaction, and particularly where serious complaints are concerned, please write to the local Tourist Board (see p. xix).

DOGS

Where dogs are permitted, owners are asked to take responsibility for pets behaviour. In particular, please keep dogs under control in the presence of farm animals.

VALUE ADDED TAX (VAT)

Please note that VAT is calculated by establishments for this publication at a rate of 15%. Any subsequent changes in this rate will affect the price you will be charged.

PRICES

To make this guide available at the earliest possible and practical time for 1987, the information contained has had to be gathered far ahead of the 1987 holiday season. Accordingly, the prices given can only be forecasts of the likely range.

Some establishments have not been able to supply advance information about prices for all of their facilities. Where this is the case, a dash (—) appears in the entry. This does not necessarily mean that the facility will not be available.

There may have been amendments subsequently and in your own interests you should check before making a booking. In addition, prices often vary according to season and are usually lower outside the peak holiday weeks.

The prices quoted in this book are per person per room and they normally represent the minimum (low season) and/or the maximum (high season) charges of the majority of rooms in the establishment and include service charges, if any, and Value Added Tax as applicable. In a few cases where normally breakfast is charged separately, the rates quoted include this charge; it is normally for full breakfast, but as some hotels only provide Continental breakfast, this should be checked at the time of booking. In many cases, double/twin bedded rooms can accommodate families: the availability of these and of family rooms is shown, along with other details.

There is a statutory requirement for establishments which have at least four bedrooms or eight beds to display overnight accommodation charges. When you arrive at a hotel it is in your interests to check prices.

The information given in this publication is as supplied to the Scottish Tourist Board and to the best of the Board's knowledge was correct at the time of going to press. The Scottish Tourist Board can accept no responsibility for any errors or omissions.

September 1986

FRANÇAIS

OÙ SE LOGER EN ECOSSE

Bienvenue en Ecosse!

Voici le guide touristique officiel des hôtels et pensions de famille en Ecosse, publié par l'Office écossais du tourisme. Revu chaque année, ce guide est reconnu depuis trente ans comme le plus complet en son genre. Des hôtels, pensions de famille et résidences universitaires de toutes les régions de l'Ecosse y sont classés selon l'ordre alphabétique des localités. Sauf indication contraire, l'indicatif téléphonique est celui de la localité.

Au moment de mettre sous presse, il ne nous est pas possible de donner des prix définitifs; il est vivement conseillé aux visiteurs de demander confirmation des prix lorsqu'ils effectuent la réservation.

Nous avons signalé à l'attention des gourmets les hôtels qui offrent les spécialités de la cuisine écossaise (recettes écossaises traditionnelles à base de produits écossais de haute qualité).

NB. L'Office écossais du tourisme (Scottish Tourist Board) décline toute responsabilité en cas d'erruers ou d'omissions.

AVERTISSEMENT: CHIENS ETC.

Il est rappelé aux visiteurs étrangers que l'introduction d'animaux domestiques en Grande-Bretagne est soumise à une réglementation très stricte, qui prévoit une longue période de quarantaine. Etant donné le danger de propagation du virus rabique, des peines très sévères sont prévues pour toute infraction aux reglements.

SUR LES ROUTES D'ECOSSE

Veillez à attacher votre ceinture de sécurité, si votre voiture en est munie. Le port de la ceinture est obligatoire en Grande Bretagne.

La légende des symboles se trouve au volet de la couverture, qui fait aussi office de signet.

Logez a l'enseigne de l'hospitalité Ecossaise voir page 220.

DEUTSCH

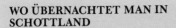

WO ÜBERNACHTET MAN IN SCHOTTLAND

Willkommen in Schottland!

Dieses Buch ist der offizielle Führer des Schottischen Touristenbüros für Ferienübernachtungen in Privatpensionen in Schottland. Seit dreißig Jahren wird dieses Buch als das umfassendste seiner Art anerkannt. Es wird jedes Jahr auf den neuesten Stand gebracht. Hotels, Gasthäuser und Unterbringung in den Universitäten in allen Teilen Schottlands sind hier nach Ortsnamen in alphabetischer Reihenfolge aufgeführt. Die jeweilige Vorwahlnummer ist unter dem Ortsnamen zu finden, außer, wenn sie extra angegeben ist.

Zu Beginn der Drucklegung dieses Buches ist es noch nicht möglich, feste Preise anzugeben, und Besuchern wird daher geraten, sich nach den Tarifen zu erkundigen, wenn sie Buchungen vornehmen.

Das Schottische Touristenbüro (Scottish Tourist Board) kann keine Verantwortung für eventuelle Fehler oder Auslassung von Preisen und Einrichtungen übernehmen.

Als weitere Hilfe haben wir die Privatpensionen gekennzeichnet, die echte schottische Küche—Taste of Scotland— anbieten. Das bedeutet, daß hier traditionell schottische Rezepte verwandt werden unter Benutzung schottischer Produkte von hoher Qualität.

HUNDE

Das Mitbringen von Tieren jeder Art aus dem Ausland ist wegen Tollwutgefahr strengstens untersagt. Die Übertretung dieses Gesetzes wird mit hohen Strafen belegt.

AUTOFAHREN IN SCHOTTLAND

Schnallen Sie sich immer an! Es wird nun zur Pflicht. (Vorausgesetzt, Ihr Auto ist mit Sicherheitsgurt ausgestattet.)

Die Zeichenerklärungen befinden sich im eingeklebten Faltblatt am Ende des Buches.

Übernachten sie dort, wo sie das Zeichen für echt Schottische Gastlichkeit Sehen Seihe Seite 222.

CLASSIFICATION AND GRADING OF ACCOMMODATION IN SCOTLAND

STAY WHERE YOU SEE THE SIGN OF A REAL SCOTTISH WELCOME

We've made sure there's a comfortable welcome waiting at hundreds of places to stay in Scotland.

Now there's no need to puzzle over which hotel, guest house, B & B or self-catering accommodation best suits you.

We've introduced a new easy to understand classification and grading scheme so you can find at a glance *exactly* what you're looking for.

WHAT DOES CLASSIFICATION MEAN?

The *classifications*, from 'Listed' to five crowns, are awarded according to the *range* of facilities available. In hotels, guest houses and B & Bs, a 'Listed' classification guarantees, for example, that your bed conforms to a minimum size, that hot and cold water is available at all reasonable times, that breakfast is provided and that there is adequate heating according to the season.

In self-catering accommodation, one crown means that you have a minimum size of unit, at least one twin or double bedroom, dining and cooking facilities suitable for the number of occupants, and a refridgerator.

Naturally, more crowns mean more facilities. A five crown establishment will provide many extras for your holiday comfort. To name just two, in five crown hotels *all* rooms have 'en suite' bathrooms, and five crown self-catering units provide the labour-saving fittings of home, including a dishwasher.

All classifications have been checked by our fully-trained team of independent officers.

CLASSIFICATION AND GRADING OF ACCOMMODATION IN SCOTLAND

WHAT ABOUT GRADING?

While classification is all about facilities, *grading* is solely concerned with their *quality*. The grades awarded—'Approved', 'Commended' or 'Highly Commended'—are based upon an independent assessment of a wide variety of items, ranging from the appearance of the buildings and tidiness of the gardens, to the quality of the furnishings, fittings and floor coverings. Cleanliness is an absolute requirement—and, of course, our officers know the value of a warm and welcoming smile.

Like classification, grading is carried out by the Scottish Tourist Board's expert team.

You can find excellent quality in all kinds of places to stay in Scotland, irrespective of the range of facilities offered: for example, a 'Listed' B & B, with the minimum of facilities, but offering excellent quality, would be awarded a 'Highly Commended' grade while a five crown self-catering property would be graded as 'Approved' if the quality of its extensive facilities was assessed as average.

SO HOW DOES THE NEW SCHEME HELP YOU PLAN YOUR HOLIDAY?

Quite simply, it offers a guarantee of both the range of facilities and their quality. Many of the establishments listed in this brochure have been inspected and this is highlighted in their entries. When you choose accommodation that has been classified, or classified and graded, you have the reassurance that what is being offered has been independently checked.

Equally, if you're on a touring holiday, and booking accommodation as you go, the new scheme can help you. All places to stay which have been inspected bear a distinctive blue oval sign by their entrance showing the classification and grade awarded. And if you call in at a Tourist Information Centre you can ask for a list of local establishments that have joined the scheme, which will include those which are shown in this brochure as *awaiting inspection* at time of going to press.

Whatever kind of accommodation you're looking for, you can be sure the new classification and grading scheme will help you find it.

Please note that where self-catering establishments offer a number of units of differing classifications and grades, their entry in this brochure is shown as 'Up to' the highest award held. You should ascertain the specific classification and grade of an individual unit at time of booking.

Please also note that establishments are visited annually and therefore classifications and grades may therefore change from year to year.

YOUR HOLIDAY IN SCOTLAND

USEFUL INFORMATION ABOUT SCOTLAND

TRAVEL

Bookings for rail, sea and air travel to Scotland and within Scotland should be made through your travel agent, or directly to British Rail, airlines and ferry companies. The Scottish Tourist Board will be glad to give you information but cannot make your bookings for you.

Seats may be booked in advance on the main long-distance coaches, aircraft and for berths and cabins in the steamers to the islands. Sleeping berths on trains should always be booked well in advance. It is necessary to book seats for 'extended' coach tours and also for day coach outings operated from most holiday and touring centres.

Car hire bookings should also be made in advance wherever possible, especially for July and August. Taxis are readily available in Edinburgh, Glasgow, and other major centres at controlled charges. Taxis are generally available in most communities, but in smaller, less populous areas charges may vary considerably.

DRIVING

The 'Rules of the Road' are the same in Scotland as in the rest of the U.K. While there is limited motorway mileage in Scotland, the roads are uniformly good. In the remoter areas there is a considerable mileage of one-way roads, with frequent passing-places. Please, *never* use these passing-places as lay-bys—or for overnight parking of caravans. Slow-moving traffic (and motorists towing caravans), are asked to pull in to passing places, where appropriate, to let faster traffic through.

When touring in the far north and west particularly, remember that petrol stations are comparatively few, and distances between them may be considerable. Some petrol stations close on Sundays. Fill your tank in good time, and keep it as full as possible.

Remember, it is now law that the driver and front passenger must wear seat belts.

SCOTLAND'S WEATHER

Did you know that in June, places in the north of Scotland have an average of 18-20 hours of daylight each day, and that resorts on the east coast are particularly noted for their hours of sunshine?

June has those marvellous long evenings when it's light till very late, and the palm trees which grow on the west coast must say something about how warm it is.

Yes, we do have to admit, it does sometimes rain in Scotland; but rainfall is surprisingly low despite the age-old myths. The rainfall in the Edinburgh area, for example, is almost exactly the same as that around London—and Rome for that matter. And don't forget, even if you do get caught in a shower, that Scotland is well-endowed with a whole host of indoor attractions to keep you entertained till long after the sun has come out again.

PUBLIC HOLIDAYS

The Bank Holidays which are also general holidays in England do not apply in Scotland. Most Bank Holidays apply to banks and to some professional and commercial offices only, although Christmas Day and New Year's Day are usually taken as holidays by everyone. Scottish banks are closed in 1987 on 1 and 2 January, 17 April, 4 and 25 May, 3 August, 25 and 28 December. In place of the general holidays, Scottish cities and towns normally have a Spring Holiday and an Autumn Holiday. The dates of these holidays vary from place to place, but they are almost invariably on a Monday.

MONEY

Currency, coinage and postal rates in Scotland are the same as in the rest of the U.K. Scotland differs from England in that Scottish banks issue their own notes. These are acceptable in England, at face value, as are Bank of England notes in Scotland. Main banks are open during the following hours:

Monday, Tuesday, Wednesday: 0930-1230; 1330-1530

Thursday: 0930-1230; 1330-1530; 1630-1800

Friday: 0930-1530

Some city centre banks are open daily 0930-1530 and on Saturdays.

In rural areas, banks post their hours clearly outside and travelling banks call regularly.

SHOPPING

The normal shopping hours in Scotland are 0900-1730, although bakeries, dairies and newsagents open earlier. Many shops have an early closing day (1300) each week, but the actual day varies from place to place and in cities from district to district.

Many city centre shops also stay open late on one evening each week.

EATING

Lunch in restaurants and hotels outside the main centres is usually served between 1230 and 1400. Dinner usually starts at 1900 or 1930 and may not be served much after 2100. Where you know you may arrive late it is advisable to make arrangements for a meal in advance. An alternative to dinner is High Tea, usually served between 1630 and 1830.

A TASTE OF SCOTLAND

When eating out, don't forget to sample a 'Taste of Scotland'. Look out for the 'Stockpot' sign at hotels and restaurants. This indicates that the establishment offers traditional Scottish recipes using the best of Scottish produce: Scottish soups with intriguing names like Powsowdie or Cullen Skink; Aberdeen Angus steaks or venison or game in season; salmon or trout from Scottish rivers, or herring or haddock cured in a variety of ways; and a choice of some 30 varieties of Scottish . cheese—these are some of the 'Tastes of

Scotland' which add to the enjoyment of a holiday. For your free copy of the 1987 booklet, write to: Taste of Scotland Ltd, 23 Ravelston Terrace, Edinburgh EH4 3EU.

LICENSING LAWS

Currently in Scotland, the hours that public houses and hotel bars are open to serve drinks are the same all over the country. 'Pubs' are open from 1100 to 1430 and from 1700 to about 2300 hours, Monday to Saturday inclusive and most are now licensed to open on Sundays. In addition, some establishments may have obtained extended licences for afternoon or late night opening.

Hotel bars have the same hours as 'pubs', and are open on Sundays from 1230 to 1430 and 1830 to 2300. Residents in licensed hotels may have drinks served at any time. Some restaurants and hotels have extended licences allowing them to serve drinks with meals until 0100 in the morning. Persons under the age of 18 are not allowed to drink in licensed premises.

CHURCHES

The established Church of Scotland is Presbyterian, but the Roman Catholic and other denominations have very considerable numbers of adherents. The Episcopal Church of Scotland is in full communion with the Church of England, and uses a similar form of worship. In the far north and west of Scotland, particularly in the islands, many people belong to the Free Church of Scotland, and appreciate it when their views on the Sabbath as a day when there should be no recreational or other unnecessary activity, are respected by visitors. Times of services of the various denominations are usually intimated on hotel notice boards, as well as outside the churches and, of course, visitors are always welcome.

COMING FROM OVERSEAS?

Visitors to Scotland from overseas require to observe the same regulations as for other parts of the U.K. As a general rule they must have a valid passport and, in certain cases, visas issued by British Consular authorities overseas: check with a local Travel Agent, or where appropriate, the overseas offices of the British Tourist Authority.

Currency: Overseas visitors who require information about the import and export of currency, cars, or other goods, on personal purchases and belongings, shopping concessions, etc., should consult a Travel Agent or Bank or the overseas offices of the B.T.A.

Driving: Motorists coming from overseas who are members of a motoring organisation in their own country may obtain from them full details of the regulations for importing cars, motor cycles, etc., for holiday and touring purposes into the U.K. They can drive in Britain on a current Driving Licence from their own country, or with an international Driving Permit, for a maximum period of 12 months. Otherwise, a British Driving Licence must be obtained: until the Driving Test is passed it is essential to be accompanied by a driver with a British licence.

Seat belts: Drivers and front seat passengers **must** wear safety belts while driving in Britain, by law.

VAT: Value Added Tax, currently charged at 15% on many goods, can sometimes be reclaimed by overseas visitors who buy items for export. Visitors should ask the shopkeeper about the retail export schemes before making a purchase, and will be required to fill in special forms.

RABIES

Britain is *very* concerned to prevent the spread of rabies. Strict quarantine regulations apply to animals brought into Britain from abroad and severe penalties are enforced if they are broken or ignored. Dogs and cats are subject to 6 months quarantine in an approved quarantine centre. Full details from the Department of Agriculture and Fisheries for Scotland, Chesser House, 500 Gorgie Road, Edinburgh EH11 3AW. The restrictions do not apply to animals from Eire, Northern Ireland, the Isle of Man or the Channel Islands.

SCOTLAND'S TOURIST AREAS

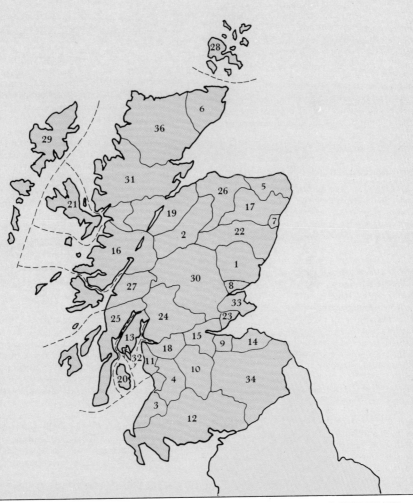

DETAILS OF SOME OF THE ATTRACTIONS OF THESE AREAS ARE TO BE FOUND ON THE FOLLOWING PAGES.

SCOTLAND'S TOURIST AREAS

1

Angus

Angus is situated on the east coast of Scotland between two rivers, the Tay and the North Esk. From the North Sea edge, with cliffs and harbours set to north and south by miles of golden sands, it stretches inland through picturesque villages and scenic glens to the foothills of the eastern Grampians. The six towns — Arbroath, Brechin, Carnoustie, Forfar, Kirriemuir and Montrose — have many interesting individual attractions and the entire district is rich in historical, literary and architectural features. A warm welcome awaits visitors to the area which offers a wide variety of recreations and pursuits together with the opportunity to relax in bracing sea breezes or balmy country air, and all compactly contained within an approximate 100-mile boundary.

2

Aviemore and Spey Valley

Dominated by tree-clad, craggy mountains, river, loch and stream, the Spey Valley offers a unique welcome. Come climbing and ski-ing in the mighty Cairngorms, sailing and canoeing on rivers and lochs and angling in the famous River Spey. History abounds with ruined castles and a relic of the Jacobite rebellion, the formidable Ruthven Barracks. Folk and clan museums, wildlife and nature parks, osprey, reindeer and breathtaking scenery provide a land of contrast. Accommodation in hotels, guest and farmhouses, caravan and campsites and the attractions of modern holiday complexes such as the Aviemore Centre offer all the year round Highland hospitality.

3

Ayrshire and Burns Country

Ayrshire and Burns Country, situated on the south-west coast of Scotland, offers something for everyone. The area's rich and colourful heritage is depicted by the many castles, both ruined and otherwise, scattered throughout the district. Robert Burns, Scotland's National Poet, was born at Alloway, the starting point for the Burns Heritage Trail. With fifteen golf courses, including three championship ones, Turnberry, Troon and Prestwick, the area is aptly described as a paradise for any golfer. With no shortage of good accommodation and entertainment facilities, why not visit ABC Land and see for yourself that it's just too good to miss!

4

Ayrshire Valleys

The Ayrshire Valleys Tourist Board Area— Kilmarnock and Loudoun and Cumnock and Doon Valley is the very heart of Scotland. Every year more and more tourists discover the special appeal of the Ayrshire Valleys. Much of the history of Scotland is here in stone and in reputation. From this area came individuals who contributed massively to the progress of mankind, inventions bringing benefits world wide, industrial innovation and literature. This heritage together with the gentle scenic beauty and the warm hospitality of Ayrshire make the Ayrshire Valleys increasingly popular for the tourist who seeks the real Scotland.

5

Banff and Buchan

Banff and Buchan is the unspoiled shoulder of Scotland which divides the North Sea from the Moray Firth. Magnificent cliffs, nesting places of the puffin, tower over picturesque fishing villages and sandy inlets. Inland, uncrowded roads lead you through the fertile, rolling countryside to the beauty of Aden Country Park, the baroque splendour of Duff House and to Fyvie Castle, the pride of the Castles of the north east. Eight good golf courses, the finest bowling greens, riding, fishing and windsurfing add to the range of activities available. The friendly local folk will welcome you with a cheery smile to a wide range of comfortable and good value accommodation, ranging from snug hotels to beach-side caravans.

Tourist Information Centres in these areas and addresses to write for further information are on pages xx to xxvi.

SCOTLAND'S TOURIST AREAS

6
Caithness

The John O'Groats Peninsula is an area of captivating contrasts. Here, craggy cliffs, spectacular rock stacks, historic harbours and beautiful beaches all contribute to some of the most magnificent coastal scenery in Europe. Many sea birds nest at Duncansby Head, and elsewhere you can see otters, seals and foxes. Caithness is a treasure house for historians, with mediaeval churches, mysterious stone circles, cairns, brochs and castles towering on cliff tops. In Thurso and Wick—the main towns in northern Scotland—you'll find a good selection of shops, and craftsmen producing woollens, pottery and the famous Caithness Glass.

7
City of Aberdeen

Aberdeen, 'Britain in Bloom' winner, Chelsea gold medal winner. All year round amazing floral displays delight the visitor — in the breathtaking Winter Gardens, or by roads, rivers, offices and houses, in parks and gardens, where crocuses, daffodils or roses carpet the ground. But there is much more to Aberdeen than flowers. A historic city with royal charters from the 12th century, Aberdeen has fascinating areas and buildings to explore; interesting museums and art galleries to browse in; sports a-plenty to try; shops and restaurants to visit; events and festivals to experience; entertainment — and Britain's most beautiful theatre — to enjoy. Aberdeen — The Flower of Scotland.

8
City of Dundee

An idyllic setting along the north bank of the River Tay Estuary, with the backcloth of the Grampian Mountains, gives Dundee one of the healthiest locations in the world. Apart from the benefits of the river — sea angling, salmon and trout fishing and sailing — it is also one of the best golf centres in the world.

Within an hour's drive there are over 40 golf courses including St Andrews, Carnoustie and Gleneagles. Three under-cover shopping malls, ample central parking. Steeped in history, Dundonians are also very friendly and proud of their parks and gardens.

9
City of Edinburgh

Edinburgh, Scotland's beautiful capital and international Festival City, is full of historic and romantic interest. It is surrounded by hills, woodlands and rivers and also features an extensive coastline. The City is dominated by its ancient fortress towering above gardens which during the summer feature a full programme of musical entertainment including Highland and Scottish country dancing. Explore the treasures of the Royal Mile or enjoy quality shopping on Princes Street. For the young, and not so young, there is always something interesting to see or do. A warm welcome awaits you.

10
Clyde Valley

The Clyde Valley — Scotland's Garden Centre linking the districts of Hamilton, Motherwell and Clydesdale stretches south east from the outskirts of Glasgow to the Lowther Hills, following the River Clyde and the A74 almost to the Border. Traditionally an area renowned for its healthy air, today the Clyde Valley is able to boast some of Scotland's best known history and scenery. Like New Lanark, Europe's most important industrial archaeological site; the famous Clydeside Orchard Country — blossom, pick-your-own fruit and garden centres. Elsewhere — castles, nature reserves, visitor centres, museums, shopping centres and acres of beautiful countryside to explore. Planning to tour Scotland? Base yourself here — Edinburgh, Glasgow, The Trossachs, Borders, Burns Country and Ayrshire are all within easy driving distance. With good road and rail connections, discovering the Clyde Valley couldn't be easier.

Tourist Information Centres in these areas and addresses to write for further information are on pages xx to xxvi.

SCOTLAND'S TOURIST AREAS

11
Cunninghame

On Scotland's west coast — encompassing north Ayrshire and the islands of Arran and Cumbrae, this area is rich in natural beauty. The mainland coastline has many fine beaches, with superb golf courses backing them. The islands have a magic of their own: peace, tranquility, yet plenty to do from cycling to mountain climbing. The Magnum Leisure Centre, with twin flumes, in Irvine's beachpark, ranks as one of the largest in Europe, and the coastal resorts of Saltcoats, Ardrossan and Largs have much to offer including Largs' world famous Viking Festival.

12
Dumfries and Galloway

This is a relatively undiscovered corner of Scotland, but for the discerning tourist looking for beaches and hills; castles and abbeys, museums and gardens; sea angling and salmon fishing; or a winter holiday away from the rigours of ski-ing: it is an area you are unlikely to forget. One of Scotland's principal highways, the A74, cuts through the area from south to north. So why don't you leave the headlong flight to others and take yourself off the dual carriageway into the quiet and meandering byways of Dumfries and Galloway. You will not regret it!

13
Dunoon and The Cowal Peninsula

Holidaying on an island stirs the romantic blood. Cowal is an island — well almost! The majority of visitors travel on one of the two short ferry crossings from Gourock to Dunoon, but you can 'Take the High Road' and be in Dunoon in under two hours from Glasgow. Being slightly off-the-beaten-track of the 'doing Scotland' tourist brigade, the Cowal Peninsula is a peaceful corner of Argyll where you can travel on quiet, uncluttered roads, where you can relax and enjoy our magnificent scenery,

our mountains, our seascapes, our lochs and glens, and the steeply wooded hillsides of the Argyll Forest Park.

14
East Lothian

East Lothian is an area rich in contrasts which provides just about everything for the family. You can be assured of a genuine welcome, good food, unspoilt scenery, historic sites, perfect stretches of golden sand, the opportunity for recreation or the relief of doing simply nothing. Hotels and guest houses, with 14 golf courses on their doorstep, specialise in catering for the golfer and his family. East Lothian — an experience you will treasure for a lifetime.

15
Forth Valley

Crowned by the magnificent Forth Bridges, Forth Valley has a wealth of history: neolithic Cairnpapple; the Antonine Wall in Falkirk; Scotland's ancient capital, Dunfermline; quaint 17th century burgh, Culross; picturesque Linlithgow Palace, birthplace of Mary Queen of Scots; elegant stately homes, The Binns, Dalmeny and Hopetoun Houses; and relics of the industrial age, the canals and Bo'ness Steam Railway. Enjoy the countryside in the beautiful parks at Muiravonside, Lochore Meadows and Beecraigs. And remember, Forth Valley is just half an hour away from Edinburgh or Glasgow and makes an ideal centre for visiting Edinburgh Castle or Glasgow's Burrell Collection.

16
Fort William and Lochaber

All the delights of Scotland and the Highlands come together in Lochaber, an area of 1,755 square miles with Fort William at the centre. From Glencoe in the south to the Small Isles of Muck, Rhum, Eigg and Canna in the west, Lochaber encompasses many of Scotland's

Tourist Information Centres in these areas and addresses to write for further information are on pages xx to xxvi.

superlatives including Ben Nevis, Britain's highest mountain, and Loch Morar, the deepest loch. The land of 'bens, glens and heroes', Lochaber is resonant with Scottish history. And there's always something to do in Fort William, with its many shops, hotels, restaurants and leisure facilities.

17
Gordon

You have to be prepared for enchantment if you choose to come to Gordon District. Gordon's countryside varies from the sandy beaches of Balmedie on the east coast to the upland terrain of the western part of Strathdon. Follow the Castle Trail and visit restored castles and romantic ruins. Age-old crafts are being revived and visitors are welcome. But Gordon is not just for the spectator — it is a paradise for anglers, golfers, skiers, hillwalkers, railway enthusiasts and malt whisky drinkers. Your holiday in Gordon District can be as quiet and relaxing or as energetic and lively as you care to make it.

18
Greater Glasgow

Glasgow, Scotland's largest city, is the cultural capital of Scotland. It is home to Scottish Opera, Scottish National Orchestra, Scottish Ballet and the Scottish Theatre Company and a priceless collection of art treasures in a number of museums. Of the top twenty tourist attractions in the country, Glasgow has six including the magnificent Burrell Collection, Scotland's No. 1 attraction. The area is also ideal for shopping and entertainment. With its many first-class hotels and excellent communications by road, rail and air, Greater Glasgow is an ideal touring base from which to explore the rest of Scotland.

19
Inverness, Loch Ness and Nairn

In Inverness, the Capital of the Highlands, the shopping and accommodation are excellent, while entertainment sparkles more brightly each year. Nearby the famous monster haunts Loch Ness and the Caledonian Canal offers passage to all types of craft. Nairn, a long time favourite for family holidays, with its glorious beaches and long hours of sunshine, is also a mecca for golfers. At Culloden Moor and Cawdor Castle the history of the area comes alive. Visit this hub of the Highlands for a combination of the best of the past and of today.

20
Isle of Arran

A Hebridean refugee sheltering in the Firth of Clyde, the Isle of Arran is only an hour's sail from the mainland port of Ardrossan, which connects with rail and road traffic. Towering mountains in the north, soft rolling lands in the south, sixty miles of glorious coastline with sub-tropical palms, glens, inland lochs and waterfalls — a veritable photographer's paradise. Past and present merge when you gaze across the Firth once scoured by the Vikings and crossed by Bruce and his 300. The energetic will appreciate the Island's hillwalking and climbing — the only problem is where to start.

21
The Isle of Skye and South West Ross

A short ferry trip from South West Ross, Skye has over 900 miles of coastline rich in bays and towering cliffs, dominated by the great ridge of the Cuillin Mountains. Rich in Bonnie Prince Charlie's history it has a romantic but awe-inspiring atmosphere which can only be felt by visiting this remarkable island. The old way of life is reflected in the Black House Museums, contemporary crafts are plentiful and unusual, from candle-making to hand-weaving. With South West Ross so close on the main land, rich too in its own history — the whole area 'comes well recommended'.

Tourist Information Centres in these areas and addresses to write for further information are on pages xx to xxvi.

SCOTLAND'S TOURIST AREAS

22
Kincardine and Deeside

Kincardine and Deeside extends a heartfelt welcome and invites you to a feast of ever changing spectacle and colour — from the regal splendour of Balmoral Castle, the Scottish summer residence of the Royal Family to the thrilling sights and sounds of the world famous Braemar Gathering, to the homeland of the sparkling Dee famous for its salmon fishing. Lush pine-clad hillsides rise from its banks, while along its length a wonderland of romantic castles speak of the sometimes turbulent past. Our coastline is as varied as it is beautiful. Kincardine and Deeside is an experience you will never forget.

23
Kirkcaldy

Kirkcaldy and District is an area rich in heritage which has been preserved to ensure you will remember your stay. In Kirkcaldy, with its fine views across the Firth of Forth, you can trace the lives of Adam Smith, the philosopher, or Robert Adam, the architect; or admire the skill of the local Wemyss Ware pottery. There are many picturesque seaside villages in the area including the holiday towns of Burntisland, Kinghorn and Leven, while inland there is plenty of scope for walks and golf. If you want to travel further afield, the attractions of the East Neuk of Fife, Perth, Falkland Palace and Loch Leven are just a short drive away.

24
Loch Lomond, Stirling and the Trossachs

Bridging the gap between highlands and lowlands lies the scenic splendour of Loch Lomond and the Trossachs combining with the excitement of historic Stirling. Underlying the visual impact, feel the brooding atmosphere of the area's heritage; the land of folk hero Rob Roy McGregor, the stirring site of

Bannockburn, and the castle homes of Scotland's royalty and aristocracy. Couple this with some of today's fascinating visitor attractions; lose yourself in the tranquility of a boat trip on one of the lochs; or walk the unspoilt country paths, all before coming home to Scottish hospitality within a superb choice of accommodation.

25
Mid Argyll, Kintyre and Islay

Situated in the South West Highlands, this holiday area has over 1,000 miles of coastline, heavily indented with attractive sea lochs and natural harbours — a yachtsman's paradise. Hillwalking and loch fishing, golf and archaeology, sub-tropical gardens and bird watching — a gentle countryside to enjoy these varied pursuits. Blessed with a temperate climate the Atlantic seaboard on Kintyre and Islay provides a habitat for many species of wintering birds, especially geese. Enjoy the colourful sub-tropical gardens which flourish on Gigha and at Crarae, all year round golf, the ultimate seclusion of exploration on Jura — holidays to suit everyone.

26
Moray

Moray District lies on the sunny southern shores of the Moray Firth, midway between Aberdeen and Inverness, embracing the ancient bishopric whose symbol is the magnificent ruined Cathedral of Elgin. Along the coast sandy beaches alternate with villages whose traditional architecture is a link with the prosperous times of the fishing industry. Inland the fertile farmlands of Moray rise gently through extensive forest and beyond the River Spey — famed among salmon fishermen — to the high Cairngorm Mountains. Moray is the heart of the whisky industry, with almost half of Scotland's distilleries within its borders, many of them open to visitors.

Tourist Information Centres in these areas and addresses to write for further information are on pages xx to xxvi.

SCOTLAND'S TOURIST AREAS

27
Oban, Mull and District

Oban is the gateway to a world of tranquillity — to the enchantment of the highlands and the Hebrides. Sail away to the dreaming isles of Mull, Coll, Tiree, Staffa and the Holy Isle of Iona — or escape to the naturalists' paradise of Colonsay. Explore the land of Lorne — the grandeur of its mountains, winding lochs, whispering forests — villages, castles, gardens — and, of course, the town of Oban itself. Wherever you go you will find traditional hospitality in the friendly shops, the Highland Games and Ceilidhs — and, from country house to country cottage, holiday accommodation to suit all tastes.

28
Orkney

Separated by a mere six miles from mainland Scotland, the low lying fertile islands that comprise Orkney have an abundance of treasures. Here is the richest historic area in Scotland, some sites being of European importance. Orkney is home to over one million seabirds and has nine RSPB reserves. The lochs of Orkney provide wild brown trout and no permits are required. The surrounding waters provide good sea angling with record-breaking Skate and Halibut. Scapa Flow and its sunken German warships is Europe's best dive site. Add to this the genuine friendliness and hospitality of the people and you can be assured of an island adventure in Britain's Treasure Islands.

29
Outer Hebrides

Due to their separation from the mainland of Scotland the Outer Hebrides have a unique character all of their own. This splintered sweep of islands, stretching 130 miles from the Butt of Lewis to Barra Head incorporates six immensely beautiful holiday islands. On the west coasts there are long stretches of pasture land with wild flowers and miles of clean sandy beaches. The eastern coasts are rugged with cliffs and small bays which have an atmosphere all their own. The islands are ideal for ornithology and archaeology, for fishing and sea angling, for the photographer, or the holidaymaker seeking peace and tranquillity.

30
Perthshire

Break away to Perthshire, the heartland of Scotland, and explore one of Europe's most beautiful holiday regions. Over 2,000 square miles of Highland lochs, hidden glens and historic lowlands are yours to discover. Whether you come by rail, air or road, we know you'll come back again to enjoy our unrivalled hospitality, superb sporting facilities, and relaxing way of life. Sir Walter Scott once wrote, "If an intelligent stranger were asked to describe the most varied and most beautiful province in Scotland, it is probable that he would name the country of Perthshire". Our visitors all agree.

31
Ross and Cromarty

Explore the coast of Wester Ross and you'll discover breathtaking mountains and great cliffs. Wander through East Ross and the Black Isle, and you'll be amid gentle hills, woods and charming Highland villages. Coast to coast — there's plenty to surprise and interest you. The incredible sub-tropical Inverewe Gardens, Torridon's mighty peaks and Hugh Miller's Cottage in Cromarty. Visit Strathpeffer, the Victorian spa village or Ullapool and enjoy a pleasure cruise to the Summer Isles. Golfers, walkers and fishers can always find new experiences or alternately just laze on sandy beaches such as the Golden Sands at Gairloch.

Tourist Information Centres in these areas and addresses to write for further information are on pages xx to xxvi.

SCOTLAND'S TOURIST AREAS

32
Rothesay and Isle of Bute

The Isle of Bute has long been one of Scotland's favourite holiday retreats, set in the heart of the glorious Firth of Clyde. Safe, sandy beaches adorn the coastline. There are enough entertainments and facilities in Rothesay alone to amuse the whole family. There's golf on three courses, each enjoying spectacular views; sailing and cruising; walking, cycling and bowling. Delve into Bute's rich history at the ancient Castle and the Bute Museum. All this just 30 minutes by ferry from Wemyss Bay (serving Central Scotland and the motorways) or only 5 minutes across the Kyles of Bute from Colintraive (Argyll).

33
St Andrews and North East Fife

North East Fife, approximately one hour from Edinburgh by road or rail, lies between the Firth of Forth and the River Tay. The coastline from Lundin Links to Crail — 'The East Neuk' — is a chain of delightful fishing villages and forms part of Scotland's Fishing Heritage Trail. Inland, the many places of interest to visitors are linked by a network of quiet country roads centred on the market town of Cupar. The university town and holiday resort of St Andrews is famous too as the 'Home of Golf' and the Old Course is the venue for many international tournaments.

34
Scottish Borders

In Scotland's south-eastern corner, the Scottish Borders is a land of rolling hills, wooded river valleys, prosperous farmland and rugged castles. A link with the region's turbulent past is evidenced by the hilltop ruins of castles and keeps, while the ruined abbeys remind the visitor of a more peaceful era, and there are houses from various times. The thriving woollen textile industry produces quality knitwear and tweeds. The River Tweed, famous for its salmon fishing, threads its way through the region, and provides a superb setting for many of the towns and villages of the region.

35
Shetland

The enchanting Shetland islands lie almost as close to Norway as to Scotland and the Viking heritage lives on in culture, dialect and place names. A scattered mosaic of 100 islands or skerries, there is so much to see and explore. Nature abounds — the cliffs are teeming with birds, the lochs are filled with trout, ponies roam the hills, and seals and otters frequent the bays. Transport to Shetland is easy with frequent daily flights and drive-on drive-off ferries. For a holiday abroad in Britain, visit Shetland — the natural holiday choice.

36
Sutherland

Sutherland is a scenic area of great beauty, with mystical sea-lochs, magnificent mountains, crystal-clear streams, rugged coastline, picturesque villages and vibrant moorlands laced with quiet meandering roads. Visit Dunrobin Castle with its fairytale turrets, marvel at our range of peaks and discover the huge sea cliffs near Cape Wrath and awesome Smoo Cave. You won't believe how clean and extensive our beaches are: fishing, golf, climbing and walking are well provided for — Royal Dornoch golf course is ranked in the top 10 in the world! So come north and visit us soon. Getting to Sutherland couldn't be easier on the new A9.

Tourist Information Centres in these areas and addresses to write for further information are on pages xx to xxvi.

TOURIST INFORMATION CENTRES

i Scotland has about 160 local Tourist Information Centres dispersed throughout many towns and villages. These Centres offer you a friendly welcome, information and help with:

* places to stay
* places to see
* things to do
* routes to take
* local events
* detailed literature

PLACES TO STAY

Almost all Centres have accommodation booking services offering both LOCAL BED-BOOKING and the BOOK-A-BED-AHEAD scheme for hotels, guest houses, and bed and breakfast.

Even at short notice, many Centres can also help you book a self catering holiday in their areas, using up-to-date lists of available accommodation. Centres marked with an asterisk * in the next few pages offer this service.

PLACES TO SEE

All Centres have friendly and well-informed staff ready to tell you about castles and abbeys, museums, walks and trails and all the special delights in the area. Many Centres have displays of local attractions and posters giving details of opening times and charges.

THINGS TO DO

Local bus, rail, ferry and air time-tables are usually available for consultation and staff will be delighted to offer their suggestions on the best way to get you to your destination. They may, too, offer you suggestions of ways you'd never thought of, like the Postbus service.

ROUTES TO TAKE

There are always maps and advice available to ensure that you discover all the delights of the local countryside for yourself. Staff will help you plan your day trips to see the sights and to take the most attractive routes in the area.

LOCAL EVENTS

Tourist Information Centres are always the best place to find out what's on in the area, particularly special events, festivals and important happenings. They get detailed day-to-day information to make sure you don't miss something which would make your stay in the area an even more memorable one.

DETAILED LITERATURE

All the information services of these Centres are backed up by a wide range of publications, some free, some saleable, which are available to you. Many Centres produce their own publications and all can offer you the local area booklets and those published by the Scottish Tourist Board.

SCOTTISH TOURIST INFORMATION CENTRES

Call in for more information on Scotland.

London: 19 Cockspur Street, tel: 01-930 8661/2/3
Southwaite: M6 Service Area, Cumbria (south of Carlisle)
Edinburgh: 14 South St Andrew Street

TOURIST INFORMATION CENTRES

1

Angus
ARBROATH ✉ 🛏
Angus Tourist Board
Information Centre
Market Place
Tel: Arbroath (0241) 72609/76680
Jan-Dec

BRECHIN
Angus Tourist Board
Information Centre
St. Ninian's Place
Tel: Brechin (03562) 3050
June-Sept
✉ Arbroath

CARNOUSTIE 🛏
Angus Tourist Board
Information Centre
24 High Street
Tel: Carnoustie (0241) 52258
Jan-Dec
✉ Arbroath

FORFAR
Angus Tourist Board
Information Centre
The Myre
Tel: Forfar (0307) 67876
June-Sept
✉ Arbroath

KIRRIEMUIR
Angus Tourist Board
Information Centre
Bank Street
Tel: Kirriemuir (0575) 74097
June-Sept
✉ Arbroath

MONTROSE 🛏
Angus Tourist Board
Information Centre
212 High Street
Tel: Montrose (0674) 72000
Jan-Dec
✉ Arbroath

2

Aviemore and Spey Valley
AVIEMORE * ✉ 🛏
Aviemore and Spey Valley
Tourist Board
Main Road
Tel: Aviemore (0479) 810363
Jan-Dec

BOAT OF GARTEN * 🛏
Boat Hotel Car Park
Tel: Boat of Garten (047983) 307
May-Sept
✉ Aviemore

CARRBRIDGE * 🛏
Information Centre
Village Car Park
Tel: Carrbridge (047 984) 630
May-Sept
✉ Aviemore

GRANTOWN-ON-SPEY * 🛏
Information Centre
54 High Street
Tel: Grantown-on-Spey (0479) 2773
Jan-Dec
✉ Aviemore

KINGUSSIE * 🛏
Information Centre
King Street
Tel: Kingussie (054 02) 297
May-Sept
✉ Aviemore

NEWTONMORE * 🛏
Information Centre
Main Street
Tel: Newtonmore (054 03) 274
May-Sept
✉ Aviemore

RALIA PICNIC SITE * 🛏
Nr. Newtonmore
Tel: Newtonmore (054 03) 253
April-Oct
✉ Aviemore

3

Ayrshire and Burns Country
AYR ✉ 🛏
Information Centre
39 Sandgate
Tel: Ayr (0292) 284196 (24-hr
answering service)
Jan-Dec

CULZEAN CASTLE 🛏
Tel: Kirkoswald (065 56) 293
Apr-Oct
✉ Ayr

GIRVAN 🛏
Information Centre
Bridge Street
Tel: Girvan (0465) 4950
Apr-Oct
✉ Ayr

PRESTWICK 🛏
Information Centre
Boydfield Gardens
Tel: Prestwick (0292) 79946
June-Sept
✉ Ayr

PRESTWICK AIRPORT 🛏
British Airports Authority
Information Desk
Tel: Prestwick (0292) 79822
Jan-Dec
✉ Ayr

TROON 🛏
Information Centre
Municipal Buildings
South Beach
Tel: Troon (0292) 317696
Apr-Oct
✉ Ayr

4

Ayrshire Valleys
CUMNOCK 🛏
Tourist Information Centre
Glaisnock Street
Tel: Cumnock (0290) 23058
Jan-Dec
✉ Kilmarnock

NEW CUMNOCK 🛏
Tourist Information Centre
Town Hall
Tel: New Cumnock (0290) 38581
April-Sept
✉ Kilmarnock

DALMELLINGTON 🛏
Tourist Information Centre
Tel: Dalmellington (0292) 550145
April-Sept
✉ Kilmarnock

DARVEL 🛏
Tourist Information Centre
April-Sept
Tel: Darvel (0560) 22780
✉ Kilmarnock

KILMARNOCK ✉ 🛏
Ayrshire Valley Tourist Board
Tourist Information Centre
62 Bank Street
Tel: Kilmarnock (0563) 39090
Jan-Dec

5

Banff and Buchan
BANFF * ✉ 🛏
Information Centre
Collie Lodge
Tel: Banff (026 12) 2419
Mid Apr-Mid Oct

FRASERBURGH ✉ 🛏
Information Centre
Saltoun Square
Tel: Fraserburgh (0346) 28315
Mid May-Sept
✉ Banff

 Shows that you can write to the Centre for information during its normal months of opening. In some cases
an alternative Centre is shown for written enquiries.   Information correct at August 1986.

FYVIE ⛵
Information Centre
Fordoun
Tel: Fyvie (06516) 597
End Apr-Sept
✉ Banff

PETERHEAD ⛵
Information Centre
Arbuthnot Museum
St Peter Street
Tel: Peterhead (0779) 71904
July-Aug incl.
✉ Banff

6

Caithness

JOHN O' GROATS ⛵
Information Centre
Tel: John o' Groats (095 581) 373
May-Sept

THURSO ⛵
Information Centre
Car Park
Riverside
Tel: Thurso (0847) 62371
May-Sept

WICK ✉ ⛵
Caithness Tourist Board
Whitechapel Road
off High Street
Tel: Wick (0955) 2596
Jan-Dec

7

City of Aberdeen

ABERDEEN ✉ ⛵
City of Aberdeen
Tourist Board
St Nicholas House
Broad Street
Tel: Aberdeen (0224) 632727/637353
Telex: 73366
Jan-Dec

Tourist Information Kiosk ⛵
(local bed-booking only)
Concourse
Railway Station
Guild Street
Jan-Dec

8

City of Dundee

DUNDEE ✉ ⛵
Information Centre
Nethergate Centre
Tel: Dundee (0382) 27723
Jan-Dec

9

City of Edinburgh

EDINBURGH ✉ ⛵
City of Edinburgh Tourist
Information and Accommodation
Service
Waverley Market
Princes Street
Tel: 031-557 2727
Telex: 727143 (Mon-Fri only)
Jan-Dec

EDINBURGH AIRPORT ✉
City of Edinburgh
Tourist Information and
Accommodation Service
Tel: 031-333 2167
Jan-Dec

10

Clyde Valley

ABINGTON ⛵
'Little Chef'
A74 Northbound
Tel: Crawford (086 42) 436
May-Sept

BIGGAR ⛵
Information Centre
High Street
Tel: Biggar (0899) 21066
May-Sept

Nr HAMILTON ⛵
(M74 Northbound)
Roadchef Service Area
Tel: Hamilton (0698) 285590
May-Sept

LANARK ✉ ⛵
Clyde Valley Tourist Board
Horsemarket
Tel: Lanark (0555) 61661
Jan-Dec

LESMAHAGOW ⛵
The Resource Centre
New Trows Road
Tel: Lesmahagow (0555) 894449
May-Sept

MOTHERWELL ⛵
The Library
Hamilton Road
Tel: Motherwell (0698) 51311
May-Sept

11

Cunninghame

LARGS ✉ ⛵
Information Centre
Promenade KA30 8BE
Tel: Largs (0475) 673765
Jan-Dec

MILLPORT ⛵
Information Centre
Guildford Street
Tel: Millport (0475) 530753
April-Oct
✉ Largs

12

Dumfries and Galloway

CASTLE DOUGLAS * ✉ ⛵
Information Centre
Markethill
Tel: Castle Douglas (0556) 2611
Easter-Oct

DALBEATTIE * ✉ ⛵
Information Centre
Car Park
Tel: Dalbeattie (0556) 610117
Easter-Oct

DUMFRIES * ✉ ⛵
Information Centre
Whitesands
Tel: Dumfries (0387) 53862
Easter-Oct

GATEHOUSE OF FLEET * ✉ ⛵
Information Centre
Car Park
Tel: Gatehouse of Fleet
(05574) 212
Easter-Oct

GRETNA * ✉ ⛵
Information Centre
Annan Road
Tel: Gretna (0461) 37834
Easter-Oct

KIRKCUDBRIGHT * ✉ ⛵
Information Centre
Harbour Square
Tel: Kirkcudbright (0557) 30494
May-Sept

LANGHOLM * ✉ ⛵
Town Hall
Tel: Langholm (0541) 80976
Easter-Oct

---

*   Self Catering Late Booking Service operated.   ⛵   Local Bed-booking and Book-a-bed Ahead.

TOURIST INFORMATION CENTRES

MOFFAT * ✉ ⌂
Information Centre
Church Gate
Tel: Moffat (0683) 20620
Easter-Oct

NEWTON STEWART * ✉ ⌂
Information Centre
Dashwood Square
Tel: Newton Stewart (0671) 2431
Easter-Oct

STRANRAER * ✉ ⌂
Information Bureau
Port Rodie
Tel: Stranraer (0776) 2595

13

Dunoon and The Cowal Peninsula

DUNOON ✉ ⌂
Dunoon & Cowal
Tourist Board
7 Alexandra Parade
Tel: Dunoon (0369) 3785
Jan-Dec

14

East Lothian

DUNBAR ✉ ⌂
Information Centre
Town House
High Street
Tel: Dunbar (0368) 63353
Jan-Dec

MUSSELBURGH ✉ ⌂
Brunton Hall
East Lothian
Tel: 031-665 6597
June-mid Sept

NORTH BERWICK * ✉ ⌂
Information Centre
Quality Street
Tel: North Berwick (0620) 2197
Jan-Dec

PENCRAIG ⌂
A1
East Linton
Tel: Pencraig (0620) 860063
Mid May-mid Sept
✉ Dunbar

15

Forth Valley

DUNFERMLINE ⌂
Information Centre
Glen Bridge Car Park
Tel: Dunfermline (0383) 720999
May-Sept
✉ Linlithgow

FORTH ROAD BRIDGE ⌂
Information Centre
Tel: Inverkeithing (0383) 417759
Easter-Sept
✉ Linlithgow

KINCARDINE BRIDGE ⌂
Tourist Information Centre
Pine 'n' Oak
Kincardine Bridge Road
Airth, Falkirk
Tel: Airth (032 483) 422
May-Sept
✉ Linlithgow

LINLITHGOW ✉ ⌂
Burgh Halls
The Cross
Tel: Linlithgow (0506) 844600
Jan-Dec

16

Fort William and Lochaber

BALLACHULISH ⌂
Tourist Office
Tel: Ballachulish (08552) 296
April-Sept
✉ Fort William

FORT WILLIAM * ✉ ⌂
Fort William and Lochaber
Tourist Board
Tel: Fort William (0397) 3781
Jan-Dec

MALLAIG ⌂
Information Centre
Tel: Mallaig (0687) 2170
April-Sept
✉ Fort William

SALEN
Tourist Office
Tel: Salen (096785) 622
Mid June-mid Sept
✉ Fort William

17

Gordon

ALFORD ⌂
Information Centre
Railway Museum
Station Yard
Tel: Alford (0336) 2052
Apr-Sept
✉ Aberdeen

ELLON ⌂
Information Caravan
Market Street Car Park
Tel: Ellon (0358) 20730
Mid May-Sept
✉ Aberdeen

HUNTLY ⌂
Information Centre
The Square
Tel: Huntly (0466) 2255
Mid May-Sept
✉ Aberdeen

INVERURIE ⌂
Information Centre
Town Hall, Market Place
Tel: Inverurie (0467) 20600
Mid May-Sept
✉ Aberdeen

18

Greater Glasgow

GLASGOW ✉ ⌂
Tourist Information Centre
35-39 St. Vincent Place
Tel: 041-227 4880
Telex: 779504
Jan-Dec

PAISLEY ⌂
Town Hall
Abbey Close
Tel: 041-889 0711
Jan-Dec
✉ Glasgow

GOUROCK ⌂
Information Centre
Municipal Buildings
Shore Street
Tel: Gourock (0475) 31126
Jan-Dec

GREENOCK ✉ ⌂
Information Centre
Municipal Buildings
23 Clyde Street
Tel: Greenock (0475) 24400

19

Inverness, Loch Ness and Nairn

DAVIOT ⌂
by Inverness
Daviot Wood Information Centre
Tel: Daviot (046385) 203
April-Sept
✉ Inverness

FORT AUGUSTUS ⌂
Information Centre
Car Park
Tel: Fort Augustus (0320) 6367
May-Sept
✉ Inverness

INVERNESS * ✉ ⌂
Inverness, Loch Ness and
Nairn Tourist Board
23 Church Street
Tel: Inverness (0463) 234353
Telex: 75114
Jan-Dec

NAIRN ⌂
Information Centre
62 King Street
Tel: Nairn (0667) 52753
May-Sept
✉ Inverness

20

Isle of Arran

BRODICK, Isle of Arran * ✉ ⌂
Tourist Information Centre
The Pier
Tel: Brodick (0770) 2140/2401
Jan-Dec

21

The Isle of Skye and South West Ross

BROADFORD, Isle of Skye * ⌂
The Isle of Skye and
South West Ross
Tourist Board
Tel: (047 12) 361/463
Easter-Sept
✉ Portree

KYLE OF LOCHALSH * ⌂
The Isle of Skye and
South West Ross Tourist Board
Tel: Kyle (0599) 4276
Easter-Sept
✉ Portree

PORTREE, Isle of Skye * ✉ ⌂
The Isle of Skye and
South West Ross Tourist Board
Tourist Information Centre
Tel: Portree (0478) 2137
Jan-Dec

SHIEL BRIDGE ⌂
Information Caravan
Tel: Glenshiel (0599) 81264
Easter-Sept
✉ Portree

22

Kincardine and Deeside

ABOYNE * ✉ ⌂
Information Caravan
Ballater Road Car Park
Tel: Aboyne (0339) 2060
Easter-Sept

BALLATER * ✉ ⌂
Information Centre
Station Square
Tel: Ballater (0338) 55306
Easter-mid Oct

BANCHORY * ✉ ⌂
Information Centre
Dee Street Car Park
Tel: Banchory (033 02) 2000
Easter-Sept

BRAEMAR * ✉ ⌂
Information Centre
Balnellan Road
Tel: Braemar (033 83) 600
Easter-Oct

STONEHAVEN * ✉ ⌂
Information Centre
The Square
Tel: Stonehaven (0569) 62806
Easter-Sept

23

Kirkcaldy

BURNTISLAND ✉
4 Kirkgate
Tel: Burntisland (0592) 872667
Jan-Dec

KIRKCALDY
Information Centre
Esplanade
Tel: Kirkcaldy (0592) 267775
Jan-Dec

LEVEN ✉
Information Centre
South Street
Tel: Leven (0333) 29464
Jan-Dec

24

Loch Lomond, Stirling and The Trossachs

ABERFOYLE ✉ ⌂
Information Centre
Main Street
Tel: Aberfoyle (087 72) 352
Apr-Sept

BALLOCH ✉ ⌂
Information Centre
Balloch Road
Tel: Alexandra (0389) 53533
Apr-Sept

BANNOCKBURN ⌂
Motorway Services Area
by Stirling
Tel: (0786) 814111
Mar-Oct

CALLANDER ✉ ⌂
Tourist Information Centre
Leny Road
Tel: Callander (0877) 30342
Apr-Sept

DUNBLANE ✉ ⌂
Tourist Information Centre
Stirling Road
Tel: Dunblane (0786) 824428
Apr-Sept

HELENSBURGH ✉ ⌂
Tourist Information Centre
The Clock Tower
Tel: Helensburgh (0436) 2642
Apr-Sept

KILLIN ✉ ⌂
Tourist Information Centre
Main Street
Tel: Killin (056 72) 254
Apr-Sept

STIRLING ✉ ⌂
Tourist Information Centre
Dumbarton Road
Tel: Stirling (0786) 75019
Jan-Dec

TARBET, Loch Lomond ✉ ⌂
Information Caravan
Pier Road
Tarbet
Loch Lomond
Tel: Arrochar (03012) 260
Apr-Sept
✉ Stirling

* Self Catering Late Booking Service operated.   ⌂ Local Bed-booking and Book-a-bed Ahead.

xxiii

TOURIST INFORMATION CENTRES

TILLICOULTRY ✉ ☎
Information Centre
Clock Mill
Upper Mill Street
Tel: Tillicoultry (0259) 52176
Apr-Sept

TYNDRUM ✉ ☎
Information Centre Car Park
Tel: Tyndrum (083 84) 246
Apr-Sept

25

Mid Argyll, Kintyre and Islay

BOWMORE, Isle of Islay ☎
Information Centre
Tel: (049 681) 254
Apr-mid Oct
✉ Campbeltown

CAMPBELTOWN * ✉ ☎
Mid Argyll, Kintyre & Islay
Tourist Board
Tel: Campbeltown (0586) 52056
Jan-Dec

INVERARAY ☎
Information Centre
Tel: Inveraray (0499) 2063
Apr-mid Oct
✉ Campbeltown

LOCHGILPHEAD ☎
Information Centre
Tel: Lochgilphead (0546) 2344
Apr-mid Oct
✉ Campbeltown

TARBERT, Loch Fyne ☎
Information Centre
Tel: Tarbert (088 02) 429
Apr-mid Oct
✉ Campbeltown

26

Moray

CULLEN ☎
20 Seafield Street
Information Centre
Tel: Cullen (0542) 40757
June-Sept
✉ Elgin

DUFFTOWN ☎
Information Centre
The Clock Tower
The Square
Tel: Dufftown (0340) 20501
May-Sept
✉ Elgin

ELGIN * ✉ ☎
Information Centre
17 High Street, IV30 1EG
Tel: Elgin (0343) 3388/2666
Jan-Dec

FORRES ☎
Information Centre
Falconer Museum
Tolbooth Street
Tel: Forres (0309) 72938
May-Sept
✉ Elgin

KEITH ☎
Information Centre
Church Road
Tel: (054 22) 2634
June-Sept
✉ Elgin

TOMINTOUL ☎
Information Centre
The Square
Tel: Tomintoul (080 74) 285
Apr-Oct
✉ Elgin

27

Oban, Mull and District

OBAN * ✉ ☎
Oban, Mull and District
Tourist Board
Argyll Square
Tel: Oban (0631) 63122
Jan-Dec

TOBERMORY ✉ ☎
Isle of Mull
Information Centre
48 Main Street
Tel: Tobermory (0688) 2182
Jan-Dec (9-11 in winter months)

28

Orkney

KIRKWALL ✉ ☎
Orkney Tourist Board
Information Centre
Broad Street KW15 1NX
Tel: Kirkwall (0856) 2856
Jan-Dec

STROMNESS ☎
Information Centre
Ferry Terminal Building
Pierhead
Tel: Stromness (0856) 850716
May-Sept
(also 2 hours per day, Oct-Apr)
✉ Kirkwall

29

Outer Hebrides

CASTLEBAY, Isle of Barra ☎
Information Centre
Tel: Castlebay (087 14) 336
May-Sept
✉ Stornoway

LOCHBOISDALE ☎
Isle of South Uist
Information Centre
Tel: Lochboisdale (087 84) 286
May-Sept
✉ Stornoway

LOCHMADDY ☎
Isle of North Uist
Information Centre
Tel: Lochmaddy (08763) 321
May-Sept
✉ Stornoway

STORNOWAY, Isle of Lewis ✉ ☎
Outer Hebrides Tourist Board
Administration and Information
Centre
4 South Beach Street
Tel: Stornoway (0851) 3088
Jan-Dec

TARBERT, Isle of Harris ☎
Information Centre
Tel: Harris (0859) 2011
May-Sept
✉ Stornoway

30

Perthshire

ABERFELDY ✉ all year ☎
Aberfeldy and District Tourist
Association
8 Dunkeld Street
Tel: Aberfeldy (0887) 20276
Easter-mid Sept

AUCHTERARDER * ✉ all
year ☎
Auchterarder and District
Tourist Association
High Street
Tel: Auchterarder (076 46) 3450
Apr-Oct (Oct-Apr open 1000-1400
daily)

BLAIRGOWRIE * ✉ all year ☎
Blairgowrie and District Tourist
Association
Wellmeadow
Tel: Blairgowrie (0250) 2960
Jan-Dec

✉ Shows that you can write to the Centre for information during its normal months of opening. In some cases an alternative Centre is shown for written enquiries. Information correct at August 1986.

CRIEFF * ✉ all year ⛵
Crieff and District Tourist Association
James Square
Tel: Crieff (0764) 2578
Apr-Oct
(Nov-Mar, open 4 hrs per day)

DUNKELD ✉ all year ⛵
Dunkeld and Birnam Tourist
Association
The Cross
Tel: Dunkeld (035 02) 688
Easter-Oct

GLENSHEE ✉ all year
Information Officer
Glenshee Tourist Association
Corsehill
Upper Allan Street
Blairgowrie
Tel: BLairgowrie (0250) 5509

KINROSS ✉ all year ⛵
Kinross-shire Tourist Association
Information Centre
Kinross Service Area,
off Junction 6, M90
Tel: Kinross (0577) 63680
(62585 when closed)
Apr-Oct

PERTH * ✉ all year ⛵
Perth Tourist Association
The Round House
Marshall Place
Tel: Perth (0738) 22900/27108
Jan-Dec

PITLOCHRY * ✉ all year ⛵
Pitlochry and District
Tourist Association
22 Atholl Road
Tel: Pitlochry (0796) 2215/2751
Jan-Dec

31

Ross and Cromarty

GAIRLOCH ✉ ⛵
Ross & Cromarty Tourist Board
Information Office
Achtercairn
Gairloch IV21 2DN
Tel: Gairloch (0445) 2130
Jan-Dec

NORTH KESSOCK ✉ ⛵
Ross & Cromarty Tourist Board
Tourist Office
North Kessock IV1 1XB
Tel: Kessock (046 373) 505
Jan-Dec

STRATHPEFFER ✉ ⛵
Ross & Cromarty Tourist Board
Information Centre
The Square
Tel: Strathpeffer (0997) 21415
Easter, May-Sept
✉ North Kessock

ULLAPOOL ⛵
Ross & Cromarty Tourist Board
Information Centre
Tel: Ullapool (0854) 2135
Easter-Sept
✉ Gairloch

32

Rothesay and Isle of Bute

ROTHESAY, Isle of Bute ✉ ⛵
Rothesay & Isle of Bute Tourist
Board
The Pier
Tel: Rothesay (0700) 2151
Jan-Dec

33

St. Andrews and North East Fife

ANSTRUTHER ⛵
East Neuk Information Centre
Scottish Fisheries Museum
Tel: (0333) 310628
May-Sept
✉ St Andrews

CUPAR ⛵
Information Centre
Fluthers Car Park
Tel: Cupar (0334) 55555
Mid June-Sept
✉ St Andrews

ST ANDREWS ✉ ⛵
Information Centre
South Street
Tel: St Andrews (0334) 72021
Jan-Dec

34

Scottish Borders

COLDSTREAM * ✉ ⛵
Henderson Park
Tel: Coldstream (0890) 2607
Apr-Oct

EYEMOUTH * ✉ ⛵
Auld Kirk
Tel: Eyemouth (0390) 50678
Apr-Oct

GALASHIELS * ✉ ⛵
Bank Street
Tel: Galashiels (0896) 55551
Apr-Oct

HAWICK * ✉ ⛵
Common Haugh
Tel: Hawick (0450) 72547
Apr-Oct

JEDBURGH * ✉ ⛵
Information Centre
Murray's Green
Tel: Jedburgh (0835)
63435/63688
Feb-Nov

KELSO * ✉ ⛵
Turret House
Tel: Kelso (0573) 23464
Apr-Oct

MELROSE * ✉ ⛵
Priorwood Gardens, nr. Abbey
Tel: Melrose (089 682) 2555
Apr-Oct

PEEBLES * ✉ ⛵
Chambers Institute
High Street
Tel: Peebles (0721) 20138
Apr-Oct

SELKIRK * ✉ ⛵
Halliwell's House
Tel: Selkirk (0750) 20054
Apr-Oct

35

Shetland

LERWICK, Shetland ✉ ⛵
Shetland Tourist Organisation
Information Centre
Tel: Lerwick (0595) 3434
Telex: 75119
Jan-Dec

36

Sutherland

BETTYHILL ⛵
Information Centre
Tel: Bettyhill (064 12) 342
May-Sept
✉ Dornoch

---

* **Self Catering Late Booking Service operated.** ⛵ **Local Bed-booking and Book-a-bed Ahead.**

TOURIST INFORMATION CENTRES

BONAR BRIDGE 🛏
Information Centre
Tel: Ardgay (08632) 333
May-Sept
✉ Dornoch

DORNOCH ✉ 🛏
Sutherland Tourist Board
The Square
Tel: Dornoch (0862) 810400
Jan-Dec

DURNESS 🛏
Information Centre
Tel: Durness (097 181) 259
April-Oct
✉ Dornoch

HELMSDALE 🛏
Information Centre
Tel: Helmsdale (043 12) 640
May-Sept
✉ Dornoch

LAIRG 🛏
Information Centre
Tel: Lairg (0549) 2160
May-Sept
✉ Dornoch

LOCHINVER 🛏
Information Centre
Tel: Lochinver (057 14) 330
April-Oct
✉ Dornoch

BOOK-A-BED-AHEAD 🛏

The Scottish Tourist Board's *Book A Bed Ahead* scheme, which operates throughout Scotland, is available at all the Tourist Information Centres where the 'bed' symbol is displayed.

You can book your accommodation ahead for the coming night and subsequent nights at any of these Centres, even if your destination is many miles away. It is a guaranteed booking. Hotels, guest houses and bed and breakfast places may all be reserved by means of the scheme.

By using this scheme, the holidaymaker may save hours which would otherwise have been spent in trying to find accommodation—and the motorist can also save petrol—and knows exactly where he is going and that a welcome awaits him.

Full details of the *Book A Bed Ahead* scheme are available at all Tourist Information Centres.

RESERVATION A L'AVANCE
Vous pouvez utiliser la formule de réservation à l'avance lancée par l'Office écossais du tourisme dans tous les bureaux d'information touristique affichant l'enseigne du lit illustrée ci-dessus.

Moyennant le paiement d'une somme modique, vous pouvez retenir votre chambre pour le soir même dans un hôtel ou une pension de n'importe quelle région de l'Ecosse.

Rien n'est plus simple, et cette formule de réservation vous permet d'économiser de précieuses heures de vacances, qui seraient sinon passées à la recherche d'un logement, sans parler de l'économie d'essence, pour les vacanciers motorisés!

Renseignez-vous donc dans un bureau d'information touristique. Faites votre réservation, et partez profiter de votre journée en toute quiétude!

VORAUSBUCHUNG
Das Schottische Touristenbüro hat ein System entwickelt, wonach Sie ein Zimmer für die kommende Nacht im voraus buchen können. Buchungen können bei jedem Touristen-Informationszentrum vorgenommen werden, an dem das "Betten-Symbol" ausgestellt ist.

Gegen eine geringe Gebühr reserviert man Ihnen dort ein Zimmer in einem Hotel, Gasthaus oder in einer Privatpension überall in Schottland.

So einfach ist das.

Durch diesen Dienst sparen Sie wertvolle Urlaubsstunden, die Sie dann nicht mit Zimmersuche verbringen müssen. Und für den Autofahrer ergibt sich auch eine erhebliche Benzinersparnis.

Sie genießen Ihren Urlaub ohne Sorgen um die nächste Unterkunft.

Erkundigen Sie sich nach dem System der "Vorausbuchung" bei jedem beliebigen Touristen-Informationszentrum, buchen Sie Ihr Zimmer im voraus und lassen Sie sich gleich beraten, wie Sie den Rest des Tages am besten verbringen.

✉ Shows that you can write to the Centre for information during its normal months of opening. In some cases an alternative Centre is shown for written enquiries. Information correct at August 1986.

xxvi

MAPS

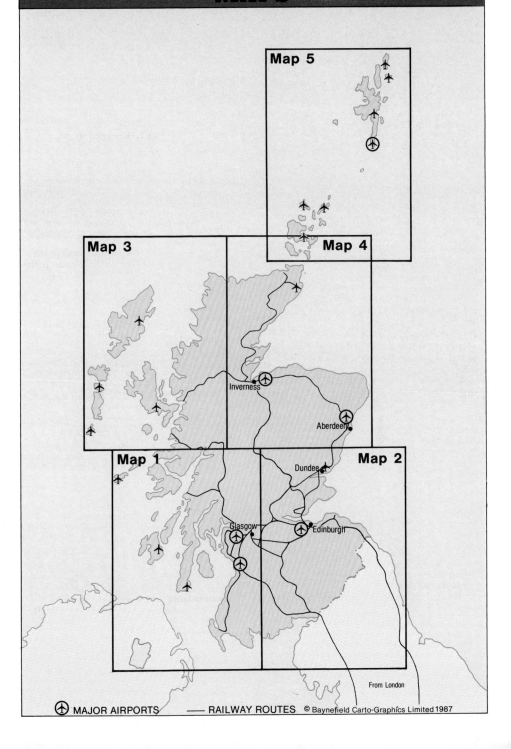

Map 5

Map 3

Map 4

Inverness

Aberdeen

Map 1

Dundee

Glasgow

Edinburgh

Map 2

From London

⊕ MAJOR AIRPORTS   —— RAILWAY ROUTES   © Baynefield Carto-Graphics Limited 1987

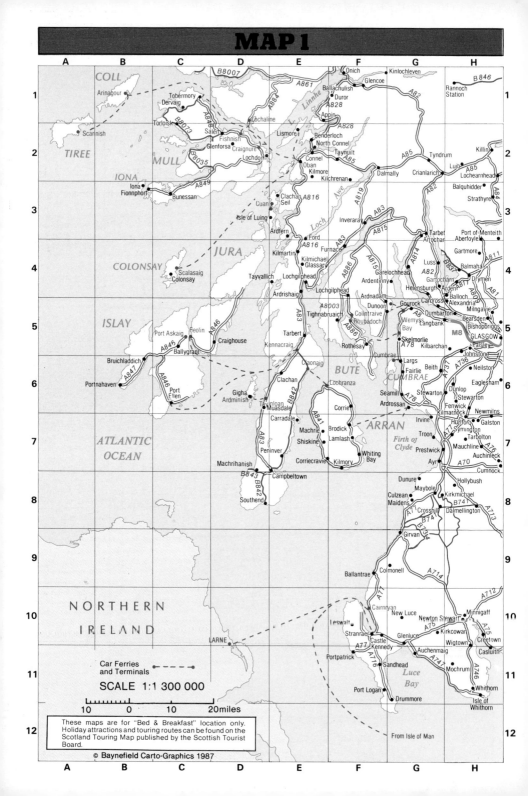

MAP 2

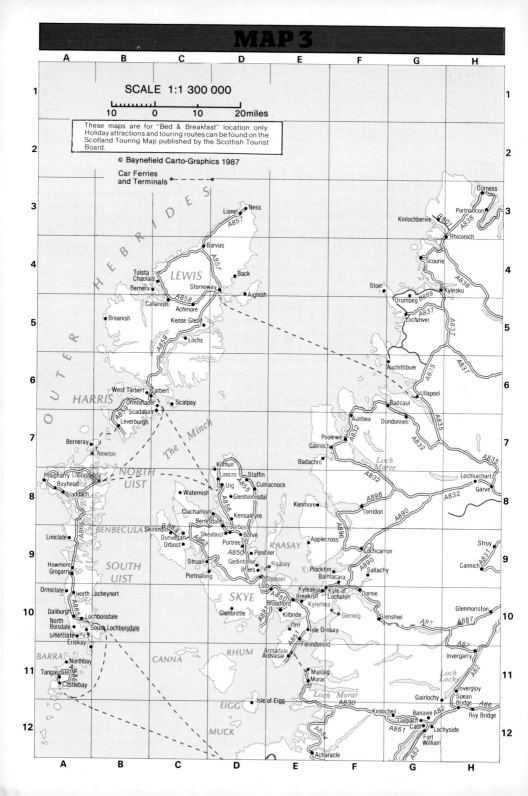

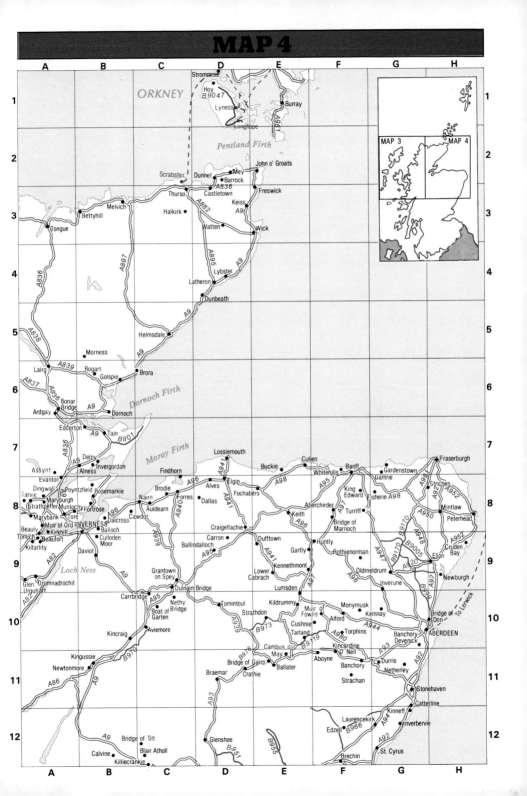

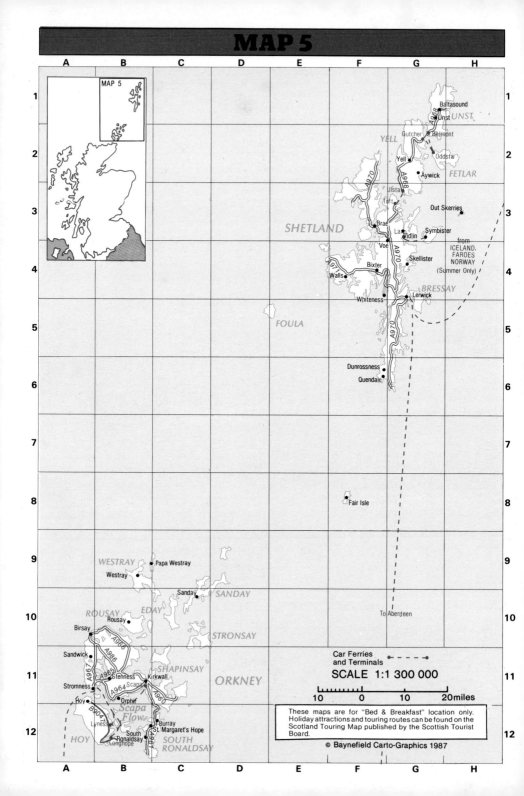

SCOTLAND
BED AND BREAKFAST
ACCOMMODATION 1987

ABERCHIRDER Banffshire Mrs S Bowie Monedie AB5 5PL Tel. Aberchirder (04665) 287	Map 4 F8		1 Single 2 Dble/Twin	1 Public Bath/Sh	B&B per person £6.00-£7.50 Single £6.00-£7.50 Double	Open May-Oct
ABERDEEN Aberdeen Springdale Guest House 404 Great Western Road AB1 6NR Tel. Aberdeen (0224) 316561	Map 4 G10		1 Single 2 Dble/Twin 1 Family	1 Private Bath/Sh 1 Public Bath/Sh	B&B per person £12.00 Single £10.00 Double	Open Jan-Dec
Aberlee Guest House 218 Great Western Road AB1 6PD Tel. Aberdeen (0224) 575973			4 Dble/Twin 2 Family	1 Public Bath/Sh	B&B per person £11.50 Single £9.00 Double	Open Jan-Dec
Arjon Guest House 394 Great Western Road AB1 6NR Tel. Aberdeen (0224) 314784			2 Dble/Twin 3 Family	2 Public Bath/Sh	B&B per person £9.00-£10.00 Double	Open Jan-Dec
Arkaig Guest House 43 Powis Terrace AB2 3PP Tel. Aberdeen (0224) 638872		**COMMENDED** Listed	2 Single 4 Dble/Twin 1 Family	1 Public Bath/Sh	B&B per person £11.00-£12.00 Single £10.00-£11.00 Double	Open Jan-Dec
		Detached, granite house centrally located within 1/2 mile (1km) of the city centre.				
Ashgrove Guest House 34 Ashgrove Road AB2 5AD Tel. Aberdeen (0224) 484861		**APPROVED** Listed	1 Single 4 Dble/Twin 2 Family	1 Public Bath/Sh	B&B per person £11.00-£12.50 Single £9.50-£10.50 Double	Open Jan-Dec
		Convenient for city centre, airport and local hospitals.				
Bon Accord Guest House 162 Bon-Accord Street AB1 7TX Tel. Aberdeen (0224) 594764			4 Single 4 Dble/Twin 3 Family	2 Public Bath/Sh	B&B per person £11.00 Single £10.00 Double	Open Jan-Dec
Bracklinn Guest House 348 Great Western Road AB1 6LX Tel. Aberdeen (0224) 317060		**COMMENDED** 👑 👑	2 Single 2 Dble/Twin 2 Family	2 Private Bath/Sh 1 Public Bath/Sh	B&B per person £16.50-£22.50 Single £12.00-£14.00 Double	Open Jan-Dec Dinner 1900
		Victorian House, elegantly furnished and decorated.				
Braeside Guest House 68 Bon-Accord Street AB1 2EL Tel. Aberdeen (0224) 581652			5 Dble/Twin 1 Family		B&B per person £9.50 Double	Open Jan-Dec
Caledonia Guest House 54 Fonthill Road AB1 2UJ Tel. Aberdeen (0224) 582488		👑 👑	3 Single 1 Dble/Twin 1 Family	1 Public Bath/Sh	B&B per person £11.50 Single £9.50 Double	Open Jan-Dec
Crynoch Guest House 164 Bon-Accord Street Tel. Aberdeen (0224) 582743			6 Single 2 Dble/Twin	4 Public Bath/Sh	B&B per person £12.50 Single £9.00 Double	Open Jan-Dec

VAT is shown at 15%: changes in this rate may affect prices. Prices shown are for guidance only. Please send SAE with each enquiry.

ABERDEEN continued	Map 4 G10						
The Four Bees Guest House 356 Holburn Street AB1 6DX Tel. Aberdeen (0224) 585110			1 Single 1 Dble/Twin 4 Family	1 Public Bath/Sh	B&B per person £11.00 Single £9.00 Double	Open Jan-Dec	🛏🧺☕🍴▦ 📺🐕✳ C
Four Ways Guest House 435 Great Western Road AB1 6NJ Tel. Aberdeen (0224) 310218		COMMENDED 👑👑	1 Single 4 Dble/Twin 2 Family	1 Private Bath/Sh 2 Public Bath/Sh	B&B per person £12.00-£14.00 Single £10.00-£11.00 Double	Open Jan-Dec	🛏🧺▦📺 P C
			Centrally situated in residential area of city. On main tourist route to Royal Deeside.				
Furain Guest House 92 N Deeside Rd, Peterculter AB1 0QW Tel. Aberdeen (0224) 732189		APPROVED Listed	6 Dble/Twin 2 Family	3 Private Bath/Sh 2 Public Bath/Sh	B&B per person £9.75-£10.25 Double	Open Jan-Dec	🛏🧺▦🐕🍴 P
			Late victorian house built of Peterhead granite. Many castles within easy motoring distance.				
Glenisla Guest House 95 Bon Accord Street AB1 2ED Tel. Aberdeen (0224) 582639/591612			2 Single 4 Dble/Twin 1 Family	1 Public Bath/Sh	B&B per person £12.50 Single £11.50 Double	Open Jan-Dec Dinner 1730	🛏🧺V🧺 ▦📺🐕P C T
Hazel-Lea Guest House 378 Great Western Road AB1 6PH Tel. Aberdeen (0224) 315872			1 Single 3 Dble/Twin 1 Family	2 Public Bath/Sh	B&B per person £12.50-£15.00 Single £10.00-£12.00 Double	Open Jan-Dec	🛏🧺☕▦📺 C
The Jays Guest House 422 King Street AB2 3BR Tel. Aberdeen (0224) 638295		Awaiting Inspection	3 Single 4 Dble/Twin	1 Public Bath/Sh	B&B per person £14.00 Single £12.00 Double	Open Jan-Dec	🛏🧺🧺☕▦ P C
Klibreck Guest House 410 Great Western Road AB1 6NR Tel. Aberdeen (0224) 316115		COMMENDED 👑👑	1 Single 4 Dble/Twin 1 Family	2 Public Bath/Sh	B&B per person £12.00-£13.00 Single £10.00-£11.00 Double	Open Jan-Dec Dinner 1800	🛏🧺V🍴▦ 📺P C
			Granite building, corner site in residential area in city's West End. Bus route to city and Deeside.				
Morrison's Guest House 444 King Street AB2 3BS Tel. Aberdeen (0224) 637809			5 Dble/Twin 2 Family	2 Public Bath/Sh	B&B per person £10.00-£12.00 Double	Open Jan-Dec	🛏🧺🧺☕V ▦P C
Nutshell Guest House 301 Holburn Street AB1 6DP Tel. Aberdeen (0224) 591991			3 Single 1 Dble/Twin 1 Family		B&B per person £10.00-£11.50 Single £7.50-£8.50 Double	Open Jan-Dec	🛏🧺🧺☕🍴 ▦📺🐕 P C
Powberry Guest House 122 Crown Street AB1 2HJ Tel. Aberdeen (0224) 589294			1 Single 4 Dble/Twin 1 Family	2 Public Bath/Sh	B&B per person £10.00 Single £8.00 Double	Open Jan-Dec	🛏🍴▦📺🐕
Ravenscraig Guest House 69 Constitution Street AB2 1ET Tel. Aberdeen (0224) 646912			1 Single 4 Dble/Twin 3 Family	2 Public Bath/Sh	B&B per person £8.00-£9.00 Single £8.00-£9.00 Double	Open Jan-Dec	M🧺V📺🐕 C

Key to symbols is on back flap. Details of Classification and Grading are on page vi.

3

ABERDEEN continued	Map 4 G10					
Salisbury Guest House 12 Salisbury Terrace AB1 6QH Tel. Aberdeen (0224) 590447		1 Single 3 Dble/Twin 1 Family	1 Public Bath/Sh	B&B per person £10.00 Single £9.50-£10.00 Double	Open Jan-Dec Dinner 1700	
Stewart Lodge Guest House 89 Bon Accord Street AB1 2ED Tel. Aberdeen (0224) 573823		3 Single 4 Dble/Twin 1 Family	2 Public Bath/Sh	B&B per person £11.00 Single £9.00 Double	Open Jan-Dec	
Strathboyne Guest House 26 Abergeldie Terrace AB1 6EE Tel. Aberdeen (0224) 593400		2 Single 3 Dble/Twin 2 Family	2 Public Bath/Sh	B&B per person £10.00-£11.00 Single £9.00-£10.00 Double	Open Jan-Dec Dinner 1750	
Terra Nova Guest House 114 Crown Street AB1 2HR Tel. Aberdeen (0224) 573096		3 Single 8 Dble/Twin 1 Family		B&B per person £14.95-£16.00 Single £9.80-£10.90 Double	Open Jan-Dec	
Trovador Guest House 158 Bon-Accord Street AB1 2TX Tel. Aberdeen (0224) 596837		2 Single 1 Dble/Twin 4 Family	1 Public Bath/Sh	B&B per person £10.00 Single £9.00 Double	Open Jan-Dec	
Vaila Guest House 111 Crown Street Tel. Aberdeen (0224) 586461		2 Single 4 Dble/Twin 2 Family	4 Private Bath/Sh 2 Public Bath/Sh	B&B per person £14.95-£16.60 Single £9.80-£11.50 Double	Open Jan-Dec	

University of Aberdeen Conference Office, Kings College AB9 1FX Tel. Aberdeen (0224) 480241 Ext 5171 Telex 73458	APPROVED ♛	1200 Single	190 Public Bath/Sh	B&B per person £12.75 Single	Open Mar-Apr Jul-Oct Dinner 1800	
		Halls of Residence situated off High St. in old town. Landscaped garden, extensive sports facilities.				
Mrs C Barnet Zenith, 16 Claremont Street AB1 6QS Tel. Aberdeen (0224) 572930		1 Single 1 Dble/Twin		B&B per person £8.50-£9.50 Single £7.50-£8.50 Double	Open Jan-Dec	
Mrs Boyd Braehead, 175 Clifton Road AB2 3RA Tel. Aberdeen (0224) 483301		1 Single 2 Dble/Twin	1 Public Bath/Sh	B&B per person £9.00-£11.00 Single £8.50-£9.50 Double	Open Jan-Dec	

	Map 4 G10						
ABERDEEN continued Mr F Cherry 427 Great Northern Road AB2 2EU Tel. Aberdeen (0224) 484084		APPROVED Listed	1 Dble/Twin	1 Public Bath/Sh	B&B per person £9.00 Double	Open Jan-Dec	🛏️🍵 Ⓡ 📺 🛋️ Ⓒ
			Convenient for city centre and airport.				
Mrs J Davidson 101 Don Street AB2 1UJ Tel. Aberdeen (0224) 486011			2 Single 1 Dble/Twin	1 Public Bath/Sh	B&B per person £10.00 Single £10.00 Double	Open Jan-Dec	🛏️🍵 Ⓡ 🖥️ 📺 Ⓟ
Mrs Dey Lilian Cottage, 442 King Street AB2 3BS Tel. Aberdeen (0224) 636947			5 Dble/Twin 1 Family	1 Private Bath/Sh 2 Public Bath/Sh	B&B per person £10.00-£12.00 Double	Open Jan-Dec	🛁 🖵 🍵 Ⓥ Ⓡ 🖥️ 📺 Ⓟ Ⓒ
Mr & Mrs J C Duffus 11 Beechgrove Terrace AB2 4DR Tel. Aberdeen (0224) 640326			1 Dble/Twin 1 Family		B&B per person £9.00 Double	Open Jul-Aug Dinner 1800	🖵 🍵 🖥️ 📺 Ⓒ
Mrs M Gallan 50 Murray Terrace AB1 2SB Tel. Aberdeen (0224) 585073		COMMENDED Listed	1 Single 1 Dble/Twin 1 Family	1 Public Bath/Sh	B&B per person £10.00 Single £9.00 Double	Open Jan-Dec	🍵 Ⓡ 🖥️ 📺 Ⓒ
			Semi-detached house close to public park and convenient for bus route to city centre.				
Mrs D Howie Jasmin Villa, 252 Victoria Road AB1 3NU Tel. Aberdeen (0224) 871680			1 Single 2 Dble/Twin	1 Public Bath/Sh	B&B per person £10.00 Single £10.00 Double	Open Jan-Dec	🛁 🖵 🍵 🖥️ Ⓒ
Mrs I Leslie 75 Dee Street AB1 2EE Tel. Aberdeen (0224) 582517			2 Single 2 Dble/Twin 2 Family	1 Public Bath/Sh	B&B per person £9.50 Single £8.50 Double	Open Jan-Dec	🛁 Ⓡ 🖥️ 📺 🖐️ Ⓒ
Mrs Mann Bellfield Farm, Kingswells AB1 8PX Tel. Aberdeen (0224) 740239			2 Dble/Twin 1 Family	2 Public Bath/Sh	B&B per person £9.50-£10.00 Double	Open Jan-Dec	🛁 Ⓥ Ⓡ 🖥️ 📺 Ⓟ Ⓒ 🛴
Mrs E Morrison Braemore, 32 Springbank Terrace AB1 2LR Tel. Aberdeen (0224) 586535			2 Dble/Twin 1 Family	1 Public Bath/Sh	B&B per person £8.00 Double	Open Mar-Apr Jun-Sep	🛁 🛏️ 🍵 Ⓡ 🖥️ 📺 🛋️ Ⓟ Ⓒ
Mrs I Mroczek Orcadia, 201 Great Western Road AB1 6PS Tel. Aberdeen (0224) 587823			2 Single 1 Dble/Twin 3 Family	2 Public Bath/Sh	B&B per person £10.00 Single £10.00 Double	Open Jan-Dec	🖵 🛏️ 🍵 🖥️ 📺 🖐️ 🍴 🐕 ✂️ 🅩 Ⓟ Ⓒ

Key to symbols is on back flap. Details of Classification and Grading are on page vi.

5

ABERDEEN continued	Map 4 G10						
Mrs E Noble 39 Desswood Place AB2 4EE Tel. Aberdeen (0224) 646571			2 Dble/Twin 1 Family	1 Public Bath/Sh	B&B per person £8.50 Double	Open Jun-Oct	🔥 M ⬜ 🍺 TV ▯ 🦮 🐕 C
Mrs C Pauline 25 Springbank Terrace AB1 2JY Tel. Aberdeen (0224) 588686			2 Dble/Twin 1 Family	1 Public Bath/Sh	B&B per person £8.00 Double	Open Jan-Dec	🔥 M 🍺 TV £ C
Mrs W Rough 402 Great Western Road AB1 6NR Tel. Aberdeen (0224) 323871			2 Dble/Twin 1 Family	1 Public Bath/Sh	B&B per person £10.00 Double	Open Jan-Dec	🔥 ▯ TV ✂ 🐕 P C
Mrs Simpson 33 Springank Terrace AB1 2LR Tel. Aberdeen (0224) 596351			1 Single 2 Dble/Twin 2 Family	2 Public Bath/Sh	B&B per person £10.00-£11.00 Single £17.00 Double	Open Jan-Dec	🔥 V ▯ TV ✂ 🐕 C
Mrs L Stevenson 3 Ashley Park South AB1 6RP Tel. Aberdeen (0224) 590901			1 Dble/Twin 1 Family	1 Public Bath/Sh	B&B per person £8.50-£9.00 Double	Open Jan-Sep	▯ TV £ P C
Mrs Charlotte Styles Dunromin, 75 Constitution St AB2 1ET Tel. Aberdeen (0224) 647995			1 Single 3 Dble/Twin 1 Family	1 Public Bath/Sh	B&B per person £10.00 Single £10.00 Double	Open Jan-Dec	🔥 ▯ TV 🐕 🐕
Mrs A Watt St Elmo, 64 Hilton Drive AB2 2NP Tel. Aberdeen (0224) 483065			3 Dble/Twin	1 Public Bath/Sh	B&B per person £8.00 Double	Open Jan-Dec	⬜ 🍺 TV 🐕 🐕 P C 🎠
ABERDOUR Fife	Map 2 C4						
Mrs E Barrie Hawkcraig House, Hawkcraig Point Tel. Aberdour (0383) 860335			1 Dble/Twin 1 Family	1 Public Bath/Sh	B&B per person £9.00 Double	Open Feb-Nov Dinner 1900-2030	🔥 V ▯ TV ✗ P ⚠
Mrs Hughes Drift Inn, 19 Main Street Tel. Aberdour (0383) 860331			1 Single 3 Dble/Twin	1 Public Bath/Sh	B&B per person £9.65-£11.50 Single £9.00-£11.00 Double	Open Jan-Dec	🍺 ▯ TV 🦮
Mrs S Knott Dunraggie, Murrell Road KY3 0XN Tel. Aberdour (0383) 860136		**APPROVED** ♔	1 Single 1 Dble/Twin 1 Family	1 Public Bath/Sh	B&B per person £8.00-£8.50 Single £8.00-£8.50 Double	Open Jan-Dec Dinner 1800	V ▯ TV ✂ 🐕 P ⚠ C
			Comfortable, warm and quiet. Ideal for all ages. Lovely views over River Forth.				
ABERFELDY Perthshire	Map 2 B1						
Caber-Feidh Guest House 56 Dunkeld Street Tel. Aberfeldy (0887) 20342			4 Dble/Twin 2 Family	1 Public Bath/Sh	B&B per person £8.00-£8.50 Double	Open Jan-Dec Dinner 1800	🔥 🍺 V ▯ TV ✂ 🐕 P ⚠ C

	Map	Rooms	Bath	B&B	Open/Dinner
ABERFELDY continued Glenburn Guest House Grandtully PH15 2QX Tel. Strathtay (08874) 330	Map 2 B1	1 Single 6 Dble/Twin 2 Family		B&B per person £9.00-£12.00 Single £7.50-£9.50 Double	Open Jan-Dec Dinner 1830
Tom-an-Droighne Guest House PH15 2JS Tel. Aberfeldy (0887) 20489		1 Single 3 Dble/Twin	2 Public Bath/Sh	B&B per person £9.00 Single £9.00 Double	Open Jan-Dec Dinner 1900
Mrs Aymer Wester Killiechassie PH15 2JR Tel. Aberfeldy (0887) 20229		1 Dble/Twin	1 Private Bath/Sh	B&B per person £6.50-£7.50 Double	Open Apr-Oct Dinner 1800
Mrs C Campbell Weem Farm, Weem PH15 2LD Tel. Aberfeldy (0887) 20228		2 Dble/Twin	1 Public Bath/Sh	B&B per person £7.00-£7.50 Double	Open May-Sep Dinner 1830
Ms K Gray Comraich, Home Street PH15 2AJ Tel. Aberfeldy (0887) 20682		1 Single 2 Dble/Twin	1 Public Bath/Sh	B&B per person £7.50 Single £7.00 Double	Open Jan-Dec Dinner 1730
Mr & Mrs J & N Kidd Crossroads, 4 Kenmore Street PH15 2BL Tel. Aberfeldy (0887) 20293		1 Single 3 Dble/Twin 1 Family	2 Public Bath/Sh	B&B per person £7.50 Single £7.50 Double	Open Mar-Dec Dinner 1830
Mrs McGregor Taycladdoch Farm, Grandtully PH15 2QX Tel. Strathtay (08874) 255		1 Dble/Twin 1 Family	1 Public Bath/Sh	B&B per person £7.00 Double	Open Apr-Sep
B McNeill & B Scott Dallavon, Taybridge Road Tel. Aberfeldy (0887) 20353		1 Single 2 Dble/Twin 1 Family	2 Public Bath/Sh	B&B per person £7.50-£8.00 Single £7.50-£8.00 Double	Open Mar-Nov Dinner 1800
Mr & Mrs G Reid Claremont, Taybridge Road PH15 2BH Tel. Aberfeldy (0887) 20724	♛ ♛	1 Single 2 Dble/Twin	1 Public Bath/Sh	B&B per person £8.00-£8.50 Single £8.00-£8.50 Double	Open Apr-Oct Dinner 1800
Mrs E C Todd Tigh-na-Caorann, Crieff Road PH15 2BJ Tel. Aberfeldy (0887) 20993		2 Dble/Twin	1 Public Bath/Sh	B&B per person £7.50-£8.00 Double	Open Apr-Oct Dinner 1900
ABERFOYLE Perthshire Mrs M More Keith House, Trossachs Rd FK8 3SX Tel. Aberfoyle (08772) 470	Map 1 H3	3 Dble/Twin	1 Public Bath/Sh	B&B per person £7.00 Double	Open Apr-Oct Dinner 1830
Mrs Orr Old Manse Garden, Manse Rd FK8 3XF Tel. Aberfoyle (08772) 532		2 Dble/Twin 1 Family	1 Public Bath/Sh	B&B per person £7.50-£8.00 Double	Open Apr-Oct

Key to symbols is on back flap. Details of Classification and Grading are on page vi.

7

ABERFOYLE continued
Map 1 H3

Mrs D Reay
Creagroineach, Trossachs Road
FK8 3SP
Tel. Aberfoyle (08772) 230

COMMENDED Listed

2 Dble/Twin — 1 Public Bath/Sh — B&B per person £9.00-£9.50 Double — Open May-Oct, Dinner 1830

1903 semi detached villa, friendly and comfortable. Home cooking and baking. Washbasins all bedrooms.

ABERLADY
East Lothian — Map 2 E4

Mrs A Cunningham
Cairnville, Main Street
Tel. Aberlady (08757) 351

3 Dble/Twin, 1 Family — 2 Public Bath/Sh — B&B per person £8.50-£9.00 Double — Open Apr-Sep

---

ABERNETHY
Perthshire — Map 2 C3

Mrs Maryon Ashford
Serendib, Perth Road
PH2 9LW
Tel. Abernethy (073885) 398

Awaiting Inspection

1 Dble/Twin — 1 Private Bath/Sh — B&B per person £9.00 Double — Open Jan-Dec, Dinner 1800

Mrs D Dowie
Glenbank, Glenfoot
PH2 9LS
Tel. Abernethy (073885) 251

1 Dble/Twin, 1 Family — 1 Public Bath/Sh — B&B per person £7.50-£8.00 Double — Open Apr-Oct

---

ABINGTON
Lanarkshire — Map 2 B7

Mrs Vicki Gallagher
The Arbory, 82 Carlisle Road
ML12 6SD
Tel. Crawford (08642) 310

Awaiting Inspection

2 Dble/Twin, 1 Family — 1 Public Bath/Sh — B&B per person £8.00-£9.00 Double — Open Jan-Dec

Mrs Mary Hodge
Craighead Farm
Tel. Crawford (08642) 356

1 Single, 1 Dble/Twin, 1 Family — 1 Public Bath/Sh — B&B per person £8.00-£8.50 Single, £8.00-£8.50 Double — Open Apr-Oct, Dinner 1800

Mrs A Hodge
Gilkerscleugh Mains Farm
Tel. Crawford (08642) 388

2 Dble/Twin — 1 Public Bath/Sh — B&B per person £8.00 Double — Open May-Oct, Dinner 1830

Mrs J Hyslop
Netherton Farm House
Tel. Crawford (08642) 321

COMMENDED

2 Dble/Twin, 1 Family — 1 Public Bath/Sh — B&B per person £9.00 Double — Open Jan-Dec, Dinner 1830

Built as a shooting lodge in 1896 for Edward VII. Countryside views.

Mrs Neilina Young
Lillievale, 17 Colebrooke Terrace
Tel. Crawford (08642) 294

1 Family — 1 Public Bath/Sh — B&B per person £8.50 Double — Open Jan-Dec

---

ABOYNE
Aberdeenshire — Map 4 F11

Mrs J Addy
Birseside, Birse
AB3 5BY
Tel. Aboyne (0330) 2000

3 Dble/Twin — 1 Public Bath/Sh — B&B per person £8.50 Double — Open Apr-Oct

---

ACHARACLE, Ardnamurchan
Argyll — Map 3 E12

Mrs M Cameron
Ardshealach
PH36 4JL
Tel. Salen (096785) 209

1 Single, 1 Dble/Twin, 1 Family — 1 Public Bath/Sh — B&B per person £7.00 Single, £7.00 Double — Open Apr-Oct, Dinner 1900

VAT is shown at 15%; changes in this rate may affect prices. Prices shown are for guidance only. Please send SAE with each enquiry.

ACHARACLE, Ardnamurchan continued Mrs Learmouth Belmont Tel. Salen (096785) 266	Map 3 E12		3 Dble/Twin	1 Public Bath/Sh	B&B per person £9.00 Double	Open Jan-Dec Dinner 1900	🛏 V ⚓ 🛏 ▥ 📺 ✦ ⏶ ⏚ ✳ P ⚠ C
ACHILTIBUIE Ross-shire Mrs M W MacLeod Dornie House Tel. Achiltibuie (085482) 271	Map 3 G6	Listed	3 Dble/Twin	1 Public Bath/Sh	B&B per person £8.00-£10.00 Double	Open Apr-Oct	🛏 ⚓ ▥ 📺 ✳ P ⚠ C 🔧
Mrs K Murray Summer Isle Marine, 119 Polglass IV26 2YG Tel. Achiltibuie (085482) 366			2 Dble/Twin	1 Public Bath/Sh	B&B per person £9.00-£10.00 Double	Open Apr-Oct Dinner 1800	⚓ V 🛏 ▥ 📺 ✦ ⏚ ✂ 🐕 ✳ P ⚠ 🔧
AIGNISH Lewis, Western Isles Mrs L G MacDonald Ceol-Na-Mara, 1a Aignish Tel. Garrabost (0851) 870339	Map 3 D4		3 Dble/Twin	1 Public Bath/Sh	B&B per person £8.00 Double	Open Jan-Dec Dinner 1830	⚓ 🛏 📺 ✦ ⏚ ⏶ 🐕 P C
AIRLIE, by Kirriemuir Angus Mrs D Grimmond Lismore Tel. Craigton (05753) 213	Map 2 D1		2 Dble/Twin	1 Public Bath/Sh	B&B per person £7.50 Double	Open Jan-Dec Dinner 1900	▱ ⚓ V 🛏 ▥ 📺 ⏚ ⏶ P C
ALEXANDRIA Dunbartonshire Mrs Janet Barr Southend Cottage, 280 Main Street Tel. Alexandria (0389) 50886	Map 1 H5		1 Dble/Twin 2 Family	1 Public Bath/Sh	B&B per person £8.00-£8.50 Double	Open Jan-Dec Dinner 1700	🛏 ▥ 📺 🐕 C
Mrs Isobel Owen 60 Luss Road Tel. Alexandria (0389) 53744			1 Dble/Twin	1 Public Bath/Sh	B&B per person £8.00 Double	Open Apr-Oct	▥ 📺
ALFORD Aberdeenshire Mrs Wink Sylvan, Main Street AB3 8QA Tel. Alford (0336) 2485	Map 4 F10		2 Dble/Twin 1 Family	1 Public Bath/Sh	B&B per person £7.50 Double	Open Jan-Dec	⚓ V 🛏 ▥ 📺 ✦ ⏚ ⏶ 🐕 P 🔧 C T
ALNESS Ross-shire Mrs J Cann Firthview, 13 Springfield Terrace IV17 0SP Tel. Alness (0349) 882346	Map 4 B7		3 Dble/Twin	1 Public Bath/Sh	B&B per person £5.50 Double	Open Jan-Dec Dinner 1800	⚓ 🛏 📺 P C
Mrs Dorothy MacDougall Averon Bank Cottage, Ardross Road IV17 0QA Tel. Alness (0349) 882392			1 Single 2 Dble/Twin	1 Public Bath/Sh	B&B per person £7.00 Single	Open Jan-Dec	▯ ⚓ V ▥ 📺 ⏚ ⏶ ✂ 🐕 P C

ALNESS continued Mrs MacPherson 29 Darroch Brae Tel. Alness (0349) 883551	Map 4 B7		2 Dble/Twin 1 Family	2 Public Bath/Sh	B&B per person £7.00-£8.00 Double	Open Jan-Dec	(symbols)
ALVES, Elgin Moray Mrs Janet E Philpott The White House, 17 Main Road IV30 3UR Tel. Alves (034385) 271	Map 4 D8		1 Single 1 Dble/Twin 2 Family		B&B per person £7.50-£8.00 Single £7.50-£8.00 Double	Open Jan-Dec Dinner 1800	(symbols)
ALYTH Perthshire Mrs Matthews The Old Parsonage, Cambridge Street PH11 8AW Tel. Alyth (08283) 2027	Map 2 C1		1 Single 3 Dble/Twin 1 Family	1 Public Bath/Sh	B&B per person £7.00 Single £7.00 Double	Open Apr-Oct	(symbols)
Mrs Mcbain Old Stables, Losset Road PH11 8BT Tel. Alyth (08283) 2547		COMMENDED Listed	1 Single 1 Dble/Twin 1 Family	1 Private Bath/Sh	B&B per person £8.00 Single £7.50 Double	Open Jan-Dec	(symbols)
			Modern, open plan house with feature log fireplace and sauna. Quiet residential area. Large garden.				
ANCRUM, Jedburgh Roxburghshire Mrs P Boyd Harrietsfield House Tel. Ancrum (08353) 327	Map 2 E7		3 Dble/Twin	1 Public Bath/Sh	B&B per person £9.00 Double	Open Apr-Oct	(symbols)
Mrs Hensens Ancrum Craig Tel. Ancrum (08353) 280		COMMENDED Listed	1 Dble/Twin 1 Family	2 Private Bath/Sh	B&B per person £10.00-£12.00 Double	Open Mar-Oct	(symbols)
			Stone built victorian house in quiet location. Magnificent views of hills and countryside.				
ANNAN Dumfriesshire Mrs F Hendry 18 St Johns Road Tel. Annan (04612) 4665	Map 2 C10		1 Single 2 Dble/Twin 1 Family	1 Public Bath/Sh	B&B per person £9.00 Single £8.00 Double	Open Jan-Dec Dinner 1800	(symbols)
Mr & Mrs J Johnston Winnyrigg Cottage Tel. Annan (04612) 4945			2 Dble/Twin	1 Public Bath/Sh	B&B per person £8.00-£8.50 Double	Open Jan-Dec Dinner 1800	(symbols)
K E Yates Beechgrove Manor Tel. Annan (04612) 2220			1 Single 4 Dble/Twin 1 Family	1 Private Bath/Sh 2 Public Bath/Sh	B&B per person £7.60 Single £7.60 Double	Open Jan-Dec Dinner 1800	(symbols)
ANSTRUTHER Fife Mrs E MacGeachy The Dykes, 69 Pittenweem Road Tel. Anstruther (0333) 310537	Map 2 E3		1 Dble/Twin 1 Family	1 Public Bath/Sh	B&B per person £8.00-£10.00 Double	Open Mar-Oct	(symbols)

ANSTRUTHER continued Mrs D Wheeler 5 Melville Terrace, Crail Road KY10 3EW Tel. Anstruther (0333) 310876	Map 2 E3		2 Dble/Twin 1 Family	1 Public Bath/Sh	B&B per person £8.00-£8.50 Double	Open Jun-Sep	▭ ⛱ ⚲ C
APPIN **Argyll** Mrs C Macmillan Shian Bay, North Shian PA38 4BA Tel. Appin (063173) 364	Map 1 E1	**COMMENDED** ♛	1 Dble/Twin	1 Private Bath/Sh	B&B per person £8.00 Double	Open Jan-Dec Dinner 1800	♟ ⚿ V ⌨ ▦ ❄ P △ ⚲ C
			Bungalow with grounds to shore. Bedroom and sunroom face south across Loch Crearan. Peaceful.				
APPLECROSS **Ross-shire** Mrs Griffin The Kennels Tel. Applecross (05204) 247	Map 3 E9		1 Family	1 Public Bath/Sh	B&B per person £7.00 Double	Open Mar-Sep Dinner 1800	V ⚿ ⌨ ⛱ ⚲ ⛅ ❄ P C
Mrs J Thomson Raon-Mor, Camustiel Tel. Applecross (05204) 260			3 Dble/Twin	1 Public Bath/Sh	B&B per person £7.00 Double	Open Apr-Oct Dinner 1830	♟ ⚿ V ⌨ ▦ TV ⛅ C
ARBIRLOT, by Arbroath **Angus** Mr G H Coulson Kelly Castle Tel. Arbroath (0241) 79765	Map 2 E1		4 Dble/Twin	4 Private Bath/Sh	B&B per person £6.00-£12.00 Double	Open May-Sep	⌨ ▦ TV ⚲ ⛱ ⛅ ❄ ✕ ⛩
ARBROATH **Angus** Harbour House Guest House 4 Shore Tel. Arbroath (0241) 78047	Map 2 E1		1 Dble/Twin 2 Family	1 Public Bath/Sh	B&B per person £8.00-£9.00 Double	Open Jan-Dec Dinner 1800	♟ ⬚ ☎ V ⌨ ▦ TV ⚲ ⛱ C
Kingsley Guest House 29-31 Marketgate Tel. Arbroath (0241) 73933			3 Single 7 Dble/Twin 4 Family	3 Public Bath/Sh	B&B per person £8.80 Single £8.00 Double	Open Jan-Dec Dinner 1730	♟ ⚿ V ⚱ ⌨ ▦ TV ⚲ ⛱ ⛅ C
Sandhutton Guest House 16 Addison Place DD11 2AX Tel. Arbroath (0241) 72007			1 Dble/Twin 2 Family	1 Public Bath/Sh	B&B per person £8.50-£9.00 Double	Open Mar-Oct Dinner 1730	♟ M ▢ ⚿ ☎ V ⌨ ▦ TV ⚲ ⛱ ⛅ ⚲ P
Mrs I Anderson Seahaven, 4 Addison Place Tel. Arbroath (0241) 72545			2 Dble/Twin 1 Family	1 Public Bath/Sh	B&B per person £7.50 Double	Open Jan-Dec Dinner 1700	V ⌨ ▦ TV ⛱ ⛅ C
Mr M Birse 6 Alexandra Place Tel. Arbroath (0241) 75660			2 Dble/Twin 1 Family	1 Public Bath/Sh	B&B per person £7.00-£7.50 Double	Open Jan-Dec	⚿ ⌨ TV ⚲ ⛱ ⛅ ⚲ P C
Mrs H M Henderson Ashlea, 27 Bellevue Gardens DD11 5BE Tel. Arbroath (0241) 74816			1 Dble/Twin 1 Family	1 Public Bath/Sh	B&B per person £7.50 Double	Open Jan-Dec	⚿ ▦ TV ⛱ ⛅ C
Mrs W G Kirkman Bankhead, Arbirlot Tel. Arbroath (0241) 75335			3 Dble/Twin	1 Private Bath/Sh 1 Public Bath/Sh	B&B per person £8.00 Double	Open Apr-Oct	♟ ⚿ V ▦ TV ❄ P C
Mrs J Paterson 60 Nolt Loan Road Tel. Arbroath (0241) 76107			2 Dble/Twin 1 Family	1 Public Bath/Sh	B&B per person £8.00 Double	Open Jan-Dec Dinner 1700	♟ ☎ ⌨ ▦ TV C

Key to symbols is on back flap. Details of Classification and Grading are on page vi.

11

ARDENTINNY Argyll Mrs Mathison Drynain Cottage PA23 8TT Tel. Ardentinny (036981) 232	Map 1 G4		1 Dble/Twin 1 Family		B&B per person £8.00 Double	Open Jan-Dec
ARDFERN, by Lochgilphead Argyll Mrs M Peterson Traighmhor Tel. Barbreck (08525) 228	Map 1 E3	APPROVED Listed	4 Dble/Twin	1 Public Bath/Sh	B&B per person £8.50 Double	Open Jan-Dec Dinner 1930
			Modern, on working croft. Picturesque site beside loch Craignish. Traditional Scottish home cooking.			
ARDGAY Sutherland Croit Mairi Guest House Kincardine Hill IV24 3DJ Tel. Ardgay (08632) 504	Map 4 A6	COMMENDED	5 Dble/Twin 1 Family	2 Public Bath/Sh	B&B per person £9.00 Double	Open Jan-Dec Dinner 1900
			Modern, purpose built, above village. Superb views to Bonar Bridge and hills beyond. Friendly home.			
Mrs C A Skinner Kincardine House Tel. Ardgay (08632) 471		Listed	3 Dble/Twin	1 Public Bath/Sh	B&B per person £7.50 Double	Open Jan-Dec
ARDRISHAIG, by Lochgilphead Argyll Mrs Briggs Canal House Tel. Lochgilphead (0546) 3212	Map 1 E4		1 Dble/Twin 2 Family	1 Public Bath/Sh	B&B per person £7.00-£7.50 Double	Open Jan-Dec Dinner 1800
ARDROSSAN Ayrshire The Beeches Guest House 56 Eglinton Road KA22 8NQ Tel. Ardrossan (0294) 64029	Map 1 G6		1 Single 2 Dble/Twin 2 Family	1 Public Bath/Sh	B&B per person £8.50 Single £7.50 Double	Open Jan-Dec Dinner 1730
Edenmore Guest House 47 Park House Road Tel. Ardrossan (0294) 62306			1 Single 4 Dble/Twin 2 Family		B&B per person £8.00-£8.50 Single £7.00-£7.50 Double	Open Jan-Dec
ARDVASAR, Sleat Isle of Skye, Inverness-shire Mrs Barton Hazelwood Tel. Ardvasar (04714) 200	Map 3 E11		2 Dble/Twin	1 Public Bath/Sh	B&B per person £8.50 Double	Open Jan-Dec
ARISAIG Inverness-shire Mrs Henderson Tigh-na-Bruaich, Traigh Tel. Arisaig (06875) 645	Map 3 E12		3 Dble/Twin	1 Public Bath/Sh	B&B per person £7.50 Double	Open Apr-Oct
ARROCHAR Dunbartonshire Fascadail House Guest House Tel. Arrochar (03012) 344	Map 1 G3		3 Dble/Twin 3 Family	1 Public Bath/Sh	B&B per person £8.00-£8.50 Double	Open Jan-Dec Dinner 1850

	Map Ref	Grading	Accommodation	Bathrooms	Prices	Opening
ARROCHAR continued Greenbank Guest House Tel. Arrochar (03012) 305	Map 1 G3		1 Single 2 Dble/Twin 1 Family	4 Private Bath/Sh 1 Public Bath/Sh	B&B per person £10.00-£11.00 Single £10.00-£11.00 Double	Open Jan-Dec Dinner 1700
Mansfield Guest House Tel. Arrochar (03012) 282		COMMENDED 👑 👑	3 Dble/Twin 1 Family Friendly, personal attention. Home cooking, log fire in lounge. Overlooks Loch Long and The Cobbler.	1 Public Bath/Sh	B&B per person £9.50 Double	Open Jan-Dec Dinner 1900
Mrs Harvey Ardvreck Tel. Arrochar (03012) 368			2 Dble/Twin 1 Family	1 Public Bath/Sh	B&B per person £8.00-£9.00 Double	Open Feb-Nov
Mrs M Rose Rossmay House & Boat Hire Centre Tel. Arrochar (03012) 250			2 Single 3 Dble/Twin 1 Family	2 Public Bath/Sh	B&B per person £9.00-£10.00 Single £8.00-£9.00 Double	Open Jan-Dec Dinner 1900
AUCHENCAIRN, by Castle Douglas **Kirkcudbrightshire** Mrs Cannon Collin House Tel. Auchencairn (055664) 242	Map 2 B11	Awaiting Inspection	2 Dble/Twin 1 Family	1 Private Bath/Sh 2 Public Bath/Sh	B&B per person £10.00 Single £8.50-£9.00 Double	Open Apr-Oct Dinner 1800
AUCHINLECK **Ayrshire** Mrs R McKinley Hillend of Heateth Farm Tel. Cumnock (0290) 22086	Map 1 H7		1 Dble/Twin 1 Family	1 Public Bath/Sh	B&B per person £8.00 Double	Open Apr-Nov Dinner 1800
AUCHTERARDER **Perthshire** Oakwood Guest House Castle Wynd PH3 1DA Tel. Auchterarder (07646) 2401	Map 2 B3		1 Single 2 Dble/Twin 1 Family	1 Public Bath/Sh	B&B per person £10.50-£12.00 Single £10.50-£12.00 Double	Open Jan-Dec Dinner 1800
Mrs Armour Deansland, 17 High Street PH3 1DB Tel. Auchterarder (07646) 2528			1 Single 2 Dble/Twin	1 Public Bath/Sh	B&B per person £10.00-£11.00 Single £10.00-£11.00 Double	Open Apr-Oct
Mrs F Hunter The Parsonage, 111 High Street Tel. Auchterarder (07646) 2062			1 Dble/Twin 2 Family	1 Private Bath/Sh 1 Public Bath/Sh	B&B per person £8.00-£9.00 Double	Open Jan-Dec
Mrs R B Mcfarlane Mamore, 10 The Grove PH3 1DB Tel. Auchterarder (07646) 2036			1 Dble/Twin	1 Public Bath/Sh	B&B per person £7.00 Double	Open Apr-Oct
Mrs S Robertson Nether Coul PH3 1NT Tel. Auchterarder (07646) 3119			1 Single 1 Dble/Twin 1 Family	1 Private Bath/Sh 1 Public Bath/Sh	B&B per person £8.00-£9.50 Single £8.50-£9.50 Double	Open Jan-Dec Dinner 1800

Key to symbols is on back flap. Details of Classification and Grading are on page vi.

13

AUCHTERARDER continued — Map 2 B3

Mrs Toms
39 Townhead
PH3 1JG
Tel. Auchterarder (07646) 2154

2 Dble/Twin
1 Family | 1 Public Bath/Sh | B&B per person £7.00-£7.50 Double | Open Jan-Dec Dinner 1750

Mrs Williams
Ben Affray House, 28 High St
PH3 1DF
Tel. Auchterarder (07646) 2457

COMMENDED 👑👑

3 Dble/Twin | 1 Public Bath/Sh | B&B per person £9.00 Double | Open Jan-Dec Dinner 1800

Family run. Garden available for guest use. Parking for 3 cars.

AUCHTERMUCHTY — Fife — Map 2 C3

Mrs Isobel J Steven
Ardchoille, Woodmill Farm
Tel. Auchtermuchty (0337) 28414

COMMENDED 👑👑👑

1 Dble/Twin
2 Family | 3 Private Bath/Sh
2 Public Bath/Sh | B&B per person £12.50 Double | Open Jan-Dec Dinner 1830

Modern farmhouse with open views. Home cooking, bread, preserves. Jersey milk and free range eggs.

AULDEARN — Nairn — Map 4 C8

Mrs E Leslie
Brightmony House
IV12 5PP
Tel. Nairn (0667) 52927

1 Single
2 Dble/Twin | 1 Public Bath/Sh | B&B per person £6.50-£7.00 Single £6.50-£7.00 Double | Open Jan-Dec Dinner 1830

AULDGIRTH — Dumfriesshire — Map 2 B9

Mrs P A Burford
Allanton House
Tel. Auldgirth (038774) 509

4 Single
7 Dble/Twin | 2 Public Bath/Sh | B&B per person £8.00 Single £8.00 Double | Open Jan-Dec Dinner 1800

AULTBEA — Ross-shire — Map 3 F7

Mrs MacDonald
6 Pier Road
IV22 2JQ
Tel. Aultbea (044582) 251

1 Single
2 Dble/Twin
1 Family | 1 Public Bath/Sh | B&B per person £6.00 Single £6.00 Double | Open Mar-Oct Dinner 1800

Mrs A MacLennan
5 Pier Road
IV22 2JQ
Tel. Aultbea (044582) 336

Listed

1 Single
1 Dble/Twin
1 Family | 1 Public Bath/Sh | B&B per person £7.50-£8.00 Single £7.50-£8.00 Double | Open Jan-Dec Dinner 1800

Mrs MacNeill
Buena Vista
Tel. Aultbea (044582) 374

1 Single
2 Dble/Twin | 1 Public Bath/Sh | B&B per person £7.50-£8.50 Single £7.50-£8.50 Double | Open Apr-Oct

---

Mrs A MacRae
Mellondale, 47 Mellon Charles
Tel. Aultbea (044582) 326

3 Dble/Twin | 2 Public Bath/Sh | B&B per person £7.50-£8.50 Double | Open Mar-Oct Dinner 1830

Mrs P Macrae
Cove View
Tel. Aultbea (044582) 351

4 Dble/Twin | 2 Public Bath/Sh | B&B per person £8.00 Double | Open Mar-Nov Dinner 1900

Mrs H McLeod
The Croft
Tel. Aultbea (044582) 352

Listed

1 Dble/Twin
2 Family | 1 Public Bath/Sh | B&B per person £7.50-£8.00 Double | Open Jan-Dec Dinner 1900

VAT is shown at 15%: changes in this rate may affect prices. Prices shown are for guidance only. Please send SAE with each enquiry.

AVIEMORE Inverness-shire	Map 4 C10						
Balavoulin Guest House Tel. Aviemore (0479) 810672		APPROVED 👑 👑	1 Single 3 Dble/Twin 3 Family	5 Private Bath/Sh 1 Public Bath/Sh	B&B per person £15.00-£17.00 Single £10.00-£11.00 Double	Open Jan-Dec Dinner 1830	
			Traditional stone building with original pine work. Close to attractions of village centre.				
Craiglea Guest House PH22 1RH Tel. Aviemore (0479) 810210			1 Single 6 Dble/Twin 4 Family	1 Private Bath/Sh 2 Public Bath/Sh	B&B per person £9.50-£10.50 Single £9.50-£10.50 Double	Open Jan-Dec	

KINAPOL GUEST HOUSE
Dalfaber Road, Aviemore, Inverness-shire.
Tel. 0479 810513

Modern, family-run guest house in quiet situation close to Aviemore Centre and Station (5 minutes' walk). All bedrooms have H&C, etc., and most have unrestricted views over Spey Valley to Cairngorm Mountains. Large bright guests' lounge with woodstove, TV, and tea/coffee-making facilities. Large garden with access to river. Drying cupboard and ski store. Some bicycles for guests' use. Reduced rates for weekly bookings.

Kinapol Guest House Dalfaber Road Tel. Aviemore (0479) 810513			5 Dble/Twin	2 Public Bath/Sh	B&B per person £8.50-£9.00 Double	Open Jan-Dec	
Ravenscraig Guest House PH22 1RP Tel. Aviemore (0479) 810278			1 Single 8 Dble/Twin 3 Family	9 Private Bath/Sh 1 Public Bath/Sh	B&B per person £10.00-£11.50 Single £10.00-£11.50 Double	Open Jan-Dec	
Mr & Mrs J H Baxter Loramore, Grampian Road Tel. Aviemore (0479) 810304			4 Dble/Twin 1 Family	1 Public Bath/Sh	B&B per person £8.00-£9.50 Double	Open Dec-Oct	
Mrs F Bruce Hame, Dalfaber Road PH22 1PY Tel. Aviemore (0479) 810822			1 Single 2 Dble/Twin	1 Public Bath/Sh	B&B per person £7.50-£8.00 Single £7.50-£8.50 Double	Open Jan-Dec	
Mrs Chalmer Avolon Tel. Aviemore (0479) 810878			1 Dble/Twin 2 Family	1 Public Bath/Sh	B&B per person £8.00-£9.00 Double	Open Jan-Dec Dinner 1700	
Mrs E Clark Sonas, 19 Muirton Tel. Aviemore (0479) 810409		APPROVED 👑	3 Dble/Twin	2 Public Bath/Sh	B&B per person £8.50-£9.00 Double	Open Jan-Dec	
			Modern establishment within easy walking distance of the centre's many amenities.				
Mrs J Cornfoot The Polchar Tel. Aviemore (0479) 810911			1 Dble/Twin 2 Family	1 Private Bath/Sh 1 Public Bath/Sh	B&B per person £8.00 Double	Open Jan-Oct Dinner 1850	
Mrs A Doherty 2 Queens Houses, Glenmore Tel. Cairngorm (047986) 210			1 Dble/Twin 1 Family	1 Public Bath/Sh	B&B per person £7.50 Double	Open Jan-Dec	

Key to symbols is on back flap. Details of Classification and Grading are on page vi.

15

AVIEMORE continued	Map 4 C10					
Mrs J R Faulkner 14 Muirton PH22 1SF Tel. Aviemore (0479) 810881		2 Dble/Twin	1 Public Bath/Sh	B&B per person £8.00 Double	Open Jan-Dec	
Mrs A M Ferguson Craigeyne, Glenmore PH22 1QU Tel. Cairngorm (047986) 223		1 Dble/Twin 1 Family	1 Public Bath/Sh	B&B per person £7.50 Double	Open Jan-Dec	
Mrs Fiona Grant Outlook, Avielochan Farm PH22 1QD Tel. Aviemore (0479) 810846		1 Dble/Twin 1 Family	1 Public Bath/Sh	B&B per person £7.00-£8.50 Double	Open Jan-Dec	
Mrs E M Grant Avielochan Tel. Aviemore (0479) 810282		2 Single 2 Dble/Twin	1 Public Bath/Sh	B&B per person £7.00-£7.50 Single £7.00-£7.50 Double	Open Jan-Dec	
Mrs M Harper 32 Seafield Place PH22 1RZ Tel. Aviemore (0479) 810433		1 Dble/Twin 1 Family	1 Public Bath/Sh	B&B per person £8.50 Double	Open Jan-Dec	
Mrs S Kennedy Ranville PH22 1RL Tel. Aviemore (0479) 810631		1 Dble/Twin 1 Family	1 Public Bath/Sh	B&B per person £8.00 Double	Open Jan-Dec	
Mrs Macpherson Laimrig, 1 Muirton PH22 1SE Tel. Aviemore (0479) 810355		2 Dble/Twin	2 Public Bath/Sh	B&B per person £8.50 Double	Open Jan-Dec	
Mrs D J McCormick Junipers, 5 Dell Mhor Tel. Aviemore (0479) 810405		3 Dble/Twin 1 Family	1 Public Bath/Sh	B&B per person £7.00-£7.50 Double	Open Jan-Dec	
Mrs Lorna McKenna 3 Dellmhor, Rothiemurchus Tel. Aviemore (0479) 810358		1 Dble/Twin 1 Family	1 Public Bath/Sh	B&B per person £8.00 Double	Open Jan-Dec	
Mrs Noble Ardlogie, Dalfaber Road Tel. Aviemore (0479) 810747	👑👑	3 Dble/Twin 1 Family	2 Public Bath/Sh	B&B per person £8.50 Double	Open Jan-Dec	
Mrs O'Donnell 3 Queens House, Glenmore Tel. Cairngorm (047986) 255		2 Dble/Twin	1 Public Bath/Sh	B&B per person £7.50 Double	Open Jan-Dec	
Mrs E Orr Carn Mhor Tel. Aviemore (0479) 810249		1 Single 4 Dble/Twin 1 Family	1 Public Bath/Sh	B&B per person £8.50-£9.00 Single £8.00 Double	Open Jan-Dec	
Mrs J Palombo Strathavon, Dalfaber Road Tel. Aviemore (0479) 810034		2 Dble/Twin 1 Family	1 Public Bath/Sh	B&B per person £8.00 Single £8.00 Double	Open Jan-Dec	

VAT is shown at 15%: changes in this rate may affect prices. Prices shown are for guidance only. Please send SAE with each enquiry.

	Map		Rooms	Bath	Price	Open	Symbols
AVIEMORE continued Mrs E Paxton 29 Craig-na-Gower Avenue PH22 1RW Tel. Aviemore (0479) 810641	Map 4 C10		1 Dble/Twin 2 Family	1 Public Bath/Sh	B&B per person £8.00-£9.50 Double	Open Jan-Dec	
Mrs W Riley Kila, Grampian Road Tel. Aviemore (0479) 810573			2 Dble/Twin 2 Family	2 Public Bath/Sh	B&B per person £8.50-£9.00 Double	Open Jan-Dec	
Mrs R Severn Ver Mont Villa, Grampian Road Tel. Aviemore (0479) 810470			3 Dble/Twin 1 Family	2 Public Bath/Sh	B&B per person £7.50-£8.50 Double	Open Jan-Dec Dinner 1900	
Mrs M Tonkin 11 Muirton Tel. Aviemore (0479) 810365			2 Dble/Twin	2 Public Bath/Sh	B&B per person £7.50 Double	Open Jan-Dec	
Mr Mark Van Twest Feithlinn, Dalfaber Road PH22 1PU Tel. Aviemore (0479) 810839			1 Single 3 Dble/Twin 1 Family	2 Public Bath/Sh	B&B per person £7.50-£8.00 Single £7.50-£8.00 Double	Open Jan-Dec	
AVONBRIDGE, by Falkirk **Stirlingshire** Mrs M Ireland Westside Farm FK1 2JP Tel. Avonbridge (032486) 424	Map 2 B5		2 Dble/Twin 1 Family	1 Public Bath/Sh	B&B per person £10.00 Double	Open Jan-Dec Dinner 1800	
Mrs Wilson Avonmill Cottage Tel. Avonbridge (032486) 592			1 Dble/Twin	1 Public Bath/Sh	B&B per person £8.50 Double	Open Jan-Dec Dinner 1700	
AYR Armadale Guest House 33 Bellevue Crescent KA7 2DP Tel. Ayr (0292) 264320	Map 1 G7		1 Single 2 Dble/Twin 1 Family	1 Private Bath/Sh 1 Public Bath/Sh	B&B per person £8.50 Single £8.50 Double	Open Jan-Dec Dinner 1800	
Craggallan Guest House 8 Queen's Terrace KA7 1DU Tel. Ayr (0292) 264998		**APPROVED** Listed	1 Single 2 Dble/Twin 2 Family	1 Public Bath/Sh	B&B per person £9.00-£10.00 Single £9.00-£10.00 Double	Open Jan-Dec Dinner 1730	
			One minute's walk from a sandy beach and a 2 mile (3km) long promenade and gardens.				
Donbar Guest House 5 Queen's Terrace KA7 1DU Tel. Ayr (0292) 265749			2 Dble/Twin 1 Family	1 Public Bath/Sh	B&B per person £8.50-£9.00 Double	Open Jan-Dec Dinner 1730	
Gargowan Guest House 35 Racecourse Road KA7 2TG Tel. Ayr (0292) 264493			2 Single 4 Dble/Twin 6 Family	2 Public Bath/Sh	B&B per person £9.00 Single £9.00 Double	Open Apr-Oct Dinner 1830	

Key to symbols is on back flap. Details of Classification and Grading are on page vi.

AYR continued	Map 1 G7						
Queen's Guest House 10 Queen's Terrace KA7 1DU Tel. Ayr (0292) 265618			1 Single 1 Dble/Twin 3 Family	1 Public Bath/Sh	B&B per person £9.00-£9.50 Single £9.00-£9.50 Double	Open Jan-Dec Dinner 1700	
Mrs Alice Abbott 22 Queen's Terrace KA7 1DX Tel. Ayr (0292) 266619			1 Dble/Twin 2 Family		B&B per person £8.50-£9.00 Double	Open Jan-Dec	
Mr & Mrs H W Anton Clyde Cottage, 1 Arran Terrace KA7 1JF Tel. Ayr (0292) 267368		👑 👑	2 Dble/Twin 1 Family	1 Public Bath/Sh	B&B per person £8.00-£10.00 Double	Open Jan-Dec Dinner 1800	
Mrs Berretti 23 Dalblair Road KA7 1UF Tel. Ayr (0292) 282227			1 Single 2 Family	1 Public Bath/Sh	B&B per person £8.00-£9.00 Single £8.00 Double	Open Apr-Oct	
Mrs Mary Boyd 52 Holmston Road KA7 3BE Tel. Ayr (0292) 266518			2 Single 2 Dble/Twin	2 Public Bath/Sh	B&B per person £10.00 Single £10.00 Double	Open Jan-Dec	
Mrs I Cairns 32 Holmston Road KA7 3BD Tel. Ayr (0292) 261520			2 Family	1 Public Bath/Sh	B&B per person £8.50-£9.00 Double	Open Jan-Dec Dinner 1800	
Mrs S Dunn The Dunn Thing, 13 Park Circus KA7 2DJ Tel. Ayr (0292) 284531			2 Dble/Twin 2 Family	2 Public Bath/Sh	B&B per person £9.00 Double	Open Jan-Dec	
Mrs Halima Erenlioglu 33 Prestwick Road KA8 8LE Tel. Ayr (0292) 266394			1 Single 2 Dble/Twin 1 Family	2 Public Bath/Sh	B&B per person £8.50-£9.00 Single £8.50-£9.00 Double	Open Jan-Dec Dinner 1700	
Mrs Fawcett 8 Holmston Road KA7 3BB Tel. Ayr (0292) 264536			1 Single 3 Family	1 Public Bath/Sh	B&B per person £8.50-£9.00 Single £8.50-£9.00 Double	Open Jan-Dec	
Mrs T Filippi Coilbank Villa, 32 Castlehill Road KA7 2HZ Tel. Ayr (0292) 262936		COMMENDED Listed	1 Single 2 Dble/Twin	1 Private Bath/Sh 1 Public Bath/Sh	B&B per person £8.50-£9.00 Single £8.00-£8.50 Double	Open Apr-Sep Dinner 1800	
			Stone built victorian town house convenient for town centre.				
Mrs J Gardner 16 Ewenfield Road KA7 2QB Tel. Ayr (0292) 262065			1 Single 4 Dble/Twin	3 Public Bath/Sh	B&B per person £12.00-£14.00 Single £10.00-£12.00 Double	Open Apr-Oct	
Mrs W Goodwin Strathyre House, 42 Prestwick Road KA8 8LB Tel. Ayr (0292) 284026			3 Dble/Twin	2 Public Bath/Sh	B&B per person £8.50 Double	Open Apr-Oct Dinner 1800	
Mrs Guthrie Dargil, 7 Queen's Terrace KA7 1DU Tel. Ayr (0292) 261955			1 Single 2 Dble/Twin	1 Public Bath/Sh	B&B per person £8.00-£9.00 Single £8.00-£9.00 Double	Open Jan-Dec Dinner 1700	

VAT is shown at 15%. changes in this rate may affect prices. Prices shown are for guidance only. Please send SAE with each enquiry.

AYR continued	Map 1 G7					
Mrs Shiona Hogg 111 Castlehill Road KA7 2LE Tel. Ayr (0292) 260660			3 Dble/Twin	1 Public Bath/Sh	B&B per person £9.00 Double	Open Apr-Oct
Mrs Howie Craig Court, 22 Eglinton Terrace KA7 1JJ Tel. Ayr (0292) 261028			1 Single 2 Dble/Twin 2 Family	1 Public Bath/Sh	B&B per person £9.00 Single £9.00 Double	Open Jan-Dec
Mrs M Jellema 69 Prestwick Road KA8 8LG Tel. Ayr (0292) 267551			1 Dble/Twin 1 Family		B&B per person £8.00 Double	Open Jan-Dec
Mrs Ian Jess The Round House, 16 Carrick Avenue KA7 2SN Tel. Ayr (0292) 266757			2 Dble/Twin 1 Family	1 Private Bath/Sh 2 Public Bath/Sh	B&B per person £9.00 Double	Open Jan-Dec
Mrs Nan MacLeod 102 Castlehill Road KA7 2LF Tel. Ayr (0292) 266723			2 Dble/Twin 1 Family	1 Private Bath/Sh 1 Public Bath/Sh	B&B per person £8.00 Double	Open Apr-Oct
Mrs J B Mair Laggan, 42 Craigie Road KA8 0EZ Tel. Ayr (0292) 264947			1 Single 1 Family	1 Public Bath/Sh	B&B per person £8.50 Single £8.50 Double	Open Apr-Oct
Mrs N McConnachie Millbank, 16 Cromwell Road KA7 1DY Tel. Ayr (0292) 268448			1 Dble/Twin 1 Family	1 Public Bath/Sh	B&B per person £8.00 Double	Open Jun-Sep
Mrs McLellan Enfield, 48 Bellevale Avenue KA7 2RP Tel. Ayr (0292) 284684			1 Dble/Twin	1 Public Bath/Sh	B&B per person £7.50-£8.50 Double	Open Apr-Sep Dinner 1730
Mrs McPherson Beechwood, 39 Prestwick Road Tel. Ayr (0292) 262093			3 Single 3 Dble/Twin 2 Family	1 Public Bath/Sh	B&B per person £8.50-£9.00 Single £8.50-£9.00 Double	Open Jan-Dec
Mrs Morton Bogend Farm, Mossblown KA6 5AZ Tel. Annbank (0292) 520327			1 Dble/Twin 1 Family	1 Public Bath/Sh	B&B per person £7.50-£8.00 Double	Open Apr-Oct Dinner 1800
Miss M Murdoch 13 Forest Way KA7 3ST Tel. Ayr (0292) 267100			1 Dble/Twin 1 Family	1 Public Bath/Sh	B&B per person £8.00-£8.50 Double	Open Apr-Oct
Mrs Mary M Paterson Balmoral, 5 Carrick Road KA7 2RA Tel. Ayr (0292) 265487			1 Single 1 Dble/Twin 1 Family	1 Public Bath/Sh	B&B per person £7.50-£8.00 Single £7.50-£8.00 Double	Open Apr-Oct
Mrs Paulin Brookholm, 15 Castlehill Road KA7 2HX Tel. Ayr (0292) 289510			1 Dble/Twin 2 Family	1 Public Bath/Sh	B&B per person £8.50-£9.50 Double	Open Jan-Dec

Key to symbols is on back flap. Details of Classification and Grading are on page vi.

Name & Address	Map	Rating	Rooms	Bath/Shower	Terms	Opening	Facilities
AYR continued Mrs M Robb Carcluie Farm, Dalrymple Road KA6 6BP Tel. Dalrymple (029256) 554	Map 1 G7		4 Dble/Twin	1 Public Bath/Sh	B&B per person £7.50-£8.50 Double	Open Mar-Oct	
Mrs Stewart Reynolds, 74 St Leonards Road KA7 2PT Tel. Ayr (0292) 267450		COMMENDED Listed	3 Dble/Twin 2 Family	2 Public Bath/Sh	B&B per person £10.00 Double	Open Jan-Dec	
			Victorian semi detached house on main road to Turnberry. Near town centre and seafront.				
Mrs Helen White Leapark, 42 Ashgove Street KA7 3BG Tel. Ayr (0292) 260575		COMMENDED 👑👑	2 Single 1 Dble/Twin 1 Family	2 Public Bath/Sh	B&B per person £9.00 Single £8.50 Double	Open Jan-Dec Dinner 1800	
			Semi detached stone built house. Quiet residential area, close to public transport. Home cooking.				
Mrs Wilson Deanbank, 44 Ashgrove Street KA7 3BG Tel. Ayr (0292) 263745			1 Single 1 Dble/Twin 1 Family	2 Public Bath/Sh	B&B per person £9.00 Single £8.00 Double	Open Jan-Dec	
AYTON Berwickshire Mrs Riach Ayton Mains Farm House Tel. Ayton (08907) 81336	Map 2 G5		1 Single 2 Dble/Twin	2 Public Bath/Sh	B&B per person £7.50-£8.00 Single £7.00-£7.50 Double	Open Apr-Oct Dinner 1800	
AYWICK, Yell Shetland Pinewood Guest House Upper Toft Tel. Mid Yell (0957) 2077	Map 5 G2		3 Dble/Twin	2 Private Bath/Sh 2 Public Bath/Sh	B&B per person £10.50-£12.50 Double	Open Jan-Dec Dinner 1900	
BACK Lewis, Western Isles Mrs MacKay 23 Back Tel. Back (085182) 212	Map 3 D4		2 Dble/Twin 1 Family	1 Public Bath/Sh	B&B per person £7.00-£7.50 Double	Open Apr-Oct Dinner 1700	
Mrs A Stewart 12 Back Tel. Back (085182) 301			2 Dble/Twin 1 Family	1 Private Bath/Sh 1 Public Bath/Sh	B&B per person £7.50 Double	Open Jan-Dec Dinner 1800	
BADACHRO Ross-shire Mrs E M Park Harbour View Tel. Badachro (044583) 213	Map 3 E7	Awaiting Inspection	1 Single 3 Dble/Twin 1 Family	1 Private Bath/Sh 1 Public Bath/Sh	B&B per person £8.00-£8.50 Single £8.00-£9.00 Double	Open Mar-Oct Dinner 1900	
BADCAUL, Dundonnell Ross-shire Mr & Mrs R Mannion Badcaul House IV23 2QY Tel. Dundonnell (085483) 213	Map 3 G6		1 Dble/Twin 2 Family	1 Public Bath/Sh	B&B per person £7.50-£8.50 Double	Open Jan-Dec Dinner 1800	

VAT is shown at 15%: changes in this rate may affect prices. Prices shown are for guidance only. Please send SAE with each enquiry.

BALERNO Midlothian Mrs Joan M Sayers 19 Marchbank Drive EH14 7ER Tel. 031 449 3095	Map 2 C5		1 Single 2 Dble/Twin	2 Public Bath/Sh	B&B per person £8.00-£9.00 Single £8.00-£9.00 Double	Open Jan-Dec Dinner 1900	⛏🖥🛏💺✂️ 🅿
BALGEDIE, by Kinross Mrs S Milne Levenbank KY13 7HE Tel. Scotlandwell (059284) 234	Map 2 C3		1 Family	1 Public Bath/Sh	B&B per person £8.00-£8.50 Double	Open Mar-Nov	⛏☕🖥💺🅿 C
BALLACHULISH Argyll Craigellachie Guest House PA39 4JB Tel. Ballachulish (08552) 531	Map 1 F1		1 Single 5 Dble/Twin 2 Family	1 Public Bath/Sh	B&B per person £7.25-£7.95 Single £7.25-£7.95 Double	Open Jan-Oct Dinner 1900	⛏🍷V🏆💺 TV 🐕✂️🅿 ⚠ C
Craiglinnhe Guest House Tel. Ballachulish (08552) 270		Listed	2 Dble/Twin 1 Family	2 Public Bath/Sh	B&B per person £7.50-£8.00 Double	Open Apr-Oct	💺🖥 TV ❄🅿 ♻ C
Mrs B Cook Fern Villa Tel. Ballachulish (08552) 393			2 Dble/Twin	1 Public Bath/Sh	B&B per person £7.50-£8.50 Double	Open Jan-Dec Dinner 1900	⛏🍷💺🖥 TV 🐕🅿 C
BALLANTRAE Ayrshire Mrs H McClung Antrim View, Seafront KA26 0NQ Tel. Ballantrae (046583) 376	Map 1 F9	COMMENDED Listed	2 Dble/Twin 1 Family	1 Public Bath/Sh	B&B per person £7.00 Double	Open Apr-Oct Dinner 1800	⛏💺V🏆🖥 TV ⚠ C
			On seafront, near ferry port to Ireland. Sea angling, golf. Tour Burn's country; see Culzean Castle.				
Mrs E McIntyre Downan Farm KA26 0PB Tel. Ballantrae (046583) 226			1 Dble/Twin 1 Family	1 Public Bath/Sh	B&B per person £7.00 Double	Open Apr-Oct	V💺 TV ✂❄🅿 ⚠ 🐕 C 🐎🎣
BALLATER Aberdeenshire The Ballater Guest House 34 Victoria Road AB3 5QX Tel. Ballater (0338) 55346	Map 4 E11		5 Single 7 Dble/Twin 1 Family	2 Public Bath/Sh	B&B per person £8.75 Single £16.50 Double	Open Mar-Oct Dinner 1900	⛏🍷V🏆💺 🖥 TV ✂🛏💺 🐕🅿 🎣 C
Dee Valley Guest House 26 Viewfield Road AB3 5RD Tel. Ballater (0338) 55408		COMMENDED 👑👑	2 Dble/Twin 2 Family	2 Public Bath/Sh	B&B per person £8.75-£10.00 Double	Open Apr-Oct Dinner 1800	⛏🍷💺V💺 TV ✂🛏🐕 🅿 C
			Detached house in quiet residential area close to village centre. Personally supervised by owners.				
Glenbardie Guest House Braemar Road AB3 5RQ Tel. Ballater (0338) 55537			4 Dble/Twin 2 Family	2 Private Bath/Sh 1 Public Bath/Sh	B&B per person £9.00-£11.00 Double	Open Apr-Oct	⛏💺🖥 TV ❄£🅿
Killarney Guest House AB3 5RS Tel. Ballater (0338) 55465		COMMENDED 👑👑	1 Single 4 Dble/Twin	1 Public Bath/Sh	B&B per person £8.00 Single £8.00 Double	Open Apr-Oct Dinner 1830	💺V💺 TV 🐕🛏 🅿
			Detached, stone built house in quiet residential area. Adjacent to golf course and bowling green.				

Key to symbols is on back flap. Details of Classification and Grading are on page vi.

21

BALLATER continued	Map 4 E11						
Mrs Beaton Cornellan, Braemar Road AB3 5RQ Tel. Ballater (0338) 55410			2 Dble/Twin 1 Family	1 Public Bath/Sh	B&B per person £7.50 Double	Open May-Sep	
Mrs J Greenlaw The Maples, 27 Braemar Road AB3 5RL Tel. Ballater (0338) 55931			3 Dble/Twin	1 Public Bath/Sh	B&B per person £8.50 Double	Open Apr-Oct	
A & P Henchie Morven Lodge, 29 Braemar Road AB3 5RQ Tel. Ballater (0338) 55373			2 Dble/Twin 1 Family	2 Public Bath/Sh	B&B per person £8.50-£10.00 Double	Open Jun-Oct	
Mrs Jeffs Bield, Braemar Road Tel. Ballater (0338) 55208			3 Dble/Twin	1 Public Bath/Sh	B&B per person £8.00 Double	Open Apr-Oct Dinner 1900	
BALLINDALLOCH Banffshire	Map 4 D9						
Mrs Halliday Woodville AB3 9AD Tel. Ballindalloch (08072) 347			3 Dble/Twin	1 Private Bath/Sh 1 Public Bath/Sh	B&B per person £7.50-£8.50 Double	Open May-Aug Dinner 1930	
BALLINLUIG Perthshire	Map 2 B1						
Tighrioch Guest House PH9 0NE Tel. Ballinluig (079682) 518			2 Single 3 Dble/Twin 2 Family	2 Public Bath/Sh	B&B per person £8.50 Single £8.50 Double	Open Jan-Dec Dinner 1800	
Mrs Hendry Wester Tulliemet, Tulliemet Tel. Ballinluig (079682) 208			1 Single 1 Dble/Twin 1 Family	1 Public Bath/Sh	B&B per person £8.50-£9.00 Single £8.50-£9.00 Double	Open Apr-Oct Dinner 1830	
Mrs Meredith Auchnaguie Farm House, Tulliemet PH9 0NZ Tel. Ballinluig (079682) 369		Listed	1 Single 2 Dble/Twin 2 Family	1 Public Bath/Sh	B&B per person £9.00 Single £9.00 Double	Open Apr-Oct Dinner 1830	
BALLINTUIM Perthshire	Map 2 C1						
Mr & Mrs Mear Merklands Tel. Strathardle (025081) 218			2 Dble/Twin 1 Family	2 Public Bath/Sh	B&B per person £8.50 Double	Open Jan-Oct	
BALLOCH Dunbartonshire	Map 1 H4						
Gowanlea Guest House Drymen Road Tel. Alexandria (0389) 52456		COMMENDED	3 Dble/Twin 1 Family	1 Public Bath/Sh	B&B per person £9.00-£10.00 Double **Close to Loch Lomond and Balloch Park. Family run.**	Open Jan-Dec Dinner 1730	
Mrs M Brown 6 McLean Cres, Lomond Rd Estate Tel. Alexandria (0389) 52855		Listed	2 Dble/Twin	1 Public Bath/Sh	B&B per person £8.00-£8.50 Double	Open Jan-Dec Dinner 1800	

VAT is shown at 15%: changes in this rate may affect prices. Prices shown are for guidance only. Please send SAE with each enquiry.

	Map		Rooms	Bath	Rates	Open	Symbols
BALLOCH continued Celia Chadwick St Blanes, Drymen Road Tel. Alexandria (0389) 52008	Map 1 H4		2 Dble/Twin		B&B per person £9.00 Double	Open Apr-Oct	
Mrs McFarlane 7 Carrochan Crescent Tel. Alexandria (0389) 57253			1 Single 2 Dble/Twin	1 Public Bath/Sh	B&B per person £7.50 Single £7.50 Double	Open Apr-Oct	
Mrs E Oultram Westville, Riverside G83 8LF Tel. Alexandria (0389) 52307			2 Dble/Twin 1 Family	1 Public Bath/Sh	B&B per person £9.00 Double	Open Jan-Dec Dinner 1800	
Mrs Margo J Ross Glyndale, 6 McKenzie Dr, Lomond Rd Est. Tel. Alexandria (0389) 58238		Listed	2 Dble/Twin	1 Public Bath/Sh	B&B per person £8.50-£8.75 Double	Open Jan-Dec	
BALLOCH Inverness-shire Mrs J Thom 47 Culloden Road IV1 2HQ Tel. Inverness (0463) 790643	Map 4 B8		3 Dble/Twin	1 Public Bath/Sh	B&B per person £7.50-£10.00 Double	Open May-Oct Dinner 1900	
BALLYGRANT Isle of Islay, Argyll Mrs Rozga Kilmeny Farm Tel. Port Askaig (049684) 668	Map 1 C5	COMMENDED Listed	1 Single 2 Dble/Twin	1 Public Bath/Sh	B&B per person £9.00 Single £9.00 Double	Open Jan-Dec Dinner 1730	
			On working farm, with excellent views over surrounding farmland. Friendly atmosphere. Home cooking.				
BALMACARA SQUARE, by Kyle of Lochalsh Ross-shire Mrs M D Macleod Camlarg Tel. Balmacara (059986) 251	Map 3 F9		3 Dble/Twin 1 Family		B&B per person £7.50-£8.50 Double	Open Jan-Dec Dinner 1800	
BALMACARA, by Kyle of Lochalsh Ross-shire Mrs Macleod The Farm, The Square IV40 8DJ Tel. Balmacara (059986) 238	Map 3 F9	Listed	1 Dble/Twin 2 Family	1 Public Bath/Sh	B&B per person £7.50-£8.50 Double	Open Jan-Dec	

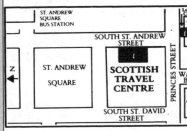
Key to symbols is on back flap. Details of Classification and Grading are on page vi.

BALMACARA, by Kyle of Lochalsh continued	Map 3 F9

Old Post Office House
Reraig, Balmacara, By Kyle, Wester Ross
Tel. 059 986 200

Situated on the shores of Lochalsh, this recently renovated cottage is three miles from the ferry for the Isle of Skye. Adjacent to shop, post office, hotel, restaurant, petrol station, caravan site and pub. Open all year round, offering special terms on stays of three nights or more. Central heating, bath/shower. Residents' lounge with tea-making facilities. Parking.

| Mrs Anne Smith
Old Post Office House
IV40 8DH
Tel. Balmacara (059986) 200 | | Listed | 4 Dble/Twin | 1 Public Bath/Sh | B&B per person
£8.50-£10.00 Double | Open Jan-Dec | |

| BALMACLELLAN
Kirkcudbrightshire | Map 2
A9 | | | | | |
| Mrs P Porritt
Craig
Tel. New Galloway (06442) 228 | | | 3 Dble/Twin | 2 Public Bath/Sh | B&B per person
£10.00 Double | Open Jan-Dec
Dinner 1830 |

High Park Farm
AA Listed   STB Listed

BALMACLELLAN, CASTLE DOUGLAS DG7 3PT

HIGH PARK is a comfortable, stone-built farmhouse built in 1838. The 171-acre Dairy, Stock-rearing and Sheep Farm is situated by Loch Ken on the A713, amidst Galloway's beautiful scenery within easy reach of hills and coast. A good variety of well cooked meals and home baking offered. Washbasins and shaver points in all bedrooms.
Pets welcome. Reduced rates for children and senior citizens.
Mrs. Jessie E. Shaw.   **TEL: New Galloway (06442) 298.**

| Mrs J Shaw
High Park
DG7 3PT
Tel. New Galloway (06442) 298 | | Listed | 2 Dble/Twin
1 Family | 1 Public Bath/Sh | B&B per person
£7.00-£7.50 Double | Open Apr-Oct
Dinner 1900 | |

| BALMAHA
Stirlingshire | Map 1
H4 | | | | | |
| Mrs E Craik
Lomond Bank
Tel. Balmaha (036087) 213 | | | 2 Dble/Twin | 1 Public Bath/Sh | B&B per person
£10.50-£12.00 Double | Open Apr-Oct
Dinner 1830 | |

| Mrs M Fraser
Arrochoile
G63 0JG
Tel. Balmaha (036087) 231 | | COMMENDED ♛ ♛ | 4 Dble/Twin
2 Family | 2 Public Bath/Sh | B&B per person
£8.00-£8.50 Double | Open Apr-Oct | |
| | | | Spacious traditional bungalow on hillside. Short walk to Loch Lomond shore. Boating and walking. | | | |

| Mrs K MacFadyen
Dunleen, Milton of Buchanan
G63 0JE
Tel. Balmaha (036087) 274 | | | 2 Dble/Twin | 1 Public Bath/Sh | B&B per person
£8.50-£9.00 Double | Open Apr-Oct | |

| Mrs Margaret Maxwell
Cashel Farm
G63 0AW
Tel. Balmaha (036087) 229 | | | 3 Family | 1 Public Bath/Sh | B&B per person
£8.00-£9.00 Double | Open Mar-Sep | |

VAT is shown at 15%: changes in this rate may affect prices. Prices shown are for guidance only. Please send SAE with each enquiry.

	Map	Grade	Accommodation	Bathrooms	Terms	Open	Facilities
BALQUHIDDER Perthshire Helensfield Guest House Tel. Lochearnhead (05673) 208	Map 1 H3		2 Dble/Twin 2 Family	2 Public Bath/Sh	B&B per person £7.50-£9.00 Double	Open Apr-Oct Dinner 1850	(symbols)
Mrs Lesley Blain Stronvar Farm Tel. Strathyre (08774) 260			2 Dble/Twin	1 Public Bath/Sh	B&B per person £8.00 Double	Open Apr-Oct	(symbols)
Mrs Jean Lewis Monachyle Mohr Tel. Strathyre (08774) 622		Awaiting Inspection	2 Dble/Twin	2 Public Bath/Sh	B&B per person £8.00-£8.50 Double	Open Jan-Dec Dinner 1850	(symbols)
Mrs V Pickering Auchtubh Mor House Tel. Strathyre (08774) 632			3 Dble/Twin 1 Family	3 Private Bath/Sh 4 Public Bath/Sh	B&B per person £10.50-£12.50 Double	Open Apr-Oct Dinner 1730	(symbols)
BALTASOUND, Unst Shetland Clingera Guest House Tel. Baltasound (095781) 579	Map 5 G1	Listed	1 Single 3 Dble/Twin	2 Public Bath/Sh	B&B per person £8.00-£9.00 Single £8.00-£9.00 Double	Open Jan-Dec Dinner 1830	(symbols)
Mrs E Nicolson 16 Nikkavord Lea ZE2 9XL Tel. Baltasound (095781) 503			2 Dble/Twin	1 Public Bath/Sh	B&B per person £9.00 Double	Open Jan-Dec Dinner 1800	(symbols)
Mrs A Priest Berrybrake Tel. Baltasound (095781) 535		COMMENDED Listed	1 Family	1 Public Bath/Sh	B&B per person £8.00 Double	Open Apr-Sep	(symbols)
			Detached bungalow, with magnificent views of hills and Loch of Cliff.				
BANAVIE, by Fort William Inverness-shire Algarve Guest House Badabrie Tel. Corpach (03977) 461	Map 3 G12		3 Dble/Twin	2 Public Bath/Sh	B&B per person £7.50-£8.50 Double	Open Apr-Oct Dinner 1900	(symbols)
Tigh-an-Tom Guest House Badabrie Tel. Corpach (03977) 426			1 Single 2 Dble/Twin 1 Family	1 Private Bath/Sh 1 Public Bath/Sh	B&B per person £7.50 Single	Open May-Sep Dinner 1900	(symbols)
Mrs L M Allan Loch Leven House Tel. Fort William (0397) 3311			1 Single 3 Dble/Twin	1 Public Bath/Sh	B&B per person £9.00 Single £8.00 Double	Open Jun-Oct	(symbols)
Mrs Campbell Lochindaal, Tomonie Tel. Corpach (03977) 478			1 Dble/Twin 2 Family	1 Public Bath/Sh	B&B per person £8.50 Double	Open Mar-Oct Dinner 1800	(symbols)
Mrs Davie Carinbrook PH33 7LX Tel. Corpach (03977) 318			2 Dble/Twin 1 Family	1 Public Bath/Sh	B&B per person £8.50 Double	Open Apr-Oct Dinner 1900	(symbols)
Mr K Johnson Serendipity, Lochiel Crescent PH33 7LX Tel. Corpach (03977) 326			1 Dble/Twin 1 Family	1 Public Bath/Sh	B&B per person £7.30-£7.80 Double	Open Feb-Nov	(symbols)

Name / Address	Map	Grade	Rooms	Bath	B&B per person	Open	Facilities
BANAVIE, by Fort William continued Mrs McInnes, Taormina, PH33 7LY, Tel. Corpach (03977) 217	Map 3 G12		1 Single, 2 Dble/Twin, 1 Family	1 Public Bath/Sh	B&B per person £7.10 Single £7.10-£7.60 Double	Open Apr-Oct Dinner 1900	
BANCHORY Kincardineshire Mrs G Adams, Amulree, Corsee Road, AB3 3RS, Tel. Banchory (03302) 2884	Map 4 F11	Awaiting Inspection	3 Dble/Twin	2 Public Bath/Sh	B&B per person £8.50 Double	Open Apr-Oct Dinner 1800	
Mrs N Boyd, Windsor House, Bridge Street, AB3 3SX, Tel. Banchory (03302) 2100			1 Dble/Twin, 1 Family	1 Public Bath/Sh	B&B per person £8.50-£9.50 Double	Open Jan-Dec Dinner 1800	
Mr & Mrs J Carnie, Pitmachie, Arbeadie Terrace, AB3 3TN, Tel. Banchory (03302) 4424		APPROVED Listed	1 Single, 2 Dble/Twin, 2 Family	2 Public Bath/Sh	B&B per person £8.50 Single £8.50 Double	Open Jan-Dec	
In an elevated position in a quiet part of town.							
Mrs McConnach, Waulkmill Farm, Strachan, AB3 3NS, Tel. Feughside (033045) 640			2 Dble/Twin	1 Public Bath/Sh	B&B per person £8.00-£9.00 Double	Open Apr-Oct	
Mrs G Milne, Towerbank, High Street, AB3 3XT, Tel. Banchory (03302) 3821			3 Dble/Twin	1 Public Bath/Sh	B&B per person £8.00 Double	Open Apr-Sep	
Mrs W Mitchell, 2 Alexandra Place, Watson Street, AB3 3UB, Tel. Banchory (03302) 2155			1 Single, 2 Dble/Twin, 1 Family	2 Public Bath/Sh	B&B per person £8.00 Single £8.00 Double	Open Apr-Oct	
BANFF Bridge Guest House, 35a Bridge Street, AB4 1HD, Tel. Banff (02612) 5075	Map 4 F7		4 Dble/Twin, 1 Family	2 Public Bath/Sh	B&B per person £9.00 Double	Open Jan-Dec Dinner 1800	
Mrs E M Montgomery, Deveronbank, 11 Old Market Place, Tel. Banff (02612) 2894			1 Single, 1 Dble/Twin, 1 Family	1 Public Bath/Sh	B&B per person £7.00-£8.00 Single £7.00-£8.00 Double	Open Jan-Dec Dinner 1700	
BANKFOOT Perthshire Mrs S Davidson, Strathcluanie, Dunkeld Road, PH1 4AJ, Tel. Bankfoot (073887) 225	Map 2 B2	COMMENDED	2 Dble/Twin, 1 Family	1 Public Bath/Sh	B&B per person £7.50-£8.00 Double	Open Apr-Sep Dinner 1800	
Comfortable, traditional stone built house in a very quiet setting.							
Mrs D McFarlane, Letham Farm, PH1 4EF, Tel. Bankfoot (073887) 322		Awaiting Inspection	2 Dble/Twin, 1 Family	2 Public Bath/Sh	B&B per person £7.50-£8.00 Double	Open Mar-Oct Dinner 1830	
Mrs C McKay, Blair Cottage, Main Street, PH1 4AB, Tel. Bankfoot (073887) 338			2 Family	1 Public Bath/Sh	B&B per person £7.50 Double	Open Apr-Oct	

VAT is shown at 15%. changes in this rate may affect prices. Prices shown are for guidance only. Please send SAE with each enquiry.

BANKFOOT continued Frank & Linda Noakes Northcote, Waterloo Tel. Bankfoot (073887) 501	Map 2 B2		3 Dble/Twin	2 Public Bath/Sh	B&B per person £7.50 Double	Open Jan-Dec Dinner 1800	symbols
BANKNOCK, by **Bonnybridge** **Stirlingshire** Mrs Pitcairn Orchard Grove Tel. Banknock (0324) 840146	Map 2 A4	**COMMENDED** Listed	3 Dble/Twin	1 Public Bath/Sh	B&B per person £10.00-£11.00 Double	Open Apr-Oct Dinner 1900	symbols
			Modern farmhouse, secluded location, excellent views. Close to major tourist routes.				
BARNBARROCH, by **Dalbeattie** **Kirkcudbrightshire**	Map 2 B10						

"SHENNAN CREEK"
Barnbarroch, by Dalbeattie,
Kirkcudbrightshire D65 4QS.
Tel. 055 662 659

"Shennan Creek" was built in the 17th century and stands in nearly two acres of secluded grounds with panoramic views. The house is fully centrally heated. Resident's TV lounge is available at all times. A friendly welcome and good food is assured.
The Stewartry is ideal for tranquil and relaxing holidays. A good centre for touring and exploring the many places of historical interest, wonderful scenery, forests, lochs, miles of unspoilt beaches and an unusually abundant range of wildlife.
We are open twelve months of the year catering for summer holidays, weekend breaks and wildfowling parties of up to six persons. Dogs welcome and kept in purpose-built granite kennels.
Brochure and terms available on request SAE.

Mrs E M Wickenden Shennan Creek D65 4US Tel. Kippford (055662) 659			3 Dble/Twin	1 Public Bath/Sh	B&B per person £8.50 Double	Open Jan-Dec Dinner 1800	symbols
BARVAS **Lewis, Western Isles** Mrs K Macdonald Rockville Tel. Barvas (085184) 286	Map 3 C4	**APPROVED** Listed	1 Single 1 Dble/Twin 1 Family	2 Public Bath/Sh	B&B per person £7.00-£8.00 Single £7.00-£8.00 Double	Open Jan-Dec Dinner 1700	symbols
			Family run, overlooking west coast of Lewis. 12 miles (19km) from the main town of Stornaway.				
BATHGATE **West Lothian** Mrs E Spalding Burnside Cottage, Starlaw Road EH48 1JU Tel. Bathgate (0506) 53188	Map 2 B5		2 Dble/Twin 1 Family	1 Public Bath/Sh	B&B per person £7.50-£9.00 Double	Open Jan-Dec Dinner 1700	symbols
BAYHEAD **N Uist, Western Isles** Mrs Rena MacDonald 4 Paiblesgarry	Map 3 A8		2 Dble/Twin 1 Family	1 Public Bath/Sh	B&B per person £7.50 Double	Open Apr-Oct	symbols

Key to symbols is on back flap. Details of Classification and Grading are on page vi.

27

			Accommodation	Bathrooms	Prices	Opening	Facilities
BEARSDEN, Glasgow Kilmardinny Riding Establishment Kilmardinny Farm, Milngavie Road G61 3DH Tel. 041 942 4404/943 1310	Map 1 H5		4 Single 4 Dble/Twin	2 Public Bath/Sh	B&B per person £10.00 Single £10.00 Double	Open Jan-Dec	
St Andrews College of Education G61 4QA Tel. 041 943 1424			280 Single	52 Public Bath/Sh	B&B per person £11.13 Single	Open Jun-Sep, Easter Dinner 1730	
BEATTOCK **Dumfriesshire** Mrs F Bell Cogries Farm DG10 9PP Tel. Johnstone Bridge (05764) 320	Map 2 C8		3 Family	1 Public Bath/Sh	B&B per person £7.50-£8.50 Double	Open Feb-Nov Dinner 1800	
BEAULY **Inverness-shire** Chrialdon Guest House Station Road IV4 7EH Tel. Beauly (0463) 782336	Map 4 A8		1 Single 6 Dble/Twin 2 Family	2 Private Bath/Sh 3 Public Bath/Sh	B&B per person £9.50 Single £9.50 Double	Open Mar-Dec Dinner 1900	
Aigas Field Centres Ltd IV4 7AD Tel. Beauly (0463) 782443			9 Single 13 Dble/Twin	1 Private Bath/Sh 14 Public Bath/Sh	B&B per person £8.50 Single £8.50 Double	Open Apr-Oct Dinner 1930	
Mrs MacKay Ellangowan, Croyard Road IV4 7DJ Tel. Beauly (0463) 782273			2 Dble/Twin 1 Family	1 Public Bath/Sh	B&B per person £7.00-£7.50 Double	Open Apr-Oct	
Mrs Munro Thornhill Farm IV4 7AS Tel. Beauly (0463) 782338		COMMENDED 👑 👑	3 Dble/Twin	1 Public Bath/Sh	B&B per person £7.50-£8.00 Double	Open May-Oct Dinner 1830	
			On arable farm; barley grown for making whisky. Views of Beauly Firth and Cabrach Hills.				
Mrs Peterkin Barnyards IV4 7AT Tel. Beauly (0463) 782317			2 Dble/Twin 1 Family	2 Public Bath/Sh	B&B per person £8.00 Double	Open Apr-Oct Dinner 1830	
Mrs M Ritchie Rheindown Farm IV4 7AB Tel. Beauly (0463) 782461		👑 👑	1 Single 1 Dble/Twin 1 Family	1 Public Bath/Sh	B&B per person £7.50 Single £7.50 Double	Open Apr-Oct Dinner 1815	
BEESWING **Kirkcudbrightshire** Mrs C M Schooling Locharthur House Tel. Dumfries (0387) 76235	Map 2 B10	COMMENDED 👑	2 Dble/Twin	1 Public Bath/Sh	B&B per person £7.00-£9.00 Double	Open Jan-Dec Dinner 1800	
			Late georgian house set in 3 acre grounds. Access off main A711. Excellent views of countryside.				

VAT is shown at 15%: changes in this rate may affect prices. Prices shown are for guidance only. Please send SAE with each enquiry.

BEITH Ayrshire Mr Colin Farrimond 7 Barrmill Road KA15 1EU Tel. Beith (05055) 2633	Map 1 G6		3 Single 3 Dble/Twin	1 Public Bath/Sh	B&B per person £9.00 Single £9.00 Double	Open Jan-Dec Dinner 1830	
BENDERLOCH, by Connel Argyll Mrs Bryson Fasgadh, South Shian Rd Tel. Ledaig (063172) 337	Map 1 E2	Awaiting Inspection	2 Dble/Twin	1 Public Bath/Sh	B&B per person £7.50-£8.50 Double	Open Apr-Oct	
BERNERA Lewis, Western Isles Mrs A A MacDonald Kelvindale, 17 Tobson PA86 9NA Tel. Great Bernera (085174) 347	Map 3 C4		1 Single 5 Dble/Twin 1 Family	2 Public Bath/Sh	B&B per person £7.50 Single £7.50 Double	Open Apr-Oct Dinner 1900	
BERNERAY N Uist, Western Isles Mrs E Macleod Cnoc Ard, Backhill Tel. Berneray (08767) 257	Map 3 A7		2 Dble/Twin	1 Public Bath/Sh	B&B per person £7.00 Double	Open Apr-Sep Dinner 1800	
BERNISDALE, by Portree Isle of Skye, Inverness- shire Mrs D Macleod Benview House Tel. Skeabost Bridge (047032) 208	Map 3 D9		1 Dble/Twin 2 Family	1 Public Bath/Sh	B&B per person £7.50 Double	Open Apr-Oct Dinner 1830	
Mrs A Rodger Cnoc Grianach, Park Tel. Skeabost Bridge (047032) 372			2 Dble/Twin	1 Public Bath/Sh	B&B per person £7.50-£8.00 Double	Open May-Sep	
BETTYHILL Sutherland Mrs I MacKay 58 Farr KW14 7TA Tel. Bettyhill (06412) 265	Map 4 B3		3 Dble/Twin	1 Public Bath/Sh	B&B per person £7.00 Double	Open May-Oct Dinner 1800	
BIGGAR Lanarkshire Mrs Isobel Burness Schoolgreen Cottage, Kirkstyle Tel. Biggar (0899) 20388	Map 2 C6		2 Dble/Twin	1 Public Bath/Sh	B&B per person £9.00 Double	Open Jan-Dec	
Mrs R Kampman Candybank Farm, Candymill Tel. Biggar (0899) 20422			1 Single 1 Dble/Twin 1 Family	2 Public Bath/Sh	B&B per person £8.50-£10.00 Single £8.50-£10.00 Double	Open Jan-Dec Dinner 1830	
Mrs I Morrison Woodgill, 12 Edinburgh Rd Tel. Biggar (0899) 20324			1 Single 2 Dble/Twin		B&B per person £9.00 Single £9.00 Double	Open Jan-Dec	

BIRNAM, by Dunkeld Perthshire	Map 2 B1						
Mrs Macdonald Glenburn, Station Road Tel. Dunkeld (03502) 755			3 Dble/Twin	1 Public Bath/Sh	B&B per person £12.00-£15.00 Double	Open Jan-Dec	🍷🛏📺 ⚡ 🅿
Mrs Morison Oronsay House, Oak Road Tel. Dunkeld (03502) 294			3 Dble/Twin	1 Private Bath/Sh 2 Public Bath/Sh	B&B per person £8.50-£10.00 Double	Open Apr-Oct	V 📺 ⚡ ❄ 🅿 C
Mrs R W Niven Elwood Villa, Perth Road Tel. Dunkeld (03502) 330		COMMENDED 👑 👑	2 Dble/Twin 1 Family	1 Public Bath/Sh	B&B per person £8.00 Double	Open May-Oct	🛏📺 ⚡ 🐕 🅿
			Edwardian, stone villa in residential area. Close to village amenities and River Tay. Forest walks.				
Mrs Walker Rathlin, Oak Road Tel. Dunkeld (03502) 693			2 Dble/Twin	1 Public Bath/Sh	B&B per person £8.00-£9.50 Double	Open Apr-Oct	🛏📺 🐕 🅿 C
BIRSAY Orkney	Map 5 A10						
Orkney Field Centre, Links House KW17 2LX Tel. Birsay (085672) 221			1 Single 4 Dble/Twin 2 Family	2 Public Bath/Sh	B&B per person £12.00 Single £9.00 Double	Open May-Oct Dinner 1930	V 🅿 C T

HEATHERLEA
Birsay, Orkney KW17 2LR
Mrs H. Balderstone   Tel. 0856 72 382
Beautiful situation in the West Mainland of Orkney, overlooking the Loch of Boardhouse. Free trout angling. Boat for hire. Warm, comfortable house. Parking. Colour TV. Open April to October. The accommodation is one double bedroom and one twin bedroom both with wash-basins. Bath and shower. Bed and Breakfast with Evening Meal, if required.

Mrs Balderstone Heatherlea KW17 2LR Tel. Birsay (085672) 382		👑	1 Dble/Twin 1 Family	1 Public Bath/Sh	B&B per person £7.50 Double	Open Apr-Oct Dinner 1900	🛏📺 ❄ 🅿 C
Mrs J A Moreton Britain Farm KW17 2NB Tel. Birsay (085672) 303			1 Dble/Twin 1 Family		B&B per person £6.50 Double	Open Apr-Oct Dinner 1800	V 🛏📺 ⚡ 🅿 C
Mrs Taylor Kirbuster Hill KW17 2LR Tel. Birsay (085672) 244		Listed	3 Dble/Twin	1 Public Bath/Sh	B&B per person £7.00 Double	Open Jan-Dec Dinner 1900	🛏📺 ❄ 🅿 C
BISHOPBRIGGS, Glasgow	Map 1 H5						
Mrs M Witton Floralbank, 21 Kirkintilloch Road G64 2AN Tel. 041 772 3037			2 Dble/Twin 1 Family	1 Public Bath/Sh	B&B per person £10.00 Double	Open Jan-Dec Dinner 1800	🛏📺 ❄ 🅿 C

VAT is shown at 15%: changes in this rate may affect prices. Prices shown are for guidance only. Please send SAE with each enquiry.

BLACKFORD Perthshire Glenmuir Guest House Stirling Street PH4 1QG Tel. Blackford (076482) 348/432	Map 2 B3	5 Dble/Twin 2 Family	1 Public Bath/Sh	B&B per person £8.50-£9.50 Double	Open Jan-Dec Dinner 1830	(symbols)
BLACKSHIELS, Pathhead Midlothian Mrs L Matthewson Soutra Mains Tel. Humbie (087533) 224	Map 2 D5	2 Dble/Twin	1 Public Bath/Sh	B&B per person £7.50 Double	Open May-Sep	(symbols)
Mrs Winthrop Fairshiels EH37 6SX Tel. Humbie (087533) 665		1 Dble/Twin 5 Family	1 Private Bath/Sh 2 Public Bath/Sh	B&B per person £8.00-£9.00 Double	Open Jan-Dec	(symbols)
BLAIR ATHOLL Perthshire Mrs D Herdman Woodlands Tel. Blair Atholl (079681) 403	Map 4 C12	1 Single 2 Dble/Twin	2 Public Bath/Sh	B&B per person £9.00 Single £8.00 Double	Open Jan-Dec Dinner 1900	(symbols)
BLAIRDRUMMOND Perthshire Mrs Inglis Briarlands Farm Tel. Doune (0786) 841309	Map 2 A4	2 Dble/Twin 1 Family	1 Public Bath/Sh	B&B per person £8.00 Double	Open Apr-Sep	(symbols)
BLAIRGOWRIE Perthshire	Map 2 C1					

GLENSHIELING

HATTON ROAD · NEW RATTRAY · BLAIRGOWRIE
PERTHSHIRE PH10 7HZ. Tel: 0250 4605
AA LISTED ● LES ROUTIERS ● RAC LISTED
Set in 2 acres of wooded grounds, facing south with views of the Sidlaw Hills. Relax and enjoy your tour of the many castles, gardens and glens. Return to the comfort and quiet of Glenshieling. For the golfer there are over 40 courses within an hour's drive. Dinner, bed and breakfast from £17 per person. Private facilities available. Contact Joan Roper.

Glenshieling Guest House Hatton Road, Rattray PH10 7HZ Tel. Blairgowrie (0250) 4605	**COMMENDED** 👑👑	2 Single 2 Dble/Twin 2 Family	1 Private Bath/Sh 2 Public Bath/Sh	B&B per person £9.00-£11.00 Single £9.00-£11.00 Double	Open Jan-Dec Dinner 1900	(symbols)
		Personally run, friendly, home cooking, honey from own bees. Imposingly sited in own grounds.				
Ivybank Guest House Boat Brae, Rattray Tel. Blairgowrie (0250) 3056	**COMMENDED** 👑👑	4 Dble/Twin 2 Family	2 Public Bath/Sh	B&B per person £9.50-£10.50 Double	Open Jan-Dec Dinner 1800	(symbols)
		Stone built 19C house with large garden and own tennis court, on edge of town. Home cooking.				
The Laurels Guest House Golf Course Road, Rosemount PH10 6LH Tel. Blairgowrie (0250) 4920	**COMMENDED** 👑👑	1 Single 3 Dble/Twin 1 Family	1 Public Bath/Sh	B&B per person £9.00 Single £9.00 Double	Open Jan-Oct Dinner 1900	(symbols)
		Originally a farmhouse dating from 1873. Set back from main road.				

BLAIRGOWRIE continued	Map 2 C1					
Rosebank Guest House, Balmoral Road, PH10 7AF, Tel. Blairgowrie (0250) 2912	Awaiting Inspection	1 Single, 4 Dble/Twin, 2 Family	5 Private Bath/Sh, 2 Public Bath/Sh	B&B per person £10.50-£11.50 Single £10.50-£11.50 Double	Open Dec-Oct Dinner 1900	
Mrs Aimer, Cromwell Villa, 25 Newton Street, PH10 6HZ, Tel. Blairgowrie (0250) 3196		1 Single, 3 Dble/Twin	1 Public Bath/Sh	B&B per person £9.00 Single £8.50-£9.00 Double	Open Feb-Dec Dinner 1830	
Mrs J Conacher, Claremont, 49 George Street, PH10 6HP, Tel. Blairgowrie (0250) 2599		3 Family	1 Public Bath/Sh	B&B per person £7.00-£7.50 Double	Open Jan-Dec Dinner 1800	
Mrs E U Edgar, Ashford, Boat Brae, Rattray, Tel. Blairgowrie (0250) 4187		1 Single, 3 Dble/Twin, 1 Family	1 Private Bath/Sh, 1 Public Bath/Sh	B&B per person £8.50-£9.00 Single £7.50-£8.00 Double	Open Jan-Dec Dinner 1900	
Mrs Hayes, Cruachan, Victoria Street, Rattray, Tel. Blairgowrie (0250) 4133		1 Single, 3 Family	2 Public Bath/Sh	B&B per person £6.50-£7.50 Single £6.50-£7.50 Double	Open Jan-Dec Dinner 1800	
Mrs Hunter, Loon Brae House, Ashgrove Road, Rattray, PH10 7BS, Tel. Blairgowrie (0250) 4170		1 Dble/Twin, 1 Family	1 Private Bath/Sh, 2 Public Bath/Sh	B&B per person £8.00-£9.00 Double	Open Apr-Oct Dinner 1800	
Mrs S Kiddy, Mullion House, Coupar Angus Road, Tel. Blairgowrie (0250) 2825	HIGHLY COMMENDED	3 Dble/Twin	3 Private Bath/Sh	B&B per person £13.00 Double	Open Jan-Dec Dinner 1900	
		Victorian country house retaining many features. 1 acre tree-lined garden. Shooting and fishing.				
Mrs Luke, Adylinn, Newton Street, PH10 6HT, Tel. Blairgowrie (0250) 3132	COMMENDED	3 Dble/Twin	1 Public Bath/Sh	B&B per person £8.50-£9.00 Double	Open Jan-Dec Dinner 1800	
		Family run, victorian villa in quiet area of town , 16 miles (26km) from Perth.				
Mrs I Macgregor, Bush House, Newton Terrace, PH10 6HJ, Tel. Blairgowrie (0250) 2219		1 Single, 1 Dble/Twin, 1 Family	1 Public Bath/Sh	B&B per person £7.00 Single £7.00 Double	Open Jan-Dec Dinner 1730	
Mrs C McClement, Duncraggan, Perth Road, Tel. Blairgowrie (0250) 2082	APPROVED	1 Single, 1 Dble/Twin, 1 Family	2 Public Bath/Sh	B&B per person £7.00-£8.50 Single £7.00-£8.50 Double	Open Jan-Dec Dinner 1800	
		Stone built house of interesting design with large garden. Conveniently sited for visiting Perth.				
Mrs Murray, Eildon Bank, Perth Road, PH10 6ED, Tel. Blairgowrie (0250) 3648		2 Dble/Twin	1 Public Bath/Sh	B&B per person £7.50-£8.00 Double	Open Jan-Dec Dinner 1800	
Mrs A M Scott, Laurel Villa, Balmoral Road, Rattray, PH10 7AE, Tel. Blairgowrie (0250) 2826	COMMENDED Listed	3 Dble/Twin	1 Public Bath/Sh	B&B per person £8.00 Double	Open Apr-Oct	
		Victorian town house in residential area with easy access to town centre.				

VAT is shown at 15%: changes in this rate may affect prices. Prices shown are for guidance only. Please send SAE with each enquiry.

Name / Address	Map	Grading	Rooms	Bathrooms	B&B	Opening	Facilities
BLAIRGOWRIE continued Mrs Wright Norwood, Park Drive PH10 6PA Tel. Blairgowrie (0250) 4146	Map 2 C1	👑👑	3 Dble/Twin 1 Family	1 Public Bath/Sh	B&B per person £8.00 Double	Open Apr-Mar Dinner 1800	(symbols)
BLAIRINGONE, Dollar Clackmannanshire Soroba Guest House Tel. Dollar (02594) 2785	Map 2 B4		2 Single 2 Dble/Twin 1 Family	2 Private Bath/Sh 1 Public Bath/Sh	B&B per person £12.00 Single £12.00 Double	Open Jan-Dec Dinner 1800	(symbols)
BLAIRLOGIE Stirlingshire Mrs S F Snowie East Gogar FK9 5QB Tel. Alloa (0259) 723240	Map 2 A4		2 Dble/Twin	1 Public Bath/Sh	B&B per person £8.50-£9.50 Double	Open Jan-Dec	(symbols)
BLANTYRE Lanarkshire Mrs R Sharp 21 Station Road Tel. Blantyre (0698) 826276	Map 2 A6		1 Single 1 Dble/Twin 1 Family	1 Public Bath/Sh	B&B per person £8.50 Single £8.50 Double	Open Jan-Dec Dinner 1700	(symbols)
BO'NESS West Lothian Whigmeleerie Guest House 151 Dean Road EH51 0HE Tel. Bo'ness (0506) 822707	Map 2 B4		3 Dble/Twin 2 Family	1 Public Bath/Sh	B&B per person £9.00 Double	Open Jan-Dec Dinner 1700	(symbols)
Mrs M Grant Graig-Ern, 34 Erngath Road Tel. Bo'ness (0506) 822149			1 Dble/Twin 1 Family	1 Public Bath/Sh	B&B per person £7.50 Double	Open Jan-Dec	(symbols)
Mrs B Kirk Kinglass Farm Tel. Bo'ness (0506) 822861		COMMENDED 👑👑	1 Single 5 Dble/Twin 1 Family	1 Public Bath/Sh	B&B per person £10.00 Single £9.00 Double	Open Jan-Dec Dinner 1900	(symbols)
On working arable farm overlooking Forth Valley. Fresh farm produce.							
BOAT OF GARTEN Inverness-shire Heather Lea Guest House PH24 3BU Tel. Boat of Garten (047983) 674	Map 4 C10		4 Dble/Twin 1 Family	2 Public Bath/Sh	B&B per person £8.00-£8.50 Double	Open Dec-Oct Dinner 1830	(symbols)
Mrs L Banks Cairnview, Balnacruie Tel. Boat of Garten (047983) 359			3 Dble/Twin	2 Public Bath/Sh	B&B per person £8.00 Double	Open Jan-Dec	(symbols)
Mrs N Clark Dochlaggie PH24 3BU Tel. Boat of Garten (047983) 242			1 Single 2 Dble/Twin 2 Family	1 Public Bath/Sh	B&B per person £8.00-£9.00 Single £8.00-£9.00 Double	Open Jan-Dec Dinner 1850	(symbols)

Key to symbols is on back flap. Details of Classification and Grading are on page vi.

33

BOAT OF GARTEN continued — Map 4 C10

Name	Inspection	Rooms	Facilities	Rates	Open
Mrs J L Davison, Locheil, Tel. Boat of Garten (047983) 603	Awaiting Inspection	2 Single, 1 Dble/Twin, 1 Family	1 Public Bath/Sh	B&B per person £6.00 Single £6.00 Double	Open Jan-Dec Dinner 1900
Mrs J A Grant, West Cullachie Farmhouse, PH24 3BY, Tel. Nethybridge (047982) 226	Listed	1 Single, 2 Dble/Twin, 1 Family	1 Public Bath/Sh	B&B per person £7.50-£8.00 Single £7.50-£8.00 Double	Open Mar-Oct

Farmhouse standing beside main road, about 2 miles from village and osprey nesting site.

Name	Inspection	Rooms	Facilities	Rates	Open
Mrs M M Grant, Mullingarroch Croft, PH24 3BY, Tel. Boat of Garten (047983) 645		2 Dble/Twin, 1 Family	1 Public Bath/Sh	B&B per person £7.50 Double	Open Dec-Oct

BONAR BRIDGE Sutherland — Map 4 A6

Name	Rooms	Facilities	Rates	Open
Kyle Guest House, IV24 3EB, Tel. Ardgay (08632) 360	1 Single, 4 Dble/Twin, 1 Family	1 Public Bath/Sh	B&B per person £8.00-£9.00 Single £8.00-£9.00 Double	Open Feb-Nov Dinner 1900
Mrs D Calder, Glengate, Dornoch Road, IV24 3EB, Tel. Ardgay (08632) 532	1 Dble/Twin, 2 Family	1 Private Bath/Sh 1 Public Bath/Sh	B&B per person £7.50-£8.00 Double	Open Apr-Oct

BONCHESTER BRIDGE Roxburghshire — Map 2 E8

Name	Rooms	Facilities	Rates	Open
Mrs Johnson, Cheviot House, Chesters, Tel. Bonchester Bridge (045086) 253	1 Dble/Twin, 1 Family	1 Private Bath/Sh 1 Public Bath/Sh	B&B per person £8.00 Double	Open Apr-Oct Dinner 1830

BORELAND OF BORGUE Kirkcudbrightshire — Map 2 A11

Name	Rooms	Facilities	Rates	Open
Mrs A Watson, Tel. Twynholm (05576) 214	1 Dble/Twin, 1 Family	1 Public Bath/Sh	B&B per person £7.00-£7.50 Double	Open Apr-Oct

BORELAND, by Lockerbie Dumfriesshire — Map 2 C9

Name	Inspection	Rooms	Facilities	Rates	Open
Mrs Isobel Maxwell, Gall Farm, DG11 2PA, Tel. Boreland (05766) 229	COMMENDED Listed	1 Dble/Twin, 2 Family	1 Private Bath/Sh 1 Public Bath/Sh	B&B per person £9.00-£9.50 Double	Open Apr-Oct Dinner 1800

Early post war farmhouse in rural setting, 8 miles/10km from Lockerbie.

Name	Inspection	Rooms	Facilities	Rates	Open
Mrs M Rae, Nether Boreland, DG11 2LL, Tel. Boreland (05766) 248	Awaiting Inspection	1 Single, 1 Dble/Twin, 1 Family	1 Public Bath/Sh	B&B per person £7.25 Single £7.25 Double	Open Apr-Oct Dinner 1830

BORGUE Kirkcudbrightshire — Map 2 A11

Name	Rooms	Facilities	Rates	Open
Mrs E Benson, Mile-End, DG6 4SU, Tel. Borgue (05577) 264	3 Dble/Twin	1 Public Bath/Sh	B&B per person £8.50 Double	Open Apr-Oct Dinner 1800

BORVE, by Portree Isle of Skye, Inverness-shire Mrs MacLean 26/27 Borve Tel. Skeabost Bridge (047032) 234	Map 3 D9		1 Single 2 Dble/Twin	1 Public Bath/Sh	B&B per person £8.50 Single £8.50 Double	Open May-Sep	
BOTHWELL Lanarkshire Mrs D Brown Leabank, 14 Uddingston Road Tel. Bothwell (0698) 853532	Map 2 A6		1 Single 2 Dble/Twin	1 Public Bath/Sh	B&B per person £9.50-£10.50 Single £9.50-£10.50 Double	Open Jan-Dec	
Mrs P Brown 24 Silverwells Crescent Tel. Bothwell (0698) 852771			1 Single 2 Dble/Twin 1 Family	1 Public Bath/Sh	B&B per person £9.50 Single £9.50 Double	Open Jan-Dec	
Mr & Mrs M Wilkinson Oriel Villa, 77 Fallside Road Tel. Bothwell (0698) 812465		COMMENDED 👑 👑	3 Dble/Twin	2 Public Bath/Sh	B&B per person £10.00 Double	Open Jan-Dec Dinner 1900	
19C stone built villa in large gardens. Convenient for M74 and touring Central Scotland.							
BRACO Perthshire Mrs Jessie Graham 3 Feddal Road Tel. Braco (078688) 236	Map 2 A3		2 Dble/Twin 2 Family	1 Public Bath/Sh	B&B per person £8.00-£9.00 Double	Open Apr-Oct	
BRAE, North Mainland Shetland Mrs H E Brown Vaddel, Busta Road Tel. Brae (080622) 407	Map 5 F3		2 Dble/Twin	2 Public Bath/Sh	B&B per person £7.00 Double	Open Jan-Dec	
BRAEMAR Aberdeenshire Cranford Guest House 15 Glenshee Road AB3 5YQ Tel. Braemar (03383) 675	Map 4 D11		2 Single 4 Dble/Twin 1 Family	2 Private Bath/Sh 1 Public Bath/Sh	B&B per person £8.50-£10.00 Single £8.50-£10.00 Double	Open Jan-Dec Dinner 1815	
Schiehallion Guest House Glenshee Road AB3 5YQ Tel. Braemar (03383) 679			1 Single 8 Dble/Twin 2 Family	5 Private Bath/Sh 2 Public Bath/Sh	B&B per person £9.00 Single £8.50 Double	Open Dec-Oct Dinner 1830	
Mrs Bernard An Cromlon, Inyercauld Farm AB3 5YQ Tel. Braemar (03383) 337			4 Dble/Twin 2 Family	2 Public Bath/Sh	B&B per person £7.80 Double	Open Jan-Dec	
Mr & Mrs D Lamont Auld Bank House, Invercauld Road AB3 5YP Tel. Braemar (03383) 336			1 Dble/Twin 2 Family	1 Public Bath/Sh	B&B per person £8.50 Double	Open Jan-Dec Dinner 1900	
Mrs S Shaw Rowan Cottage Tel. Braemar (03383) 393			1 Single 1 Dble/Twin 1 Family	1 Public Bath/Sh	B&B per person £6.70 Single £6.70 Double	Open Jan-Dec	

Key to symbols is on back flap. Details of Classification and Grading are on page vi.

BRAES, by Portree Isle of Skye, Inverness-shire	Map 3 D9						
Mrs Bruce Cruachanlea, Lower Ollach Tel. Sligachan (047852) 233			2 Dble/Twin 2 Family	1 Public Bath/Sh	B&B per person £8.00-£8.50 Double	Open Jan-Dec Dinner 1830	
Mrs S MacDonald Upper Ollach IV51 9LJ Tel. Sligachan (047852) 225			3 Dble/Twin	2 Public Bath/Sh	B&B per person £8.00 Double	Open Apr-Sep Dinner 1800	
Mrs R Macdonald Camusmor, Gedintailler Tel. Sligachan (047852) 252			1 Single 1 Dble/Twin	1 Public Bath/Sh	B&B per person £7.00-£8.00 Single £7.00-£8.00 Double	Open May-Oct Dinner 1830	
BREAKISH Isle of Skye, Inverness-shire	Map 3 E10						
Langdale Guest House Waterloo IV42 8QE Tel. Broadford (04712) 376		**COMMENDED** 👑👑	4 Dble/Twin	1 Public Bath/Sh	B&B per person £10.00 Double	Open Jan-Dec Dinner 1800	
Modern bungalow, superb views of sea and mountains. Motor boat available for nature watching cruises.							
Ceol-na-Mara Waterloo Tel. Broadford (04712) 323			4 Dble/Twin 1 Family	1 Public Bath/Sh	B&B per person £7.50-£8.50 Double	Open Apr-Sep Dinner 1900	

Mrs Nicolson Scorrybreac, Scullamis Tel. Broadford (04712) 525		2 Dble/Twin 1 Family	1 Public Bath/Sh	B&B per person £8.50 Double	Open Apr-Oct Dinner 1830	
BREANISH, Uig Lewis, Western Isles	Map 3 B5					
Mrs K Gillies 19 Breanish Tel. Timsgarry (085175) 300		2 Dble/Twin	1 Public Bath/Sh	B&B per person £7.00 Double	Open Apr-Dec Dinner 1800	
BRECHIN Angus	Map 4 F12					
Mrs Philp Kalulu Cottage, Woodend, Farnell Tel. Brechin (03562) 3947		1 Dble/Twin 1 Family	1 Public Bath/Sh	B&B per person £6.50-£7.50 Double	Open Apr-Oct	

VAT is shown at 15%: changes in this rate may affect prices. Prices shown are for guidance only. Please send SAE with each enquiry.

BRECHIN continued	Map 4 F12		

Wood of Auldbar · Brechin
Proprietor: Mrs J. STEWART.   TEL: 030 783 218

Mixed arable farm of 187 acres, set in lovely rural countryside near to Glens and Castles.
Fishing and Golf nearby.
All home cooking in comfortable surroundings.

Mrs J Stewart Wood of Auldbar Tel. Aberlemno (030783) 218	COMMENDED Listed	1 Single 1 Dble/Twin 1 Family	1 Public Bath/Sh	B&B per person £7.50 Single £7.50 Double	Open Jan-Dec

On working farm, rural setting in heart of Angus. Views from new sun lounge. Near golf, fishing etc.

Blibberhill Farm, Brechin
Telephone: 030 783 225 (Mrs M. Stewart)

Blibberhill is a spacious, well appointed farmhouse set in peaceful surroundings and within easy access to Angus Glens and Glamis Castle, and Pictish Stones at Aberlemno. Excellent fishing (by permit) near by; also central to many golf courses.
All rooms with H&C, 1 with private facilities.
Bed and Breakfast, Dinner optional.

Mrs M Stewart Blibberhill Farm DD9 6TH Tel. Aberlemno (030783) 225	APPROVED 👑 👑	3 Dble/Twin	1 Private Bath/Sh 2 Public Bath/Sh	B&B per person £8.00 Double	Open Jan-Dec Dinner 1800

Farmhouse, situated in peaceful surroundings.

BRIDGE OF ALLAN Stirlingshire	Map 2 A4				
Mrs Allison Claremont, 24 Kenilworth Road FK9 4DU Tel. Bridge of Allan (0786) 832101		3 Dble/Twin 3 Family	2 Public Bath/Sh	B&B per person £8.50-£9.00 Double	Open Jan-Dec
E Anderton Ferniebank, 5 Sunnylaw Road FK9 4QA Tel. Stirling (0786) 833423	👑 👑	1 Dble/Twin	1 Public Bath/Sh	B&B per person £8.50-£10.00 Double	Open Jan-Dec
Mrs Linda George Kilronan, 15 Kenilworth Road Tel. Bridge of Allan (0786) 833254		2 Dble/Twin 1 Family	2 Public Bath/Sh	B&B per person £7.50-£8.50 Double	Open Jan-Dec
BRIDGE OF CALLY, Blairgowrie Perthshire	Map 2 C1				
Miss Hackett Ardle Cottage PH10 7JG Tel. Bridge of Cally (025086) 351		3 Dble/Twin	1 Public Bath/Sh	B&B per person £8.00 Double	Open Jan-Dec

Key to symbols is on back flap. Details of Classification and Grading are on page vi.

37

BRIDGE OF CALLY, Blairgowrie continued
Map 2 C1

Mrs L Stephen
Inverardle
PH10 7JL
Tel. Bridge of Cally (025086) 227

Awaiting Inspection

3 Dble/Twin | 2 Public Bath/Sh | B&B per person £8.50-£9.00 Double | Open Jan-Dec Dinner 1830

BRIDGE OF DON, Aberdeen Aberdeenshire
Map 4 H10

Mrs Goudriaan
Blackdog Heights
AB2 8BT
Tel. Aberdeen (0224) 704287

1 Single 3 Dble/Twin | 1 Public Bath/Sh | B&B per person £9.00-£10.00 Single £8.50-£9.00 Double | Open Jan-Dec Dinner 1800

Mrs E Lochrie
3 Newburgh Crescent
AB2 8ST
Tel. Aberdeen (0224) 824638

1 Single 2 Dble/Twin | 2 Public Bath/Sh | B&B per person £6.50 Single £6.50 Double | Open Jan-Dec

---

BRIDGE OF EARN Perthshire
Map 2 C2

Rockdale Guest House
Dunning Street
PH2 9AA
Tel. Bridge of Earn (0738) 812281

2 Single 5 Dble/Twin 2 Family | 1 Public Bath/Sh | B&B per person £8.00-£9.50 Single £8.00-£8.50 Double | Open Jan-Dec Dinner 1700

Mrs A F Fulton
Mayfield, Station Road
PH2 9EA
Tel. Bridge of Earn (0738) 812790

1 Dble/Twin 1 Family | 1 Public Bath/Sh | B&B per person £7.50 Double | Open Apr-Oct

---

BRIDGE OF MARNOCH, by Aberchirder Banffshire
Map 4 F8

Mrs Stephen
Myreside Farm
Tel. Aberchirder (04665) 832

1 Dble/Twin 1 Family | 1 Public Bath/Sh | B&B per person £6.50 Double | Open Apr-Sep Dinner 1800

BRIDGE OF TILT, Blair Atholl Perthshire
Map 4 C12

The Firs
ST ANDREWS CRESCENT, BLAIR ATHOLL
TEL: 0796 81 256

Close to Pitlochry, Blair Atholl is an ideal, quiet holiday centre. Home of the Duke of Atholl, the village caters for all with shops, hotels and most outdoor pursuits available.

Set in ⅔ of an acre, The Firs is a friendly, family-run guest house recently taken over by Geoff and Kirstie Crerar who look forward to welcoming you.

Mr Geoff Crerar
The Firs, St Andrews Crescent,
Tel. Blair Atholl (079681) 265

Awaiting Inspection

1 Single 2 Dble/Twin 2 Family | 1 Public Bath/Sh | B&B per person £8.50-£10.50 Single £8.00-£9.00 Double | Open Jan-Dec Dinner 1900

VAT is shown at 15%: changes in this rate may affect prices. Prices shown are for guidance only. Please send SAE with each enquiry.

BROADFORD Isle of Skye, Inverness-shire Mrs J Donaldson Fairwinds, Elgol Road Tel. Broadford (04712) 270	Map 3 E10		3 Dble/Twin	1 Public Bath/Sh	B&B per person £8.50-£9.00 Double	Open Apr-Oct

Isle of Skye

Ashgrove, Black Park, Broadford. Tel. 047 12 327

Comfortable accommodation in three-bedroomed bungalow. Hot and cold in all rooms. Colour TV lounge. Nice situation, 8 miles from Kyle-Kyleakin ferry, 16 miles from Mallaig-Armadale ferry. Turn off main road at Lime Park/Black Park junction.

Bed and Breakfast £8 per person.

Mrs M Fletcher Ashgrove, 11 Black Park Tel. Broadford (04712) 327	2 Dble/Twin 1 Family	1 Public Bath/Sh	B&B per person £8.00 Double	Open Mar-Nov
Mr & Mrs Ford Green Gables, Harrapool IV49 9AQ Tel. Broadford (04712) 592	2 Single 4 Dble/Twin	1 Public Bath/Sh	B&B per person £8.50-£9.00 Single £8.50-£9.00 Double	Open Jan-Dec
Mrs M J Heenan Amulree Tel. Broadford (04712) 432	2 Dble/Twin 1 Family	1 Public Bath/Sh	B&B per person £8.50-£9.00 Double	Open Apr-Oct
Mrs MacKay Strathnaver, Harrapool Tel. Broadford (04712) 406	3 Dble/Twin	1 Private Bath/Sh 1 Public Bath/Sh	B&B per person £8.50 Double	Open Jan-Nov Dinner 1830
Mrs MacKinnon Failte, 6 Heaste Tel. Broadford (04712) 268	1 Single 2 Dble/Twin	1 Public Bath/Sh	B&B per person £8.00-£8.50 Single £8.00-£8.50 Double	Open Apr-Oct Dinner 1900
Mrs Flora A MacLeod 12 Heaste Tel. Broadford (04712) 294	3 Dble/Twin	1 Public Bath/Sh	B&B per person £8.00-£8.50 Double	Open May-Oct
Mrs MacRae Hillcrest, Black Park Tel. Broadford (04712) 375	2 Dble/Twin 1 Family	2 Public Bath/Sh	B&B per person £7.50 Double	Open Jan-Dec
Mrs Maclennan Effron Tel. Broadford (04712) 404	2 Dble/Twin 2 Family	1 Public Bath/Sh	B&B per person £6.50-£7.50 Double	Open Jan-Dec
Mrs D Robertson Westside, Elgol Road IV49 9AB Tel. Broadford (04712) 320	1 Single 1 Dble/Twin 1 Family	1 Public Bath/Sh	B&B per person £9.00-£9.50 Single £9.00-£9.50 Double	Open Apr-Oct Dinner 1830
Mrs Doreen Smith Blairmore, Harrapool Tel. Broadford (04712) 208	1 Single 2 Dble/Twin 1 Family	1 Public Bath/Sh	B&B per person £8.00-£8.50 Single £8.00-£8.50 Double	Open Apr-Oct
Mrs F Sutherland Ailean Cottage Tel. Broadford (04712) 278	1 Single 3 Dble/Twin	1 Private Bath/Sh 1 Public Bath/Sh	B&B per person £7.50-£10.50 Single £7.00-£10.50 Double	Open Apr-Oct

	Map 1 F7						
BRODICK Isle of Arran Allandale Guest House KA27 8BJ Tel. Brodick (0770) 2278		COMMENDED ♛ ♛	1 Single 3 Dble/Twin 2 Family	6 Private Bath/Sh 1 Public Bath/Sh	B&B per person £10.25-£11.00 Single £10.25-£11.00 Double	Open Jan-Oct Dinner 1900	
			Comfortable house, all rooms with private facilities. Feature rambling holidays. Ridge walking.				

Glencloy Farm Guesthouse

GLENCLOY, BRODICK, ISLE OF ARRAN. 0770 2351

Glencloy Farm Guesthouse is situated in a peaceful glen just outside Brodick. We have superb views of the hills and sea and offer large comfortable bedrooms, log fire, and excellent food prepared by the chef proprietor.

Arran is a beautiful island in the Firth of Clyde and has nine golf courses, sandy beaches, pony trekking and lovely walks.

Glencloy Farm Guest House Tel. Brodick (0770) 2351		COMMENDED ♛ ♛	5 Dble/Twin 2 Family	1 Public Bath/Sh	B&B per person £9.50 Double	Open Jan-Dec Dinner 1900	
			Farmhouse set in peaceful glen with views of hills and sea. Within easy reach of Brodick ferry.				
Mrs S Macmillan Glenard Tel. Brodick (0770) 2318			1 Single 2 Family	1 Public Bath/Sh	B&B per person £8.00 Single £8.00 Double	Open Apr-Oct	
Mrs J McClure The Sheilin, Corriegills Tel. Brodick (0770) 2456			2 Single 2 Dble/Twin 1 Family	1 Private Bath/Sh 1 Public Bath/Sh	B&B per person £7.00-£8.00 Single £7.00-£12.00 Double	Open Jan-Dec Dinner 1800	
Mrs Wilkie Cala Sona, Alma Park Tel. Brodick (0770) 2353		APPROVED ♛ ♛ ♛	2 Dble/Twin	1 Public Bath/Sh	B&B per person £7.75 Double	Open Jan-Dec Dinner 1950	
			Traditional unit on seafront. Paved and walled yard looking south.				
BRODIE, Forres Moray Mrs Anne Campbell Invercairn House IV36 0TD Tel. Brodie (03094) 261	Map 4 C8		1 Single 3 Family	1 Public Bath/Sh	B&B per person £8.00 Single £8.00 Double	Open Jan-Dec Dinner 1800	
BRORA Sutherland Mrs J Ballantyne Clynelish Farm KW9 6LR Tel. Brora (0408) 21265	Map 4 C6		1 Single 2 Dble/Twin	2 Public Bath/Sh	B&B per person £8.00 Single £8.00 Double	Open Apr-Oct	
Mr & Mrs C H Berthelot Ard Beag, Badnellan KW9 6NQ Tel. Brora (0408) 21300			1 Single 1 Dble/Twin 1 Family	1 Public Bath/Sh	B&B per person £8.00 Single £8.00 Double	Open Jan-Dec Dinner 1900	

| BRORA continued | Map 4
C6 | | | | |

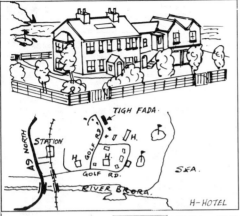

NON-SMOKERS' HAVEN

"Tigh Fada" Golf Road, Brora
Telephone: 0408 21332

Proprietors: **John & Ishbel Clarkson**

Good old-fashioned Highland hospitality in warm home. Personal attention from Scots couple. Super situation, convenient for rail, bus, hotels, restaurants, tennis, bowling, curling (winter), fishing, riding etc. plus, garden gate to golf course and sandy beach.

Comfortable beds, electric blankets, clock radios, adjacent shower/WC and bath/shower/WC. Plenty hot water. Evening cuppa and home baking in lounge by peat fire — no TV to hinder conversation! Good "menu and time" choice for breakfast.

Open all year. Advance booking recommended.
S.A.E. for brochure.

Mrs Clarkson Tigh Fada, Golf Road KW9 6QS Tel. Brora (0408) 21332		COMMENDED ♔♔	2 Dble/Twin 1 Family	2 Public Bath/Sh	B&B per person £7.50 Double	Open Jan-Dec	
			A non smokers haven. Welcoming peat fires, fine sea views. Good breakfast table. Own beach hut. Golf.				
BRUICHLADDICH **Isle of Islay, Argyll**	Map 1 B6						
Miss M Fletcher Failte, Main Street Tel. Port Charlotte (049685) 412			2 Dble/Twin 1 Family	1 Public Bath/Sh	B&B per person £7.00-£7.50 Double	Open Jan-Dec	
Stuart & Wesley Taylor Kilchoman House Tel. Port Charlotte (049685) 382			2 Dble/Twin	1 Public Bath/Sh	B&B per person £10.00 Double	Open Jan-Dec	
BUCKIE **Banffshire**	Map 4 E7						
Mrs Jennifer Marnie Arradoul House, Arradoul AB5 2BB Tel. Buckie (0542) 31552		Listed	2 Dble/Twin 2 Family	2 Public Bath/Sh	B&B per person £8.50-£10.00 Double	Open Apr-Oct Dinner 1800	
BUNESSAN **Isle of Mull, Argyll**	Map 1 C3						
Assapol Guest House Assapol House Tel. Fionnphort (06817) 258			2 Single 3 Dble/Twin 2 Family	6 Private Bath/Sh 1 Public Bath/Sh	B&B per person £17.71 Single £17.71 Double	Open Apr-Feb Dinner 1900	
Mrs E Cruden 3 Fountainhead Tel. Fionnphort (06817) 225			3 Dble/Twin	1 Public Bath/Sh	B&B per person £8.00-£8.50 Double	Open Apr-Oct Dinner 1800	

BUNESSAN continued	Map 1 C3					
Mrs M MacLean Rhumhor Tel. Fionnphort (06817) 275			1 Single 1 Dble/Twin 1 Family	1 Public Bath/Sh	B&B per person £8.00-£8.50 Single £8.00-£8.50 Double	Open Jan-Dec
Mrs A MacNeill Ardness, Tiraghoil Tel. Fionnphort (06817) 260			2 Dble/Twin	1 Public Bath/Sh	B&B per person £9.00-£10.00 Double	Open Mar-Nov Dinner 1900
BURNMOUTH, Eyemouth Berwickshire	Map 2 G5					
Mrs Foster Harbour View TD14 5ST Tel. Ayton (08907) 81213			2 Dble/Twin	1 Public Bath/Sh	B&B per person £7.50-£8.00 Double	Open Jan-Dec
CALLANDER Perthshire	Map 2 A3					
Abbotsford Lodge Guest House Stirling Road FK17 8DA Tel. Callander (0877) 30066			1 Single 11 Dble/Twin 7 Family	2 Private Bath/Sh 4 Public Bath/Sh	B&B per person £9.00-£9.50 Single £9.00-£9.50 Double	Open Jan-Dec Dinner 1900
Arden House Guest House Bracklinn Road FK17 8EQ Tel. Callander (0877) 30235	COMMENDED		2 Single 5 Dble/Twin 2 Family	3 Private Bath/Sh 2 Public Bath/Sh	B&B per person £8.50-£9.50 Single £8.50-£9.50 Double	Open Feb-Nov Dinner 1900
		Family run, peacefully situated. Own grounds. Superb panoramic views to Ben Ledi and the Trossachs.				
Edina Guest House 111 Main Street FK17 8BQ Tel. Callander (0877) 30004			2 Single 8 Dble/Twin 1 Family	3 Private Bath/Sh 1 Public Bath/Sh	B&B per person £7.77-£8.35 Single £7.77-£8.35 Double	Open Jan-Dec Dinner 1830
Greenbank Guest House 143 Main Street FK17 8BH Tel. Callander (0877) 30296			4 Dble/Twin 2 Family	2 Public Bath/Sh	B&B per person £9.00-£10.00 Double	Open Jan-Dec Dinner 1900
Kinnell Guest House 24 Main Street FK17 8BB Tel. Callander (0877) 30181			2 Single 4 Dble/Twin 2 Family	2 Public Bath/Sh	B&B per person £9.00-£9.50 Single £8.75-£9.25 Double	Open Jan-Dec Dinner 1900
Linley Guest House 139 Main Street FK17 8BH Tel. Callander (0877) 30087			3 Dble/Twin 2 Family	2 Public Bath/Sh	B&B per person £8.00 Double	Open Jan-Dec
The Old Rectory Guest House Leny Road Tel. Callander (0877) 30787			5 Dble/Twin 1 Family	2 Private Bath/Sh 1 Public Bath/Sh	B&B per person £8.00-£9.50 Double	Open Jan-Dec Dinner 1845
Rock Villa Guest House Bracklinn Road FK17 8EH Tel. Callander (0877) 30331			1 Single 4 Dble/Twin 1 Family	1 Public Bath/Sh	B&B per person £9.50 Single £8.50 Double	Open Jan-Dec Dinner 1830
White Shutters Guest House South Church Street FK17 8BN Tel. Callander (0877) 30442			1 Single 3 Dble/Twin	1 Public Bath/Sh	B&B per person £8.00-£9.00 Single £8.00-£9.00 Double	Open Apr-Oct

VAT is shown at 15%: changes in this rate may affect prices. Prices shown are for guidance only. Please send SAE with each enquiry.

CALLANDER continued	Map 2 A3	Grading	Rooms	Baths	B&B	Open	Facilities
Mrs S Collier, Spinningdale, Stirling Road, Tel. Callander (0877) 30494			5 Dble/Twin, 1 Family	2 Public Bath/Sh	B&B per person £8.00-£8.50 Double	Open Mar-Dec, Dinner 1800	(symbols)
Mrs Cummins, Ancaster Cottage, Aveland Road, FK17 8EN, Tel. Callander (0877) 30146		COMMENDED Listed	1 Single, 2 Dble/Twin	1 Public Bath/Sh	B&B per person £8.50-£9.00 Single £8.50-£9.00 Double	Open May-Sep	(symbols)
			Traditionally built house in quiet area of town. 10 minutes walk from centre. Close to golf course.				
Mrs E J Easton, The Priory, Bracklinn Road, Tel. Callander (0877) 30001			2 Single, 4 Dble/Twin, 1 Family	2 Private Bath/Sh, 2 Public Bath/Sh	B&B per person £8.50-£9.95 Single £8.50-£9.95 Double	Open Apr-Oct, Dinner 1900	(symbols)
Mrs L D Ferguson, Roslin Cottage, Stirling Road, Tel. Callander (0877) 30638			2 Single, 2 Dble/Twin	1 Public Bath/Sh	B&B per person £7.00-£9.00 Single £7.00-£8.00 Double	Open Jan-Dec, Dinner 1900	(symbols)
Mrs C C Frerichs, Gart House, FK17 8LE, Tel. Callander (0877) 31055			2 Single, 2 Dble/Twin, 2 Family	3 Public Bath/Sh	B&B per person £9.00-£12.00 Single £9.00-£12.00 Double	Open Jan-Dec	(symbols)
Mrs Greenfield, Annfield House, North Church Street, FK17 8EG, Tel. Callander (0877) 30204		Awaiting Inspection	1 Single, 7 Dble/Twin	2 Public Bath/Sh	B&B per person £7.50 Single £7.50 Double	Open Mar-Oct	(symbols)
Mrs Hamilton, Westcot, Leny Road, Tel. Callander (0877) 30293		COMMENDED ♛	2 Dble/Twin	1 Public Bath/Sh	B&B per person £7.00-£7.50 Double	Open Mar-Oct, Dinner 1900	(symbols)
			Detached, period cottage. Open outlook to River Teith and park. Close to town centre.				
Mrs Kennett, Ramona, 3-5 North Church Street, FK17 8EE, Tel. Callander (0877) 30208			2 Single, 2 Dble/Twin, 1 Family		B&B per person £8.00 Single £7.50 Double	Open Apr-Oct	(symbols)
Mr & Mrs J Lamb, Greenholme, Leny Road, Tel. Callander (0877) 30999			2 Dble/Twin, 1 Family	1 Private Bath/Sh, 1 Public Bath/Sh	B&B per person £8.00 Double	Open Apr-Oct, Dinner 1800	(symbols)
Mrs MacKenzie, Auchinlea, Ancaster Road, Tel. Callander (0877) 30769			1 Dble/Twin, 1 Family	1 Public Bath/Sh	B&B per person £7.00-£7.50 Double	Open Apr-Oct	(symbols)
Mrs McAlpine, Craigburn House, North Church Street, Tel. Callander (0877) 30332			1 Single, 3 Dble/Twin, 1 Family	1 Public Bath/Sh	B&B per person £7.00 Single £7.00 Double	Open Apr-Oct	(symbols)
Mrs Potts, Woodvale, Lagrannoch, FK17 8LE, Tel. Callander (0877) 30862		♛	2 Dble/Twin, 1 Family	1 Public Bath/Sh	B&B per person £9.00 Double	Open Jun-Sep	(symbols)
A & F Roebuck, Leny House, FK17 8HA, Tel. Callander (0877) 31078			4 Dble/Twin, 2 Family	1 Private Bath/Sh, 2 Public Bath/Sh	B&B per person £9.00 Double	Open Apr-Sep	(symbols)

Key to symbols is on back flap. Details of Classification and Grading are on page vi.

43

CALLANDER continued Mrs Scott Craig Villa, Leny Road Tel. Callander (0877) 30195	Map 2 A3		2 Dble/Twin	1 Public Bath/Sh	B&B per person £9.00-£10.00 Double	Open Apr-Oct Dinner 1900	
Mrs Smillie Auchyle, Stirling Road Tel. Callander (0877) 31062			1 Dble/Twin 1 Family	2 Public Bath/Sh	B&B per person £8.00 Double	Open Apr-Oct	
CALLANISH Lewis, Western Isles Mrs B A Barrett 24 Callanish Tel. Callanish (08502) 341	Map 3 C5	COMMENDED 👑 👑	3 Dble/Twin	1 Private Bath/Sh 1 Public Bath/Sh	B&B per person £7.00-£8.00 Double	Open May-Sep Dinner 1900	
			Modern bungalow on edge of small township. About 1 mile (2km) from Standing Stones of Callanish.				
Mrs A MacLeod The Cairns, 32 Callanish Tel. Callanish (085172) 248		Listed	1 Single 3 Dble/Twin	2 Private Bath/Sh 1 Public Bath/Sh	B&B per person £7.00 Single £7.00 Double	Open Jan-Dec Dinner 1900	
CALVINE Perthshire Mrs Stewart Clachan of Struan PH18 5UB Tel. Calvine (079683) 207	Map 4 B12		1 Dble/Twin 1 Family	1 Public Bath/Sh	B&B per person £8.00 Double	Open May-Oct	
CAMBUS O'MAY, by Ballatter Aberdeenshire Mrs Williams The Willows AB3 5SD Tel. Ballater (0338) 55892	Map 4 E11		2 Dble/Twin 1 Family	1 Private Bath/Sh	B&B per person £9.50-£10.50 Double	Open Jan-Dec Dinner 1900	
CAMPBELTOWN Argyll Mrs Armour High Knockrioch Farm Tel. Campbeltown (0586) 52094	Map 1 E7		2 Dble/Twin 1 Family	1 Public Bath/Sh	B&B per person £7.00-£8.00 Double	Open May-Oct	
Mrs Bell Sandiway, Fort Argyll Rd, Low Askomil Tel. Campbeltown (0586) 52280		COMMENDED 👑 👑	1 Dble/Twin	1 Public Bath/Sh	B&B per person £8.00 Double	Open Jan-Dec Dinner 1800	
			Modern bungalow in quiet residential area on edge of town. Sheltered garden. Home cooking.				

CAMPBELTOWN continued	Map 1 E7

OATFIELD HOUSE
CAMPBELTOWN, ARGYLL PA28 6PH
Tel: 0586 52601 Gordon & Muriel Staples

A lovely country house in extensive gardens, Oatfield offers large comfortable heated rooms and a guests' lounge with log fire and TV. Facilities are provided for tea/coffee making, and for laundry. Within easy reach are Campbeltown, fine beaches and golf, and Kintyre is superb for hill-walking, bird watching, or just relaxing in peaceful countryside. 👑👑 **Commended**

Mrs C M Staples Oatfield House, Southend Road PA28 6PH Tel. Campbeltown (0586) 52601	**APPROVED** 👑👑	1 Single 3 Dble/Twin	1 Public Bath/Sh	B&B per person £8.50-£9.50 Single £8.50-£9.50 Double	Open Jan-Dec

18 c manor house in 7 acres ground, 3 miles/5 km from town. Views of Jura and Islay islands.

CANNICH Inverness-shire Westward Guest House Tel. Cannich (04565) 225	Map 3 H9 👑👑	3 Dble/Twin	1 Private Bath/Sh 1 Public Bath/Sh	B&B per person £9.50 Double	Open Mar-Nov

Mrs S McRae Kerrow House IV4 7NA Tel. Cannich (04565) 243		2 Dble/Twin	1 Public Bath/Sh	B&B per person £9.00-£11.00 Double	Open Mar-Nov

CANONBIE Dumfriesshire Mrs Ruth Williams Caulside Head DG14 0RT Tel. Canonbie (05415) 452	Map 2 D9	2 Dble/Twin 1 Family	1 Public Bath/Sh	B&B per person £8.00 Single £8.00 Double	Open Jan-Dec

CAOL, by Fort William Inverness-shire Mrs I Payne 71 Kilmallie Road Tel. Fort William (0397) 4660	Map 3 G12	1 Dble/Twin 1 Family	1 Public Bath/Sh	B&B per person £5.50-£7.00 Double	Open Apr-Oct

CARBOST Isle of Skye, Inverness-shire Mrs R Grant Glenview Tel. Carbost (047842) 279	Map 3 D9	2 Dble/Twin	1 Public Bath/Sh	B&B per person £8.00-£9.00 Double	Open Apr-Oct Dinner 1800

CARDROSS Dunbartonshire Mrs G Macdonald Kirkton House, Darleith Road Tel. Cardross (0389) 841951	Map 1 G5 **COMMENDED**	2 Family	1 Public Bath/Sh	B&B per person £9.00-£9.50 Double	Open Jan-Dec Dinner 1800

Elevated rural site. Magnificent views of the Firth of Clyde and the Argyll Hills.

Key to symbols is on back flap. Details of Classification and Grading are on page vi.

45

CARGILL
Perthshire — Map 2 C2

Miss K Matthew
Cargil House
PH2 6DT
Tel. Meikleour (025083) 334

1 Single
2 Dble/Twin
1 Family
1 Private Bath/Sh
1 Public Bath/Sh
B&B per person
£8.50-£9.50 Single
£7.50-£8.50 Double
Open Apr-Oct

CARLOPS
Peeblesshire — Map 2 C5

Mrs Jane Aitken
Carlophill Farm
EH26 9NQ
Tel. West Linton (0968) 60340

3 Dble/Twin
1 Public Bath/Sh
B&B per person
£8.00-£10.00 Double
Open May-Oct

Mrs A Smith
Amulree
EH26 9NF
Tel. Penicuik (0968) 60271

COMMENDED 🏆🏆

2 Dble/Twin
1 Public Bath/Sh
B&B per person
£9.50-£10.50 Double
Open Jan-Dec
Dinner 1900

18C weavers cottage in small village. Scottish gourmet breakfast, supper, dinners. Hillwalking.

CARLUKE
Lanarkshire — Map 2 B6

Mrs Mary Scott
Dunvegan, 45 Carnwath Road
Tel. Carluke (0555) 50636

1 Single
1 Dble/Twin
1 Family
1 Public Bath/Sh
B&B per person
£8.00 Single
£8.00 Double
Open Jan-Dec
Dinner 1700

CARNOUSTIE
Angus — Map 2 E2

Mrs Elder
8 Mariner Street
Tel. Carnoustie (0241) 59589

1 Dble/Twin
1 Family
2 Public Bath/Sh
B&B per person
£8.00 Double
Open Apr-Oct

Mrs M Hancox
37 Westfield Place
Tel. Carnoustie (0241) 54288/59804

1 Dble/Twin
1 Family
1 Public Bath/Sh
B&B per person
£8.00 Double
Open Jan-Dec
Dinner 1830

CARNWATH
Lanarkshire — Map 2 B6

Mrs M Thomson
Medwyn House, 48 Main Street
Tel. Carnwath (0555) 840526

3 Dble/Twin
1 Public Bath/Sh
B&B per person
£8.00-£10.00 Double
Open Jan-Dec
Dinner 1830

CARRADALE
Argyll — Map 1 E7

Dunvalanree Guest House
Portrigh Bay
PA28 6SE
Tel. Carradale (05833) 226

COMMENDED
Listed

2 Single
8 Dble/Twin
2 Family
3 Public Bath/Sh
B&B per person
£8.50-£9.50 Single
£8.50-£9.50 Double
Open Apr-Oct
Dinner 1800

Purpose built, set in peaceful location. Large garden with superb outlook over Port Righ Bay.

Mrs Henderson
Feoirlinn, School Park
Tel. Carradale (05833) 250

Listed

1 Dble/Twin
1 Family
1 Public Bath/Sh
B&B per person
£7.50 Double
Open Apr-Oct
Dinner 1730

Mrs McCormick
The Mains Farm
Tel. Carradale (05833) 216

Listed

1 Single
1 Dble/Twin
1 Family
1 Public Bath/Sh
B&B per person
£7.50 Single
£7.50 Double
Open Apr-Oct
Dinner 1800

	Map	Grading	Accommodation	Bathroom	Price	Open	Facilities
CARRBRIDGE **Inverness-shire** Ard-na-Coille Guest House Station Road Tel. Carrbridge (047984) 239	Map 4 C10		1 Single 5 Dble/Twin	2 Public Bath/Sh	B&B per person £8.50-£9.50 Single £8.50-£9.50 Double	Open Jan-Dec Dinner 1800	
Carrmoor Guest House Carr Road PH23 3AD Tel. Carrbridge (047984) 244		COMMENDED 👑 👑	3 Dble/Twin 1 Family	1 Public Bath/Sh	B&B per person £9.00-£10.00 Double	Open Jan-Dec Dinner 1900	
		Small pebbledash house away from main roads in a residential area near Landmark Visitor Centre.					
Craigellachie Guest House PH23 3AS Tel. Carrbridge (047984) 641			1 Single 6 Dble/Twin 1 Family	2 Public Bath/Sh	B&B per person £8.50-£9.50 Single £8.50-£9.50 Double	Open Jan-Dec Dinner 1800	
Crannich Guest House Tel. Carrbridge (047984) 620			1 Single 1 Dble/Twin 3 Family	3 Public Bath/Sh	B&B per person £8.50-£9.50 Single £8.50-£9.50 Double	Open Jan-Dec Dinner 1900	
Dalrachney Beag Guest House PH23 3AX Tel. Carrbridge (047984) 250			2 Single 5 Dble/Twin 2 Family	4 Public Bath/Sh	B&B per person £9.00-£9.50 Single £8.50-£9.00 Double	Open Dec-Oct Dinner 1900	
Mountain Thyme Guest House Station Road PH23 3AP Tel. Carrbridge (047984) 696		COMMENDED 👑 👑	1 Single 3 Dble/Twin 2 Family	2 Public Bath/Sh	B&B per person £9.50-£11.50 Single £9.50-£11.50 Double	Open Dec-Oct Dinner 1800	
		Personally run 19c stone built house in own grounds with fine views. 1 mile (2 km) from Carrbridge.					
The Pines Guest House The Pines, Duthill Tel. Carrbridge (047984) 220		Listed	2 Dble/Twin 1 Family	1 Public Bath/Sh	B&B per person £8.00-£9.00 Double	Open Jan-Dec Dinner 1900	
Mrs H Marshall Ell-Mar, Station Road PH23 3AN Tel. Carrbridge (047984) 284			3 Dble/Twin	1 Public Bath/Sh	B&B per person £7.50-£8.50 Double	Open Jan-Dec	
Mrs F Ritchie Pine View, Carr Road PH23 3AB Tel. Carrbridge (047984) 217			1 Dble/Twin 2 Family	1 Public Bath/Sh	B&B per person £8.00 Double	Open Jan-Oct	
Mrs K Sandilands Ryna Clarsach, Sloch PH23 3AY Tel. Carrbridge (047984) 263			1 Single 2 Dble/Twin 1 Family	1 Public Bath/Sh	B&B per person £7.50 Single £7.50 Double	Open Jan-Dec Dinner 1900	
CARRON, Aberlour **Moray** Mrs Rosemary L MacLeod Westview IV34 7QP Tel. Carron (03406) 415	Map 4 D9		1 Dble/Twin 2 Family	1 Public Bath/Sh	B&B per person £7.50 Double	Open Jan-Dec	

Key to symbols is on back flap. Details of Classification and Grading are on page vi.

47

Name / Address	Map Ref	Classification	Rooms	Bath	B&B	Open
CARRUTHERSTOWN Dumfriesshire Mrs J Brown Domaru DG1 4JX Tel. Carrutherstown (038784) 260	Map 2 C10		3 Dble/Twin	2 Public Bath/Sh	B&B per person £7.50 Double	Open Apr-Oct Dinner 1800
CASLUITH, by Creetown Kirkcudbrightshire Mrs J Henry Rambank Tel. Creetown (067182) 216	Map 1 H10		2 Dble/Twin	1 Private Bath/Sh 1 Public Bath/Sh	B&B per person £9.00-£10.50 Double	Open Mar-Dec Dinner 1830
CASTLE DOUGLAS Kirkcudbrightshire	Map 2 A10					
Coila Guest House 39 St Andrew Street Tel. Castle Douglas (0556) 2601		Awaiting Inspection	1 Single 2 Dble/Twin 2 Family	2 Public Bath/Sh	B&B per person £8.50-£9.00 Single £8.50-£9.00 Double	Open Jan-Nov Dinner 1700
Cuil Park Guest House Bridge of Dee Tel. Bridge of Dee (055668) 213			1 Single 9 Dble/Twin 2 Family	4 Private Bath/Sh 1 Public Bath/Sh	B&B per person £10.00 Single £10.00 Double	Open Jan-Dec Dinner 1800
Longacre Guest House Ernespie Road Tel. Castle Douglas (0556) 3576		COMMENDED 👑👑👑	3 Dble/Twin 1 Family	4 Private Bath/Sh	B&B per person £12.00-£15.00 Double	Open Jan-Dec Dinner 1930
			Family run, in own grounds overlooking town. All rooms with private facilities and colour TV.			
Mr & Mrs Brown 18 Queen Street Tel. Castle Douglas (0556) 3157			1 Single 2 Dble/Twin	1 Public Bath/Sh	B&B per person £7.50 Single £7.50 Double	Open Jan-Dec
Mrs Gibson Craignar, 32 Abercromby Road DG7 1BA Tel. Castle Douglas (0556) 2112			1 Single 3 Dble/Twin	1 Public Bath/Sh	B&B per person £8.00 Single £8.00 Double	Open Jan-Dec
Mrs J Hunter Windyridge, 48 Abercromby Road DG7 1BA Tel. Castle Douglas (0556) 2700			1 Single 2 Dble/Twin	1 Public Bath/Sh	B&B per person £7.25 Single £7.25 Double	Open Mar-Oct
Mrs M Hunter Benmore, 5 King Street Tel. Castle Douglas (0556) 2693			1 Single 2 Dble/Twin	2 Public Bath/Sh	B&B per person £7.50 Single £7.50 Double	Open Feb-Nov Dinner 1750
Mrs G MacFarlane Markfast, Haugh-of-Urr DG7 3LE Tel. Haugh-of-Urr (055666) 220		COMMENDED 👑👑	2 Dble/Twin 1 Family	1 Public Bath/Sh	B&B per person £8.00 Double	Open Jan-Dec Dinner 1800
			Victorian house on working farm. Peaceful rural setting, 3 miles from A75, 7 miles Castle Douglas.			
Mrs Anne Mundell Norwood, Abercromby Road Tel. Castle Douglas (0556) 2683			1 Single 2 Dble/Twin 1 Family	1 Public Bath/Sh	B&B per person £7.50-£8.00 Single £7.50 Double	Open Apr-Oct Dinner 1800

	Map	Classification	Rooms	Bath	Rates	Opening	Symbols
CASTLE DOUGLAS continued Mrs D J Smith Ingleston Farm DG7 1SW Tel. Castle Douglas (0556) 2936	Map 2 A10	Awaiting Inspection	2 Dble/Twin	2 Private Bath/Sh	B&B per person £7.50 Double	Open Apr-Oct Dinner 1830	(symbols)
CASTLEBAY Isle of Barra, Western Isles An Calla Guest House Tel. Castlebay (08714) 270	Map 3 A11		1 Single 5 Dble/Twin	2 Public Bath/Sh	B&B per person £9.00 Single £9.00 Double	Open Apr-Oct Dinner 1800	(symbols)
Mrs Katie Galbraith Terra Nova, Nask Tel. Castlebay (08714) 458			2 Dble/Twin 1 Family	1 Public Bath/Sh	B&B per person £8.00-£8.50 Double	Open Apr-Oct	(symbols)
Mrs L MacLean Tigh-na-Mara Tel. Castlebay (08714) 304			1 Single 1 Dble/Twin 1 Family	1 Public Bath/Sh	B&B per person £8.00 Single £8.00 Double	Open Jan-Dec Dinner 1900	(symbols)
Mrs M S MacNeil Ceol Mara Tel. Castlebay (08714) 294			3 Dble/Twin	2 Public Bath/Sh	B&B per person £8.00 Double	Open Jan-Dec Dinner 1800	(symbols)
CASTLETOWN Caithness Mrs G Custer Greenland House, Main Street Tel. Castletown (084782) 215	Map 4 D3		1 Single 1 Dble/Twin 3 Family	1 Public Bath/Sh	B&B per person £8.00 Single £9.00 Double	Open Jan-Dec Dinner 1830	(symbols)
CATTERLINE Kincardineshire Mrs D Knight Old Schoolhouse AB3 2UN Tel. Catterline (05695) 262	Map 4 G11		2 Dble/Twin	1 Public Bath/Sh	B&B per person £8.50-£9.50 Double	Open Apr-Oct Dinner 1800	(symbols)
CAWDOR Nairn Mrs Jennifer Macleod Dallaschyle IV12 5XS Tel. Croy (06678) 422	Map 4 B8		1 Dble/Twin 1 Family	1 Public Bath/Sh	B&B per person £8.00 Double	Open Apr-Oct	(symbols)
CERES Fife Mrs E Kay Blebo Mains Farm Tel. Ceres (033482) 266	Map 2 D3	Listed	1 Single 1 Dble/Twin 1 Family	1 Public Bath/Sh	B&B per person £8.00-£10.00 Single £8.50-£9.50 Double	Open Apr-Oct	(symbols)
CLACHAMISH, by Portree Isle of Skye, Inverness-shire Mrs H M Campbell 2 Suladale Tel. Edinbane (047082) 251	Map 3 D8		1 Single 2 Dble/Twin	1 Public Bath/Sh	B&B per person £6.50-£7.00 Single £6.50-£7.00 Double	Open Apr-Oct Dinner 1900	(symbols)

Key to symbols is on back flap. Details of Classification and Grading are on page vi.

49

CLACHAN SEIL, by Oban Argyll	Map 1 E3

ACHRAICH   Tel: Balvicar (085 23) 259

Clachan Seil, by Oban, Argyll PA34 4TN

Achraich is 13 miles from Oban across 'Atlantic Bridge', in a beautiful situation on the road to Ardencaple, just off the main B844 to Easdale. Extensive views over Balvicar Bay and Seil Sound. Convenient for visiting the islands of Luing and Easdale.

Accommodation consists of one double bedroom (downstairs) and one twin-bedded room. Both rooms have H&C.

Mrs J Butler Achraich, Ardencaple Road PA34 4TN Tel. Balvicar (08523) 259	♛	2 Dble/Twin	1 Public Bath/Sh	B&B per person £7.50 Double	Open Apr-Oct	🐟 🛁 🖥 🐎 ❄ P C

CLACHAN, by Tarbert Argyll	Map 1 E6

BATTERY POINT

CLACHAN, by TARBERT, ARGYLL. Tel. 08804 226

Comfortable, well appointed house in secluded situation by fine beach on the lovely unspoiled peninsula of Kintyre. Impressive outlook and convenient day trip access to the islands of Jura, Islay, Gigha and Arran, the latter two having famous National Trust gardens. Area rich in bird, plant and animal shore/moorland wildlife.

Mrs Dale Battery Point Tel. Clachan (08804) 226		3 Dble/Twin	1 Public Bath/Sh	B&B per person £8.00 Double	Open Jan-Dec Dinner 1830	🛁 V ✂ ❄ ⚘ P △ C 🏤
Mrs Moller Old Smithy Tel. Clachan (08804) 635		3 Dble/Twin 1 Family	1 Public Bath/Sh	B&B per person £7.50-£8.00 Double	Open Jan-Dec	🛁 V ✦ ⚘ 🖥 ✂ 🐎 P C 🎠

CLARENCEFIELD Dumfriesshire	Map 2 C10					
Mrs J McGaw Kirkbeck Farm Tel. Clarencefield (038787) 671		2 Dble/Twin 1 Family	1 Public Bath/Sh	B&B per person £7.50 Double	Open Jan-Dec Dinner 1700	🐟 🛁 V 🛁 ⌂ 🖥 📺 🐎 ❄ P C 🎠

Comlongon Castle

CLARENCEFIELD · DUMFRIES · Tel: 038 787 283

Situated in 50 acres of secluded grounds, between Dumfries and Annan on B724. Enjoy a truly relaxing break in this historic mansion. Rooms with four-poster beds/private bathrooms. Before a candlelit dinner join us on our tour of the dungeons, great hall, battlements etc.

Bed and Breakfast £20. Dinner £10.

Mr & Mrs Ptolomey Comlongon Castle Tel. Clarencefield (038787) 283	COMMENDED ♛♛♛	4 Dble/Twin	4 Private Bath/Sh	B&B per person £20.00 Double	Open Mar-Dec Dinner 1930	🐟 📺 🖥 V 🛁 🍴 🖥 📺 ✦ ⚘ 🎠 ✂ ❄ P / 🏤
		Elegant period mansion set in 50 acres of parkland. Adjoining original medieval castle.				

VAT is shown at 15%: changes in this rate may affect prices. Prices shown are for guidance only. Please send SAE with each enquiry.

CLEISH, Kinross Kinross-shire	**Map 2** C3						
Mrs Alcock Bowood Tel. Cleish Hills (05575) 213			1 Dble/Twin	1 Private Bath/Sh	B&B per person £8.50-£9.25 Double	Open Mar-Nov Dinner 1830	
COLDSTREAM Berwickshire	**Map 2** F6						
Kengarth Guest House 7 Market Street TD12 4BU Tel. Coldstream (0890) 2477			1 Single 1 Dble/Twin 1 Family	2 Public Bath/Sh	B&B per person £7.00 Single £7.00 Double	Open Apr-Oct Dinner 1700	
Mrs J Bowie Iolair, Victoria Place Tel. Coldstream (0890) 2084		**COMMENDED** 👑👑	4 Dble/Twin	3 Public Bath/Sh	B&B per person £10.00 Double	Open Jan-Dec Dinner 1900	
			Elegantly furnished victorian house, in side street opposite Post Office in centre of town.				
COLMONELL Ayrshire	**Map 1** G9						

BURNFOOT FARM
Burnfoot, Colmonell, Girvan KA26 0SQ, Ayrshire
Tel: 046 588 220/265

A warm welcome awaits you at Burnfoot Farm, a family-run dairy and beef unit of 157 acres, nestled in the beautiful Stinchar Valley. It is an ideal base for touring the Ayrshire and Wigtownshire coasts, Burns Country and Galloway Hills. Many beautiful gardens and interesting places to visit. Home cooking and baking a speciality using fresh garden produce. A place where friendliness cleanliness and comfort are guaranteed.

Mrs Shankland Burnfoot Farm KA26 0SQ Tel. Colmonell (046588) 220/265		**COMMENDED** Listed	1 Dble/Twin 2 Family	1 Public Bath/Sh	B&B per person £8.00-£8.50 Double	Open Apr-Oct Dinner 1830	
			Farmhouse on 150 acre dairy farm. Ideally situated for touring Ayrshire coast and Burns Country.				
COLONSAY, Isle of Argyll	**Map 1** C4						
Mrs A Clark Baleromindobh Farm Tel. Colonsay (09512) 305			1 Single 1 Dble/Twin 1 Family	1 Public Bath/Sh	B&B per person £8.00-£9.00 Single £8.00-£9.00 Double	Open Jan-Dec Dinner 1800	
Mr & Mrs Lawson Seaview Tel. Colonsay (09512) 315			2 Dble/Twin 1 Family	1 Public Bath/Sh	B&B per person £7.50 Double	Open Apr-Oct Dinner 1900	
COLVEND, by Dalbeattie Kirkcudbrightshire	**Map 2** B10						
Mrs A Douglas Anchordale DG5 4PU Tel. Southwick (038778) 240			1 Single 2 Dble/Twin	1 Public Bath/Sh	B&B per person £7.00 Single £7.00 Double	Open Apr-Oct	
COMRIE Perthshire	**Map 2** A2						
Mossgiel Guest House Burrell Street PH6 2JP Tel. Comrie (0764) 70567			6 Dble/Twin	1 Public Bath/Sh	B&B per person £7.00 Double	Open Apr-Oct Dinner 1930	

Key to symbols is on back flap. Details of Classification and Grading are on page vi.

51

COMRIE continued	Map 2 A2						
Mrs S Bradley Larklea, Barrack Road Tel. Comrie (0764) 70467			2 Dble/Twin	2 Public Bath/Sh	B&B per person £7.00-£7.50 Double	Open Jan-Dec	
Mr N Leigh St Kessacs, Dunira Street Tel. Comrie (0764) 70233			1 Single 1 Dble/Twin 2 Family	1 Public Bath/Sh	B&B per person £8.50 Single £7.50 Double	Open Jan-Dec Dinner 1830	

West Ballindalloch Farm
GLENLEDNOCK, COMRIE, BY CRIEFF, PERTHSHIRE PH6 2LY   Tel: 0764 70282

Enjoy a holiday in Perthshire Glen. Ideal touring, walking or golf on the many courses. Bed and breakfast, bedtime snack and early morning tea served. Tea/coffee making facilities available. Electric blankets on all beds. Open March to November. Terms sent on request. **AA Listed.**

Mrs Rimmer West Ballindalloch Farm, Glenlednock PH6 2LY Tel. Comrie (0764) 70282			1 Dble/Twin 1 Family	1 Public Bath/Sh	B&B per person £8.00-£8.50 Double	Open Mar-Nov	
CONNEL **Argyll**	Map 1 E2						
Mrs Gravell Lora House Tel. Connel (063171) 456			2 Single 2 Dble/Twin	1 Public Bath/Sh	B&B per person £9.00 Single £9.00 Double	Open Apr-Oct Dinner 1800	
Mr J Lawson Rughriach House PA37 1PT Tel. Connel (063171) 485			2 Dble/Twin 1 Family	2 Public Bath/Sh	B&B per person £9.00 Double	Open Jan-Dec Dinner 1830	
Mrs Pollock Lusragan Lodge PA37 1PH Tel. Connel (063171) 488			2 Single 5 Dble/Twin 1 Family	2 Public Bath/Sh	B&B per person £8.50-£10.50 Single £8.50-£10.50 Double	Open Jan-Dec	
CORPACH, by Fort William **Inverness-shire**	Map 3 G12						
Ben Nevis View Guest House Tel. Corpach (03977) 760			1 Dble/Twin 2 Family	3 Public Bath/Sh	B&B per person £9.00-£9.50 Double	Open Mar-Oct Dinner 1800	
Mansfield Guest House Tel. Corpach (03977) 262		APPROVED 👑👑	2 Dble/Twin 3 Family	2 Public Bath/Sh	B&B per person £9.50 Double	Open Jan-Dec Dinner 1900	
Victorian house standing in own grounds, 3 miles/5 km from Fort William on road to Mallaig.							
Mrs Dunlop Migarna Tel. Corpach (03977) 220			1 Dble/Twin 1 Family	1 Public Bath/Sh	B&B per person £7.50 Double	Open Apr-Oct	
Mrs B Grieve 14 Farrow Drive Tel. Corpach (03977) 447			1 Single 1 Family		B&B per person £8.50 Single £8.50 Double	Open Jan-Dec	

CORPACH, by Fort William continued Mrs McLeod Clintwood, 23 Hillview Drive Tel. Corpach (03977) 680	Map 3 G12		4 Dble/Twin	1 Public Bath/Sh	B&B per person £8.50 Double	Open Apr-Oct	♿ 🍽 🛏 TV P
Mrs K Moran 18 Lady Maraget Drive Tel. Corpach (03977) 506			2 Dble/Twin	1 Public Bath/Sh	B&B per person £6.50 Double	Open May-Sep	
Mr Steel 6 Lady Margaret Drive Tel. Corpach (03977) 430			2 Dble/Twin 1 Family	1 Public Bath/Sh	B&B per person £8.00 Double	Open Apr-Oct Dinner 1900	♿ 🛏 TV ✎ £ C
CORRIE **Isle of Arran** Mr Hunter Heathfield Tel. Corrie (077081) 286	Map 1 F6		1 Single 1 Dble/Twin 1 Family	1 Public Bath/Sh	B&B per person £8.00-£8.50 Single £8.00-£8.50 Double	Open Jan-Dec Dinner 1800	♿ ♨ V ♨ ♨ TV ✎ ♨ ✎ 🐕 ※ P ⚠ ⚘ C ⚘ T
CORRIECRAVIE **Isle of Arran** Mrs Kelso Hillside Tel. Sliddery (077087) 274	Map 1 E7	Awaiting Inspection	1 Dble/Twin 1 Family	1 Public Bath/Sh	B&B per person £9.00 Double	Open Jan-Dec Dinner 1730	V ♨ TV ✎ P C ⚘ 🐾
CORSOCK, by Castle Douglas **Kirkcudbrightshire** Mrs Wilson Auchenvey Farm Tel. Corsock (06444) 268	Map 2 B9		1 Dble/Twin 1 Family	1 Public Bath/Sh	B&B per person £7.50 Double	Open Apr-Oct Dinner 1800	V ♨ ♨ TV 🐕 P ⚠ ⚘ C 🐾
COUPAR ANGUS **Perthshire** Mrs MacFarlane Rabana, Caddam Road PH13 9EF Tel. Coupar Angus (0828) 27767	Map 2 C1		1 Family	1 Private Bath/Sh 1 Public Bath/Sh	B&B per person £7.50-£8.00 Double	Open Jan-Dec Dinner 1730	♨ 🛏 TV P C
Mrs J G Shaw Boatlands House, Blairgowrie Road Tel. Coupar Angus (0828) 28385			1 Single 2 Dble/Twin 1 Family		B&B per person £9.50-£11.00 Single £8.50-£9.50 Double	Open Jan-Dec Dinner 1700	🍽 V ♨ ♨ 🛏 TV ♨ ✎ 🐕 ※ £ P ⚘ C T
COWDENBEATH **Fife** Glenbank Guest House 36 Foulford Road Tel. Cowdenbeath (0383) 515466	Map 2 C4	COMMENDED 👑 👑	1 Single 1 Dble/Twin 3 Family	1 Public Bath/Sh	B&B per person £8.50-£10.00 Single £8.00-£9.50 Double	Open Jan-Dec Dinner 1800	♿ 🍽 🏆 ♨ 🛏 TV ♨ 🐕 ※ P C
			19th century dressed stone house in quiet area above town. Warm and friendly atmosphere.				
Marchmont Guest House 91 Broad Street KY4 8JR Tel. Cowdenbeath (0383) 510823			3 Single 1 Dble/Twin 2 Family	1 Private Bath/Sh 1 Public Bath/Sh	B&B per person £8.50 Single £8.00 Double	Open Jan-Dec Dinner 1800	♿ 🍽 ♨ 🛏 TV ✎ ✂ P C

CRAIGELLACHIE, Aberlour Banffshire	Map 4 D8						
Mrs Fiona Ogilvie Tanzie AB3 9RL Tel. Craigellachie (03404) 214			1 Dble/Twin 1 Family	1 Public Bath/Sh	B&B per person £10.00 Double	Open Apr-Oct	
Mrs Iris Wilson Sabhal, Brickfield AB3 9TD Tel. Craigellachie (03404) 207			1 Single 2 Dble/Twin 1 Family	1 Private Bath/Sh 1 Public Bath/Sh	B&B per person £8.00 Single £8.00 Double	Open Apr-Oct Dinner 1900	
CRAIL Fife	Map 2 E3	**COMMENDED** ♔ ♔					
Caiplie Guest House 51-53 High Street KY10 3RA Tel. Crail (0333) 50564			1 Single 6 Dble/Twin		B&B per person £9.50-£12.50 Single £9.50-£12.50 Double	Open Feb-Oct Dinner 1900	
Compact, privately owned, in main street of fishing village. Home cooking. Taste of Scotland.							
Mrs E B Clarkson Westgarth, Kirkmay Road KY10 8SF Tel. Crail (0333) 50289			2 Dble/Twin 1 Family		B&B per person £8.00 Double	Open Apr-Oct	
CRATHIE Aberdeenshire	Map 4 D11						
Mrs M Fraser Rhynabaich Tel. Crathie (03384) 237			2 Dble/Twin 2 Family	1 Public Bath/Sh	B&B per person £7.50 Double	Open Apr-Nov Dinner 1900	
Mrs I Fraser Balnault Farm AB3 5TP Tel. Crathie (03384) 223			1 Dble/Twin 1 Family	1 Public Bath/Sh	B&B per person £8.50 Double	Open Jan-Dec	
CRAWFORD Lanarkshire	Map 2 B7	**APPROVED** ♔ ♔					
Field End Guest House ML12 6TN Tel. Crawford (08642) 276			2 Single 2 Dble/Twin 1 Family	2 Private Bath/Sh 1 Public Bath/Sh	B&B per person £9.00-£12.00 Single £9.00-£12.00 Double	Open Jan-Dec Dinner 1830	
Stone villa overlooking fields. Games room and evening meal available.							

VAT is shown at 15%; changes in this rate may affect prices. Prices shown are for guidance only. Please send SAE with each enquiry.

CREETOWN, by Newton Stewart Wigtownshire	Map 1 H10

The Boathouse
Creetown, Newton Stewart, Wigtownshire
Telephone: 065 182 335

Good food together with comfortable accommodation awaits you at this small private guest house. All rooms have superb views overlooking the River Cree which is famous for its salmon fishing.

If you are just passing why not stop for morning coffee and admire the scenic views of the salt marshes and surrounding countryside. The Boathouse is an ideal base for touring beautiful Dumfries and Galloway and taking part in countryside activities, i.e. Fishing, Golfing, Riding, Walking and Birdwatching.

The Boathouse Guest House DG8 7DE Tel. Creetown (067182) 335	**COMMENDED** Listed	3 Dble/Twin	1 Public Bath/Sh	B&B per person £8.50 Double	Open Jan-Dec Dinner 1930	
		Converted cottage and boathouse on banks of River Cree. Village 1 mile, Newton Stewart 6 miles.				
CRIANLARICH Perthshire	Map 1 G2					
Craigbank Guest House FK20 8QS Tel. Crianlarich (08383) 279		3 Dble/Twin 1 Family	1 Public Bath/Sh	B&B per person £9.00 Double	Open Jan-Dec Dinner 1900	
Glenardran Guest House Tel. Crianlarich (08383) 236		1 Single 2 Dble/Twin 3 Family	1 Public Bath/Sh	B&B per person £8.50-£9.00 Single £8.50-£9.00 Double	Open Jan-Dec Dinner 1915	
Mountgreenan Guest House FK20 8RU Tel. Crianlarich (08383) 286		1 Single 3 Dble/Twin 1 Family	2 Public Bath/Sh	B&B per person £9.50-£10.00 Single £8.50-£9.00 Double	Open Jan-Dec Dinner 1930	

Key to symbols is on back flap. Details of Classification and Grading are on page vi.

CRIANLARICH continued	Map 1 G2	

Portnellan Guest House

Lochdochart, by Crianlarich, Perthshire
Telephone: 08383 284

Climb Ben More, go fishing on Loch Dochart or play golf at Killin and return to the warmth and comfort of this family-run, 19th-century house, and sit before a roaring log fire with a dram and good company.

Centrally located for touring, ½ hour south of Glen Coe with Fort William, Oban and Perth within an hour's drive.

All rooms have private baths, tea and coffee-making facilities and central heating. Residents' lounge and sun lounge, private gardens extending to 60 acres.

All this from £10 per person/night including full Scottish breakfast.

Brochure: Elaine and Trevor Taylor, Portnellan House, Loch Dochart, by Crianlarich FK20 8QS. Tel: 08383 284.
♛ ♛ ♛ *Commended*

Portnellan House Guest House Glendochart FK20 8QS Tel. Crianlarich (08383) 284	COMMENDED ♛ ♛ ♛	2 Dble/Twin 1 Family	2 Private Bath/Sh 1 Public Bath/Sh	B&B per person £10.00-£12.50 Double	Open Jan-Dec Dinner 1900	
		Family run, 19C shooting lodge on private estate. Fine views, free fishing, boats available.				
The Riverside Guest House Tigh Na Struith Tel. Crianlarich (08383) 235		4 Dble/Twin 2 Family		B&B per person £9.00-£9.50 Double	Open Apr-Oct	
CRIEFF Perthshire	Map 2 B2					
Comely Bank Guest House 32 Burrell Street PH7 4DT Tel. Crieff (0764) 3409		1 Single 3 Dble/Twin 2 Family	3 Public Bath/Sh	B&B per person £7.50-£8.25 Single £7.50-£8.25 Double	Open Jan-Dec Dinner 1830	
Dalchonzie House Guest House 28 Burrell Street PH7 4DT Tel. Crieff (0764) 3423		4 Dble/Twin	1 Public Bath/Sh	B&B per person £8.00-£9.00 Double	Open Apr-Oct Dinner 1830	
Heatherville Guest House 31 Burrell Street PH7 4DT Tel. Crieff (0764) 2825	COMMENDED ♛ ♛	1 Single 3 Dble/Twin 1 Family	2 Public Bath/Sh	B&B per person £8.00-£8.50 Single £8.00-£8.50 Double	Open Jan-Dec Dinner 1830	
		Terraced house with attractive garden near shops and park. Golf holidays. Special diets available.				
Mrs B Kelly Mill House, South Bridgend Tel. Crieff (0764) 4700	COMMENDED Listed	1 Single 2 Dble/Twin	2 Public Bath/Sh	B&B per person £8.00-£9.00 Single £8.00-£9.00 Double	Open Jan-Dec Dinner 1830	
		18th century building on banks of River Earn. On A823 tourist route, on the outskirts of town.				
Mrs O J Mill The Heugh, Gwydyr Road PH7 4BS Tel. Crieff (0764) 2523		1 Single 2 Dble/Twin	1 Public Bath/Sh	B&B per person £7.50-£9.00 Single £7.50-£9.00 Double	Open Jan-Dec	
Mrs Oliver 83 East High Street PH7 3JA Tel. Crieff (0764) 3020		3 Dble/Twin 2 Family	1 Public Bath/Sh	B&B per person £8.00 Double	Open Jan-Dec Dinner 1800	

CRIEFF continued Miss B Sim Craigally, 1 Addison Crescent PH7 5AU Tel. Crieff (0764) 2434	Map 2 B2		1 Single 2 Dble/Twin	1 Public Bath/Sh	B&B per person £7.00 Single £7.00 Double	Open Apr-Oct

CROCKETFORD, by Dumfries
Kirkcudbrightshire — Map 2 B10

Brandedleys

Crocketford, by Dumfries.   Tel. 055 669 250

The farmhouse of Brandedleys is situated on a hill overlooking Auchenreoch Loch. All meals are available in the adjacent restaurant and lounge. Fishing, golfing, walking and shopping are all nearby. There are castles, museums, villages and gardens to visit and in the grounds a heated swimming pool, tennis court and games room offer recreation.

Mr & Mrs Mcdonald Brandedleys Tel. Crocketford (055669) 250	1 Single 1 Dble/Twin 1 Family	1 Public Bath/Sh	B&B per person £9.50-£11.00 Single £9.50-£11.00 Double	Open Apr-Oct Dinner 1800	
CROOK OF DEVON, Kinross Kinross-shire Mrs Mercer The Poplars KY13 7PR Tel. Fossoway (05774) 202	Map 2 B3		2 Family	1 Public Bath/Sh	B&B per person £8.00-£9.00 Double	Open Jan-Dec
CROSSHILL, by Maybole Ayrshire Mrs Morton Ashlea, 18 Kirkmichael Road KA19 7RJ Tel. Crosshill (06554) 251	Map 1 G8		1 Dble/Twin 1 Family	1 Public Bath/Sh	B&B per person £8.00 Double	Open Apr-Oct Dinner 1800
Mrs Young Gartlea, Garpin Farm KA19 7PX Tel. Crosshill (06554) 381			2 Dble/Twin	1 Public Bath/Sh	B&B per person £8.50 Double	Open Apr-Oct Dinner 1800
CROSSMICHAEL, by Castle Douglas Kirkcudbrightshire Crawford & Margaret Masson Kenloch House Tel. Crossmichael (055667) 452	Map 2 A10		2 Dble/Twin 1 Family	2 Private Bath/Sh 3 Public Bath/Sh	B&B per person £8.50 Double	Open Jan-Dec Dinner 1900
Mrs B McBride Airds Farm DG7 3BG Tel. Crossmichael (055667) 418		COMMENDED	3 Dble/Twin 1 Family	2 Public Bath/Sh	B&B per person £8.00-£9.00 Double	Open Apr-Oct Dinner 1850

On working farm with young stock, 4 miles from Castle Douglas. Pony trekking, views of Loch Ken.

Key to symbols is on back flap. Details of Classification and Grading are on page vi.

57

Location	Map	Rating	Rooms	Bath	B&B	Open
CRUDEN BAY Aberdeenshire Mrs J Blackburn Dunroy, Aulton Road AB4 7NJ Tel. Cruden Bay (077981) 2686	Map 4 H9		2 Family	2 Public Bath/Sh	B&B per person £7.00 Double	Open Jan-Dec Dinner 1900
CULLEN, Buckie Banffshire Mrs S Seivwright Drummore House, York Place AB5 2UW Tel. Cullen (0542) 40304	Map 4 E7		2 Dble/Twin 1 Family	1 Public Bath/Sh	B&B per person £8.50 Double	Open Apr-Oct
Mrs Marian Sleightholm Norwood, 11 Seafield Place AB5 2TE Tel. Cullen (0542) 40314			2 Single 3 Dble/Twin 1 Family	1 Public Bath/Sh	B&B per person £6.50-£8.50 Single	Open Jan-Dec Dinner 1830
CULLODEN MOOR, by Inverness Inverness-shire Mrs E M C Alexander Culdoich Farm IV1 2EP Tel. Inverness (0463) 790268	Map 4 B9	COMMENDED 👑👑	1 Dble/Twin 1 Family	1 Public Bath/Sh	B&B per person £8.00-£9.00 Double	Open Apr-Oct Dinner 1900
On mixed arable and livestock farm, on hillside near Culloden Battlefield. Home baking and cooking.						
CULNACNOCK, Portree Isle of Skye, Inverness-shire Mrs K Macleod Blaracrian House Tel. Staffin (047062) 208	Map 3 D8		1 Single 4 Dble/Twin 1 Family	2 Public Bath/Sh	B&B per person £7.50 Single £7.50 Double	Open Mar-Sep Dinner 1830
CULROSS Fife Mrs K Peddie The Cottage, Blairburn KY12 8JN Tel. Newmills (0383) 880704	Map 2 B4		2 Dble/Twin		B&B per person £7.50 Double	Open Apr-Sep Dinner 1800
CUMBERNAULD Dunbartonshire Mrs M Abercrombie 68 Lammermoor Drive, Greenfaulds G67 4BE Tel. Cumbernauld (02367) 21307	Map 2 A5	Listed	1 Dble/Twin 1 Family	1 Public Bath/Sh	B&B per person £10.00 Double	Open Jan-Dec
CUMMERTREES, by Annan Dumfriesshire Mrs Forest Hurkledale Farm Tel. Cummertrees (04617) 228	Map 2 C10		1 Single 3 Dble/Twin	1 Public Bath/Sh	B&B per person £8.00 Single £8.00 Double	Open Apr-Oct Dinner 1830
CUMNOCK Ayrshire Stepends Guest House 6 Auchinleck Road Tel. Cumnock (0290) 25238	Map 1 H7		1 Single 2 Dble/Twin 1 Family	2 Private Bath/Sh 1 Public Bath/Sh	B&B per person £14.50-£16.50 Single £14.50-£16.50 Double	Open Mar-Jan Dinner 1730

VAT is shown at 15%. changes in this rate may affect prices. Prices shown are for guidance only. Please send SAE with each enquiry.

	Map	Grading	Rooms	Bathrooms	Prices	Opening	Symbols
CUMNOCK continued Mrs Mckinlay Meikle Heateth Farm, Auchinleck Tel. Mauchline (0290) 51279	Map 1 H7	Awaiting Inspection	1 Dble/Twin 2 Family	1 Public Bath/Sh	B&B per person £8.00 Double	Open Mar-Nov Dinner 1700	
CUPAR Fife Lynda M Gibson Easterhills, Castlebank Road Tel. Cupar (0334) 54275	Map 2 D3		1 Single 2 Dble/Twin 1 Family	2 Public Bath/Sh	B&B per person £10.00-£10.50 Single £10.00-£10.50 Double	Open Jan-Dec	
Mrs L Smith Myrecairnie Farm Tel. Cupar (0334) 53266		COMMENDED Listed	1 Single 2 Dble/Twin	2 Public Bath/Sh	B&B per person £10.00 Single £10.00 Double	Open Jan-Dec Dinner 1800	
Comfortable farmhouse with home cooking in the centre of Fife. Large garden, highland cattle nearby.							
Mrs H Weller Kemback Beg KY15 5TS Tel. Cupar (0334) 52056			1 Dble/Twin 1 Family	1 Public Bath/Sh	B&B per person £8.00-£8.50 Double	Open Jul-Aug	
Mrs S Whiten Mayfield, Craigrothie KY15 5QA Tel. Ceres (033482) 551			2 Dble/Twin	1 Public Bath/Sh	B&B per person £8.00 Double	Open May-Sep	
CUSHNIE, by Alford Aberdeenshire Mrs Robertson Struan AB3 8LH Tel. Muir of Fowlis (03364) 330	Map 4 F10		1 Single 2 Dble/Twin	1 Public Bath/Sh	B&B per person £6.00 Single £6.00 Double	Open Apr-Oct Dinner 1800	
DALBEATTIE Kirkcudbrightshire Galla Guest House Haugh-of-Urr Road DG5 4LP Tel. Dalbeattie (0556) 610425	Map 2 B10		4 Dble/Twin	1 Public Bath/Sh	B&B per person £10.00 Double	Open Jan-Dec Dinner 1800	
Mrs Johnston Lower Porterbelly DG5 4NJ Tel. Kirkgunzeon (038776) 245			2 Dble/Twin 1 Family	2 Public Bath/Sh	B&B per person £8.00 Double	Open Apr-Oct Dinner 1800	
Mrs V Johnstone Mimosa, Barrhill Road Tel. Dalbeattie (0556) 610073			2 Family	1 Public Bath/Sh	B&B per person £7.00-£8.00 Single £7.00-£8.00 Double	Open Mar-Oct	
Mr & Mrs M Kirkpatrick Michilly, 5 John Street Tel. Dalbeattie (0556) 611346			2 Dble/Twin 2 Family		B&B per person £9.00 Double	Open Jan-Dec Dinner 1630	
DALCROSS, by Inverness Inverness-shire Mrs Pottie Easter Dalziel Farm IV1 2JL Tel. Ardersier (0667) 62213	Map 4 B8	COMMENDED	2 Dble/Twin 1 Family	2 Public Bath/Sh	B&B per person £8.50-£10.00 Double	Open Apr-Oct Dinner 1900	
On 200 acre working farm, warm friendly atmosphere, good farmhouse food. Near for Cawdor Castle.							

DALIBURGH S Uist, Western Isles Mrs C Walker 277 Daliburgh PA81 5AS Tel. Lochboisdale (08784) 330	Map 3 A10		2 Dble/Twin	1 Public Bath/Sh	B&B per person £7.50-£8.00 Double	Open Apr-Oct Dinner 1800
DALKEITH Midlothian	Map 2 D5					
Birchlea Guest House 127 High Street Tel. 031 663 4280			1 Single 5 Dble/Twin 2 Family	1 Public Bath/Sh	B&B per person £9.00 Single £9.00 Double	Open Jan-Dec
Newbattle Abbey College EH22 3LL Tel. 031 663 1921			59 Single 11 Dble/Twin	25 Public Bath/Sh	B&B per person £9.20 Single £9.20 Double	Open Jan-Dec Dinner 1800
Mrs Hodkinson 63 Hadfast Road, Cousland Tel. 031 663 2933		Listed	2 Dble/Twin	1 Public Bath/Sh	B&B per person £8.50-£9.00 Double	Open May-Oct
Mrs Margaret Jarvis Belmont, 47 Eskbank Road EH22 3BH Tel. 031 663 8676			1 Single 4 Dble/Twin	1 Private Bath/Sh 1 Public Bath/Sh	B&B per person £10.00 Single £10.00-£12.00 Double	Open Jan-Dec
DALMALLY Argyll	Map 1 F2					

Craig Villa Guest House
Dalmally, by Loch Awe, Argyll PA33 1AX
Telephone: 08382 255 and 06313 63255

Come to the Highlands and discover the breathtaking scenery of Argyll. Dalmally is an ideal centre for touring and we place great emphasis on good food and a homely atmosphere.

Amenities include private suites, residents' lounge, colour TV, tea/coffee facilities. Activities available: Salmon and Trout Fishing, Deer Stalking, Pony Trekking, Boat Cruises, Bird Watching and Hill Walking. SAE for details.

Craig Villa Guest House Tel. Dalmally (08382) 255		COMMENDED 👑👑	4 Dble/Twin 2 Family	2 Private Bath/Sh 1 Public Bath/Sh	B&B per person £9.00-£10.00 Double	Open Apr-Oct Dinner 1900
Personally run in own grounds amidst breathtaking scenery. Good touring base. Home cooking.						
Mrs H MacPhail The Old School House, Main Road PA33 1AX Tel. Dalmally (08382) 470			1 Dble/Twin 2 Family	1 Public Bath/Sh	B&B per person £8.00-£9.00 Double	Open Jan-Dec Dinner 1900
DALMELLINGTON Ayrshire	Map 1 H8					
Mrs M Coughtrie The Mill KA6 7QT Tel. Dalmellington (0292) 550357		Listed	3 Dble/Twin	2 Public Bath/Sh	B&B per person £9.00 Double	Open Jan-Dec Dinner 1800
Mrs Jean Murdoch Bellsbank Farm House KA6 7PR Tel. Dalmellington (0292) 550248			1 Single 4 Dble/Twin 1 Family	2 Public Bath/Sh	B&B per person £8.50 Single £8.50 Double	Open Apr-Oct Dinner 1800

VAT is shown at 15%: changes in this rate may affect prices. Prices shown are for guidance only. Please send SAE with each enquiry.

	Map	Grading	Accommodation	Facilities	B&B	Opening	Symbols
DALRY Kirkcudbrightshire Mrs M Findlay 59 Main Street Tel. Dalry (06443) 420	Map 2 A9		1 Dble/Twin 1 Family	1 Public Bath/Sh	B&B per person £8.00 Double	Open Apr-Oct	
DAVIOT Inverness-shire John & Amanda Burgess Bonnie View Tel. Daviot (046385) 265	Map 4 B9		2 Single 2 Dble/Twin 1 Family		B&B per person £8.00 Single £8.00 Double	Open Jan-Dec Dinner 1830	
Mrs E Macpherson Lairgandour Farmhouse IV1 2XH Tel. Daviot (046385) 207			1 Dble/Twin 2 Family	1 Public Bath/Sh	B&B per person £8.50-£9.00 Double	Open Apr-Oct Dinner 1900	
DELNY Ross-shire Mrs O Horn Under Beechwood, Non Smokers Retreat Tel. Kildary (086284) 2685	Map 4 B7		1 Single 1 Dble/Twin 1 Family	1 Public Bath/Sh	B&B per person £7.50 Single £7.50 Double	Open Jan-Dec Dinner 1900	
DENNY Stirlingshire Mrs Morton Lochend Farm, Carronbridge FK6 5JJ Tel. Denny (0324) 822778	Map 2 A4	COMMENDED Listed	2 Dble/Twin	1 Public Bath/Sh	B&B per person £8.00-£8.50 Double	Open Jan-Dec Dinner 1830	
Stone built farmhouse. Countryside views over Loch Coulter. 6 miles (10kms) from Stirling.							
Mrs Jennifer Steel The Topps Farm, Fintry Road Tel. Denny (0324) 822471			3 Dble/Twin	2 Private Bath/Sh 1 Public Bath/Sh	B&B per person £8.50 Double	Open Jan-Dec Dinner 1730	
DERVAIG, by Tobermory Isle of Mull, Argyll Quinish House Guest House Quinish Estate Tel. Dervaig (06884) 223	Map 1 C1		1 Single 4 Dble/Twin 1 Family	3 Private Bath/Sh 1 Public Bath/Sh	B&B per person £15.00-£17.00 Single £13.50-£20.00 Double	Open Apr-Oct Dinner 1930	
Mrs Boa Antuim Farm Tel. Dervaig (06884) 230			2 Dble/Twin 1 Family	1 Public Bath/Sh	B&B per person £9.00-£9.50 Double	Open Apr-Oct	
Mick & Ursula Bradley Torr a'Chlachainn PA75 6QR Tel. Dervaig (06884) 229			2 Single 3 Dble/Twin	1 Private Bath/Sh 1 Public Bath/Sh	B&B per person £7.00-£8.50 Single £7.00-£10.50 Double	Open Apr-Oct Dinner 1800	
J L Caskie Kengharair Farm Tel. Dervaig (06884) 251			1 Dble/Twin 1 Family	1 Public Bath/Sh	B&B per person £8.00 Double	Open May-Oct Dinner 1800	
Mrs J Matthew Ardrioch Tel. Dervaig (06884) 264		COMMENDED	1 Single 3 Dble/Twin	1 Public Bath/Sh	B&B per person £9.00 Single £9.00 Double	Open May-Oct Dinner 1830	
Farmhouse situated 1 ml from village, 2mls from shore. Views across loch to hills. Home cooking.							

Key to symbols is on back flap. Details of Classification and Grading are on page vi.

61

Name & Address	Map	Category	Rooms	Bath	B&B	Open	Facilities
DERVAIG, by Tobermory continued Mr & Mrs D Stewart Achnadrish Lodge PA75 6QF Tel. Dervaig (06884) 287	Map 1 C1	Listed	3 Dble/Twin	2 Public Bath/Sh	B&B per person £9.00-£10.00 Double	Open Jan-Dec	
DEVONSIDE, by Saline **Fife** Mrs J Stark Devonlea Cottage KY12 9LN Tel. New Oakley (0383) 852367	Map 2 B4		1 Dble/Twin 1 Family	1 Public Bath/Sh	B&B per person £8.00 Double	Open Apr-Oct Dinner 1900	
DINGWALL **Ross-shire** Mrs C Carbarns Norville, Craig Road Tel. Dingwall (0349) 64998	Map 4 A8		1 Dble/Twin 1 Family	1 Public Bath/Sh	B&B per person £7.00 Double	Open Apr-Oct	
Mrs I Fox Victoria Lodge, Mill Street IV15 9PZ Tel. Dingwall (0349) 62494			1 Single 1 Dble/Twin 2 Family	1 Public Bath/Sh	B&B per person £7.00-£7.50 Single £7.00-£7.50 Double	Open Apr-Oct	
Mrs A Gunn Fyrish, Ferry Road Tel. Dingwall (0349) 64233			1 Dble/Twin 1 Family	1 Public Bath/Sh	B&B per person £7.50-£8.00 Double	Open Jan-Dec Dinner 1800	
Mrs E Lauder Kinnairdie House, Kinnairdie Avenue Tel. Dingwall (0349) 61044			2 Dble/Twin		B&B per person £7.50 Double	Open May-Sep	
Mrs J Maclean Westfield, Mill Street IV15 9PZ Tel. Dingwall (0349) 62387		Awaiting Inspection	2 Dble/Twin 1 Family		B&B per person £7.00 Double	Open Jan-Nov Dinner 1800	
Mrs K Thomson Fairfield, Craig Road Tel. Dingwall (0349) 64936			1 Dble/Twin 1 Family	1 Public Bath/Sh	B&B per person £7.50 Double	Open Apr-Oct	
Mrs Vipond The Croft, Castle Street Tel. Dingwall (0349) 63319		Awaiting Inspection	1 Single 1 Dble/Twin 1 Family	1 Public Bath/Sh	B&B per person £7.00-£8.50 Single £7.00-£8.50 Double	Open Jan-Dec	
DOLLAR **Clackmannanshire** Mrs A K J Hern Eastfield, 4 Manse Road FK14 7AJ Tel. Dollar (02594) 2545	Map 2 B4		1 Dble/Twin 1 Family	1 Public Bath/Sh	B&B per person £8.50-£9.00 Double	Open Feb-Nov	
Mrs F Hutton Kellybank House, Muckhart Road Tel. Dollar (02594) 2081		Awaiting Inspection	1 Dble/Twin 2 Family	1 Private Bath/Sh 1 Public Bath/Sh	B&B per person £9.50-£10.00 Double	Open Mar-Nov	
Mrs Y Nicol Strathdevon House Tel. Dollar (02594) 2320			1 Dble/Twin 1 Family	2 Public Bath/Sh	B&B per person £8.50 Double	Open Jan-Nov	

VAT is shown at 15%; changes in this rate may affect prices. Prices shown are for guidance only. Please send SAE with each enquiry.

			Accommodation	Bathrooms	Prices	Opening	Facilities
DORNIE, by Kyle of Lochalsh Ross-shire	Map 3 F10						
Camuslongart Guest House Ardelve Tel. Dornie (059985) 357		COMMENDED ♔	1 Single 2 Dble/Twin 1 Family	2 Public Bath/Sh	B&B per person £10.00-£12.00 Single £8.50-£10.00 Double	Open Apr-Oct	
			House with adjacent cottage, at end of small road. By picturesque Loch Long. Superb views of hills.				
Mrs Brownlee Suidhe Ban, Carr Brae Tel. Dornie (059985) 370			1 Dble/Twin	1 Public Bath/Sh	B&B per person £7.00 Double	Open May-Oct Dinner 1900	
Mrs M Graham Cuileann Cottage Tel. Dornie (059985) 224			2 Dble/Twin	1 Public Bath/Sh	B&B per person £8.50 Double	Open Apr-Oct	
Mrs Gray Mira House, 15 Francis Street IV40 8DT Tel. Dornie (059985) 221			1 Single 2 Dble/Twin 1 Family	2 Public Bath/Sh	B&B per person £7.50 Single £7.50 Double	Open Jan-Dec	
Mr F E Kitchen Caberfeidh, Ardelve IV40 8DY Tel. Dornie (059985) 293			1 Single 3 Dble/Twin 2 Family	1 Public Bath/Sh	B&B per person £8.00-£8.50 Single £8.00-£8.50 Double	Open Mar-Oct	
Mrs M Macrae Rock House IV40 8DX Tel. Dornie (059985) 268			1 Dble/Twin 1 Family	1 Public Bath/Sh	B&B per person £7.50 Double	Open Jan-Dec	
Mrs T Matheson Woodroyd, 11 Sallachy Tel. Killilan (059988) 212			1 Single 2 Dble/Twin		B&B per person £7.00-£8.00 Single £7.00-£8.00 Double	Open May-Sep Dinner 1900	
DORNOCH Sutherland	Map 4 B6						
Fearn Guest House High Street IV25 3SH Tel. Dornoch (0862) 810249			2 Dble/Twin 2 Family	1 Public Bath/Sh	B&B per person £8.50-£9.00 Double	Open Jan-Dec Dinner 1830	
Mrs M Alford Tigh Ruaraidh, Well Street IV25 3LU Tel. Dornoch (0862) 810415			1 Dble/Twin	1 Private Bath/Sh	B&B per person £7.00 Double	Open Apr-Oct	
Mrs Bowie Whinhill, Sutherland Road IV25 3RW Tel. Dornoch (0862) 810533			2 Dble/Twin	2 Private Bath/Sh	B&B per person £7.00-£7.50 Double	Open Jan-Dec Dinner 1800	
Mrs Carter Rosebank House, Clashmore IV25 3RW Tel. Whiteface (086288) 273			2 Dble/Twin 1 Family	2 Public Bath/Sh	B&B per person £8.00 Double	Open Apr-Oct Dinner 1800	
Mrs A Freeman Rosslyne, Castle Street Tel. Dornoch (0862) 810893			1 Single 1 Dble/Twin 1 Family	1 Public Bath/Sh	B&B per person £8.00 Single £8.00 Double	Open Jan-Dec Dinner 1900	
Mrs N Grieve Croft 312-313, Hilton IV25 3PW Tel. Dornoch (0862) 810259			2 Single 2 Dble/Twin	1 Public Bath/Sh	B&B per person £8.00-£8.50 Single £8.00-£8.50 Double	Open Apr-Oct	

Key to symbols is on back flap. Details of Classification and Grading are on page vi.

63

DOUGLAS Lanarkshire Mrs J Shanks West Glespin Farm Tel. Douglas (Lanark) (0555) 851349	Map 2 B7		1 Dble/Twin 2 Family	1 Public Bath/Sh	B&B per person £8.00-£8.50 Double	Open Jun-Sep	
DRINISHADER Harris, Western Isles Mrs Christine Mackay 8 Drinishader Tel. Drinishader (085981) 211	Map 3 C6		1 Single 2 Dble/Twin 1 Family	1 Public Bath/Sh	B&B per person £6.50 Single	Open Jan-Dec Dinner 1830	
DRUMBEG, by Lairg Sutherland Mrs M L Roy Craigdarroch, Glen Learig Tel. Drumbeg (05713) 254	Map 3 G4		1 Single 4 Dble/Twin	1 Public Bath/Sh	B&B per person £7.00-£8.00 Single £7.00-£8.00 Double	Open Jan-Dec	
DRUMNADROCHIT Inverness-shire Mrs C Graham An Clutha, Balmacaan Road IV3 6UR Tel. Drumnadrochit (04562) 392	Map 4 A9		2 Dble/Twin	1 Public Bath/Sh	B&B per person £7.00-£7.50 Double	Open Apr-Oct	
Mrs D MacColl Woodlands, East Lewiston Tel. Drumnadrochit (04562) 235			3 Dble/Twin 2 Family	3 Public Bath/Sh	B&B per person £8.50-£9.00 Double	Open Jan-Dec	
Mrs H MacDonald Ardwell, Lewiston IV3 6UW Tel. Drumnadrochit (04562) 382			1 Single 1 Dble/Twin 1 Family	1 Public Bath/Sh	B&B per person £7.00 Single £7.00 Double	Open Mar-Oct	
Mrs MacKenzie Carrachan, Milton IV3 6UA Tel. Drumnadrochit (04562) 254		COMMENDED ♛	1 Single 2 Family **19c house with garden in peaceful village; at entrance to Glen Urquhart. Near Loch Ness and fishing.**	1 Public Bath/Sh	B&B per person £7.50-£8.50 Single £7.50-£8.50 Double	Open Jan-Dec Dinner 1800	
Mrs MacLennan Benview, Lewiston IV3 6UW Tel. Drumnadrochit (04562) 379			2 Dble/Twin	1 Public Bath/Sh	B&B per person £7.00-£7.50 Double	Open Jan-Dec	
Mrs V Macdonald Haig Borlum Farm IV3 6XN Tel. Drumnadrochit (04562) 434			3 Dble/Twin	1 Public Bath/Sh	B&B per person £10.00-£12.50 Double	Open Mar-Oct	
DRYMEN Stirlingshire Mrs Jean W Duncan The Bridge House G63 0EY Tel. Drymen (0360) 60355	Map 1 H4		2 Dble/Twin 1 Family	1 Public Bath/Sh	B&B per person £7.50 Double	Open Jan-Dec Dinner 1750	

	Map 4 E9					
DUFFTOWN, Keith Banffshire						
Strathdullan Guest House Fife Street AB5 4AP Tel. Dufftown (0340) 20619		1 Single 4 Family		B&B per person £8.50 Single £8.50 Double	Open Jan-Dec Dinner 1830	▯ ▯ TV ▯ ▯ ▯ ▯ ▯ ▯ ▯ P C
Mrs E Munro St Michael's, Conval Street AB5 4AH Tel. Dufftown (0340) 20450		2 Dble/Twin 1 Family	1 Public Bath/Sh	B&B per person £7.00 Double	Open Jan-Dec Dinner 1900	▯ ▯ TV ▯ ▯ ▯ ▯ ▯ P C ▯
Mrs Mary M Robertson Bregach Farm, Glen Rinnes AB5 4DB Tel. Dufftown (0340) 20818		1 Single 1 Dble/Twin 1 Family	1 Public Bath/Sh	B&B per person £7.00 Single £7.00 Double	Open Apr-Oct Dinner 1800	▯ ▯ ▯ ▯ TV ▯ ▯ ▯ P C ▯
Mrs Jean D Smart Errolbank, 134 Fife Street AB5 4DP Tel. Dufftown (0340) 20229		1 Single 1 Dble/Twin 3 Family	1 Public Bath/Sh	B&B per person £8.50-£10.00 Single £8.50-£10.00 Double	Open Jan-Dec Dinner 1700	▯ ▯ ▯ ▯ ▯ TV ▯ ▯ ▯ ▯ P ▯ C

	Map 4 C9					
DULNAIN BRIDGE, by Grantown-on-Spey Moray						
Rose Grove Guest House Skye of Curr Tel. Dulnain Bridge (047985) 335	**COMMENDED** ♛ ♛	1 Single 4 Dble/Twin 1 Family	1 Public Bath/Sh	B&B per person £11.50-£12.50 Single £10.00-£12.00 Double	Open Jan-Dec Dinner 1800	▯ ▯ ▯ ▯ ▯ TV ▯ ▯ ▯ ▯ ▯ ▯ P ▯ ▯ ▯ C ▯ T ▯
		Modern, personally run. Situated on 7 acre croft and short distance from village.				
Mr R J Allston Balnacrive Tel. Dulnain Bridge (047985) 228		1 Single 1 Dble/Twin 3 Family		B&B per person £8.00 Single £8.00 Double	Open Jan-Dec Dinner 1900	▯ ▯ ▯ ▯ TV ▯ P ▯ C T

	Map 1 H5					
DUMBARTON Dunbartonshire						

KILMALID HOUSE
17 Glenpath, off Barnhill Road, Dumbarton
Telephone: 0389 32836
A pleasant house on a hill overlooking Dumbarton Castle and River Clyde. Situated adjacent to the A82 Loch Lomond road, Loch Lomond only being 5 miles north. Ideal base for touring the Trossachs, Inveraray, Dunoon, Clyde Coast and Glasgow. Full central heating. Residents' lounge with TV. Tea or coffee in the evening and Bed and Breakfast. SAE please for prompt reply.

Mrs G Gourlie Kilmalid Hse, 17 Glenpath, Barnhill Rd G82 2QL Tel. Dumbarton (0389) 32836		1 Dble/Twin 1 Family	1 Public Bath/Sh	B&B per person £10.00 Double	Open Jan-Dec	▯ ▯ ▯ TV ▯ ▯ P C

	Map 2 B9					
DUMFRIES						
Redlands Guest House 54 Rae Street Tel. Dumfries (0387) 52612		1 Single 2 Dble/Twin 1 Family	1 Public Bath/Sh	B&B per person £7.50 Single £7.50 Double	Open Jan-Dec Dinner 1800	▯ ▯ ▯ TV ▯ C
Dumfries & Galloway Coll of Tech Heathhall Tel. Dumfries (0387) 65621		80 Single	12 Public Bath/Sh	B&B per person £8.60 Single	Open Jul-Aug Dinner 1700	▯ ▯ ▯ ▯ ▯ ▯ ▯ TV ▯ ▯ ▯ ▯ P ▯ ▯ ▯

DUMFRIES continued	Map 2 B9	

ST MARGARET'S

67 Rotchell Road, Dumfries DG2 7SA. Tel. (0387) 53932

Comfortable B&B accommodation in quiet residential area convenient for touring and within walking distance of town centre. H&C in twin and double rooms with tea-making facilities in all bedrooms. Electric blankets on all beds, fully centrally heated. TV lounge and separate breakfast room, private parking.

Open all year. From £8.50 per person.

Name/Address	Status	Rooms	Baths	B&B Rates	Opening	Facilities
Mrs G M Henderson St Margarets, 67 Rotchell Rd DG2 7SA Tel. Dumfries (0387) 53932	♛ ♛	1 Single 2 Dble/Twin	1 Public Bath/Sh	B&B per person £9.00-£10.50 Single £9.00-£10.50 Double	Open Jan-Dec	
Mrs J Jardine Dhu Course, 107 Edinburgh Road Tel. Dumfries (0387) 55941		1 Single 1 Dble/Twin 2 Family	2 Private Bath/Sh 1 Public Bath/Sh	B&B per person £9.00 Single £9.00 Double	Open Jan-Dec Dinner 1800	
Mrs P Linton 38 Lovers Walk		2 Dble/Twin 1 Family	1 Public Bath/Sh	B&B per person £8.00-£8.50 Double	Open Apr-Oct Dinner 1830	
Mr D MacLachlan Northfield, 26 Georgetown Road DG1 4BL Tel. Dumfries (0387) 62724		1 Single 2 Dble/Twin	1 Public Bath/Sh	B&B per person £8.00-£9.50 Double	Open Jan-Dec Dinner 1830	
Mrs MacRory Midrig, Irongary Tel. Lochfoot (038773) 361		1 Dble/Twin 1 Family		B&B per person £7.50 Double	Open Apr-Oct	
Mrs Shona McLachlan The Neuk, 59 Moffat Road Tel. Dumfries (0387) 61949		1 Dble/Twin 1 Family	1 Public Bath/Sh	B&B per person £7.50 Double	Open Jan-Dec Dinner 1700	
Mrs McTier Oaklea, New Abbey Rd, Cargenholm DG2 8ER Tel. Dumfries (0387) 53944		2 Dble/Twin 1 Family	1 Private Bath/Sh 1 Public Bath/Sh	B&B per person £7.50-£8.50 Double	Open Apr-Oct	
Mrs A Prentice North Laurieknowe, 3 North Laurieknowe Pl DG2 7AL Tel. Dumfries (0387) 54136	Awaiting Inspection	1 Single 1 Dble/Twin 1 Family	1 Public Bath/Sh	B&B per person £7.50-£8.00 Single £7.50-£8.00 Double	Open Jan-Dec	
Mrs Smyth Henderland Farm, Crocketford Rd Tel. Lochfoot (038773) 270		1 Single 2 Family		B&B per person £7.50-£8.50 Single £7.50-£8.50 Double	Open Jan-Dec Dinner 1730	
Mrs C Stewart 38 The Grove, Heathhall, Edinburgh Road DG1 1TN Tel. Dumfries (0387) 52868	Awaiting Inspection	1 Single 1 Dble/Twin	1 Public Bath/Sh	B&B per person £7.50 Single £7.50 Double	Open Apr-Oct Dinner 1800	
Mrs Thomson Laurelbank, 7 Laurieknowe Tel. Dumfries (0387) 69388	Awaiting Inspection	1 Single 4 Dble/Twin 1 Family	1 Public Bath/Sh	B&B per person £9.00-£10.00 Single £9.00-£10.00 Double	Open Apr-Oct	

VAT is shown at 15%; changes in this rate may affect prices. Prices shown are for guidance only. Please send SAE with each enquiry.

	Map	Grading	Rooms	Bath	Price	Opening	Symbols
DUMFRIES continued Mrs M G Wilson Beaumaris House, Carsethorn Tel. Kirkbean (038788) 268	Map 2 B9		2 Dble/Twin 1 Family	1 Private Bath/Sh 2 Public Bath/Sh	B&B per person £8.50-£9.50 Double	Open Jan-Dec Dinner 1700	
DUNBAR **East Lothian** Kiloran Guest House 9 Marine Road EH42 1AR Tel. Dunbar (0368) 62286	Map 2 E4		1 Single 3 Dble/Twin 2 Family	3 Public Bath/Sh	B&B per person £10.00-£12.00 Single £9.00-£10.00 Double	Open Jan-Dec Dinner 1800	
Marine Guest House Marine Road EH42 1AR Tel. Dunbar (0368) 63315		👑👑	2 Single 4 Dble/Twin 3 Family	2 Public Bath/Sh	B&B per person £8.75-£10.00 Single £9.00-£10.00 Double	Open Jan-Dec Dinner 1800	
Springfield Guest House Belhaven Road EH42 1NH Tel. Dunbar (0368) 62502		COMMENDED 👑👑	1 Single 2 Dble/Twin 2 Family	2 Public Bath/Sh	B&B per person £12.00 Single £11.00 Double	Open Mar-Oct Dinner 1800	
			Elegant 19th century villa with garden. Under owner's personal supervision.				
St Beys Guest House Bayswell Road Tel. Dunbar (0368) 63571		COMMENDED 👑👑	1 Single 3 Dble/Twin 2 Family	3 Private Bath/Sh 1 Public Bath/Sh	B&B per person £16.50-£18.50 Single £12.50-£13.50 Double	Open Jan-Dec Dinner 1830	
			Family-run, overlooking Dunbar seafront.				
Mrs Kit Blyth St Helens, Queens Road EH42 1LN Tel. Dunbar (0368) 63716			1 Single 2 Dble/Twin 3 Family	1 Private Bath/Sh 1 Public Bath/Sh	B&B per person £8.50 Single £8.50 Double	Open Jan-Dec	
Mrs Hickman Overcliffe, 11 Bayswell Park EH42 1AE Tel. Dunbar (0368) 64004			1 Single 4 Dble/Twin 1 Family	2 Public Bath/Sh	B&B per person £9.00-£9.50 Single £9.00-£9.50 Double	Open Jan-Dec	
DUNBEATH **Caithness** Mrs E Fraser Market Place KW6 6EJ Tel. Dunbeath (05933) 328	Map 4 D4	COMMENDED Listed	2 Dble/Twin 1 Family	1 Public Bath/Sh	B&B per person £8.50 Double	Open May-Oct Dinner 1800	
			Traditional working farmhouse (sheep and beef cattle). Evening meal. Rural outlook, sea views.				
DUNBLANE **Perthshire** Mrs Bennett Mossgiel, Doune Road Tel. Dunblane (0786) 824325	Map 2 A3		2 Dble/Twin 1 Family	1 Public Bath/Sh	B&B per person £9.00 Single £8.00 Double	Open Apr-Oct Dinner 1830	
Mrs Ciccu Claredon House, Claredon Place FK15 9HB Tel. Dunblane (0786) 822621			1 Dble/Twin 1 Family	1 Public Bath/Sh	B&B per person £7.00-£10.00 Double	Open Jan-Dec Dinner 1830	

Key to symbols is on back flap. Details of Classification and Grading are on page vi.

67

DUNBLANE continued	Map 2 A3	

WESTWOOD

**Doune Road, Dunblane, Perthshire
FK15 9ND   Tel: 0786 822579**

Westwood is a modern house set in an acre of pleasant gardens in a peaceful rural setting. It offers superb views of the surrounding countryside yet it is only 1 mile from the historic city of Dunblane. Westwood provides an ideal base for touring Central Scotland and the Southern Highlands. The house is furnished to a high standard with central heating, wash-basins, tea/coffee-making facilities, radio, electric blankets and ample parking. One bedroom also offers private WC. Large, comfortable lounge with colour TV.

Our aim is to make your stay as comfortable and enjoyable as possible.

Mrs Elizabeth J Duncan Westwood, Doune Road FK15 9ND Tel. Dunblane (0786) 822579	**HIGHLY COMMENDED** ♕ ♕	2 Dble/Twin	1 Public Bath/Sh	B&B per person £8.50 Double	Open Apr-Oct Dinner 1830	
		Modern, in rural and peaceful setting; attractive garden. Offering relaxed stay, friendly atmosphere.				
Mr & Mrs R Lyall Morven, Doune Road Tel. Stirling (0786) 822954		1 Single 1 Dble/Twin 1 Family	1 Public Bath/Sh	B&B per person £8.00-£9.00 Single £8.00-£9.00 Double	Open Apr-Oct	
Mrs G L Peggie Birchbrook, Doune Road Tel. Dunblane (0786) 822638		2 Dble/Twin 1 Family	2 Public Bath/Sh	B&B per person £8.50 Double	Open Apr-Oct Dinner 1830	
Mr & Mrs D Strathdee Capelrig, Doune Road FK15 9AR Tel. Dunblane (0786) 822131		1 Single 2 Dble/Twin 2 Family	1 Public Bath/Sh	B&B per person £9.00 Single £8.50 Double	Open Apr-Oct Dinner 1800	

BLAIRGARRY

**DOUNE ROAD · DUNBLANE
Tel: 0786 823379 — MRS MAY TAYLOR**

Traditional stone-built family house — corner site. Spacious bedrooms with H&C. Large lounge with TV, large dining room. Bathroom and shower rooms/WC.   Few minutes' walk from town, shops and main line station. On A820. Good touring centre. Evening meals on request. Friendly reception and attention.

Mrs W D Taylor Blairgarry, Doune Road FK15 9AR Tel. Dunblane (0786) 823379		1 Single 1 Dble/Twin 1 Family	1 Public Bath/Sh	B&B per person £9.00 Single £9.00 Double	Open May-Oct Dinner 1830	
Mrs M Wilson Leewood, Leewood Road Tel. Dunblane (0786) 823057		1 Dble/Twin 1 Family	1 Public Bath/Sh	B&B per person £8.50-£10.00 Double	Open Jan-Dec	

DUNDEE Angus	Map 2 D2						
Beach Guest House 22 Esplanade, Broughty Ferry Tel. Dundee (0382) 76614		COMMENDED ♛ ♛	3 Dble/Twin 1 Family	4 Private Bath/Sh 1 Public Bath/Sh	B&B per person £10.00-£12.50 Double	Open Jan-Dec Dinner 1800	🛁📠🍴🍵🛏️📺
			Attractive terraced house opposite beach. All rooms with shower, colour TV and teamaking.				
The Birks Guest House 149 Arbroath Road Tel. Dundee (0382) 44693			1 Dble/Twin 3 Family	1 Public Bath/Sh	B&B per person £9.00-£12.00 Double	Open Jan-Dec	🛁🍴🍵🛏️📺 ♨🛏️🅿️C
Raewood Guest House 105 Magdalen Yard Road DD2 1BD Tel. Dundee (0382) 646576			2 Single 2 Dble/Twin		B&B per person £8.00-£9.00 Single £8.00-£9.00 Double	Open Jan-Dec Dinner 1800	M🛏️📺🛏️C🏫
Halls of Residence The University of Dundee DD1 4HN Tel. Dundee (0382) 23181 Ext 4040 Telex 76293			670 Single 60 Dble/Twin 10 Family	100 Public Bath/Sh	B&B per person £10.00-£11.00 Single £10.00-£11.00 Double	Open Jun-Sep Dinner 1800	(symbols)
Mrs M Alcock 58 Dalkeith Road Tel. Dundee (0382) 44013			1 Single 2 Dble/Twin 1 Family	1 Public Bath/Sh	B&B per person £8.00-£9.00 Single £8.00-£9.00 Double	Open Jan-Dec Dinner 1700	🍵🛏️📺🅿️C
Mrs Anderson 1 Rosemount Terr, Upper Constitution St Tel. Dundee (0382) 22154			2 Single 1 Dble/Twin 1 Family		B&B per person £7.50-£8.00 Single £7.50-£8.00 Double	Open Jan-Dec Dinner 1700	🛁🍴🛏️
Mrs E Buchan 22 Forfar Road DD4 7AS Tel. Dundee (0382) 41109			3 Dble/Twin	1 Public Bath/Sh	B&B per person £8.00 Double	Open Jan-Dec Dinner 1700	🍵🛏️📺
Mrs Carroll 65 Monifieth Road, Broughty Ferry Tel. Dundee (0382) 730381			2 Dble/Twin 1 Family	2 Public Bath/Sh	B&B per person £10.00-£12.00 Double	Open Jan-Dec Dinner 1730	(symbols)
Mrs A Dunbar St Leonards, 22 Albany Terrace Tel. Dundee (0382) 24612			3 Dble/Twin 1 Family		B&B per person £7.50-£8.50 Double	Open Jan-Dec Dinner 1700	(symbols)
Mrs H Macfarlane 56 Forfar Road Tel. Dundee (0382) 453918			2 Single 2 Dble/Twin		B&B per person £7.50 Single £7.50 Double	Open May-Sep	M🛏️📺C
Mrs E McCorkindale 17 Davidson St, Broughty Ferry DD5 3AT Tel. Dundee (0382) 730543			2 Dble/Twin	1 Public Bath/Sh	B&B per person £7.50-£9.50 Double	Open Jan-Dec	🍵🛏️🛏️ C🏫
Mrs C Millar Elm Lodge, 49 Seafield Road DD1 4NW Tel. Dundee (0382) 28402			3 Dble/Twin 4 Family	2 Public Bath/Sh	B&B per person £8.50 Double	Open Jan-Dec	(symbols)
Mrs M Mudie 20 Park Place, Ancrum Road DD2 2H5 Tel. Dundee (0382) 65898			1 Single 2 Dble/Twin	1 Public Bath/Sh	B&B per person £7.00 Single £7.00 Double	Open Jan-Dec	🛏️📺🅿️

DUNDEE continued — Map 2 D2

Mrs E Pirie
334 Blackness Road
DD2 1SD
Tel. Dundee (0382) 60783

1 Single
2 Dble/Twin — 1 Public Bath/Sh — B&B per person £8.50-£9.00 Single £8.00 Double — Open Jan-Dec

Mrs J Slane
The Old Manse, 46
Shaftesbury Road
Tel. Dundee (0382) 67631

1 Single
2 Dble/Twin — 1 Private Bath/Sh 2 Public Bath/Sh — B&B per person £8.50 Single £8.50-£9.00 Double — Open Jan-Dec

Mrs Thomson
251 Perth Road
Tel. Dundee (0382) 66175

1 Single
1 Dble/Twin
1 Family — 1 Public Bath/Sh — B&B per person £8.50-£9.50 Single £8.50-£9.50 Double — Open Jan-Dec Dinner 1800

DUNDONNELL — Ross-shire — Map 3 G7

Mrs S G Reeves
Seaview, Durnamuck
IV23 2QZ
Tel. Dundonnell (085483) 221

COMMENDED Listed

1 Dble/Twin — 1 Public Bath/Sh — B&B per person £7.50-£8.00 Double — Open Feb-Nov Dinner 1900

Original crofting cottage, now modernised. Peaceful rural site, wide views over little Loch Broom.

Mrs A Ross
4 Camusnagaul
Tel. Dundonnell (085483) 237

2 Dble/Twin
1 Family — 1 Public Bath/Sh — B&B per person £8.00 Single £7.50 Double — Open Jan-Dec

DUNFERMLINE — Fife — Map 2 C4

Garvock Guest House
82 Halbeath Road
KY12 7RS
Tel. Dunfermline (0383) 734689

COMMENDED

1 Single
3 Dble/Twin
1 Family — 2 Public Bath/Sh — B&B per person £10.00 Single £9.00 Double — Open Jan-Dec Dinner 1800

19C house, modernised and converted, 1 mile/ 2km from town. Convenient for M90. On bus route.

Haven Guest House
82 Pilmuir Street
Tel. Dunfermline (0383) 729039

1 Single
1 Dble/Twin
2 Family — 1 Public Bath/Sh — B&B per person £8.50 Single £8.50 Double — Open Jan-Dec

Pitreavie Guest House
3 Aberdour Road
KY11 4PB
Tel. Dunfermline (0383) 724244

1 Single
3 Dble/Twin
1 Family — 2 Public Bath/Sh — B&B per person £10.00-£11.00 Single £9.50-£10.50 Double — Open Jan-Dec

Mrs Hutton
Lassodie Mill Farm, Lassodie
KY12 0SW
Tel. Kelty (0383) 830202

1 Dble/Twin
1 Family — 1 Public Bath/Sh — B&B per person £7.50 Double — Open Apr-Oct

Mrs Hutton
7 Beck Crescent
KY12 0BA
Tel. Dunfermline (0383) 729229

1 Single
1 Dble/Twin
1 Family — 2 Private Bath/Sh 1 Public Bath/Sh — B&B per person £8.50 Single £8.50 Double — Open Apr-Oct

Mrs Jeanne E Lawrie
7 Garvock Hill
KY12 7TZ
Tel. Dunfermline (0383) 729644

COMMENDED

2 Dble/Twin — 1 Public Bath/Sh — B&B per person £8.00-£8.50 Double — Open Jan-Dec

Personally run in quiet residential area close to town centre.

DUNFERMLINE continued Mrs E Lindsay Ealasaid, 38 Tremayne Place, Baldridge Tel. Dunfermline (0383) 734354	Map 2 C4		1 Dble/Twin	1 Public Bath/Sh	B&B per person £9.50-£11.50 Double	Open Jan-Dec Dinner 1900	
Mrs D Phillips Pitsulie Cottage, Shiresmill KY12 8ER Tel. Newmills (0383) 880381			2 Dble/Twin 1 Family	1 Public Bath/Sh	B&B per person £8.00 Double	Open Apr-Oct	
Mrs J Strang 87 Halbeath Road KY12 7RE Tel. Dunfermline (0383) 722026			1 Dble/Twin	1 Public Bath/Sh	B&B per person £7.00 Double	Open Apr-Oct	
Mrs S Telford Ardenlea, 1 Castleblair Park Tel. Dunfermline (0383) 729553/822965		Awaiting Inspection	1 Single 2 Dble/Twin	1 Public Bath/Sh	B&B per person £9.00-£10.00 Single £9.00-£10.00 Double	Open Jan-Dec	
DUNKELD Perthshire Waterbury Guest House Murthly Terrace, Birnam PH8 0BG Tel. Dunkeld (03502) 324	Map 2 B1		1 Single 4 Dble/Twin 1 Family	1 Public Bath/Sh	B&B per person £9.00-£11.00 Single £9.00-£11.00 Double	Open Jan-Dec Dinner 1800	
Mrs E Christie Culcabock, 4 Murthly Ter, Birnam PH8 0BG Tel. Dunkeld (03502) 628		COMMENDED 👑 👑	1 Single 2 Dble/Twin 2 Family	1 Public Bath/Sh	B&B per person £7.50 Single £7.50 Double	Open Apr-Sep	
			1864 listed building in centre of village. Good walking area of historical interest.				
Mrs M R B Edwards Hillview, Perth Rd, Birnam PH8 0BH Tel. Dunkeld (03502) 239			2 Dble/Twin 1 Family	2 Public Bath/Sh	B&B per person £8.00 Double	Open Mar-Sep	
Joanne & Gordon Gerrie Byways, Perth Rd, Birnam PH8 0DH Tel. Dunkeld (03502) 542			3 Dble/Twin	1 Public Bath/Sh	B&B per person £8.00-£9.00 Double	Open May-Oct	
Mrs MacMillan Ninewells Farm PH8 0RD Tel. Caputh (073871) 272			2 Dble/Twin 1 Family	1 Public Bath/Sh	B&B per person £7.50 Double	Open Apr-Oct Dinner 1800	
Mrs Jessie Mathieson Inchmagrannachan Farm PH8 0JS Tel. Dunkeld (03502) 372			1 Single 1 Dble/Twin	1 Public Bath/Sh	B&B per person £6.50 Single £6.50 Double	Open Apr-Oct Dinner 1830	
DUNLOP Ayrshire Struther Farm Guest House 17 Newmill Road KA3 4DT Tel. Stewarton (0560) 84946	Map 1 H6	COMMENDED 👑 👑	4 Dble/Twin 2 Family	2 Public Bath/Sh	B&B per person £9.50 Double	Open Jan-Dec Dinner 1830	
			Old Scottish farmhouse; large garden. 'Tastle of Scotland'; fresh seafood and meat in season.				

Key to symbols is on back flap. Details of Classification and Grading are on page vi.

71

DUNNET Caithness	Map 4 D2						
Mrs Manson Arion, West Side Tel. Barrock (084785) 369			3 Single 1 Dble/Twin		B&B per person £7.50 Single £7.00 Double	Open Jan-Dec Dinner 1800	
Mrs C Nicolson Kariba Tel. Barrock (084785) 201		**COMMENDED** Listed	2 Dble/Twin 1 Family	1 Public Bath/Sh	B&B per person £7.00 Double	Open Apr-Oct Dinner 1830	
			Well furnished bungalow with central heating. 1 ml/2 km from sandy beach. Garden with country views.				
DUNOON Argyll	Map 1 G5						
Sebright Guest House 41 Alexandra Parade PA23 8AF Tel. Dunoon (0369) 2099			3 Dble/Twin 2.Family	1 Public Bath/Sh	B&B per person £9.50-£11.00 Double	Open Jan-Dec Dinner 1800	
Mrs J Anderson Argyll Lodge, 245 Marine Prd, Hunter Quay Tel. Dunoon (0369) 2587			2 Dble/Twin 1 Family	1 Public Bath/Sh	B&B per person £8.00 Double	Open May-Sep	
Mrs M Connor Dunarras, Alexandra Parade, East Bay Tel. Dunoon (0369) 3928		**APPROVED**	2 Dble/Twin 1 Family	1 Public Bath/Sh	B&B per person £8.00-£9.50 Double	Open Jan-Dec	
			Semi detached house with large garden in quiet area close to town. Superb views over Firth of Clyde.				
Mrs T Keith Livingston House, Victoria Rd Tel. Dunoon (0369) 2107			1 Single 1 Dble/Twin 1 Family	2 Public Bath/Sh	B&B per person £8.00-£9.00 Single £8.00-£9.00 Double	Open Jan-Dec Dinner 1800	
Mrs Maclean Auchendarroch, 17 Kilbride Rd, West Bay Tel. Dunoon (0369) 6048		Listed	3 Dble/Twin	1 Public Bath/Sh	B&B per person **£7.50 Double**	Open Jan-Dec	
Mrs F Maxwell Mhorlarich, 123 Auchamore Road			1 Single 1 Dble/Twin	2 Public Bath/Sh	B&B per person £8.00-£8.50 Double	Open Jan-Dec	
Mrs McDonald Tigh Ban, 51 Bullwood Rd, West Bay Tel. Dunoon (0369) 4138			1 Single 2 Dble/Twin	1 Public Bath/Sh	B&B per person £8.00 Single £8.00 Double	Open Jan-Dec Dinner 1800	
Mrs Murchison Foxbank, Hunter's Quay Tel. Dunoon (0369) 3858			2 Dble/Twin 1 Family	1 Public Bath/Sh	B&B per person £8.00 Double	Open Jan-Dec Dinner 1800	
Mrs L Pursley Glenville, Kilbride Avenue Tel. Dunoon (0369) 3586			1 Dble/Twin 1 Family	1 Public Bath/Sh	B&B per person £7.50-£8.50 Double	Open Jan-Dec	
Mr & Mrs Renachowski Pitcairlie House, Alexandra Parade Tel. Dunoon (0369) 4122			4 Dble/Twin 1 Family	1 Public Bath/Sh	B&B per person £10.50-£11.00 Double	Open Jan-Dec	
Mrs P M Stirling Glenlea, 57 Edward Street Tel. Dunoon (0369) 3414			1 Dble/Twin 2 Family	1 Public Bath/Sh	B&B per person £7.50-£8.50 Double	Open Jan-Dec	

VAT is shown at 15%: changes in this rate may affect prices. Prices shown are for guidance only. Please send SAE with each enquiry.

DUNROSSNESS Shetland Mainland Guest House Tel. Sumburgh (0950) 60517	Map 5 G6		1 Single 6 Dble/Twin	2 Public Bath/Sh	B&B per person £10.00-£12.00 Single £9.00-£10.00 Double	Open Jan-Dec Dinner 1800	
Mrs R Burgess Lunnabister Tel. Lerwick (0595) 60480		Listed	2 Dble/Twin 1 Family	1 Public Bath/Sh	B&B per person £6.50 Double	Open Apr-Oct Dinner 1850	
DUNS Berwickshire Mrs W M Kenworthy St Albans, Clouds Tel. Duns (0361) 83285	Map 2 F5		1 Single 1 Dble/Twin	1 Public Bath/Sh	B&B per person £9.00 Single £7.50 Double	Open Feb-Nov	
Mr King The Hunt, 19 Newtown Street Tel. Duns (0361) 82693			2 Single 2 Dble/Twin	1 Private Bath/Sh 1 Public Bath/Sh	B&B per person £11.50 Single £11.00 Double	Open Jan-Dec	
DUNSYRE, Carnwath Lanarkshire Mrs Margaret Armstrong Dunsyre Mains Farm ML11 8NQ Tel. Dunsyre (089981) 251	Map 2 C6	Awaiting Inspection	2 Dble/Twin 1 Family	1 Public Bath/Sh	B&B per person £8.50-£9.00 Double	Open Apr-Oct Dinner 1900	
DUNURE Ayrshire Mrs Reid Lagg Farm KA7 4LE Tel. Dunure (029250) 647	Map 1 G8	Awaiting Inspection	3 Dble/Twin	1 Public Bath/Sh	B&B per person £8.50 Double	Open Apr-Oct Dinner 1800	
DUNVEGAN Isle of Skye, Inverness-shire Roskhill Guest House Roskhill Tel. Dunvegan (047022) 317	Map 3 C9		3 Dble/Twin 2 Family	1 Public Bath/Sh	B&B per person £9.00-£9.50 Double	Open Mar-Oct Dinner 1915	
M Campbell Argyll House Tel. Dunvegan (047022) 230			1 Single 3 Dble/Twin 1 Family	1 Public Bath/Sh	B&B per person £8.00 Single £8.00 Double	Open Apr-Sep	
Mrs A E Gracie 14 Skinidin Tel. Dunvegan (047022) 251			2 Single 2 Dble/Twin	1 Public Bath/Sh	B&B per person £8.00 Single £8.00 Double	Open Jan-Dec Dinner 1900	
Mrs M MacPhee Kilmuir House Tel. Dunvegan (047022) 430			1 Single 5 Dble/Twin	1 Private Bath/Sh 2 Public Bath/Sh	B&B per person £7.50 Single £7.50 Double	Open Apr-Oct Dinner 1900	
Mrs Munro Feorlig Farmhouse, Feorlig Tel. Dunvegan (047022) 232			2 Family	1 Public Bath/Sh	B&B per person £8.00-£8.50 Double	Open Apr-Oct	

Key to symbols is on back flap. Details of Classification and Grading are on page vi.

73

Location	Map	Name / Address	Rooms	Bath	Terms	Open
DURNESS Sutherland	Map 3 H3	Mrs M Hames, Old Manse, Sangomore, IV27 4PW, Tel. Durness (097181) 223	2 Dble/Twin 1 Family	1 Public Bath/Sh	B&B per person £7.00 Double	Open May-Sep Dinner 1830
		Mrs L Mackay, Sarsgrum, IV27 4SN, Tel. Durness (097181) 374	1 Dble/Twin 1 Family	1 Public Bath/Sh	B&B per person £7.00 Double	Open Jan-Dec
		Mrs W Morrison, Morven, Lerin, IV27 4QB, Tel. Durness (097181) 252	1 Dble/Twin 2 Family	1 Public Bath/Sh	B&B per person £7.00-£8.00 Double	Open Apr-Oct Dinner 1800
DUROR, Appin Argyll	Map 1 F1	Mrs F Macdonald, Don-Lee, Achindarroch, Tel. Duror (063174) 303	2 Dble/Twin	1 Public Bath/Sh	B&B per person £8.00-£9.00 Double	Open Apr-Oct Dinner 1800
		Mrs Munro, Glen Duror House, Tel. Duror (063174) 312	1 Dble/Twin 2 Family	1 Public Bath/Sh	B&B per person £8.50-£9.50 Double	Open Jan-Dec Dinner 1900
DURRIS, by Banchory Kincardineshire	Map 4 G11	Mrs P Law, Monthammock Farm, AB3 3DX, Tel. Drumoak (03308) 421	2 Dble/Twin	1 Public Bath/Sh	B&B per person £10.00-£12.00 Double	Open May-Oct Dinner 1900
EAGLESFIELD, by Lockerbie Dumfriesshire	Map 2 D9	Mr & Mrs Ellis, Douglas House, Tel. Kirtlebridge (04615) 215	3 Dble/Twin 2 Family	1 Public Bath/Sh	B&B per person £8.00-£8.50 Double	Open Jan-Dec Dinner 1800
		Mrs A Fletcher, Broadlea Farm, DG11 3LU, Tel. Kirtlebridge (04615) 335	1 Single 2 Dble/Twin 2 Family	2 Public Bath/Sh	B&B per person £8.00-£9.00 Single £8.00 Double	Open Jan-Dec Dinner 1800
EAGLESHAM Renfrewshire	Map 1 H6					

		Mr & Mrs A F Bewick, 6 Polnoon Street, G76 0BH, Tel. Eaglesham (03553) 2321	1 Single 1 Dble/Twin	1 Private Bath/Sh 1 Public Bath/Sh	B&B per person £12.50 Single £12.50 Double	Open Jan-Dec Dinner 1800

VAT is shown at 15%; changes in this rate may affect prices. Prices shown are for guidance only. Please send SAE with each enquiry.

EAST CALDER, Livingston Midlothian	Map 2 C5

"WHITECROFT FARM"
EAST CALDER, Nr. EDINBURGH
Telephone: Midcalder (0506) 881810

Large bungalow, centrally heated throughout, surrounded by farmland, yet only 10 miles from Edinburgh City Centre; Edinburgh Airport and Inglinston (5 miles); Almondell Country Park nearby; M8/M9 motorways (3 miles); Livingston (4 miles). For sports enthusiasts: golf, fishing, squash, riding, swimming (indoor), trimcourse, etc., all within 4 miles.
Mrs Scott runs a Farm Shop on the farm. Fire certificate.

Mrs Scott Whitecroft Tel. Mid Calder (0506) 881810		Awaiting Inspection	2 Dble/Twin 1 Family	1 Public Bath/Sh	B&B per person £9.00 Double	Open Jan-Dec	
ECCLEFECHAN Dumfriesshire Mrs M Martin Carlyle House Tel. Ecclefechan (05763) 322	Map 2 C9		1 Single 2 Dble/Twin 1 Family	1 Public Bath/Sh	B&B per person £7.00 Single £7.00 Double	Open Jan-Dec Dinner 1800	
EDDERTON, by Tain Ross-shire Mrs Priestley Balblair House Tel. Edderton (086282) 272	Map 4 B7		1 Dble/Twin 2 Family	3 Public Bath/Sh	B&B per person £8.50 Double	Open Jan-Dec	
EDDLESTON Peeblesshire Mrs E McTeir Colliedean, 4 Elibank Road Tel. Eddleston (07213) 281	Map 2 C6		2 Dble/Twin	1 Public Bath/Sh	B&B per person £7.50-£8.00 Double	Open Apr-Oct	
EDINBURGH Abbotsford Guest House 36 Pilrig Street Tel. 031 554 2706	Map 2 D5		7 Dble/Twin 1 Family	2 Public Bath/Sh	B&B per person £10.00-£12.50 Double	Open Jan-Dec	
Aberiour Guest House 119 Mayfield Road EH9 3AJ Tel. 031 667 3908			2 Single 4 Dble/Twin 1 Family	1 Public Bath/Sh	B&B per person £9.00-£10.00 Single £9.00-£10.00 Double	Open Jan-Dec Dinner 1700	
Abileen Guest House 46 Minto Street EH9 2BR Tel. 031 667 8995			3 Dble/Twin 2 Family	3 Public Bath/Sh	B&B per person £8.50-£10.50 Double	Open Jan-Dec	
Alexander Guest House 21 Spring Gardens EH8 8HU Tel. 031 661 1157			1 Single 5 Dble/Twin 1 Family		B&B per person £9.50-£13.00 Single £9.00-£12.50 Double	Open Jan-Dec	
Allanbank Guest House 3 Leamington Terrace EH10 4JW Tel. 031 229 2772			1 Single 1 Dble/Twin 1 Family	1 Public Bath/Sh	B&B per person £9.00-£11.00 Single £8.50-£9.50 Double	Open Jan-Dec	

Key to symbols is on back flap. Details of Classification and Grading are on page vi.

EDINBURGH continued	Map 2 D5					
Alness Guest House 27 Pilrig Street EH6 5AN Tel. 031 554 1187			1 Single 3 Dble/Twin 3 Family	2 Public Bath/Sh	B&B per person £9.50-£12.00 Single £9.50-£12.00 Double	Open Jan-Dec
Amaragua Guest House 10 Kilmaurs Terrace EH16 5DR Tel. 031 667 6775	COMMENDED ♛		2 Single 2 Dble/Twin 2 Family		B&B per person £10.00-£14.00 Single £10.00-£14.00 Double	Open Jan-Dec
			Victorian terraced house in residential area. Close to golf course, Holyrood Park, Commonwealth Pool.			
The Ard Thor Guest House 10 Mentone Terr, Newington EH9 2DG Tel. 031 667 1647	COMMENDED ♛		1 Single 2 Dble/Twin 2 Family	1 Private Bath/Sh 1 Public Bath/Sh	B&B per person £10.00-£14.50 Single £9.00-£13.50 Double	Open Jan-Dec
			End-terraced villa in quiet residential area. Close to frequent bus route to city centre.			
Ardblair Guest House 1 Duddingston Cres, Milton Road EH15 3AS Tel. 031 669 2384	APPROVED ♛		2 Dble/Twin 2 Family	2 Public Bath/Sh	B&B per person £10.00-£12.00 Double	Open Jan-Dec Dinner 1800
			On city outskirts with friendly atmosphere.			
Ashling Guest House 47 Castle Street EH2 3BG Tel. 031 225 7796	Awaiting Inspection		4 Single 3 Dble/Twin		B&B per person £11.00-£16.00 Single £10.00-£13.00 Double	Open Jan-Dec
Ashwood Guest House 20 Minto Street EH9 1RQ Tel. 031 667 8024	Listed		2 Dble/Twin 2 Family	1 Private Bath/Sh 1 Public Bath/Sh	B&B per person £9.00-£11.00 Double	Open Jan-Dec
Averon Guest House 44 Gilmore Place EH3 9NQ Tel. 031 229 9932			3 Dble/Twin 2 Family	1 Public Bath/Sh	B&B per person £9.00-£10.50 Double	Open Jan-Dec
Balmoral Guest House 32 Pilrig Street EH6 5AL Tel. 031 554 1857			1 Single 4 Dble/Twin 2 Family		B&B per person £11.00-£14.00 Single £10.00-£13.00 Double	Open Jan-Dec
Balquhidder Guest House 94 Pilrig Street EH6 5AY Tel. 031 554 3377			1 Single 4 Dble/Twin 1 Family	3 Private Bath/Sh 1 Public Bath/Sh	B&B per person £10.00-£12.00 Single £9.00-£12.00 Double	Open Jan-Dec Dinner 1800
Barrosa Guest House 21 Pilrig Street EH6 5AN Tel. 031 554 3700			1 Single 4 Dble/Twin 3 Family	4 Private Bath/Sh 2 Public Bath/Sh	B&B per person £10.50-£19.00 Single £10.75-£16.50 Double	Open Jan-Dec
Bellrock Guest House 105 Ferry Road EH6 4ET Tel. 031 554 2604			1 Single 3 Dble/Twin 3 Family	2 Public Bath/Sh	B&B per person £10.00-£20.00 Single £10.00-£20.00 Double	Open Jan-Dec Dinner 1800
Ben Doran Guest House 11 Mayfield Gardens EH9 2AX Tel. 031 667 8488			1 Single 3 Dble/Twin 5 Family	3 Public Bath/Sh	B&B per person £12.00-£14.00 Single £10.00-£12.00 Double	Open Jan-Dec Dinner 1830
Blairhaven Guest House 5 Eyre Place EH3 5ES Tel. 031 556 3025			1 Single 5 Dble/Twin 4 Family		B&B per person £10.00-£12.00 Single £10.00-£12.00 Double	Open Jan-Dec Dinner 1730

EDINBURGH continued	Map 2 D5					
Blantyre Guest House 10 Blantyre Terrace EH10 5AE Tel. 031 447 5761			1 Single 4 Dble/Twin 1 Family	2 Public Bath/Sh	B&B per person £8.50-£16.00 Single £8.00-£15.00 Double	Open May-Oct
Bonnington Guest House 202 Ferry Road EH6 4NW Tel. 031 554 7610			3 Dble/Twin 3 Family	2 Public Bath/Sh	B&B per person £10.00-£11.00 Double	Open Jan-Dec Dinner 1830
The Brae Guest House 119 Willowbrae Road EH8 7HN Tel. 031 661 0170			4 Dble/Twin	1 Public Bath/Sh	B&B per person £8.50-£10.00 Double	Open Jan-Dec
Braemar Guest House 17 Henderson Terrace EH11 2JY Tel. 031 337 8087			3 Dble/Twin	2 Public Bath/Sh	B&B per person £10.50 Double	Open Jun-Aug
Brig O'Doon Guest House 262 Ferry Road EH5 3AN Tel. 031 552 3953			4 Dble/Twin 2 Family	2 Public Bath/Sh	B&B per person £10.00-£12.00 Double	Open Jan-Dec
Brunswick Guest House 7 Brunswick Street EH7 5JB Tel. 031 556 1238	COMMENDED 👑👑		5 Dble/Twin 3 Family	4 Private Bath/Sh 1 Public Bath/Sh	B&B per person £18.00-£32.00 Double	Open Jan-Dec
Georgian stone listed building. Convenient to bus and railway station. Good street parking.						
Buchan Guest House 3 Coates Gardens EH12 5LG Tel. 031 337 1045	COMMENDED 👑👑		2 Single 5 Dble/Twin 3 Family	1 Private Bath/Sh 2 Public Bath/Sh	B&B per person £12.50-£16.50 Single £11.50-£15.00 Double	Open Jan-Dec Dinner 1800
Family run, former merchants house. Centrally situated, within easy reach of Princes Street.						
Buxstone Guest House 2 Hartington Gardens EH10 4LD Tel. 031 229 8664	👑		2 Single 2 Dble/Twin 3 Family	1 Public Bath/Sh	B&B per person £8.50-£10.50 Single £17.00-£21.00 Double	Open Jan-Dec
Carrington Guest House 38 Pilrig Street EH6 5AN Tel. 031 554 4769			1 Single 5 Dble/Twin 1 Family	5 Private Bath/Sh 3 Public Bath/Sh	B&B per person £12.50-£19.00 Single £10.75-£15.50 Double	Open Jan-Dec

Castle Guest House
38 CASTLE STREET, EDINBURGH EH2 3BN
Telephone: 031-225 1975

In the city centre, off Princes Street, within easy reach of most places of interest.
TV and tea-making facilities in all rooms. Quiet and comfortable. Access to rooms all day. H&C and showers. Full central heating. Highly recommended. Good choice of breakfast.
Proprietors: Mr and Mrs J. C. Ovens

Castle Guest House 38 Castle Street EH2 3BN Tel. 031 225 1975			1 Single 5 Dble/Twin 1 Family	2 Public Bath/Sh	B&B per person £8.50-£10.50 Single £8.50-£10.50 Double	Open Jan-Dec

Key to symbols is on back flap. Details of Classification and Grading are on page vi.

EDINBURGH continued	Map 2 D5	Grade	Rooms	Bathrooms	Prices	Opening	Facilities
Claymore Guest House 68 Pilrig Street EH6 5AS Tel. 031 554 2500		COMMENDED ♔	3 Dble/Twin 1 Family	2 Public Bath/Sh	B&B per person £9.50 Double	Open Jan-Dec	
Red sandstone victorian villa; a former manse. Close to city centre, on bus route.							
Crion Guest House 33 Minto Street EH9 2BT Tel. 031 667 2708			1 Single 4 Dble/Twin 1 Family	1 Public Bath/Sh	B&B per person £11.50-£12.50 Single £9.00-£11.00 Double	Open Jan-Dec Dinner 1800	
Daisy Park Guest House 41 Abercorn Terrace EH15 2DG Tel. 031 669 2503		COMMENDED ♔ ♔	6 Dble/Twin 1 Family	2 Public Bath/Sh	B&B per person £9.00-£12.00 Double	Open Jan-Dec Dinner 1800	
Semi-detached victorian house close to promenade and Portobello beach. 20 mins. bus route to city.							
Dargil Guest House 16 Mayfield Gardens EH9 2BZ Tel. 031 667 6177			1 Dble/Twin 3 Family	1 Public Bath/Sh	B&B per person £9.00-£13.00 Double	Open Jan-Dec	
Dene Guest House 7 Eyre Place EH3 5ES Tel. 031 556 2700		Listed	2 Single 2 Dble/Twin 2 Family	2 Public Bath/Sh	B&B per person £10.00-£12.50 Single £9.00-£11.50 Double	Open Jan-Dec	
Dickie Guest House 22 East Claremont Street EH7 4JP Tel. 031 556 4032		Awaiting Inspection	1 Single 2 Dble/Twin 1 Family	2 Private Bath/Sh 1 Public Bath/Sh	B&B per person £12.00-£13.00 Single £11.00-£16.00 Double	Open Jan-Dec	
Figgete Lodge Guest House 40 Bath Street, Portobello Tel. 031 669 0613			1 Single 3 Dble/Twin 1 Family	2 Public Bath/Sh	B&B per person £14.00-£17.00 Single £11.00-£14.00 Double	Open Jan-Dec Dinner 1700	
Fountainhall Guest House 40 Fountainhall Road EH9 2LW Tel. 031 667 2544			4 Dble/Twin 3 Family	1 Public Bath/Sh	B&B per person £11.00-£14.00 Double	Open Jan-Dec	
Galloway Guest House 22 Dean Park Crescent EH4 1PH Tel. 031 332 3672 Telex 72165 Att Gal		COMMENDED ♔ ♔ ♔	1 Single 6 Dble/Twin 3 Family	5 Private Bath/Sh 3 Public Bath/Sh	B&B per person £12.00-£22.00 Single £12.00-£14.00 Double	Open Jan-Dec Dinner 1800	
Family-run, in residential area close to city centre.							
Garfield Guest House 264 Ferry Road EH5 3AN Tel. 031 552 2369			1 Single 4 Dble/Twin 2 Family	2 Public Bath/Sh	B&B per person £11.00-£15.00 Single £10.00-£12.00 Double	Open Jan-Dec	
Gil Dun Guest House 9 Spence Street EH16 6AG Tel. 031 667 1368			2 Dble/Twin 4 Family	2 Public Bath/Sh	B&B per person £9.00-£11.00 Double	Open Jan-Dec	
Granville Guest House 13 Granville Terrace EH10 4PQ Tel. 031 229 1676			2 Single 4 Dble/Twin 1 Family	2 Public Bath/Sh	B&B per person £11.00-£12.00 Single £10.50-£11.00 Double	Open Jan-Dec	
Grosvenor Guest House 1 Grosvenor Gardens EH12 5JU Tel. 031 337 4143		APPROVED Listed	1 Single 4 Dble/Twin 2 Family	2 Private Bath/Sh 2 Public Bath/Sh	B&B per person £11.50-£15.00 Single £23.00-£25.00 Double	Open Jan-Dec	
Very quiet victorian town house, in residential area close to city centre.							

VAT is shown at 15%: changes in this rate may affect prices. Prices shown are for guidance only. Please send SAE with each enquiry.

EDINBURGH continued	Map 2 D5						
Hamilton House Guest House 12 Moston Terrace EH9 2DE Tel. 031 667 2540		COMMENDED ♛	1 Single 2 Dble/Twin 2 Family	2 Public Bath/Sh	B&B per person £10.50-£14.00 Single £10.00-£12.50 Double	Open Jan-Dec Dinner 1800	♣ V ⅀ ▦ 📺 🛏 🐾 ⚲ C T
			Elegant victorian villa; many original features. In quiet residential area close to city centre.				

Hillview Guest House
92 DALKEITH ROAD, EDINBURGH. Tel: 031-667 1523
AA and RAC Listed
Our guests are provided with a well-appointed house for their stay, nicely situated in a residential area on the main A68 road, a few yards from the Commonwealth Swimming Pool and Holyrood Park. About a mile from city centre shops, bus and rail stations which guests can reach using an excellent bus service or a leisurely stroll.
Dinner by arrangement.

Hillview Guest House 92 Dalkeith Road EH16 5AF Tel. 031 667 1523			3 Single 4 Dble/Twin 2 Family	1 Private Bath/Sh 2 Public Bath/Sh	B&B per person £9.00-£12.00 Single £9.00-£12.00 Double	Open Jan-Dec Dinner 1800	♣ ▭ 🍴 ▦ 📺 P C
Hopetoun Guest House 15 Mayfield Road EH9 2NG Tel. 031 667 7691			2 Dble/Twin 1 Family	1 Public Bath/Sh	B&B per person £9.00-£11.00 Double	Open Jan-Dec	♣ M ☕ V ▦ P C
Kaimes Guest House 12 Granville Terrace EH10 4PQ Tel. 031 229 3401		Listed	5 Dble/Twin 3 Family	8 Private Bath/Sh	B&B per person £12.00-£16.00 Double	Open Jan-Dec	♣ ▭ V ▦ 🐾 P C T
Kariba Guest House 10 Granville Terrace EH10 4PQ Tel. 031 229 3773			1 Single 4 Dble/Twin 2 Family	8 Private Bath/Sh 1 Public Bath/Sh	B&B per person £12.00-£15.00 Single £12.50-£15.00 Double	Open Jan-Dec	♣ ▭ 🍴 ☕ V ▦ 📺 🛏 ⚲ 🐾 P C T
Kenvie Guest House 16 Kilmaurs Road EH16 5DA Tel. 031 668 1964		APPROVED ♛	3 Dble/Twin 2 Family	2 Public Bath/Sh	B&B per person £10.00-£12.00 Double	Open Jan-Dec	♣ ▭ ☕ V ⅀ ▦ 📺 ▱ 🐾 P C T
			Personally run, in quiet residential area close to city centre.				
Kilmaurs Guest House 9 Kilmaurs Road EH16 5DA Tel. 031 667 8315			1 Single 3 Dble/Twin 2 Family	2 Public Bath/Sh	B&B per person £10.00-£10.50 Single £10.00-£10.50 Double	Open Jan-Dec	♣ ☕ V ▦ 📺 ⚲ 🛏 🐾 C T

Kingsway House
5 EAST MAYFIELD, EDINBURGH EH9 1SD
Telephone: 031-667 5029
Situated just off A78 and A68, near centre of town. Family-run business.
All rooms have H/C, C/H, SH/P, colour TV and tea/coffee-making facilities.
Small groups catered for at reduced costs. Private parking.
For colour brochure phone Mrs Brown.

Kingsway Guest House 5 East Mayfield EH9 1SD Tel. 031 667 5029			5 Dble/Twin 2 Family	1 Public Bath/Sh	B&B per person £10.00-£11.00 Double	Open Jan-Dec Dinner 1800	♣ ▭ ☕ V ▦ 📺 ⚲ 🛏 🐾 P C T

Key to symbols is on back flap. Details of Classification and Grading are on page vi.

EDINBURGH continued	Map 2 D5	Grading	Rooms	Bath	B&B	Opening	Facilities
Kinneil Guest House 1 Bonnington Terrace EH6 4BP Tel. 031 554 4107			1 Single 3 Dble/Twin 3 Family	2 Public Bath/Sh	B&B per person £10.00 Single £9.00 Double	Open Jan-Dec	
Kirtle Guest House 8 Minto Street EH9 1RG Tel. 031 667 2813/5353		COMMENDED ♛	3 Dble/Twin 4 Family	7 Private Bath/Sh 2 Public Bath/Sh	B&B per person £10.00-£15.00 Double	Open Jan-Dec	
			Convenient for city centre. Some private car parking available.				
Kreigie Guest House 50 Mayfield Road EH9 2NH Tel. 031 667 5847			3 Single 3 Dble/Twin 1 Family	2 Public Bath/Sh	B&B per person £9.00-£10.50 Single £9.00-£10.50 Double	Open Jan-Sep	
Lantern Guest House 3 Windsor Street EH7 5LE Tel. 031 556 8170			1 Single 3 Dble/Twin 1 Family		B&B per person £10.00-£11.50 Single £10.00-£11.50 Double	Open Jan-Dec	
Lauderville Guest House 52 Mayfield Road EH9 2NH Tel. 031 667 7788			1 Single 4 Dble/Twin 3 Family	1 Public Bath/Sh	B&B per person £11.00-£13.00 Single £10.00-£11.00 Double	Open Jan-Dec	
Lindsay Guest House 108 Polwarth Terrace EH11 1NN Tel. 031 337 1580		APPROVED ♛ ♛	2 Single 2 Dble/Twin 3 Family	2 Public Bath/Sh	B&B per person £10.00-£12.00 Single £8.50-£10.00 Double	Open Jan-Dec	
			Beautiful sandstone house in quiet residential area. Private parking, TV, tea-making in all rooms.				
Marakech Guest House 30 London Street EH3 6NA Tel. 031 556 4444/7293			1 Single 5 Dble/Twin 2 Family	2 Private Bath/Sh 2 Public Bath/Sh	B&B per person £10.00-£15.00 Single £9.00-£15.00 Double	Open Jan-Dec Dinner 1900	
Maranatha Guest House 90 Pilrig Street EH6 5AY Tel. 031 554 2106			5 Dble/Twin 5 Family	1 Private Bath/Sh	B&B per person £7.00-£12.00 Double	Open Jan-Dec Dinner 1800	
The Mayfield Guest House 15 Mayfield Gardens EH9 2AX Tel. 031 667 8049			3 Single 4 Dble/Twin 4 Family	7 Private Bath/Sh 3 Public Bath/Sh	B&B per person £12.00-£24.00 Single £11.50-£18.00 Double	Open Jan-Dec	
The Meadows Guest House 17 Glengyle Terrace EH3 9LN Tel. 031 229 9559		COMMENDED ♛ ♛ ♛	1 Single 4 Dble/Twin 2 Family	2 Private Bath/Sh 2 Public Bath/Sh	B&B per person £14.00-£18.00 Single £10.00-£16.00 Double	Open Jan-Dec	
			Quietly situated, terraced house overlooks Bruntsfield Links. Near theatre and shops. Personally run.				
Palmerston Guest House 44 Colinton Road EH14 1AH Tel. 031 337 1861			4 Dble/Twin 1 Family	1 Public Bath/Sh	B&B per person £10.00-£14.00 Double	Open Jan-Dec Dinner 1900	
Park View Villa Guest House 254 Ferry Road EH5 3AN Tel. 031 552 3456			2 Dble/Twin 4 Family	2 Public Bath/Sh	B&B per person £24.00-£28.00 Double	Open Jan-Dec	
Parklands Guest House 20 Mayfield Gardens EH9 2BZ Tel. 031 667 7184			5 Dble/Twin 1 Family	2 Private Bath/Sh 1 Public Bath/Sh	B&B per person £10.00-£16.00 Double	Open Jan-Dec	

VAT is shown at 15%: changes in this rate may affect prices. Prices shown are for guidance only. Please send SAE with each enquiry.

EDINBURGH continued	Map 2 D5					
Pringle Guest House 4 Hartington Place EH10 4LE Tel. 031 229 1620			1 Single 5 Dble/Twin 1 Family	2 Public Bath/Sh	B&B per person £9.50-£10.50 Single £9.50-£10.50 Double	Open Jan-Dec
Ravensdown Guest House 248 Ferry Road EH5 3AN Tel. 031 552 5438			2 Dble/Twin 5 Family	2 Public Bath/Sh	B&B per person £9.50-£12.50 Double	Open Jan-Dec
Ravensneuk Guest House 11 Blacket Avenue EH9 1RR Tel. 031 667 5347		COMMENDED ♛	4 Dble/Twin 3 Family	2 Public Bath/Sh	B&B per person £9.50-£11.50 Double	Open Jan-Dec
		Close to city centre in quiet residential street.				
Rigville Guest House 1 Pilrig Street EH6 5AH Tel. 031 554 1116			1 Single 4 Dble/Twin	1 Public Bath/Sh	B&B per person £9.00-£9.50 Single £9.00-£9.50 Double	Open Jan-Dec
Rosebank Guest House 5 Upper Gilmore Place EH3 9NW Tel. 031 229 4669			4 Dble/Twin	1 Public Bath/Sh	B&B per person £8.50-£9.50 Double	Open Jan-Dec
Rosebery Guest House 13 Rosebery Crescent EH12 5JY Tel. 031 337 1085			4 Dble/Twin 1 Family	1 Public Bath/Sh	B&B per person £11.00-£12.00 Double	Open Jan-Oct
Rosedene Guest House 4 Queens Crescent EH9 2AZ Tel. 031 667 5806			1 Single 5 Dble/Twin 3 Family	1 Public Bath/Sh	B&B per person £10.00-£12.00 Single £9.00-£12.00 Double	Open Mar-Nov
Roselea Guest House 11 Mayfield Road EH9 2NH Tel. 031 667 6115			3 Dble/Twin 4 Family	2 Public Bath/Sh	B&B per person £9.50-£11.00 Double	Open Jan-Dec Dinner 1800
Roselea Guest House 4 Kew Terrace EH12 5JE Tel. 031 337 8396		♛	1 Single 2 Dble/Twin 2 Family	2 Private Bath/Sh 1 Public Bath/Sh	B&B per person £10.00-£12.00 Single £10.00-£12.00 Double	Open Mar-Nov
Rowan Guest House 13 Glenorchy Terrace EH9 2DQ Tel. 031 667 2463		COMMENDED ♛	2 Single 5 Dble/Twin 2 Family	1 Public Bath/Sh	B&B per person £10.00-£12.50 Single £9.50-£12.00 Double	Open Jan-Dec
		Victorian building in quiet residential area. Easy access to city centre and all its amenities.				
Shalimar Guest House 20 Newington Road EH9 1QS Tel. 031 667 2827/0789			1 Single 4 Dble/Twin 4 Family	6 Private Bath/Sh 1 Public Bath/Sh	B&B per person £12.00-£14.00 Single £10.00-£11.00 Double	Open Jan-Dec
Sonas Guest House 3 East Mayfield EH9 1SD Tel. 031 667 2781			3 Dble/Twin 4 Family	2 Public Bath/Sh	B&B per person £9.00-£14.00 Double	Open Jan-Dec
Southdown Guest House 20 Craigmillar Park EH16 5PS Tel. 031 667 2410		Awaiting Inspection	5 Dble/Twin 2 Family	7 Private Bath/Sh 3 Public Bath/Sh	B&B per person £10.50-£11.50 Double	Open Jan-Dec

Key to symbols is on back flap. Details of Classification and Grading are on page vi.

81

EDINBURGH continued	Map 2 D5						
St Bernard's Guest House 22 St Bernards Crescent EH4 1NS Tel. 031 332 2339		COMMENDED ♛♛	2 Single 6 Dble/Twin 3 Family	4 Public Bath/Sh	B&B per person £10.00-£12.00 Single £10.00-£12.00 Double	Open Jan-Dec	
			Recently refurbished victorian town house in residential area of city, convenient for Princes Street.				

St Conan

30 MINTO STREET, EDINBURGH EH9 1SB
Telephone: 031-667 8393

St Conan is situated on the A7 near centre of town. It offers friendly accommodation and is personally run by owner. All rooms H/C, SH/P, C/H, colour TV and tea-making facilities. Some rooms with private showers and private bathrooms available.
Small groups catered for at reduced costs. Private parking.
Phone Mrs Flynn, resident owner, for colour brochure.

Guest House			Rooms	Bath	B&B	Open	Facilities
St Conans Guest House 30 Minto Street EH9 1SB Tel. 031 667 8393			5 Dble/Twin 2 Family	5 Private Bath/Sh 2 Public Bath/Sh	B&B per person £10.00-£11.00 Double	Open Jan-Dec Dinner 1800	
St Margaret's Guest House 18 Craigmillar Park EH16 5PS Tel. 031 667 2202		Awaiting Inspection	5 Dble/Twin 3 Family	2 Public Bath/Sh	B&B per person £8.50-£10.00 Double	Open Jan-Dec	
Sylvern Guest House 22 West Mayfield EH9 1TQ Tel. 031 667 1241			7 Dble/Twin 4 Family		B&B per person £9.50-£10.50 Double	Open Jan-Dec Dinner 1800	
Tania Guest House 19 Minto Street EH9 1RQ Tel. 031 667 4144			1 Single 1 Dble/Twin 4 Family	1 Private Bath/Sh 1 Public Bath/Sh	B&B per person £10.00-£14.00 Single £9.00-£11.00 Double	Open Jan-Dec	
Tankard Guest House 40 East Claremont Street EH7 4JR Tel. 031 556 4218			1 Single 3 Dble/Twin 3 Family	1 Public Bath/Sh	B&B per person £11.00-£14.00 Single £11.00-£14.00 Double	Open Mar-Nov	
The Thirty-Nine Steps Guest House 62 South Trinity Road EH5 3NX Tel. 031 552 1349			1 Single 3 Dble/Twin 3 Family	1 Public Bath/Sh	B&B per person £10.00-£12.00 Single £9.00-£10.00 Double	Open Jan-Dec Dinner 1800	
Tiree Guest House 26 Craigmillar Park EH16 5PE Tel. 031 667 7477			1 Single 4 Dble/Twin 2 Family	5 Private Bath/Sh 1 Public Bath/Sh	B&B per person £9.00-£12.00 Single £8.50-£16.00 Double	Open Jan-Dec	
Turret Guest House 8 Kilmaurs Terrace EH16 5DR Tel. 031 667 6704			2 Single 3 Dble/Twin 2 Family	2 Public Bath/Sh	B&B per person £10.00-£14.00 Single £9.00-£12.00 Double	Open Jan-Dec Dinner 1630	
Villa Nina Guest House 39 Leamington Terrace EH10 4JS Tel. 031 229 2644			5 Dble/Twin 1 Family	2 Public Bath/Sh	B&B per person £8.50-£9.50 Double	Open Jan-Dec Dinner 1800	

VAT is shown at 15%: changes in this rate may affect prices. Prices shown are for guidance only. Please send SAE with each enquiry.

EDINBURGH continued	Map 2 D5					
Villa San Monique Guest House 4 Wilton Road EH16 5NY Tel. 031 667 1403			4 Dble/Twin 1 Family	2 Public Bath/Sh	B&B per person £9.00-£11.00 Double	Open May-Oct
Zetland Guest House 186 St Johns Road EH12 8SG Tel. 031 334 3898		♛	2 Single 2 Dble/Twin 5 Family	2 Public Bath/Sh	B&B per person £9.00-£10.00 Single £9.00-£10.00 Double	Open Jan-Dec
(Senior Warden) Carlyle Hall East Suffolk Road EH16 5PH Tel. 031 667 2262			260 Single 45 Dble/Twin 5 Family	25 Public Bath/Sh	B&B per person £10.00 Single £9.00 Double	Open Jul-Sep Dinner 1800
Dunfermline College Cramond Road North Tel. 031 336 6001			175 Single	36 Public Bath/Sh	B&B per person £12.65 Single	Open Mar-Apr Jul-Sep Dinner 1730
P McMillan, High St., Independant Hostel Blackfriars Street Tel. 031 557 3984			10 Family	9 Public Bath/Sh	B&B per person £4.00-£4.50 Double	Open Jan-Dec
·Pollock Halls of Residence 18 Holyrood Park Road EH16 5AY Tel. 031 667 1971 Telex 72165			1570 Single 30 Dble/Twin	90 Public Bath/Sh	B&B per person £9.85-£14.60 Single £9.85-£14.60 Double	Open Mar-Apr Jun-Sep Dinner 1800
Y W C A of Scotland Francis Kinnaird, 13-14 Coates Cres EH3 7AG			9 Single 8 Dble/Twin 3 Family	3 Public Bath/Sh	B&B per person £8.00-£8.50 Single £7.00-£7.50 Double	Open Jan-Dec Dinner 1730

Mrs Adam-Saunders 11 Mcdonald Road EH7 4LX Tel. 031 556 3434			2 Dble/Twin	1 Public Bath/Sh	B&B per person £10.00-£12.00 Double	Open Apr-Oct
Mrs Aubeeluck Lanara, 21 McDonald Road EH7 4LX Tel. 031 556 2395			2 Dble/Twin 1 Family	2 Public Bath/Sh	B&B per person £8.00-£12.00 Double	Open Jan-Dec Dinner 1800
Mrs P Birnie 8 Kilmaurs Road EH16 5DA Tel. 031 667 8998			2 Dble/Twin 2 Family	2 Public Bath/Sh	B&B per person £7.00-£8.00 Double	Open May-Oct

Key to symbols is on back flap. Details of Classification and Grading are on page vi.

83

EDINBURGH continued	Map 2 D5						
Mrs N Brown Mayfield Cottage, 26 East Mayfield EH9 1SD Tel. 031 667 0304			1 Dble/Twin 1 Family	1 Public Bath/Sh	B&B per person £8.00-£10.00 Double	Open May-Sep Dinner 1750	
Mr & Mrs K J Bruno Georgian House, 34 Blacket Place EH9 1RL Tel. 031 667 2625			1 Single 1 Dble/Twin 3 Family		B&B per person £8.50-£9.00 Single £8.00-£9.00 Double	Open Jan-Dec	
Mrs M Burns 67 Gilmore Place EH3 9NU Tel. 031 229 1669	COMMENDED		2 Dble/Twin 1 Family	1 Public Bath/Sh	B&B per person £8.00-£10.00 Double	Open Jan-Dec	
			Victorian terraced house within easy reach of city centre, stations and tourist attractions.				
Alison Burns 29 East Trinity Road EH5 3DL Tel. 031 552 5876			2 Dble/Twin	2 Public Bath/Sh	B&B per person £10.00-£12.00 Double	Open Apr-Oct	
Mrs R Caine Four Seasons, 47 Minto Street EH9 2BR Tel. 031 667 2963			1 Single 2 Dble/Twin 2 Family	2 Public Bath/Sh	B&B per person £8.00-£10.00 Single £8.00-£10.00 Double	Open Apr-Oct	
Mrs E Carmichael 568 Queensferry Road EH4 6AT Tel. 031 339 2557			1 Dble/Twin 1 Family	2 Public Bath/Sh	B&B per person £8.00-£10.00 Double	Open Jan-Dec	
Mrs E Caven Carronvale, 38 Corstorphine Bank Dr EH12 8RN Tel. 031 334 3291			2 Dble/Twin 1 Family	1 Public Bath/Sh	B&B per person £8.00-£9.50 Double	Open Jan-Dec	
Mrs Christine Cocking 7 Woodfield Avenue, Colinton EH13 0HX Tel. 031 441 2364			1 Single 2 Dble/Twin	1 Public Bath/Sh	B&B per person £8.50-£9.00 Single £7.50-£8.50 Double	Open May-Sep	
Mrs M Conway Crannoch, 467 Queensferry Road EH4 7ND Tel. 031 336 5688			2 Dble/Twin 1 Family	3 Private Bath/Sh 1 Public Bath/Sh	B&B per person £11.00-£13.00 Double	Open May-Sep	
Mr D Crerar 3 Mayfield Road EH9 2NG Tel. 031 667 2394			2 Dble/Twin 2 Family	3 Private Bath/Sh 1 Public Bath/Sh	B&B per person £9.00-£12.00 Double	Open May-Oct Dinner 1830	
Mrs I R Donaldson 134 Craigleith Road EH4 2EQ Tel. 031 332 6340			2 Dble/Twin		B&B per person £8.50-£9.00 Double	Open Jan-Dec	

EDINBURGH continued | Map 2 D5

Mrs H Donaldson Invermark, 60 Polwarth Terrace EH11 1NJ Tel. 031 337 1066	♛	1 Single 1 Dble/Twin 1 Family	1 Public Bath/Sh	B&B per person £9.00-£10.00 Single £9.00-£10.00 Double	Open Jan-Dec	
Dr R Donnelly 3 Duddingston Crescent EH15 3AS Tel. 031 669 4874		3 Dble/Twin 1 Family	1 Public Bath/Sh	B&B per person £8.00-£13.00 Double	Open Apr-Oct	
Mrs D Douglas Dundalk, 86 Milton Road West EH15 1RD Tel. 031 669 9518	COMMENDED ♛	1 Dble/Twin	1 Private Bath/Sh	B&B per person £24.00-£25.00 Double **Modern bungalow in own grounds, 2 miles (3kms) from city centre.**	Open Apr-Sep	
Mrs Downey 528 Ferry Road EH5 2DJ Tel. 031 552 6647		1 Dble/Twin	1 Public Bath/Sh	B&B per person £10.00 Double	Open May-Oct	
Mrs Dunlop 63 Glasgow Road Tel. 031 334 2306		2 Dble/Twin	1 Public Bath/Sh	B&B per person £8.50-£9.00 Double	Open Apr-Oct	
Mr & Mrs T A Ewing 36 Minto Street EH9 2BS Tel. 031 667 5966		1 Family	1 Public Bath/Sh	B&B per person £12.00-£17.00 Double	Open Jan-Dec	
Mrs Foley Seaforth, 6 Esplanade Terrace EH15 2ES Tel. 031 669 5493		1 Single 2 Dble/Twin		B&B per person £8.00-£8.50 Single £8.00-£8.50 Double	Open Jan-Dec	
Mrs C Forsyth 10 Queens Gardens EH4 2DA Tel. 031 332 1926		1 Single 2 Dble/Twin	1 Public Bath/Sh	B&B per person £10.50-£12.00 Single £9.25-£10.00 Double	Open Apr-Oct	

EDINBURGH continued	Map 2 D5	

AUCHENDINNY

20B Polwarth Terrace, Merchiston, Edinburgh EH11 1NB
Enjoy your stay in Edinburgh in a friendly and helpful home.
Merchiston is a quiet and very attractive conservation area of
fine Victorian houses just to the south-west of the city centre.
Easy access by bus or car (5 mins.). Private parking. Each
bedroom has a television set and washing facilities. Evening
meals by request. **Mrs Maria Franklin. Telephone: 031-229 3802**

Mrs M F Franklin Auchendinny, 20b Polwarth Terrace EH11 1NB Tel. 031 229 3802	APPROVED ♔	1 Single 1 Dble/Twin 1 Family	1 Public Bath/Sh	B&B per person £8.50-£11.00 Single £8.50-£11.00 Double	Open Jan-Dec
		Upper flat in detached victorian house. Quiet residential area; bus routes to city centre.			
Mrs M Fraser Torivane, 1 Morton Street EH15 2EW Tel. 031 669 1648		1 Single 1 Dble/Twin 1 Family	1 Public Bath/Sh	B&B per person £7.50-£8.00 Single £7.00-£7.50 Double	Open May-Oct Dinner 1800
Mr & Mrs D R Gibb Silver Strand, 3 Alfred Place EH9 1RX Tel. 031 667 1866		3 Single 2 Dble/Twin	1 Public Bath/Sh	B&B per person £9.00-£12.50 Single £9.00-£12.50 Double	Open Jan-Dec
Mrs Hall 55 Barnton Avenue, Davidson's Mains EH4 6JJ Tel. 031 336 1685	COMMENDED ♔	3 Dble/Twin	1 Public Bath/Sh	B&B per person £12.00-£12.50 Double	Open Mar-Oct
		Stone-built house with large garden. Overlooks golf course. Quiet area, 3 mls (5kms) to city centre.			
Mrs A Hamilton 6 Cambridge Gardens EH6 5DJ Tel. 031 554 3113		1 Single 1 Dble/Twin 1 Family		B&B per person £8.00-£9.00 Single £16.00-£18.00 Double	Open Apr-Oct
Mrs C Hanratty 6 Kilmaurs Road EH16 5DA Tel. 031 667 4135		1 Single 1 Dble/Twin 1 Family	1 Public Bath/Sh	B&B per person £8.50-£10.00 Single £8.00-£8.50 Double	Open Jan-Dec Dinner 1800
Mrs E Hay 6 Sciennes Road EH9 1LE Tel. 031 667 8735		1 Single 2 Dble/Twin		B&B per person £9.00-£11.00 Single £9.00-£10.00 Double	Open May-Oct
Mrs N Hendrie 20 St Catherines Place EH9 1NU Tel. 031 667 4785		2 Dble/Twin 1 Family	2 Public Bath/Sh	B&B per person £8.00-£10.00 Double	Open Jan-Dec
Mr & Mrs Hepburn No 5, 5, 7 Abercorn Terrace EH15 2DD Tel. 031 669 1044		1 Single 3 Dble/Twin 4 Family	1 Private Bath/Sh 2 Public Bath/Sh	B&B per person £8.00-£10.00 Single £7.50-£10.00 Double	Open Jan-Dec
Dr H Hills 13 Corrennie Drive EH10 6EG Tel. 031 447 1260	COMMENDED Listed	1 Dble/Twin	1 Private Bath/Sh	B&B per person £18.00-£20.00 Double	Open Jan-Dec
		Edwardian house with original features. Quiet residential area, near Braid Hills. Bus route to city.			

VAT is shown at 15%: changes in this rate may affect prices. Prices shown are for guidance only. Please send SAE with each enquiry.

	Map 2 D5						
EDINBURGH continued Mrs Y Innes Cleveland, 590 Queensferry Road EH4 6AT Tel. 031 339 2195			1 Single 2 Dble/Twin	2 Public Bath/Sh	B&B per person £10.00 Single £10.00 Double	Open Apr-Sep	
William Jack 1 Mayfield Road EH9 2NE Tel. 031 667 2755			3 Dble/Twin 2 Family	2 Public Bath/Sh	B&B per person £8.50-£9.50 Double	Open Jun-Sep	
Mrs S James 24 Cairnmuir Road EH12 6LP Tel. 031 334 4256			2 Single 2 Dble/Twin	2 Public Bath/Sh	B&B per person £12.00 Single £12.00 Double	Open Jul-Sep	
Mrs Jameson 1 Salisbury Place EH9 1SL Tel. 031 667 1585			2 Dble/Twin	1 Public Bath/Sh	B&B per person £7.75-£8.25 Double	Open Jul-Sep	
Mrs S Johnston 61 Lothian Road EH1 2DJ Tel. 031 229 4054			1 Single 2 Dble/Twin	1 Public Bath/Sh	B&B per person £11.00-£13.00 Single £11.00-£13.00 Double	Open Jan-Dec	
Mr & Mrs Jones 7 Grange Terrace EH9 2LD Tel. 031 667 1834			1 Single 1 Dble/Twin	2 Public Bath/Sh	B&B per person £10.00-£12.00 Single £9.00-£11.00 Double	Open May-Sep	
Mrs J Kelly 38 Piersfield Terrace EH8 7BJ Tel. 031 657 2418			4 Single 1 Dble/Twin	2 Public Bath/Sh	B&B per person £8.00-£11.00 Single £7.50-£10.00 Double	Open May-Sep	
Mrs V Kynoch Kirklea, 11 Harrison Road EH11 1EG Tel. 031 337 1129		**COMMENDED** Listed	1 Single 1 Dble/Twin 1 Family	2 Public Bath/Sh	B&B per person £10.50 Single £9.50 Double	Open Apr-Oct	
			Modernised victorian terraced house, close to city centre. Easy access to all amenities.				
Mrs Pauline MacDonald 24 Duddingston Crescent EH15 3AT Tel. 031 669 4072			3 Dble/Twin	1 Public Bath/Sh	B&B per person £9.50-£11.00 Double	Open Apr-Oct	
Mrs G MacIntyre 15 MacDonald Road EH7 4NN Tel. 031 556 4967			3 Dble/Twin 1 Family	2 Private Bath/Sh 2 Public Bath/Sh	B&B per person £10.00-£12.00 Double	Open Jan-Dec Dinner 1800	
Ann MacQueenie 51 Mortonhall Park Crescent EH17 8SX Tel. 031 664 8621			1 Single 1 Dble/Twin	1 Public Bath/Sh	B&B per person £7.00-£9.00 Single £7.00-£10.00 Double	Open Apr-Oct	
Mr & Mrs I Mackenzie 116 Gilmore Place EH3 9PL Tel. 031 229 4396			1 Dble/Twin 1 Family	1 Public Bath/Sh	B&B per person £8.00-£9.00 Double	Open Apr-Oct	

EDINBURGH continued	Map 2 D5					
Mrs Marion Mackintosh 4 Drummond Place EH3 6PH Tel. 031 556 1657		1 Single 1 Dble/Twin	1 Public Bath/Sh	B&B per person £12.00-£14.00 Single £11.00-£13.00 Double	Open Jan-Sep	☕ ▥ TV 🛏 🍴 🏠
Mrs C Major 41 Abercorn Terrace	COMMENDED ♕♕	6 Dble/Twin 1 Family	2 Public Bath/Sh	B&B per person £9.00-£12.00 Double	Open Jan-Dec Dinner 1800	☕ V ▥ TV 🏠 ⚠ C
		Semi detached victorian house close to promenade and Portobello beach. 20 min. bus route to city				
Mrs Mallon 9 Canaan Lane, Morningside Tel. 031 447 4697	Awaiting Inspection	3 Dble/Twin	1 Public Bath/Sh	B&B per person £10.50 Double	Open Apr-Oct	🚿 ☕ ▥ TV
Mrs Moira Maxwell 3 John Street, Portobello EH15 2ED Tel. 031 669 8397		2 Single 2 Dble/Twin	2 Public Bath/Sh	B&B per person £9.00-£11.00 Single £9.00-£11.00 Double	Open Jan-Dec	🚿 ☕ ▥ V ▥ 🏠 C

Ben-Aven
Proprietor: Mrs D. McConnachie

3 Shandon Road, Edinburgh. Tel: 031-337 8839

Ben-Aven is a Georgian Town House close to the centre of Edinburgh. The accommodation comprises freshly decorated rooms (with wash-hand basin) one large room with private en-suite.

Prices: £7.00-£9.00 p.p. with weekly reductions.

Mrs D A McConnachie 3 Shandon Road EH11 1QG Tel. 031 337 8839	♕	3 Dble/Twin	1 Private Bath/Sh 1 Public Bath/Sh	B&B per person £6.50-£10.00 Double	Open Apr-Oct Dinner 1800	🚿 ☕ V TV 🏠 P ⚠ C
Dorothy M G McKay 41 Corstorphine Bank Drive EH12 8RH Tel. 031 334 4100		2 Dble/Twin	1 Private Bath/Sh 1 Public Bath/Sh	B&B per person £8.00-£9.00 Double	Open May-Oct	☕ V ▥ 🏠 P
Miss E McLean 52 East Claremont Street Tel. 031 441 2638		7 Dble/Twin	2 Public Bath/Sh	B&B per person £7.00-£9.00 Double	Open Jan-Dec	🚿 TV 🏠 ⚠
Mrs S J McLennan 29 Kilmaurs Road EH16 5DB Tel. 031 668 2336	♕	3 Dble/Twin	1 Public Bath/Sh	B&B per person £8.50-£9.50 Double	Open Jun-Sep	V ▥ TV 🏠 🐕 C
Mrs M Mccormack 9 Melville Terrace EH9 1ND Tel. 031 667 3065		1 Dble/Twin 1 Family	1 Public Bath/Sh	B&B per person £7.50-£8.00 Double	Open Apr-Oct Dinner 1800	TV C
Mrs H Mckellar 64 Glasgow Road EH12 8LN Tel. 031 334 2610		1 Single 2 Dble/Twin	1 Public Bath/Sh	B&B per person £9.50-£10.00 Single £8.50-£9.00 Double	Open Apr-Oct	▥ TV P
Mr W Mckinlay 1a Granville Terrace Tel. 031 228 3381		3 Single 3 Dble/Twin	1 Public Bath/Sh	B&B per person £10.00-£12.00 Single £10.00-£11.00 Double	Open May-Sep	☕ 🏠

VAT is shown at 15%: changes in this rate may affect prices. Prices shown are for guidance only. Please send SAE with each enquiry.

EDINBURGH continued	**Map 2 D5**						
Mr J Mees 37 London Street EH3 6LX Tel. 031 556 6698			1 Dble/Twin 1 Family	1 Public Bath/Sh	B&B per person £8.00-£11.00 Double	Open May-Sep	[symbols]
Mrs M Melrose 26 Dudley Avenue EH6 4PN Tel. 031 554 1915			1 Single 2 Dble/Twin	1 Public Bath/Sh	B&B per person £7.50 Single £7.50 Double	Open Jun-Sep	[symbols]
Mrs L Murray 31 Regent Street, Portobello EH15 2AY Tel. 031 669 1501			1 Dble/Twin 2 Family	1 Public Bath/Sh	B&B per person £7.00-£8.00 Double	Open Jul-Sep Dinner 1800	[symbols]
Mrs A K Nale 7 Whitehorse Close, Holyrood EH8 8BU Tel. 031 556 8974			1 Dble/Twin	1 Private Bath/Sh	B&B per person £10.00-£12.00 Double	Open Jan-Dec Dinner 1800	[symbols]
Mrs Nisbet 9B Scotland Street Tel. 031 556 5080			3 Dble/Twin	2 Public Bath/Sh	B&B per person £8.00-£10.00 Double	Open Jun-Oct	[symbols]
Mr & Mrs O'Donnell 5 Sciennes Road, Marchmont EH9 1LE Tel. 031 667 7634			1 Single 1 Dble/Twin 1 Family	2 Public Bath/Sh	B&B per person £10.00-£12.00 Single £9.00-£10.00 Double	Open Apr-Oct	[symbols]
Mrs Pederson 166 Craigleith Road EH4 2EQ Tel. 031 343 2819			1 Single	1 Public Bath/Sh	B&B per person £9.00-£12.00 Single	Open Apr-Oct	
Mrs Reid 8 Eyre Crescent Tel. 031 556 2922			2 Dble/Twin	1 Public Bath/Sh	B&B per person £8.50-£10.00 Double	Open Apr-Oct	[symbols]
Mrs M Ritchie 61 East Restalrig Terrace EH6 8EE Tel. 031 554 6796			1 Single 2 Dble/Twin 1 Family	1 Public Bath/Sh	B&B per person £7.00-£10.00 Single £7.00-£10.00 Double	Open Apr-Oct	[symbols]
Mrs Roden Aldaniti Villa, 36 Shandon Crescent EH11 1QF Tel. 031 337 2181			2 Dble/Twin 3 Family	2 Public Bath/Sh	B&B per person £10.00 Double	Open May-Sep Dinner 1800	[symbols]
Mrs Patricia Rosa 1 Savile Terrace EH9 3AD Tel. 031 667 5157			3 Dble/Twin 1 Family	2 Public Bath/Sh	B&B per person £7.50-£10.00 Double	Open Jun-Sep	[symbols]
Mrs V Ross Glen-Affric, 39 Queens Crescent EH9 2BA Tel. 031 667 2907		COMMENDED 👑	2 Dble/Twin 1 Family	1 Public Bath/Sh	B&B per person £18.00-£20.00 Double	Open Jan-Dec	[symbols]

Mrs V Ross: Victorian house in quiet, conservation area with park. Convenient for bus routes to city centre.

EDINBURGH continued	Map 2 D5					
Mrs A M Royden 5 Polwarth Grove EH11 1LZ Tel. 031 337 9866		1 Dble/Twin 1 Family	1 Public Bath/Sh	B&B per person £8.50-£9.50 Double	Open Jun-Aug	
Kit Russell 10 Brougham Place EH3 9HW Tel. 031 229 4439		1 Single 1 Dble/Twin 1 Family	1 Public Bath/Sh	B&B per person £10.00 Single £8.50 Double	Open Jun-Sep	
Mrs H Russell 9 Lonsdale Terrace EH3 9HN Tel. 031 229 7219		2 Dble/Twin	1 Public Bath/Sh	B&B per person £7.00-£9.00 Double	Open Jan-Dec Dinner 2030	
Mrs A Sibbet (Edinburgh Holidays) 26 Northumberland Street EH3 6LS Tel. 031 556 1078	COMMENDED 👑 👑 👑	2 Dble/Twin 1 Family	3 Private Bath/Sh	B&B per person £12.00-£14.00 Double	Open Jan-Oct	
		Personal attention in georgian townhouse of character. Art/design interest. Bagpipes.				
Mrs E C Simpson 17 Crawfurd Road EH16 5PQ Tel. 031 667 1191	Listed	1 Dble/Twin 1 Family	2 Public Bath/Sh	B&B per person £7.50-£10.50 Double	Open May-Sep	

LANSDOWNE
👑 👑 *Commended*

1 WESTER COATES ROAD, EDINBURGH EH12 5LU
Telephone: 031-337 5002   *Proprietor:* **Mrs R. Sinclair**

A pleasantly situated detached villa in a quiet residential area near West End just off bus route, five minutes from Princes Street. Convenient for Stations and Airport.

Single, double, twin or family bedrooms, all with wash-hand basins, and spacious lounge with TV. Private parking. French, German, Italian spoken.
You are assured of a warm welcome!

Mrs R Sinclair Lansdowne, 1 Wester Coates Road EH12 5LU Tel. 031 337 5002	COMMENDED 👑	1 Single 1 Dble/Twin 1 Family	2 Public Bath/Sh	B&B per person £8.50-£12.00 Single £8.50-£12.00 Double	Open Jan-Dec Dinner 1800	
		Detached victorian sandstone house; garden. Residential area in city's West End. Bus route to centre.				
Mrs J Skidmore 2 Braid Hills EH10 6EZ Tel. 031 447 8848		1 Single 3 Dble/Twin	1 Public Bath/Sh	B&B per person £12.00 Single £13.00 Double	Open Apr-Oct Dinner 1800	
Mr & Mrs J M F Skinner 64 East Claremont Street EH7 4JR Tel. 031 556 2705		2 Dble/Twin 2 Family	2 Public Bath/Sh	B&B per person £10.00-£11.00 Double	Open Jan-Dec Dinner 1800	
Mrs C Skivington 7 Polwarth Grove EH11 1LZ Tel. 031 337 1174		2 Dble/Twin 2 Family	1 Public Bath/Sh	B&B per person £10.00 Double	Open Jun-Sep	
Mrs E Steedman 10 Hailes Street EH3 9NF Tel. 031 229 2251		1 Single 1 Dble/Twin 1 Family	1 Public Bath/Sh	B&B per person £6.00-£7.50 Single £6.00-£7.50 Double	Open Apr-Oct	

EDINBURGH continued	Map 2 D5		Rooms	Bath	B&B	Open	Symbols
Mrs E Sterling 90 Liberton Brae EH16 6LB Tel. 031 664 2398			1 Single 2 Dble/Twin 1 Family	1 Public Bath/Sh	B&B per person £8.50-£10.00 Single £8.00-£10.00 Double	Open Apr-Oct	▥ TV C
Mrs M J Stevens 39 Inverleith Gardens EH3 5PR Tel. 031 552 6549			1 Single 1 Dble/Twin 1 Family	1 Public Bath/Sh	B&B per person £9.00-£12.00 Single £10.00-£12.00 Double	Open Jan-Dec	🍴 V ♨ ▥ TV
Mrs B C Stone 20 McLaren Road EH9 2BN Tel. 031 668 2584			2 Dble/Twin	1 Public Bath/Sh	B&B per person £9.50-£10.50 Double	Open May-Sep	🏋 V ▥ C
Mrs Roxane Thompson Camelot, 31 Duddingston Crescent Tel. 031 669 3695			2 Dble/Twin 1 Family	1 Public Bath/Sh	B&B per person £8.00-£10.00 Double	Open Jan-Dec	🏋 🍴 V ▥ TV ✳ £ P C
Mrs L Toolin 28 Mayfield Gardens EH9 2BZ Tel. 031 667 6029			3 Dble/Twin	1 Public Bath/Sh	B&B per person £8.50-£10.00 Double	Open Apr-Oct	🏋 🍴 V ♨ ▥ TV
Mrs R C Torrance 15 Viewforth Terrace EH10 4LJ Tel. 031 229 1776		Listed	3 Dble/Twin	1 Public Bath/Sh	B&B per person £7.00-£9.00 Double	Open May-Sep	M 🍴 V ▭ 🔌 P C
Mrs June Tulloch 24 Summerside Street EH6 4NU Tel. 031 554 8652			3 Dble/Twin	1 Public Bath/Sh	B&B per person £7.00-£10.00 Double	Open May-Sep	▭ 🍴 ▥ TV
Gill Vale 92 Corstorphine Road Tel. 031 337 7418			1 Single 2 Dble/Twin 1 Family	1 Public Bath/Sh	B&B per person £11.00-£12.00 Single £11.00-£12.00 Double	Open Jan-Dec	🏋 V ♨ ▥ TV ▭ 🔌 P C
Mrs Vance 21 Murieston Crescent EH11 2LL Tel. 031 337 7108			2 Dble/Twin	1 Public Bath/Sh	B&B per person £6.50-£7.00 Double	Open Apr-Oct	♨ ▥ TV ▭ 🔌 C
Mrs S Virtue The Town House, 65 Gilmore Pl EH3 9NU Tel. 031 229 1985			1 Single 2 Dble/Twin 1 Family	1 Public Bath/Sh	B&B per person £8.00-£10.50 Single £8.00-£10.50 Double	Open May-Sep	🏋 ▭ 🍴 V ▥ TV 🐕 P C
Mr & Mrs L Walker Appin House, 4 Savile Terrace EH9 3AD Tel. 031 667 2104			1 Single 2 Dble/Twin 1 Family	1 Public Bath/Sh	B&B per person £9.00-£12.00 Single £9.00-£12.00 Double	Open Jan-Dec	🏋 M 🍴 ▥ TV 🐕 P C T
Mrs Morag S Waterson 27 Newington Road EH9 1QR Tel. 031 668 2270			2 Single 2 Dble/Twin 1 Family	1 Public Bath/Sh	B&B per person £10.00-£12.00 Single £20.00-£24.00 Double	Open Apr-Oct	🏋 ▭ 🍴 V 🐕 ✂ C 🎴
Mr & Mrs F Westbury 116 Braid Road EH10 6AS Tel. 031 447 3695			2 Dble/Twin	2 Private Bath/Sh 1 Public Bath/Sh	B&B per person £9.00 Double	Open Jul-Sep	🏋 ♨ ▥ TV ▭

Key to symbols is on back flap. Details of Classification and Grading are on page vi.

	Map Ref	Rooms	Bathrooms	Prices	Opening	
EDINBURGH continued Mrs J Williamson Hopebank, 33 Hope Lane, Portobello Tel. 031 657 1149	Map 2 D5	2 Dble/Twin 1 Family	3 Private Bath/Sh 1 Public Bath/Sh	B&B per person £8.50-£11.00 Double	Open Apr-Oct	
Mrs J Wilson 21 Esplanade Terrace EH15 2ES Tel. 031 669 8585/443 4743		1 Single 1 Dble/Twin	1 Public Bath/Sh	B&B per person £12.00 Single £12.00 Double	Open Jul-Aug	
Mrs E Young Birch House, 51 Minto Street EH9 2BR Tel. 031 667 0306		1 Single 3 Dble/Twin 1 Family	1 Private Bath/Sh 2 Public Bath/Sh	B&B per person £9.50 Double	Open May-Sep	
EDZELL **Angus** Mrs A De Costa Doune House, High Street DD9 7TA Tel. Edzell (03564) 201	Map 4 F12	1 Dble/Twin 2 Family	1 Public Bath/Sh	B&B per person £8.00-£9.00 Double	Open Jan-Dec	
EIGG, Isle of **Inverness-shire** Mr A J MacKinnon Cleadale Tel. Mallaig (0687) 82433	Map 3 D12	2 Dble/Twin 1 Family	1 Public Bath/Sh	B&B per person £9.50 Double	Open Jan-Dec Dinner 1900	
ELGIN **Moray** Mrs Agnes C Bulloch Town House, 42 Batchen Street IV30 1BH Tel. Elgin (0343) 49557	Map 4 D8	7 Dble/Twin	1 Public Bath/Sh	B&B per person £7.50 Double	Open Jan-Dec Dinner 1800	
Mrs E Cox Thornhill Farm, Longmorn IV30 3RJ Tel. Longmorn (034386) 428		2 Dble/Twin	2 Public Bath/Sh	B&B per person £7.00-£8.00 Double	Open Apr-Oct	
Mrs Isobel McGowan Non-Smokers' Haven, 63 Moss St IV30 1LT Tel. Elgin (0343) 41993		2 Family		B&B per person £7.50-£8.00 Double	Open Jan-Dec	
Mrs Anne Munn Carronvale, 18 South Guildry Street IV30 1QN Tel. Elgin (0343) 46864		3 Dble/Twin	1 Public Bath/Sh	B&B per person £7.50 Double	Open Jan-Dec Dinner 1800	
Mrs W G Ross The Bungalow, 7 New Elgin Road IV30 3BE Tel. Elgin (0343) 2035		1 Single 2 Dble/Twin 1 Family	2 Public Bath/Sh	B&B per person £7.50 Single £7.50 Double	Open Jan-Dec	

VAT is shown at 15%: changes in this rate may affect prices. Prices shown are for guidance only. Please send SAE with each enquiry.

ELIE Fife	Map 2 E3					

ELMS GUEST HOUSE
Park Place, Elie, Fife KY9 1DH   Tel: Elie (0333) 330404

The Elms Guest House in the peaceful East Neuk village of Elie offers traditional Scottish food and hospitality. Close to beautiful beaches, fine golf courses and lovely walks. All rooms with H&C, some with private facilities. Full central heating and tea-making facilities. Dinner, Bed and Breakfast from £95.000 per person weekly. Children half price. Phone or write for brochure.

Establishment			Rooms	Bath	B&B	Open	
The Elms Guest House 12 Park Place KY19 1DH Tel. Elie (0333) 330404			1 Single 3 Dble/Twin 3 Family	2 Private Bath/Sh 2 Public Bath/Sh	B&B per person £9.50-£10.00 Single £9.50-£10.00 Double	Open Jan-Dec Dinner 1800	
Mrs Black Ampersano, The Shore, Earlsferry Tel. Elie (0333) 330482			3 Dble/Twin	1 Public Bath/Sh	B&B per person £8.50-£9.50 Double	Open Apr-Oct	
Mrs V Harmes 23 Wadeslea Road Tel. Elie (0333) 330917			1 Dble/Twin	1 Public Bath/Sh	B&B per person £9.00 Double	Open Mar-Nov	
Mrs P Knottenbelt 33 Park Place Tel. Elie (0333) 330391			2 Single 1 Dble/Twin	1 Public Bath/Sh	B&B per person £8.50 Single £8.50 Double	Open Jan-Dec Dinner 1800	
ELLON Aberdeenshire Mrs H M Asbey 43 Station Road AB4 9AR Tel. Ellon (0358) 22737	Map 4 H9		2 Single 2 Family		B&B per person £7.50 Single £7.00 Double	Open Jan-Dec Dinner 1700	
Mrs Thomson 58 Station Road AB4 9AL Tel. Ellon (0358) 20263			2 Dble/Twin		B&B per person £7.00 Double	Open Apr-Sep	
ELSRICKLE, by Biggar Lanarkshire Mrs Alice Barrie Howburn Farm Tel. Dunsyre (089981) 276	Map 2 C6		1 Dble/Twin 1 Family	1 Public Bath/Sh	B&B per person £8.50 Double	Open May-Oct	
Mrs W Ramsay Townfoot Tel. Dunsyre (089981) 200			3 Dble/Twin	1 Public Bath/Sh	B&B per person £7.50-£8.50 Double	Open May-Oct Dinner 1800	
ERISKAY S Uist, Western Isles Mrs C Rusk 10 Port Patrick Tel. Eriskay (08786) 233	Map 3 A11		2 Single 2 Dble/Twin	1 Public Bath/Sh	B&B per person £9.50-£11.50 Single £9.50-£11.50 Double	Open Jan-Dec Dinner 1800	

ETTRICK BRIDGE, by Selkirk Selkirkshire	Map 2 D7		

FIR COTTAGE
ETTRICK BRIDGE
Mr & Mrs T. Mitchell
☎ (0750) 52236
Bedrooms 2T. IF.
Bath/Shower rooms, H&C
Categories 3.2.2.

House in quiet country village. All home cooking. Disabled and children welcome, also pets.
House open all day.
Parking front of house.
Open all year. Tourist Board Listed.
Relais Routier Recommended.
Prices: B&B £8.50; EM £6.00 per person.
Tourist Board Listed.

Mr T Mitchell Fir Cottage Tel. Ettrick Bridge (0750) 52236		Listed	2 Dble/Twin 1 Family	1 Public Bath/Sh	B&B per person £8.25 Double	Open Jan-Dec Dinner 1800	
ETTRICK VALLEY Selkirkshire	Map 2 D7						
Mrs Jean Kaler Glenkerry Tel. Selkirk (0750) 62244			2 Dble/Twin 2 Family	1 Public Bath/Sh	B&B per person £7.50 Double	Open Apr-Oct	
EVANTON Ross-shire	Map 4 A8						
Mrs Budd The Corner House, Assynt Street Tel. Evanton (0349) 830157			1 Single 1 Dble/Twin	1 Public Bath/Sh	B&B per person £7.00-£8.00 Single £7.00-£8.00 Double	Open Apr-Oct	
Miss M MacKay Cairnmhor, 39 Camden Street IV16 9XX Tel. Evanton (0349) 830333			2 Dble/Twin	1 Public Bath/Sh	B&B per person £7.50 Double	Open Jan-Dec Dinner 1800	
Mrs Annik Mowat 1 Ash Hill Tel. Evanton (0349) 830503		Listed	1 Family	1 Public Bath/Sh	B&B per person £7.50 Double	Open Jan-Dec Dinner 1800	
EYEMOUTH Berwickshire Mrs Bowie Alt-na-Craig, Coldingham Road Tel. Eyemouth (08907) 50862	Map 2 G5	COMMENDED Listed	2 Dble/Twin 1 Family	1 Public Bath/Sh	B&B per person £7.50-£8.50 Double	Open May-Sep Dinner 1800	

Pleasantly situated home overlooking tennis court. Short walk to harbour and town centre.

Mrs E G Boyton Ning, 5 Pocklan Slap Tel. Eyemouth (08907) 50553			1 Single 1 Dble/Twin	1 Public Bath/Sh	B&B per person £7.50-£8.50 Single £7.50-£8.50 Double	Open Apr-Sep Dinner 1800	
Mrs McGovern Ebba House, Upper Houndlaw Tel. Eyemouth (08907) 50350		COMMENDED Listed	1 Single 1 Dble/Twin 1 Family	1 Public Bath/Sh	B&B per person £8.00-£8.50 Single £8.00-£8.50 Double	Open Apr-Oct Dinner 1730	

Centrally located terraced house in quiet street. Short walk to beach, harbour and shops.

FAIRLIE Ayrshire Mrs Gardner Mon A Brie, 12 Main Road KA29 0DP Tel. Fairlie (047556) 241	Map 1 G6	♛	1 Single 3 Dble/Twin	1 Public Bath/Sh	B&B per person £7.50-£8.00 Single £7.50-£8.00 Double	Open Jan-Dec Dinner 1800
FALKIRK Stirlingshire Ivanhoe Guest House 60 Stirling Road, Camelon FK1 4ER Tel. Falkirk (0324) 23034	Map 2 B4		1 Single 4 Dble/Twin 2 Family	1 Public Bath/Sh	B&B per person £9.00 Single £9.00 Double	Open Jan-Nov
Mrs Joanna Mucha 5 Maggiewoods Loan EH3 5PS Tel. Falkirk (0324) 23241			1 Single 3 Dble/Twin 1 Family	1 Public Bath/Sh	B&B per person £8.00-£10.00 Single £8.00-£10.00 Double	Open Apr-Oct Dinner 1800
FALKLAND Fife Mrs Sarah G McGregor Templelands Farm KY7 7DE Tel. Falkland (0337) 57383	Map 2 C3	COMMENDED ♛ ♛	1 Dble/Twin 1 Family	2 Public Bath/Sh	B&B per person £8.00 Double	Open Apr-Oct Dinner 1900
			Farmhouse on side of Lomond Hills with superb views over Howe of Fife. Working farm. Home cooking.			
FEARNAN, Aberfeldy Perthshire Mr O B Clapham Easter Auchtar PH15 2PG Tel. Kenmore (08873) 316	Map 2 A1		3 Dble/Twin	2 Public Bath/Sh	B&B per person £10.00 Double	Open Apr-Sep Dinner 1930
FENWICK Ayrshire Mr & Mrs T McKellar Langside Cottage Tel. Fenwick (05606) 601	Map 1 H6		3 Dble/Twin	2 Public Bath/Sh	B&B per person £9.50 Double	Open Jan-Dec
Mr A Peaston Horsehill Farm Tel. Moscow (05607) 658			1 Single 1 Dble/Twin 1 Family	1 Public Bath/Sh	B&B per person £9.50 Single £9.50 Double	Open Jan-Dec Dinner 1730
FERINDONALD, Sleat Isle of Skye, Inverness-shire B & J Shaw Alltan House Tel. Ardvasar (04714) 342	Map 3 E10		1 Single 3 Dble/Twin 1 Family	2 Public Bath/Sh	B&B per person £8.50-£9.50 Single £8.50-£9.50 Double	Open Mar-Nov Dinner 1800
FINDO GASK, by Crieff Perthshire R & J Kinloch Clathybegg Tel. Gask (073873) 213	Map 2 B2		1 Single 2 Dble/Twin	2 Public Bath/Sh	B&B per person £9.00 Single £8.50 Double	Open Jun-Aug
FINTRY Stirlingshire Mrs Mitchell Netherglinns Farm Tel. Fintry (036086) 207	Map 2 A4		2 Dble/Twin 1 Family	2 Public Bath/Sh	B&B per person £8.00 Double	Open Apr-Sep

Key to symbols is on back flap. Details of Classification and Grading are on page vi.

	Map		Rooms	Bath	B&B	Open	Facilities
FINTRY continued Jill Proctor Riverside Cottage, Main Street Tel. Fintry (036086) 271	Map 2 A4		2 Dble/Twin	2 Public Bath/Sh	B&B per person – £7.50 Double	Open Jan-Dec	
Mrs A Willison Craigend Farm G63 0LS Tel. Fintry (036086) 257			1 Single 1 Dble/Twin 1 Family	1 Public Bath/Sh	B&B per person £7.50-£8.00 Single £7.50-£8.00 Double	Open May-Sep	
FIONNPHORT **Isle of Mull, Argyll** Mrs Greenhalgh Seaview Tel. Fionnphort (06817) 235	Map 1 B3	Awaiting Inspection	2 Dble/Twin	2 Public Bath/Sh	B&B per person £8.00 Double	Open Jan-Dec Dinner 1830	
Mrs H J Heald Bruach Mhor PA66 6BL Tel. Fionnphort (06817) 276			3 Dble/Twin	1 Public Bath/Sh	B&B per person £8.00-£8.50 Double	Open Jan-Dec Dinner 1900	
John & Ruth Wagstaff Red Bay Cottage, Deargphort Tel. Fionnphort (06817) 396			3 Dble/Twin 1 Family	2 Public Bath/Sh	B&B per person £9.00 Double	Open Jan-Dec Dinner 1900	
FISHERIE, by Turriff **Aberdeenshire** Mrs E Irvine Deneila, Fisherie Green Tel. Gardenstown (02615) 571	Map 4 G8		1 Dble/Twin 1 Family	1 Public Bath/Sh	B&B per person £7.50 Double	Open Jan-Dec Dinner 1700	
FOCHABERS **Moray** Mr T A Howe Tugnet House, Spey Bay IV30 7PJ Tel. Fochabers (0343) 821277	Map 4 E8		4 Dble/Twin 1 Family	1 Public Bath/Sh	B&B per person £8.50 Double	Open Jun-Sep	
Mrs Linda Rawlinson Braemuir, Spey Bay IV32 7PJ Tel. Fochabers (0343) 820430		Awaiting Inspection	2 Dble/Twin 1 Family	1 Private Bath/Sh 1 Public Bath/Sh	B&B per person £8.00 Double	Open Jan-Dec	
Mrs Morag Scott Monair, 83 High Street IV32 7PR Tel. Fochabers (0343) 820079			2 Dble/Twin 1 Family	1 Public Bath/Sh	B&B per person £8.00 Double	Open Jan-Dec Dinner 1730	
FORFAR **Angus** Mrs Craig Haven Cottage, 20 Craig O' Loch Road Tel. Forfar (0307) 67768	Map 2 D1	COMMENDED Listed	2 Dble/Twin 1 Family	1 Private Bath/Sh 1 Public Bath/Sh	B&B per person £8.00 Double	Open Jan-Dec Dinner 1800	

Personally run, home cooking. Near town centre.

FORGANDENNY Perthshire	Map 2 C3						
Mrs M J D Fotheringham Craighall Farm House PH2 9DF Tel. Bridge of Earn (0738) 2415			1 Single 2 Dble/Twin 1 Family	2 Private Bath/Sh 1 Public Bath/Sh	B&B per person £8.00 Single £7.50 Double	Open Mar-Nov Dinner 1800	
FORRES Moray	Map 4 C8						
Mr & Mrs W Bannerman Moray Park, Findhorn Road IV36 0TP Tel. Forres (0309) 72793			1 Single 3 Dble/Twin 1 Family	1 Public Bath/Sh	B&B per person £7.80-£8.00 Single £7.80-£8.00 Double	Open Apr-Oct Dinner 1730	
Mrs Flora Barclay Moss-Side Farm, Rafford IV36 0SL Tel. Forres (0309) 72954			1 Dble/Twin 1 Family	1 Public Bath/Sh	B&B per person £8.00 Double	Open May-Sep Dinner 1900	
Mrs K Elder Barleymill, Brodie IV36 0TE Tel. Brodie (03094) 218			3 Dble/Twin		B&B per person £8.50 Double	Open Jun-Sep	
Mrs Marian W Evans Cluny Bank, St Leonards Road IV36 0DW Tel. Forres (0309) 74676			5 Single 5 Dble/Twin 1 Family	4 Public Bath/Sh	B&B per person £10.00 Single £10.00 Double	Open Apr-Oct	
Mrs J Greene Lower Hempriggs Farm IV36 0UB Tel. Alves (034385) 252			1 Single 1 Dble/Twin 1 Family	1 Public Bath/Sh	B&B per person £6.50 Single £6.50 Double	Open Jan-Dec Dinner 1730	
Mrs Barbara Macdonald Morven, Caroline Street IV36 0AN Tel. Forres (0309) 73788			2 Dble/Twin	1 Public Bath/Sh	B&B per person £7.50-£8.00 Double	Open Jan-Dec	
Mrs S Morgan Arosdail, Woodhead, Kinloss IV36 0UE Tel. Forres (0309) 73303			1 Dble/Twin 1 Family	1 Public Bath/Sh	B&B per person £8.50 Double	Open May-Nov	
Mrs Alma Rhind Woodside, Kinloss IV36 0UA Tel. Forres(0309) 30258			2 Dble/Twin	2 Public Bath/Sh	B&B per person £7.50 Double	Open Apr-Oct	
Mrs Lindsay N Ross Tormhor, High Street IV36 0BU Tel. Forres (0309) 73837		Awaiting Inspection	1 Single 2 Family	1 Public Bath/Sh	B&B per person £8.00-£8.50 Single £8.00-£8.50 Double	Open Apr-Oct	
Mrs M Taylor The Bungalow, Lower Hempriggs Farm IV36 0UB Tel. Alves (034385) 252			1 Single 1 Dble/Twin 1 Family	1 Public Bath/Sh	B&B per person £7.00 Single £6.50 Double	Open Jan-Dec Dinner 1800	
Miss N Van Hurck Mayfield, Victoria Road IV36 0BN Tel. Forres (0309) 74863			2 Dble/Twin 1 Family	1 Public Bath/Sh	B&B per person £8.00-£8.25 Double	Open Jan-Dec	

FORT WILLIAM Inverness-shire	Map 3 G12					
Achintee Farm Guest House Achintee Tel. Fort William (0397) 2240/3667		👑👑	1 Single 4 Dble/Twin 1 Family	1 Public Bath/Sh	B&B per person £7.50-£10.00 Single £7.50-£10.00 Double	Open Jan-Dec Dinner 1800
Ben View Guest House Belford Road Tel. Fort William (0397) 2966			2 Single 12 Dble/Twin 1 Family	1 Private Bath/Sh 6 Public Bath/Sh	B&B per person £9.20-£12.65 Single £9.20-£12.00 Double	Open Mar-Dec Dinner 1845
Charlecote Guest House Alma Road Tel. Fort William (0397) 3288			2 Dble/Twin 3 Family	2 Private Bath/Sh 1 Public Bath/Sh	B&B per person £7.00-£8.00 Double	Open Jan-Dec Dinner 1830
Craig Nevis West Guest House Belford Road PH33 6BU Tel. Fort William (0397) 2023			4 Dble/Twin 2 Family	2 Public Bath/Sh	B&B per person £8.50-£9.00 Double	Open Jan-Dec Dinner 1815

DARAICH GUEST HOUSE
Cameron Road, Fort William, Inverness-shire.

"Daraich" is a granite-stone house built in 1892, set in an elevated situation, overlooking Loch Linnhe, and approximately 10 minutes' walk from Travel Centre and shops. Three bedrooms with electric blankets, wall heaters, shaver points and H&C are available for guests. There are 2 toilets and shower. Car parking in own ground at rear. Terms: B&B from £8.00
Telephone: 0397 2644.

Daraich Guest House Cameron Road Tel. Fort William (0397) 2644		Listed	1 Single 3 Family		B&B per person £8.00-£9.00 Single £8.00-£9.00 Double	Open Apr-Oct
Glen Shiel Guest House Achintore Road PH33 6RW Tel. Fort William (0397) 2271		COMMENDED 👑👑	4 Dble/Twin 1 Family	1 Private Bath/Sh 1 Public Bath/Sh	B&B per person £8.00 Double	Open Mar-Nov
			Modern, purpose built, situated on shore line with panoramic views over Loch Linnhe and mountains.			
Glenlochy Guest House Nevis Bridge Tel. Fort William (0397) 2909			6 Dble/Twin 2 Family	8 Private Bath/Sh 1 Public Bath/Sh	B&B per person £11.50-£11.80 Double	Open Mar-Nov
Guisachan Guest House Alma Road Tel. Fort William (0397) 3797/4447			3 Single 9 Dble/Twin 3 Family	4 Private Bath/Sh 3 Public Bath/Sh	B&B per person £9.00-£13.00 Single £9.00-£13.00 Double	Open Jan-Dec Dinner 1830
Hillview Guest House Achintore Road Tel. Fort William (0397) 4349		COMMENDED 👑	1 Single 6 Dble/Twin 2 Family	3 Public Bath/Sh	B&B per person £8.50 Single £8.50 Double	Open Jan-Dec Dinner 1830
			Family run, overlooking Loch Linnhe. About 2 mls (3 km) from town.			

FORT WILLIAM continued	Map 3 G12						
Kismet Villa Guest House Heathercroft, off Argyll Terrace Tel. Fort William (0397) 4476			3 Dble/Twin 1 Family	1 Public Bath/Sh	B&B per person £8.00 Double	Open Jan-Dec Dinner 1900	
Lochview Guest House Heathercroft, off Argyll Terrace PH33 6RE Tel. Fort William (0397) 3149		COMMENDED 👑 👑 👑	4 Dble/Twin 2 Family	4 Private Bath/Sh 2 Public Bath/Sh	B&B per person £8.50-£10.00 Double	Open Apr-Oct Dinner 1830	
			On hillside above town, giving panoramic views over Loch Linnhe and Ardgour Hills.				
Rhu Mhor Guest House Alma Road PH33 6BP Tel. Fort William (0397) 2213			5 Dble/Twin 2 Family	2 Public Bath/Sh	B&B per person £8.50-£9.00 Double	Open Apr-Sep Dinner 1900	
Stronchreggan View Guest House Achintore Road PH33 6RW Tel. Fort William (0397) 4644			4 Dble/Twin 3 Family	2 Public Bath/Sh	B&B per person £8.50-£9.50 Double	Open Apr-Oct Dinner 1900	
Torosay Guest House Cameron Road Tel. Fort William (0397) 4545			2 Dble/Twin 1 Family	1 Public Bath/Sh	B&B per person £9.00-£9.50 Double	Open Apr-Oct Dinner 1900	
Viewfield Guest House Alma Road Tel. Fort William (0397) 4763			2 Single 4 Dble/Twin	1 Public Bath/Sh	B&B per person £7.50-£8.50 Single £7.50-£8.50 Double	Open Jan-Dec Dinner 1830	
Mrs M Bruce 11 Mossfield Drive, Lochyside Tel. Fort William (0397) 3532			2 Dble/Twin	1 Public,Bath/Sh	B&B per person £7.50 Double	Open Apr-Oct	
Mrs Cameron Camanguseron, Achintore Road Tel. Fort William (0397) 4029			1 Single 1 Dble/Twin 1 Family	1 Public Bath/Sh	B&B per person £8.00 Single £8.00 Double	Open Mar-Oct	
Mrs I Campbell Dykelands, Camaghael Tel. Fort William (0397) 3819			2 Dble/Twin	1 Public Bath/Sh	B&B per person £9.00 Double	Open Apr-Aug Dinner 1830	
Mrs C Campbell 2 Caberfeidh, Fassifern Road Tel. Fort William (0397) 2533			2 Dble/Twin 1 Family	1 Public Bath/Sh	B&B per person £7.50 Double	Open Jan-Dec	
Mrs H Carabine Allt-Conasg, 13 Zetland Avenue Tel. Fort William (0397) 2771			3 Dble/Twin	1 Public Bath/Sh	B&B per person £7.50 Double	Open May-Oct	
Mrs F A Cook Melantee, Achintore Road PH33 6RW Tel. Fort William (0397) 5329			2 Dble/Twin 2 Family	1 Public Bath/Sh	B&B per person £7.50-£8.50 Double	Open Jan-Dec	

Key to symbols is on back flap. Details of Classification and Grading are on page vi.

99

	Map 3 G12						
FORT WILLIAM continued							
Mrs M Easson 13 Renfrew Place Tel. Fort William (0397) 2896			1 Single 2 Dble/Twin 1 Family	1 Private Bath/Sh 1 Public Bath/Sh	B&B per person £8.00-£8.50 Single £7.50-£8.00 Double	Open Apr-Oct Dinner 1830	
Mrs Gray The Birches, Lundavra Road PH33 6RD Tel. Fort William (0397) 2427			2 Dble/Twin 1 Family	1 Public Bath/Sh	B&B per person £7.50 Double	Open Apr-Oct	
Mrs M Hall 15 Banff Crescent Tel. Fort William (0397) 3654			2 Dble/Twin	1 Public Bath/Sh	B&B per person £7.50 Double	Open Jan-Dec Dinner 1830	
Mr P Hamilton 4 Caithness Place Tel. Fort William (0397) 4163			1 Single 1 Dble/Twin 3 Family		B&B per person £8.00 Double	Open Jan-Dec	
Mr & Mrs Hawkes Ballindalloch, 6 Galloway Place Tel. Fort William (0397) 4336	COMMENDED		2 Dble/Twin		B&B per person £7.50-£8.50 Double	Open Mar-Oct Dinner 1830	
			Modern, situated above town, with excellent views of surrounding countryside.				
Mrs M B Howie Glenfalloch, Argyll Road PH33 6LD Tel. Fort William (0397) 2592			2 Dble/Twin 1 Family	1 Public Bath/Sh	B&B per person £8.00 Double	Open Jan-Dec	
Mrs E Kearney 14 Dumbarton Road Tel. Fort William (0397) 2712			1 Single 1 Dble/Twin	1 Public Bath/Sh	B&B per person £7.50 Single	Open Jan-Dec Dinner 1830	
Mrs MacNicol 10 Henderson Row Tel. Fort William (0397) 5466			1 Single 2 Dble/Twin	1 Public Bath/Sh	B&B per person £7.50 Single £7.50 Double	Open Jan-Dec Dinner 1900	
Mrs Macdonald 23 Alma Road Tel. Fort William (0397) 3172			1 Family	1 Public Bath/Sh	B&B per person £7.00 Double	Open Jan-Dec	
Mrs Macdonald Glenmoidart, Fassifern Road Tel. Fort William (0397) 2016			1 Single 3 Dble/Twin	1 Public Bath/Sh	B&B per person £7.50 Single £7.50 Double	Open Jan-Dec	
Mrs Shirley Macpherson Rose Arden, Lochyside PH33 7NX Tel. Fort William (0397) 2800			3 Dble/Twin 1 Family	2 Public Bath/Sh	B&B per person £8.00 Double	Open Apr-Oct	
Mrs McMorris Roseburn, Seafield Gardens Tel. Fort William (0397) 4192			2 Dble/Twin	1 Private Bath/Sh 1 Public Bath/Sh	B&B per person £7.50 Double	Open Apr-Oct	
Mrs M Sandison Roanne, 4 Cromarty Crescent Tel. Fort William (0397) 4735			2 Dble/Twin	2 Public Bath/Sh	B&B per person £8.00-£8.50 Double	Open Jan-Dec	

VAT is shown at 15%; changes in this rate may affect prices. Prices shown are for guidance only. Please send SAE with each enquiry.

	Map	Grading	Rooms	Bath	B&B	Open	
FORT WILLIAM continued Mrs Winifred Seaman Ceol-na-Mara, 7 Kinross Pl, Upr Achintore Tel. Fort William (0397) 3771	Map 3 G12		2 Dble/Twin	1 Public Bath/Sh	B&B per person £7.00 Double	Open Apr-Oct	(symbols)
Mrs J Simpson The Tryst, 2 Mossfield Drive Tel. Fort William (0397) 3605			3 Dble/Twin	1 Public Bath/Sh	B&B per person £8.50 Double	Open May-Sep Dinner 1800	(symbols)
Mrs Wardle 16 Perth Place Tel. Fort William (0397) 4392			1 Dble/Twin	1 Public Bath/Sh	B&B per person £6.50 Double	Open Jan-Dec	(symbols)
Mrs Wiseman 17 Mossfield Drive, Lochyside Tel. Fort William (0397) 3502			1 Dble/Twin 1 Family	1 Private Bath/Sh 1 Public Bath/Sh	B&B per person £7.50-£8.00 Double	Open Apr-Oct	(symbols)
Mrs R Wynne St Andrews East, Fassfern Road Tel. Fort William (0397) 2337			1 Single 2 Dble/Twin 1 Family	2 Public Bath/Sh	B&B per person £6.50-£7.00 Single £7.00-£8.00 Double	Open Jun-Sep	(symbols)
FORTINGALL Perthshire Mrs Tulloch Fendoch PH15 2LL Tel. Kenmore (08873) 322	Map 2 A1		2 Dble/Twin 1 Family	1 Public Bath/Sh	B&B per person £8.00-£9.00 Double	Open Mar-Oct Dinner 1800	(symbols)
FORTROSE Ross-shire Saint Katherines Guest House Union Street Tel. Fortrose (0381) 20949	Map 4 B8	COMMENDED 👑 👑	3 Dble/Twin	1 Public Bath/Sh	B&B per person £10.00 Double	Open Apr-Oct Dinner 1830	(symbols)
Period house of historical interest standing in own large garden, near Fortrose Cathedral.							
FOYERS Inverness-shire Mr & Mrs Boag Loch Ness Leathercraft, 14/17 Glenlia IV1 2XX Tel. Gorthleck (04563) 367	Map 4 A10		2 Single 3 Dble/Twin	2 Public Bath/Sh	B&B per person £8.50-£9.50 Single £8.50-£9.50 Double	Open Mar-Nov Dinner 1800	(symbols)
FRASERBURGH Aberdeenshire Mrs J Alexander Lancaster House, 14 Victoria Street AB4 5PJ Tel. Fraserburgh (0346) 23612	Map 4 H7		1 Single 2 Dble/Twin 1 Family	1 Public Bath/Sh	B&B per person £8.00 Single £8.00 Double	Open May-Sep Dinner 1800	(symbols)
Mrs M Greig Clifton House, 131 Charlotte Street Tel. Fraserburgh (0346) 28365		APPROVED 👑 👑	1 Single 1 Dble/Twin 1 Family		B&B per person £8.50 Single £8.50 Double	Open Jan-Dec Dinner 1700	(symbols)
In modern housing scheme. Close to shops and town's conservation area.							

Key to symbols is on back flap. Details of Classification and Grading are on page vi.

101

	Map						
FRASERBURGH continued	Map 4 H7						
Mrs Lovie 13 Philorth Avenue Tel. Fraserburgh (0346) 28523			2 Dble/Twin	1 Public Bath/Sh	B&B per person £7.00 Double	Open Jan-Dec Dinner 1730	♨ ▥ 📺 🐎 ❄ P C
Mrs H Wadsworth 61a Saltoun Place, Middle Flat AB4 5RY Tel. Fraserburgh (0346) 28884			1 Dble/Twin	1 Public Bath/Sh	B&B per person £7.50 Double	Open Jan-Dec	V ♨ 📺 🐎 ✂ P C
FRESWICK, by Wick Caithness	Map 4 E3						
A M Wares Tofts House Tel. John O'Groats (095581) 204			4 Dble/Twin 2 Family	1 Public Bath/Sh	B&B per person £7.00 Double	Open Jan-Dec Dinner 1800	♠ ♨ V ♨ ▥ 📺 ⚲ 🐎 ✂ P C ⚲
FURNACE Argyll	Map 1 F4						
Mrs Goodheir Woodside Cottage Tel. Furnace (04995) 258			1 Dble/Twin	1 Public Bath/Sh	B&B per person £7.50 Double	Open Apr-Oct	▥ ✂ △ C
GAIRLOCH Ross-shire	Map 3 F7	COMMENDED ♛					
Charleston Guest House IV21 2AH Tel. Gairloch (0445) 2497			2 Single 4 Dble/Twin 3 Family	2 Public Bath/Sh	B&B per person £8.00 Single £8.00 Double	Open Apr-Oct Dinner 1900	♠ V ♨ ▥ 📺 ⚲ ♨ 🐎 P △ C
			Modernised 18C house, situated on loch side with excellent views over loch and hills beyond.				

HORISDALE HOUSE

Strath, Gairloch, Ross-shire IV21 2DA
Telephone: 0445 2151

Purpose-built guest house with panoramic views of sea and mountains. We offer comfortably furnished bedrooms equipped with tea/coffee-making facilities; spacious lounge with open fire; separate dining room where traditional Scottish breakfasts are served. Our imaginative evening meals by prior arrangement only.

Reduced terms for five-night stays. Special consideration given to non-smokers. Early bookings advised.

S.A.E. please, for details.   *AA LISTED*

Horisdale House Strath IV21 2DA Tel. Gairloch (0445) 2151		COMMENDED ♛ ♛	2 Single 4 Dble/Twin 3 Family	3 Public Bath/Sh	B&B per person £11.50 Single £11.00 Double	Open May-Sep Dinner 1900	♠ ♨ ⬛ V ♨ ▥ ⚲ ♨ ⚲ ❄ ✂ P
			Modern detached house with attractive garden. Home cooking; emphasis on fresh produce. TV on request.				
Mrs A Elder Arlberg, Achtercairn Tel. Gairloch (0445) 2482			3 Dble/Twin	1 Public Bath/Sh	B&B per person £7.00-£8.00 Double	Open Apr-Oct Dinner 1900	♠ ♨ ⬛ V ♨ ▥ 📺 ♨ ♨ ❄ P △ ⚲ C

   VAT is shown at 15%: changes in this rate may affect prices. Prices shown are for guidance only. Please send SAE with each enquiry.

	Map	Grading	Rooms	Bath	Rates	Open/Dinner	Symbols
GAIRLOCH continued Mrs J Elder 33 Big Sand Tel. Gairloch (0445) 2080	Map 3 F7	Listed	3 Dble/Twin	1 Private Bath/Sh 1 Public Bath/Sh	B&B per person £8.00-£8.50 Double	Open Apr-Oct Dinner 1800	[symbols]
Mrs J Hirst 13 Big Sand Tel. Gairloch (0445) 2033			2 Dble/Twin 1 Family	1 Public Bath/Sh	B&B per person £7.50-£8.00 Double	Open Jan-Dec Dinner 1800	[symbols]
Mrs I Hunter Myrtle Croft, 20 Big Sand IV21 2DD Tel. Gairloch (0445) 2129			2 Dble/Twin 1 Family	1 Public Bath/Sh	B&B per person £9.00 Single £9.00 Double	Open May-Oct Dinner 1800	[symbols]
Miss I MacKenzie Duisary, 24 Strath IV21 2DA Tel. Gairloch (0445) 2252			1 Single 1 Dble/Twin 1 Family	1 Public Bath/Sh	B&B per person £7.00 Single £7.00 Double	Open May-Oct	[symbols]
Mrs M A L Mackenzie 6 Mihol Road, Strath IV21 2BX Tel. Gairloch (0445) 2162			1 Single 1 Dble/Twin 1 Family	1 Public Bath/Sh	B&B per person £7.50-£8.00 Single £7.50-£8.00 Double	Open May-Sep	[symbols]
Mrs McDaniel Beaufort, Lonemore Tel. Gairloch (0445) 2060			1 Single 2 Dble/Twin		B&B per person £7.50-£8.00 Single £7.50-£8.00 Double	Open Mar-Nov Dinner 1900	[symbols]
Mrs Spalding Askernish, Strath IV21 2BZ Tel. Gairloch (0445) 2189			1 Single 1 Dble/Twin 1 Family	1 Public Bath/Sh	B&B per person £8.50 Single £8.00 Double	Open Apr-Oct	[symbols]
Miss I M Wylie Strathgair House IV21 2BT Tel. Gairloch (0445) 2118			3 Dble/Twin	1 Public Bath/Sh	B&B per person £8.50-£9.00 Double	Open Apr-Aug Dinner 1830	[symbols]
GAIRLOCHY, by Spean Bridge **Inverness-shire** Old Pines Guest House Tel. Spean Bridge (039781) 324	Map 3 H11	Awaiting Inspection	1 Single 4 Dble/Twin		B&B per person £7.50-£8.50 Single £7.50-£8.50 Double	Open Apr-Oct Dinner 1900	[symbols]
GALASHIELS **Selkirkshire** Buckholmburn Guest House & Coffee Shop Edinburgh Road TD1 2EY Tel. Galashiels (0896) 2697	Map 2 E6	COMMENDED 👑 👑	1 Single 4 Dble/Twin 3 Family	4 Private Bath/Sh 1 Public Bath/Sh	B&B per person £15.00 Single £13.00 Double	Open Jan-Dec Dinner 1800	[symbols]
			Substantial victorian building in own grounds overlooking River Gala. Under owners supervision.				
Osmond House Guest House Bank Street Tel. Galashiels (0896) 56437		Awaiting Inspection	4 Single 3 Dble/Twin	1 Public Bath/Sh	B&B per person £8.50 Single £8.00 Double	Open Jan-Dec Dinner 1700	[symbols]
Mr Brown Island House, 65 Island Street Tel. Galashiels (0896) 2649		COMMENDED Listed	1 Single 2 Family	1 Public Bath/Sh	B&B per person £8.00-£9.00 Single £8.00-£9.00 Double	Open Jan-Dec	[symbols]
			Stone semi villa with many attractive features. Near River Gala and short walk to town centre.				

Key to symbols is on back flap. Details of Classification and Grading are on page vi.

103

	Map		Rooms	Bath	B&B	Open	Facilities
GALASHIELS continued Mrs S Field Ettrickvale, 33 Abbotsford Road TD1 3HW Tel. Galashiels (0896) 55224	Map 2 E8		3 Dble/Twin	1 Public Bath/Sh	B&B per person £8.50 Double	Open Jan-Dec	
Mrs S Jamieson Monorene, 23 Stirling Street TD1 1BY Tel. Galashiels (0896) 3073			3 Dble/Twin 2 Family	1 Public Bath/Sh	B&B per person £9.00-£10.00 Double	Open Jan-Dec Dinner 1800	
Mrs J McLaren Dungallan, 30 Abbotsford Road Tel. Galashiels (0896) 4257			1 Dble/Twin 1 Family		B&B per person £8.00-£9.00 Double	Open Apr-Oct Dinner 1800	
Mrs M V Park Parkvilla, 69 Gala Park TD1 1EZ Tel. Galashiels (0896) 3437			1 Single 2 Dble/Twin 1 Family	1 Private Bath/Sh 1 Public Bath/Sh	B&B per person £8.50-£9.50 Single £8.50-£9.50 Double	Open Jan-Dec	
Mrs A M Platt Wakefield Bank, 9 Abbotsford Road TD1 3DP Tel. Galashiels (0896) 2641			2 Dble/Twin 1 Family	2 Public Bath/Sh	B&B per person £8.50-£9.50 Double	Open Apr-Oct Dinner 1800	
GALSTON Ayrshire Mrs J Bone Auchencloigh Farm KA4 8NP Tel. Galston (0563) 820567	Map 1 H7	Listed	1 Dble/Twin 1 Family	1 Public Bath/Sh	B&B per person £8.50 Double	Open Apr-Oct Dinner 1830	
GAMRIE, by Banff Banffshire	Map 4 G7						

Bankhead Croft (MRS SMITH)
GARDENSTOWN   Telephone: (02615) 584
Delightful modern country cottage in peaceful surroundings.
Two double bedrooms and shared bathroom. Bed and breakfast
plus half or full board if required. Home baking a speciality.
Banff 6 miles, Gardenstown and Pennan 4 miles.
Large caravan also available.
Come for a country holiday in "Local Hero" country.

	Map		Rooms	Bath	B&B	Open	Facilities
Mrs L Smith Bankhead Croft AB4 3HN Tel. Gardenstown (02615) 584			2 Dble/Twin	1 Public Bath/Sh	B&B per person £7.00-£7.50 Double	Open Jan-Dec Dinner 1800	
GARDENSTOWN Banffshire Mrs Fraser Cottage Farm Tel. Gardenstown (02615) 580	Map 4 G7		2 Dble/Twin 2 Family	1 Public Bath/Sh	B&B per person £8.00-£9.50 Double	Open Apr-Oct Dinner 1800	

GARELOCHHEAD Dunbartonshire Mrs Tamara Lepp The Old Manse G84 0AY Tel. Garelochhead (0436) 810226	Map 1 G4		1 Dble/Twin 1 Family	1 Public Bath/Sh	B&B per person £8.50-£10.50 Double	Open Apr-Oct Dinner 1830
GARRION BRIDGE, Wishaw Lanarkshire Mrs J S Pinkerton The Mill House ML2 0RR Tel. Larkhall (0698) 881166	Map 2 A6		2 Dble/Twin 2 Family	1 Public Bath/Sh	B&B per person £8.50-£9.00 Double	Open Jan-Dec
GARTLY, by Huntly Aberdeenshire Mrs Margaret I Grant Faich Hill AB5 4RR Tel. Gartly (046688) 240	Map 4 F9		1 Single 2 Dble/Twin	2 Public Bath/Sh	B&B per person £8.00-£9.00 Single £8.00-£9.00 Double	Open Jan-Dec Dinner 1830
GARTMORE, by Stirling Perthshire Mrs H M Graham The Lochans, Main Street FK8 3RJ Tel. Aberfoyle (08772) 318	Map 1 H4		1 Single 2 Dble/Twin	1 Public Bath/Sh	B&B per person £8.00 Single £8.00 Double	Open Apr-Oct Dinner 1800
Mrs Matheson Errigal Tel. Aberfoyle (08772) 472			2 Dble/Twin	1 Public Bath/Sh	B&B per person £7.50 Double	Open Jan-Dec Dinner 1900
Mrs J Samwell-Smith Forth House FK8 3RW Tel. Aberfoyle (08772) 646			2 Dble/Twin	1 Public Bath/Sh	B&B per person £8.50 Double	Open Jan-Dec Dinner 1800
GARTOCHARN, by Alexandria Dunbartonshire Mrs M L Hill Gowk Inn G83 8ND Tel. Gartocharn (038983) 224	Map 1 H4		2 Dble/Twin 1 Family	2 Public Bath/Sh	B&B per person £9.50 Double	Open Apr-Oct
GARVE Ross-shire Mrs J Hollingdale The Old Manse Tel. Garve (09974) 201	Map 3 H8		2 Dble/Twin	1 Public Bath/Sh	B&B per person £7.00 Double	Open Jan-Dec Dinner 1900
Mrs J. Wilcox Keepers House, Strathgarve IV23 2PU Tel. Garve (09974) 301			2 Dble/Twin	1 Public Bath/Sh	B&B per person £7.00 Double	Open Jan-Dec Dinner 1900
GATEHOUSE-OF-FLEET Kirkcudbrightshire The Bobbin Guest House 36 High Street DG7 2HP Tel. Gatehouse (05574) 229	Map 2 A10		1 Single 3 Dble/Twin 3 Family	1 Private Bath/Sh 1 Public Bath/Sh	B&B per person £8.50-£10.00 Single £8.50-£10.00 Double	Open Jan-Dec Dinner 1830

GATEHOUSE-OF-FLEET continued	Map 2 A10						
Mrs W Johnstone High Auchenlarie Farmhouse Tel. Mossyard (055724) 231		APPROVED ♛	2 Dble/Twin 1 Family	1 Public Bath/Sh	B&B per person £8.00 Double	Open Mar-Oct Dinner 1800	🚜 ♨ 📺 🐾 🅿 ⓒ 🐖
			Working farm in prominent setting with views of the Fleet and Wigtown Bays.				
Mr & Mrs I Kerr Girthon Kirk House, Sandgreen Road Tel. Gatehouse of Fleet (05574) 770			2 Dble/Twin 1 Family	1 Private Bath/Sh 1 Public Bath/Sh	B&B per person £8.50-£10.00 Double	Open Apr-Oct Dinner 1900	🚜 ☕ Ⓥ ♨ 📺 🖥 🅿 ⓒ
Mrs Taylor Disdow Farm Tel. Gatehouse (05574) 286			3 Dble/Twin	1 Public Bath/Sh	B&B per person £8.00 Double	Open Apr-Oct	✳ 🅿 🐖
GATTONSIDE, by Melrose Roxburghshire	Map 2 E6						
Mrs Wilkie Derwent Villa Tel. Melrose (089682) 2472			1 Single 1 Dble/Twin	1 Public Bath/Sh	B&B per person £9.00-£9.50 Single £11.00 Double	Open Apr-Oct	🛏 🖥 ✳ 🅿
GIRVAN Ayrshire	Map 1 G9						

Appin Cottage ♛ ♛ ♛ COMMENDED

27/29 Ailsa Street West, Girvan.   Tel. 0465 3214

A warm Scottish welcome awaits you in our small guest house. Home cooking, individual attention. Central for harbour, beach and town centre. HC, CH, colour TV and tea/coffee making facilities in all bedrooms. Ideal centre for touring the Burns Country and South West Scotland. Resident owners. Open all year.

Bed, Breakfast from £8; Bed, Breakfast, Evening Dinner from £12.

Appin Cottage Guest House 27/29 Ailsa Street West KA26 9AD Tel. Girvan (0465) 3214	COMMENDED ♛ ♛ ♛	1 Single 1 Dble/Twin 1 Family	1 Public Bath/Sh	B&B per person £10.00 Single £8.00-£10.00 Double	Open Jan-Dec Dinner 1830	🚜 📼 □ ☕ Ⓥ 🛏 ♨ 🖥 📺 🅿 ⓒ
		Converted fishermen's cottages. Dinner including vegetarian meals available.				
Gowanbrae Guest House 45 Henrietta Street KA26 9AL Tel. Girvan (0465) 2316		1 Single 3 Dble/Twin 2 Family	1 Public Bath/Sh	B&B per person £8.00-£8.50 Single £8.00-£8.50 Double	Open Jan-Dec Dinner 1730	🛏 Ⓥ ♨ 🖥 📺 🐾 🅿 ⓒ
Thistleneuk Guest House 19 Louisa Drive KA26 9AH Tel. Girvan (0465) 2137	COMMENDED ♛ ♛	1 Single 3 Dble/Twin 3 Family	1 Public Bath/Sh	B&B per person £9.00-£10.00 Single £8.50-£9.50 Double	Open Jan-Dec Dinner 1800	🚜 🛏 Ⓥ ♨ 📺 ✳ 🅿 ⓒ 📺 🏙
		19C terraced house on seafront overlooking Ailsa Craig. Within easy walking distance of town centre.				
Troohrogue Guest House KA26 9QA Tel. Girvan (0465) 2074		9 Single 9 Dble/Twin 5 Family	2 Private Bath/Sh 6 Public Bath/Sh	B&B per person £15.00-£17.00 Single £15.00-£17.00 Double	Open Jan-Nov Dinner 1800	🚜 🛏 Ⓥ 🛏 🍷 ♨ 🖥 ⬆ 📺 🖥 🅿 ✂ ✳ 🍽 🅿 🔍 ⓒ
Mrs Hughes Blair Farm, Barrhill KA26 0RD Tel. Barrhill (046582) 247	Awaiting Inspection	1 Dble/Twin 1 Family	1 Public Bath/Sh	B&B per person £7.50-£8.00 Double	Open May-Sep Dinner 1800	♨ 🖥 📺 🐾 🅿 🐖 🔺 ⓒ

VAT is shown at 15%; changes in this rate may affect prices. Prices shown are for guidance only. Please send SAE with each enquiry.

	Map 1					
GIRVAN continued Mr & Mrs McIntosh Glendrissaig House KA26 0HU Tel. Girvan (0465) 4631	G9		2 Dble/Twin 1 Family	1 Private Bath/Sh 1 Public Bath/Sh	B&B per person £9.00-£12.00 Double	Open Mar-Nov Dinner 1830
Mrs M Wilson Dunrovyn, 41 Henrietta St Tel. Girvan (0465) 2196			1 Dble/Twin 1 Family	1 Public Bath/Sh	B&B per person £10.00-£11.00 Double	Open Apr-Oct Dinner 1700
GLASGOW The Alamo Guest House 46 Gray Street G3 7SE Tel. 041 339 2395	Map 1 H5		2 Single 4 Dble/Twin 2 Family	2 Public Bath/Sh	B&B per person £8.00 Single £7.00 Double	Open Jan-Dec
Aldara Guest House 5 Bentinck Street G3 7SB Tel. 041 339 0852/0928	APPROVED Listed		2 Dble/Twin 3 Family	2 Public Bath/Sh	B&B per person £8.50-£9.50 Double	Open Jan-Dec
		Traditional tenement in quiet street near Kelvingrove Park.				
Belle Vue Guest House 163 Hamilton Road, Mount Vernon G32 9QT Tel. 041 778 1077	Listed		3 Single 7 Dble/Twin 2 Family	1 Private Bath/Sh 1 Public Bath/Sh	B&B per person £12.50 Single £9.50 Double	Open Jan-Dec Dinner 1750
Charing Cross Guest House 310 Renfrew Street Tel. 041 332 7894			2 Single 4 Dble/Twin 2 Family	1 Public Bath/Sh	B&B per person £11.00-£12.00 Single £10.00 Double	Open Jan-Dec
Chez Nous Guest House 33 Hillhead Street G12 8PX Tel. 041 334 2977			7 Single 7 Dble/Twin 3 Family	4 Public Bath/Sh	B&B per person £10.50 Single £9.00 Double	Open Jan-Dec
Glades Guest House 142 Albert Road G42 8UF Tel. 041 423 4911	Listed		1 Single 5 Dble/Twin 2 Family	2 Public Bath/Sh	B&B per person £8.50-£9.00 Single £8.00-£9.00 Double	Open Jan-Dec
Iona Guest House 39 Hillhead Street G12 8TX Tel. 041 334 2346			3 Single 3 Dble/Twin 3 Family	2 Public Bath/Sh	B&B per person £12.00 Single £9.00 Double	Open Jan-Dec Dinner 1800
McLays Guest House 268 Renfrew Street G3 6TT Tel. 041 332 4796	APPROVED 👑 👑		6 Single 10 Dble/Twin 4 Family	4 Private Bath/Sh 5 Public Bath/Sh	B&B per person £12.00 Single £12.00 Double	Open Jan-Dec
		Quiet yet close to city centre, convenient for all amenities and main routes.				
Peveril Guest House 16 Onslow Drive G31 2LX Tel. 041 554 5481/041 556 1413			2 Dble/Twin 1 Family	1 Public Bath/Sh	B&B per person £9.00 Double	Open Jan-Dec Dinner 1700
Rosemundy Guest House 50 Bentinck Street G3 7TT Tel. 041 339 8220			2 Single 5 Dble/Twin 2 Family	2 Public Bath/Sh	B&B per person £10.00 Single £8.00 Double	Open Jan-Dec

Key to symbols is on back flap. Details of Classification and Grading are on page vi.

107

GLASGOW continued	Map 1 H5					
Wilkies Guest House 16 Hillhead Street G12 8PY Tel. 041 339 6898		2 Single 9 Dble/Twin 2 Family	6 Private Bath/Sh 4 Public Bath/Sh	B&B per person £9.50-£10.00 Single £9.50-£10.50 Double	Open Jan-Dec	

Jordanhill College of Education
76 Southbrae Drive, Glasgow G13 1PP

170 rooms in 120 acres of parkland, 10 minutes from city centre on train and bus routes. Families and groups enjoy swimming, tennis, table tennis, squash, weights room, sports pitch and games hall. Resident sports coaches. Visit the pleasures and treasures of Glasgow, tour Burns' country and the West Highlands. Friendly staff welcome you to a unique holiday. Bed and Breakfast from £12.25. Group rates available.

For full details: Mr D. C. Wilkie, telephone 041-959 1232, ext. 292.

Hostel Accommodation Jordanhill College, 76 Southbrae Drive G13 1PP Tel. 041 959 1232 Ext 292		170 Single 2 Dble/Twin	18 Public Bath/Sh	B&B per person £12.25 Single £10.00 Double	Open Apr, Jul-Sep Dinner 1730	
Garnett Hall, Univ of Strathclyde Cathedral Street Tel. 041 552 4400 Ext 3560		124 Single	38 Public Bath/Sh	B&B per person £13.50 Single	Open Jun-Sep Dinner 1900	
Dalrymple Hall, University of Glasgow 22 Belhaven Terrace West G12 0UW Tel. 041 339 5271		77 Single 52 Dble/Twin 4 Family	19 Public Bath/Sh	B&B per person £11.00-£13.00 Single £11.00-£13.00 Double	Open Mar-Apr Jun-Sep Dinner 1730	
Univ. of Glasgow Queen Margaret Hall 55 Bellshaugh Road G12 0SQ Tel. 041 334 2192		330 Single 15 Dble/Twin	50 Public Bath/Sh	B&B per person £11.00-£13.00 Single £11.00-£13.00 Double	Open Mar-Apr Jun-Sep Dinner 1800	
University of Glasgow, Reith Hall 10-13 Botanic Crescent Tel. 041 945 1636		75 Single 15 Dble/Twin	25 Public Bath/Sh	B&B per person £11.00-£13.00 Single £11.00-£13.00 Double	Open Mar-Apr, Jul-Sep Dinner 1730	
The Warden Glasgow University Horslethill House, 7 Horslethill Road G12 9LY Tel. 041 339 9943		7 Single 22 Dble/Twin	8 Public Bath/Sh	B&B per person £11.00-£13.00 Single £11.00-£13.00 Double	Open Mar-Apr, Jul-Sep Dinner 1800	
University of Glasgow, Wolfson Hall Garscube Estate, Maryhill Road G20 0TH Tel. 041 946 5252		213 Single 18 Dble/Twin	39 Public Bath/Sh	B&B per person £11.00-£13.00 Single £11.00-£13.00 Double	Open Mar-Apr, Jul-Sep Dinner 1730	
Baird Hall, Univ. of Strathclyde 460 Sauchiehall Street Tel. 041 552 4400 Ext 3560 Telex 77472		65 Single 115 Dble/Twin 5 Family	25 Public Bath/Sh	B&B per person £13.75 Single	Open Jan-Dec Dinner 1730	

VAT is shown at 15%: changes in this rate may affect prices. Prices shown are for guidance only. Please send SAE with each enquiry.

Name	Map	Grading	Rooms	Bath	B&B	Opening	Symbols
GLASGOW continued Forbes Hall, Univ. of Strathclyde Rottenrow East Tel. 041 552 4400 Ext 3560	Map 1 H5		104 Single	32 Public Bath/Sh	B&B per person £13.50 Single	Open Jun-Sep Dinner 1900	
Business School Univ. of Strathclyde 130 Rottenrow G4 0HG Tel. 041 552 4400 Ext 3560 Telex 77472			80 Single	80 Private Bath/Sh	B&B per person £19.26 Single	Open Jan-Dec Dinner 1800	
Murray Hall, Univ of Strathclyde Collins Street G4 0NG Tel. 041 552 4400 Ext 3560 Telex 77472			94 Single		B&B per person £13.75 Single	Open Mar-Apr Jul-Sep Dinner 1730	
Y M C A Glasgow, Residential Club David Naismith Ct, 33 Petershill Dr G21 4QH Tel. 041 558 6166			12 Single 4 Dble/Twin	4 Public Bath/Sh	B&B per person £6.50 Single £6.50 Double	Open Jul-Sep	
Mrs I Adey 21 Hayburn Crescent G11 5AY Tel. 041 357 2097		Listed	2 Dble/Twin 1 Family	1 Public Bath/Sh	B&B per person £9.00-£10.00 Double	Open May-Sep	
Mrs K Boyle 31 Berelands Cres, Rutherglen Tel. 041 647 8464			2 Dble/Twin	1 Public Bath/Sh	B&B per person £7.50-£8.00 Double	Open Jan-Dec	
Mrs C Divers Kirkland House, 42 St Vincent Crescent G3 8NG Tel. 041 248 3458			2 Single 2 Dble/Twin 1 Family	3 Private Bath/Sh 1 Public Bath/Sh	B&B per person £16.00 Single £15.00 Double	Open Jan-Dec	
Mrs R Easton 148 Queen's Drive G42 8QN Tel. 041 423 3143		COMMENDED	1 Dble/Twin 1 Family	1 Public Bath/Sh	B&B per person £9.00 Double	Open Jan-Dec	
			Part of 19C tenement, overlooking Queens Park. Convenient for the Burrell Collection and city centre.				
Mrs J Freebairn-Smith 14 Prospect Avenue, Cambuslang G72 8BW Tel. 041 641 5055			1 Single 2 Dble/Twin	1 Public Bath/Sh	B&B per person £8.50 Single £8.50 Double	Open Jan-Dec Dinner 1700	
Mrs N Nalliah 609 Coatbridge Road, Bargeddie G69 7PH Tel. 041 771 0515			4 Dble/Twin	2 Public Bath/Sh	B&B per person £7.50-£8.50 Double	Open Jan-Dec	
GLEN LYON, Aberfeldy **Perthshire** Mrs K A Conway Dalchiorlich PH15 2PX Tel. Bridge of Balgie (08876) 226	Map 2 A1	Listed	1 Dble/Twin 1 Family	1 Public Bath/Sh	B&B per person £6.50-£7.00 Double	Open Jan-Dec Dinner 1800	

Key to symbols is on back flap. Details of Classification and Grading are on page vi.

109

	Map	Award	Rooms	Bath/Shower	Prices	Open	Facilities
GLEN LYON, Aberfeldy continued Mrs M Holroyd Easter Invervar PH15 2PL Tel. Glen Lyon (08877) 214	Map 2 A1		2 Dble/Twin	1 Public Bath/Sh	B&B per person £11.50 Double	Open Jan-Dec Dinner 1900	
GLENBRITTLE **Isle of Skye, Inverness-shire** Mrs J Akroyd Stac Lee Tel. Carbost (047842) 289	Map 3 D10		3 Dble/Twin	2 Public Bath/Sh	B&B per person **£7.50 Double**	Open Jan-Oct Dinner 1830	
Mr Robert Van der Vliet 3 Forestry Cottages, Eynort Tel. Carbost (047842) 320			3 Dble/Twin	1 Public Bath/Sh	B&B per person £7.00 Double	Open Jan-Dec Dinner 1800	
GLENCOE **Argyll** Scorry Breac Guest House Tel. Ballachulish (08552) 354	Map 1 F1		4 Dble/Twin 1 Family	1 Public Bath/Sh	B&B per person £8.50-£9.50 Double	Open Jan-Dec Dinner 1800	
GLENDEVON, Dollar **Clackmannanshire** Mrs P M Forrester St Serfs FK14 7JX Tel. Muckhart (025981) 438	Map 2 B3	⬥ (crown)	1 Single 2 Family	1 Public Bath/Sh	B&B per person £9.00 Single £9.00 Double	Open Apr-Oct Dinner 1900	
Mrs M Taylor Rosslyn House FK14 7JY Tel. Glendevon (025982) 254			1 Single 3 Dble/Twin 1 Family	1 Private Bath/Sh 2 Public Bath/Sh	B&B per person £8.50-£9.00 Single £8.00-£12.50 Double	Open Jan-Dec Dinner 1800	
GLENFARG **Perthshire** Mrs Lawrie Candy Farm Tel. Glenfarg (05773) 217	Map 2 C3	COMMENDED ⬥ (crown)	3 Dble/Twin	1 Public Bath/Sh	B&B per person £9.00 Double	Open Apr-Oct Dinner 1830	
On 520 acre farm east of Ochil Hills; views from sun lounge. Fishing boat for hire on reservoir.							
GLENFORSA, by Salen **Isle of Mull, Argyll** Mrs D Macgilvary The Bungalow PA72 6JN Tel. Aros (06803) 335	Map 1 D2		2 Dble/Twin	1 Public Bath/Sh	B&B per person £8.50-£9.00 Double	Open Apr-Oct	
Mrs Macphail Callachally Farm Tel. Aros (06803) 424			2 Dble/Twin 1 Family	1 Public Bath/Sh	B&B per person £8.50-£9.00 Double	Open Apr-Oct	
GLENHINNISDAL, **Snizort** **Isle of Skye, Inverness-shire** Mrs Wilson Garrybuie, 4 Balmeanach Tel. Uig (047042) 310	Map 3 D8		1 Single 1 Dble/Twin 2 Family	1 Private Bath/Sh 1 Public Bath/Sh	B&B per person £8.00 Single £8.00 Double	Open Apr-Oct Dinner 1830	

VAT is shown at 15%: changes in this rate may affect prices. Prices shown are for guidance only. Please send SAE with each enquiry.

GLENISLA **Perthshire** Highland Adventure Activity Centre Knockshannoch PH11 8PE Tel. Glenisla (057582) 207/238	Map 2 C1		10 Family		B&B per person £7.50 Double	Open Jan-Dec Dinner 1800
Mrs L MacPherson Reekie Linn House, Kilry PH11 8MP Tel. Lintrathen (05756) 219			2 Dble/Twin	1 Private Bath/Sh 2 Public Bath/Sh	B&B per person £6.50 Double	Open Jan-Dec Dinner 1700
GLENLUCE **Wigtownshire** Rowantree Guest House 38 Main Street Tel. Glenluce (05813) 244	Map 1 G10		4 Dble/Twin	1 Public Bath/Sh	B&B per person £8.50 Double	Open Jan-Dec Dinner 1830
Mrs A Marshall Kirkland, 14 North Street Tel. Glenluce (05813) 270			2 Dble/Twin	1 Public Bath/Sh	B&B per person £8.00 Double	Open Jan-Dec Dinner 1800
Mrs M Stewart Bankfield Farm DG8 0JF Tel. Glenluce (05813) 281			3 Dble/Twin 1 Family	1 Public Bath/Sh	B&B per person £7.50 Double	Open Apr-Oct Dinner 1800
Mrs Wilson Ardville Tel. Glenluce (05813) 240			2 Dble/Twin 1 Family	1 Public Bath/Sh	B&B per person £8.00 Double	Open Jan-Dec Dinner 1800
GLENMAVIS, Airdrie Mrs M Dunbar Braidenhill Farm ML6 0PJ Tel. Glenboig (0236) 872319	Map 2 A5		1 Single 1 Dble/Twin 1 Family	1 Public Bath/Sh	B&B per person £8.50 Single	Open Jan-Dec
GLENMORISTON **Inverness-shire** Mrs Smart Rhialdt, Bhlaraidh IV3 6YH Tel. Glenmoriston (0320) 51269	Map 3 H10		1 Dble/Twin 1 Family	2 Public Bath/Sh	B&B per person £8.00 Single £8.00 Double	Open Apr-Oct Dinner 1845
Mrs M Templeton Alt Darach, Bhlaraidh Tel. Glenmoriston (0320) 51239			2 Dble/Twin	2 Public Bath/Sh	B&B per person £7.50 Double	Open Apr-Oct Dinner 1830
Mrs W Tomlin Redburn House IV3 6YJ Tel. Dalchreichart (0320) 40229			1 Dble/Twin 1 Family	1 Public Bath/Sh	B&B per person £7.50-£8.50 Double	Open Jan-Dec Dinner 1900
GLENROTHES **Fife** Kenmill Guest House 73 Marmion Drive Tel. Glenrothes (0592) 750358	Map 2 C3		3 Dble/Twin	2 Public Bath/Sh	B&B per person £7.00 Double	Open Apr-Oct Dinner 1700

Key to symbols is on back flap. Details of Classification and Grading are on page vi.

111

	Map Ref		Accommodation	Facilities	Prices	Opening
GLENROTHES continued	Map 2 C3					
Mrs Givans, 141 Altyre Avenue, Pittenchar Est. Tel. Glenrothes (0592) 771087			1 Single, 1 Dble/Twin, 1 Family	1 Public Bath/Sh	B&B per person £5.50 Single £5.50 Double	Open Jan-Dec Dinner 1700
O & H Robertson, 13 Laxford Road, Tel. Glenrothes (0592) 754513			1 Single, 2 Dble/Twin	1 Public Bath/Sh	B&B per person £7.00 Single £6.00-£7.00 Double	Open Jan-Dec Dinner 1730
GLENSHEE Perthshire	Map 4 D12					
The Compass Christian Centre, Glenshee Lodge, PH10 7QD, Tel. Glenshee (025085) 209			1 Dble/Twin, 6 Family	1 Public Bath/Sh	B&B per person £6.50-£7.75 Double	Open Jan-Dec Dinner 1800
GLENSHIEL, by Kyle of Lochalsh Ross-shire	Map 3 F10					
Mrs I Campbell, Shiel House, Tel. Glenshiel (059981) 282			2 Dble/Twin, 1 Family	1 Public Bath/Sh	B&B per person £8.50 Double	Open Apr-Oct Dinner 1900
Mrs J Macintosh, Foresters Bungalow, Inverinate, Tel. Glenshiel (059981) 329			2 Dble/Twin	1 Public Bath/Sh	B&B per person £7.00-£8.00 Double	Open Apr-Sep Dinner 1900
GLENURQUHART Inverness-shire	Map 4 A9					
Mrs Miles, Meiklie House, IV3 6TJ, Tel. Glenurquhart (04564) 265			3 Dble/Twin		B&B per person £8.00-£9.00 Double	Open Jan-Dec
GOLSPIE Sutherland	Map 4 B6					
Mrs N Grant, Deo Greine Farm, Backies, KW10 6SE, Tel. Golspie (04083) 3106		Listed	3 Dble/Twin, 2 Family	3 Private Bath/Sh, 2 Public Bath/Sh	B&B per person £8.00 Double	Open May-Oct Dinner 1800
Mrs N R Lochore, Tulachard, Fountain Road, KW10 6TH, Tel. Golspie (04083) 3808			2 Dble/Twin	1 Public Bath/Sh	B&B per person £7.00 Double	Open Apr-Oct
Mrs F MacLeod, West Dean, Station Road, KW10 6SN, Tel. Golspie (04083) 3400			2 Dble/Twin	1 Public Bath/Sh	B&B per person £6.50-£7.00 Double	Open May-Oct
Mr I W B & Mrs S A Paterson, Granite Villa, Fountain Road, KW10 6TH, Tel. Golspie (04083) 3146			1 Single, 1 Dble/Twin, 2 Family	1 Public Bath/Sh	B&B per person £8.00-£9.00 Single £8.00-£9.00 Double	Open Jan-Dec Dinner 1800

VAT is shown at 15%: changes in this rate may affect prices. Prices shown are for guidance only. Please send SAE with each enquiry.

GOUROCK **Renfrewshire** Mrs E Crawford Ellerslie, 56 Manor Crescent Tel. Gourock (0475) 31439	Map 1 G5	COMMENDED ♕	1 Single 2 Dble/Twin	1 Public Bath/Sh	B&B per person £11.00-£11.20 Single £11.00-£11.20 Double	Open Jan-Dec	

Detached house on hill overlooks Clyde Estuary. Good touring base for Ayr coast and Central Scotland.

GRANGEMOUTH **Stirlingshire** Mr Robertson Kylie House, 55 Boness Road Tel. Grangemouth (0324) 471301	Map 2 B4	Listed	3 Dble/Twin	1 Public Bath/Sh	B&B per person £8.50-£10.00 Double	Open Jan-Dec Dinner 1800	

GRANTOWN-ON-SPEY **Moray** Culdearn Guest House Woodlands Terrace Tel. Grantown-on-Spey (0479) 2106	Map 4 C9		3 Dble/Twin 4 Family	2 Public Bath/Sh	B&B per person £7.50-£12.00 Double	Open Jan-Dec Dinner 1900	

DAR-IL-HENA
Grant Road, Grantown-on-Spey. Tel: 0479 2929
This very well appointed property, renowned for its beautiful woodwork, has a very friendly atmosphere, elegant lounge and dining room, and very comfortable bedrooms. This well situated house is away from the noise of the High Street, and yet is within comfortable walking distance. The house itself is set in approximately 1 acre of mature gardens and has ample parking space.

Dar-il-Hena Guest House Grant Road PH26 3LA Tel. Grantown-on-Spey (0479) 2929			1 Single 3 Dble/Twin 3 Family	2 Public Bath/Sh	B&B per person £8.50 Single £8.50 Double	Open Apr-Oct Dinner 1900	

Dunallan Guest House Woodside Avenue PH26 3JW Tel. Grantown-on-Spey (0479) 2140			1 Single 3 Dble/Twin 1 Family	1 Public Bath/Sh	B&B per person £7.50-£8.00 Single £7.50-£8.00 Double	Open Jan-Nov Dinner 1800	

Firhall Guest House PH26 3LD Tel. Grantown-on-Spey (0479) 3097		COMMENDED ♕ ♕	1 Single 3 Dble/Twin 3 Family	2 Public Bath/Sh	B&B per person £8.00 Single £8.00 Double	Open Jan-Dec Dinner 1900	

Stone house of character. Original cornicing, pine woodwork, marble fireplaces. Personal attention.

Forest Park Guest House Woodside Avenue Tel. Grantown-on-Spey (0479) 2000		Awaiting Inspection	6 Dble/Twin	2 Public Bath/Sh	B&B per person £9.50 Single £9.50 Double	Open Jan-Dec Dinner 1800	

Kinross Guest House Woodside Avenue PH26 3JR Tel. Grantown-on-Spey (0479) 2042		COMMENDED ♕ ♕	1 Single 3 Dble/Twin 2 Family	2 Public Bath/Sh	B&B per person £8.30 Double	Open Jan-Dec Dinner 1900	

19c stone house built with original features in quiet area close to River Spey. Home cooking & baking.

Key to symbols is on back flap. Details of Classification and Grading are on page vi.

113

GRANTOWN-ON-SPEY continued	Map 4 C9					
Ravenscourt Guest House Seafield Avenue PH26 3JG Tel. Grantown-on-Spey (0479) 2286	COMMENDED 👑 👑	4 Dble/Twin 2 Family	2 Public Bath/Sh	B&B per person £7.00-£7.75 Double	Open Jan-Oct Dinner 1900	🐴 V ⚲ 🏠 ▥ 📺 ⚙ 🔥 🐕 ❄ P 🔺 🐾 C
		Former stone built manse, with large garden, in quiet area. Family run. Home cooking.				
Riversdale Guest House Grant Road PH26 31D Tel. Grantown-on-Spey (0479) 2648	APPROVED 👑	1 Single 4 Dble/Twin 2 Family	2 Public Bath/Sh	B&B per person £7.75-£8.00 Single £7.75-£8.00 Double	Open Jan-Dec Dinner 1900	🐴 🖐 V 🏠 ▥ 📺 ⚙ 🏠 🐕 P 🐾 C 🍽 &A
		Situated in quiet area of town but convenient for local shops.				

Rossmor

WOODLANDS TERRACE
GRANTOWN-ON-SPEY
Telephone: (0479) 2201

Beautiful 19th-century house of architectural interest furnished to a high standard, set in ½ acre landscaped garden overlooking pine woods and Cromdale Hills.

Excellent centre for birdwatching, hill-walking, fishing and ski-ing and ideal base for exploring Central Highlands, Royal Deeside and North-East coast.

A friendly home, where we offer a varied Scottish breakfast and optional evening meal using home produce.

Rossmor Guest House Woodlands Terrace PH26 3JU Tel. Grantown-on-Spey (0479) 2201	COMMENDED 👑 👑	1 Single 3 Dble/Twin 2 Family	2 Public Bath/Sh	B&B per person £7.50 Single £7.50 Double	Open Jan-Dec Dinner 1830	▶ V 🏠 ▥ 📺 ⚙ 🔥 🐕 ❄ 🍽 P 🔺 🐾 C
		Victorian detached house with own large garden. Excellent views to hills beyond.				

UMARIA
Guest House 👑 👑 Commended
Woodlands Terrace, Grantown-on-Spey
Morayshire PH26 3JU
Telephone: (0479) 2104

Our friendly, Scottish-owned, Highland Guest House overlooking beautiful hill and woodland surroundings is an ideal centre for active or restful holidays and for touring.

Detached, in large gardens, our comfortable accommodation has tea-making, H&C and electric blankets and radiators in all bedrooms. Home cooking and log fires if the evenings are chilly.

For bookings or any further information please contact Brenda or Brian Brodie who will be happy to help you.

Umaria Guest House Woodlands Terrace PH26 3JU Tel. Grantown-on-Spey (0479) 2104	COMMENDED 👑 👑	1 Single 4 Dble/Twin 3 Family	2 Public Bath/Sh	B&B per person £7.50 Single £7.50 Double	Open Jan-Dec Dinner 1830	🐴 🖐 ▶ V ▥ 📺 🏠 ❄ 🍽 P 🔺 🐾 C
		Stone built victorian house with large garden. On edge of village with views of hill and woodland.				

GRANTOWN-ON-SPEY continued	Map 4 C9						
Willowbank Guest House PH26 3HN Tel. Grantown-on-Spey (0479) 2089			6 Dble/Twin 2 Family	2 Public Bath/Sh	B&B per person £7.00 Double	Open Jan-Dec Dinner 1800	symbols
Mr & Mrs D Thomson Brooklynn, Grant Road Tel. Grantown-on-Spey (0479) 3113			1 Single 3 Dble/Twin 1 Family	1 Public Bath/Sh	B&B per person £7.50 Single £7.50 Double	Open Jan-Oct	symbols
Mrs R Donaldson The Hawthorns, Old Spey Bridge Tel. Grantown-on-Spey (0479) 2016			1 Dble/Twin 1 Family	1 Public Bath/Sh	B&B per person £8.00 Double	Open Jan-Dec Dinner 1900	symbols
GRANTSHOUSE Berwickshire	Map 2 F5						
Mrs Margaret Fleming Renton House			2 Dble/Twin 1 Family	2 Public Bath/Sh	B&B per person £8.50-£9.50 Double	Open Jan-Dec Dinner 1800	symbols
GREENLAW, Duns Berwickshire	Map 2 F6						
Mrs J D Lockie 8 Wester Row Tel. Greenlaw (03616) 337		Listed	2 Dble/Twin	1 Public Bath/Sh	B&B per person £7.50-£8.00 Double	Open Apr-Sep	symbols
GRETNA Dumfriesshire	Map 2 D10						
The Gables Guest House The Gables Tel. Gretna (0461) 38300			3 Dble/Twin 2 Family	2 Private Bath/Sh 2 Public Bath/Sh	B&B per person £12.00-£14.00 Double	Open Jan-Dec Dinner 1830	symbols
Mrs Donabie The Beeches, Loanwath Road Tel. Gretna (0461) 37448		Listed	1 Dble/Twin 1 Family	1 Public Bath/Sh	B&B per person £8.50-£9.00 Double	Open Mar-Oct	symbols
Mrs J Hodgson Davall, 26 Sarkfoot Road Tel. Gretna (0461) 37049			1 Dble/Twin	1 Public Bath/Sh	B&B per person £8.00 Double	Open Jan-Dec	symbols
Mrs A M Oldham Gordon House, 168 Central Avenue Tel. Gretna (0461) 37365			4 Dble/Twin		B&B per person £9.00 Double	Open May-Oct	symbols
GRETNA GREEN Dumfriesshire	Map 2 D10						
Greenlaw Guest House Tel. Gretna (0461) 38361			1 Single 6 Dble/Twin 1 Family	1 Public Bath/Sh	B&B per person £9.00-£9.50 Single £9.00-£9.50 Double	Open Jan-Dec Dinner 1800	symbols
Mrs B Moffat Kirkcroft, Glasgow Road Tel. Gretna (0461) 37403			2 Dble/Twin 1 Family	1 Public Bath/Sh	B&B per person £9.00-£9.50 Double	Open Jan-Dec	symbols
GROGARRY, Howmore S Uist, Western Isles	Map 3 A9						
Mrs E M MacAskill Drimsdale House Tel. Grogarry (08705) 231			2 Single 4 Dble/Twin 1 Family	2 Public Bath/Sh	B&B per person £6.50-£7.50 Single £7.50-£8.50 Double	Open Jan-Dec Dinner 1830	symbols

Key to symbols is on back flap. Details of Classification and Grading are on page vi.

	Map	Rating	Rooms	Bath	Price	Open	

GRUINART, Bridgend
Isle of Islay, Argyll — Map 1 B5

Loch Gruinart Guest House
Tel. Port Charlotte (049685)
212

1 Single / 4 Dble/Twin — 1 Public Bath/Sh — B&B per person £7.00-£8.00 Single £7.00-£8.00 Double — Open Jan-Dec Dinner 1800

GUARDBRIDGE, by St Andrews
Fife — Map 2 D2

COMMENDED 👑👑

Heather Christie Douglas
Seggie House, Cupar Road
KY16 0UP
Tel. Leuchars (033483) 209

2 Dble/Twin / 4 Family — 4 Private Bath/Sh / 3 Public Bath/Sh — B&B per person £9.00-£11.00 Double — Open Apr-Oct

Gracious victorian mansion in 5 acres wooded ground with walled garden. St Andrews 4 miles (6 km).

GULLANE
East Lothian — Map 2 E4

👑

Mrs R MacGregor
Langhills West, Whim Road
EH31 2BD
Tel. Gullane (0620) 842166

3 Dble/Twin — 2 Public Bath/Sh — B&B per person £8.50-£9.50 Double — Open Mar-Oct

---

COMMENDED Listed

Mrs McGowan
Glen Averon, Broadgait
EH31 2DJ
Tel. Gullane (0620) 842160

2 Dble/Twin — 1 Public Bath/Sh — B&B per person £9.00 Double — Open Jan-Dec

Edwardian semi detached house, in quiet area, near village centre. Golf courses and beach nearby.

Mrs Mcrae
Glebewood, Marine Terrace
Tel. Gullane (0620) 842593

1 Single / 1 Dble/Twin — 1 Public Bath/Sh — B&B per person £9.00 Single £9.00 Double — Open Apr-Oct

---

HADDINGTON
East Lothian — Map 2 E5

Mrs MacFadyen
46 Seggarsdean Park
EH41 4NB
Tel. Haddington (062082) 2272

1 Dble/Twin — 1 Public Bath/Sh — B&B per person £8.50-£10.00 Double — Open Jan-Dec Dinner 1800

HALKIRK
Caithness — Map 4 C3

Mrs M Banks
Glenlivet, Fairview
Tel. Halkirk (084783) 302

1 Single / 4 Dble/Twin / 1 Family — 2 Public Bath/Sh — B&B per person £7.50 Single £7.50 Double — Open Jan-Dec

---

HAMILTON
Lanarkshire — Map 2 A6

Mr & Mrs Wm Jones
5A Auchingramont Road
Tel. Hamilton (0698) 285230

2 Single / 2 Dble/Twin — 1 Private Bath/Sh / 1 Public Bath/Sh — B&B per person £10.00-£12.00 Single £10.00-£12.00 Double — Open Jan-Dec

---

HAWICK
Roxburghshire — Map 2 E8

Bridge House Guest House
Sandbed
TD9 0HE
Tel. Hawick (0450) 73351

2 Single / 6 Dble/Twin / 2 Family — 2 Public Bath/Sh — B&B per person £10.00 Single £10.00 Double — Open Jan-Dec

---

COMMENDED 👑👑

Oakwood Guest House
Buccleuch Road
Tel. Hawick (0450) 72896/72814

3 Dble/Twin — 1 Public Bath/Sh — B&B per person £9.00-£11.00 Double — Open Jan-Dec Dinner 1730

Large stone built house situated just off A7, on edge of town overlooking garden and bowling green.

	Map 2 E8						
HAWICK continued Mrs A Borthwick Hope Hill Tel. Hawick (0450) 75042		COMMENDED ♛♛♛	3 Dble/Twin	2 Private Bath/Sh 2 Public Bath/Sh	B&B per person £8.50-£10.00 Double	Open Jan-Dec Dinner 1730	
			Detached victorian house in large secluded gardens. Near centre of town, views of hills from bedrooms.				
Mrs M Jackson Colterscleugh, Teviotdale TD9 0LF Tel. Teviotdale (045085) 247			2 Dble/Twin 1 Family	1 Public Bath/Sh	B&B per person £7.50-£8.00 Double	Open Jan-Dec Dinner 1900	
Miss Elspeth Scott Burnside Cottage, Wilton Dean TD9 7HY Tel. Hawick (0450) 73378		Awaiting Inspection	2 Dble/Twin	1 Public Bath/Sh	B&B per person £10.00 Double	Open Jan-Dec	
Mrs Telfer Craig-Ian, 6 Weensland Road TD9 9NP Tel. Hawick (0450) 73506			3 Dble/Twin	1 Public Bath/Sh	B&B per person £8.00 Double	Open Apr-Oct	
Mrs White Craik Farm, Roberton Tel. Borthwickbrae (045088) 251		COMMENDED Listed	1 Single 1 Dble/Twin 1 Family	1 Public Bath/Sh	B&B per person £7.50-£8.50 Single £7.50-£8.50 Double	Open May-Oct Dinner 1800	
			On a working farm, on the edge of Craik Forest. Approximately 14 miles (22 km) from Hawick.				
HELENSBURGH Dunbartonshire Ardmore Guest House 98 West Clyde Street Tel. Helensburgh (0436) 3461	Map 1 G4	APPROVED ♛♛	4 Dble/Twin 1 Family	1 Public Bath/Sh	B&B per person £8.00-£9.00 Double	Open Jan-Dec	
			On seafront close to town centre. Family run. Most bedrooms double glazed.				
Carnmoss Guest House Station Road, Shandon Tel. Rhu (0436) 820817			1 Single 2 Dble/Twin 1 Family	1 Private Bath/Sh 1 Public Bath/Sh	B&B per person £9.50-£10.50 Single £9.00-£10.00 Double	Open Jan-Dec Dinner 1800	
Mrs E Blackwell Longleat, 39 East Argyle St G84 7EN Tel. Helensburgh (0436) 2465		COMMENDED ♛♛	3 Dble/Twin	1 Public Bath/Sh	B&B per person £8.50-£9.50 Double	Open Jan-Dec Dinner 1800	
			Privately owned family house. Spacious grounds. Quiet residential area overlooking Firth of Clyde.				
Mrs H Fraser 1 Craigendoran Avenue Tel. Helensburgh (0436) 6482			3 Dble/Twin	1 Public Bath/Sh	B&B per person £8.00-£9.00 Double	Open Jan-Dec Dinner 1700	
Mrs A McGill 50 William Street Tel. Helensburgh (0436) 3306			2 Dble/Twin		B&B per person £8.00 Double	Open May-Oct	
Mrs Paton Kyra, 100 West Clyde Street Tel. Helensburgh (0436) 5576			3 Dble/Twin 1 Family	2 Public Bath/Sh	B&B per person £8.00-£10.00 Double	Open Jan-Dec	
Mrs M K Paul Middledrift, 85 James Street Tel. Helensburgh (0436) 4867		Listed	1 Single 2 Dble/Twin	1 Public Bath/Sh	B&B per person £8.50-£9.00 Single £8.50-£9.00 Double	Open Jan-Dec	

Key to symbols is on back flap. Details of Classification and Grading are on page vi.

117

HELENSBURGH continued	Map 1 G4

CALADH LODGE Tel: 0436 2231

2 Havelock Street, Helensburgh, Dunbartonshire

CALADH LODGE is an attractive house set in a large secluded garden above the Firth of Clyde, within easy walking distance of the centre of Helensburgh.

It offers well-appointed accommodation and a warm, friendly atmosphere.

Mrs Stewart Caladh Lodge, 2 Havelock Street Tel. Helensburgh (0436) 2231		COMMENDED ♕ ♕	3 Dble/Twin	1 Public Bath/Sh	B&B per person £8.50-£9.00 Double Dinner 1800	Open Jan-Dec
			Comfortable detatched house in residential area. Attractive garden with croquet lawn.			
Mrs Anne Urquhart Upper Ericstane, 7 West Montrose Street Tel. Helensburgh (0436) 4922		COMMENDED Listed	1 Single 1 Dble/Twin 1 Family	2 Public Bath/Sh	B&B per person £9.50-£11.00 Single £8.50-£10.00 Double	Open Jan-Dec Dinner 1900
			Attractive family home of architectural interest on quiet street. Large garden.			
HELMSDALE Sutherland	Map 4 C5					
A Blance Green Table View, Navidale KW8 6JS Tel. Helmsdale (04312) 259			2 Dble/Twin	1 Public Bath/Sh	B&B per person £7.00 Double	Open Apr-Sep Dinner 1700
Mrs M L Cowie 33 Dunrobin Street KW8 6JX Tel. Helmsdale (04312) 661			1 Single 1 Family	1 Public Bath/Sh	B&B per person £7.50 Single £7.50 Double	Open Jan-Dec Dinner 1800
Mrs E Mcangus Glebe House, Sutherland Street KW8 6LQ Tel. Helmsdale (04312) 682			2 Dble/Twin	2 Public Bath/Sh	B&B per person £7.00 Double	Open May-Oct
HOLLYBUSH Ayrshire	Map 1 H8					
Mrs M M Drummond Malcolmston Farm Tel. Dalrymple (029256) 238			2 Dble/Twin 1 Family	1 Public Bath/Sh	B&B per person £8.50 Double	Open May-Sep
HOUGHGARRY N Uist, Western Isles	Map 3 A8					
Mrs Deans The Cottage			1 Dble/Twin 1 Family	1 Public Bath/Sh	B&B per person £10.00 Double	Open Jan-Dec Dinner 1800
HOWMORE S Uist, Western Isles	Map 3 A9					
Mrs MacDonald Ben More House Tel. Grogarry (08705) 283			2 Dble/Twin 1 Family	1 Public Bath/Sh	B&B per person £8.50 Single	Open Apr-Oct Dinner 1600

VAT is shown at 15%: changes in this rate may affect prices. Prices shown are for guidance only. Please send SAE with each enquiry.

HOWNAM Roxburghshire	Map 2 F7		

Greenhill
Hownam, by Kelso, Roxburghshire
Tel. Morebattle (05734 505)   Mrs Julia Harris
STB COMMENDED
Peace and tranquillity. Shooting lodge built for Duke of Roxburgh amid scenic beauty of Cheviot foothills. Ideal base for walking, birdwatching or exploring the Border countryside with its many varied historical sites. The lodge offers very comfortable accommodation with good home cooking using vegetables and soft fruits from our kitchen garden.
Prices per person, Dinner, Bed and Breakfast £15-£16.50.

Mrs J Harris Greenhill Tel. Morebattle (05734) 505	COMMENDED Listed	2 Single 2 Dble/Twin 1 Family	2 Public Bath/Sh	B&B per person £9.00-£10.50 Single £9.00-£10.50 Double	Open Jan-Dec Dinner 1900	
		Once shooting lodge, now family home, nestling at foot of Cheviots. Large garden, fresh home cooking.				

HOY Orkney	Map 5 A11					
Burnmouth Guest House Tel. Hoy (085679) 297	COMMENDED Listed	1 Single 1 Dble/Twin 1 Family		B&B per person £8.00 Single £8.00 Double	Open Jan-Dec Dinner 1800	
		Stone cottage of character by waters edge. Free trout fishing, good walking and near RSPB reserve.				
W O Lancaster Rysa Lodge, Lyness Tel. Hoy (085679) 248	👑👑	1 Single 3 Dble/Twin	1 Private Bath/Sh 2 Public Bath/Sh	B&B per person £8.00 Single £8.00 Double	Open Jan-Dec Dinner 2200	
Mrs McLaren Northness, Lyness Tel. Hoy (0856) 70301		3 Family	1 Public Bath/Sh	B&B per person £6.00 Double	Open Jan-Dec	
Mrs Morris The Garrison, Lyness KW16 3NX Tel. Hoy (085679) 312		1 Single 2 Dble/Twin	2 Public Bath/Sh	B&B per person £7.00-£8.00 Single £6.50-£7.00 Double	Open Jan-Dec Dinner 1700	
Mrs Rendall Glen, Rackwick KW16 3NJ Tel. Hoy (085679) 262		1 Dble/Twin	1 Public Bath/Sh	B&B per person £8.00-£9.00 Double	Open May-Aug Dinner 1830	

HUNTLY Aberdeenshire	Map 4 F9					
Mrs I Bell Glenburn, 19 Castle Street AB5 5BP Tel. Huntly (0466) 2798		2 Dble/Twin 1 Family	1 Public Bath/Sh	B&B per person £7.00 Double	Open Jan-Dec	
Miss J Davidson 29 Deveron Street AB5 5BY Tel. Huntly (0466) 3265		4 Dble/Twin 1 Family	1 Public Bath/Sh	B&B per person £8.00 Double	Open Jan-Dec Dinner 1700	
Mrs Lyon Aldie House, Battlehill AB5 5HX Tel. Huntly (0466) 4209		1 Single 5 Dble/Twin	2 Public Bath/Sh	B&B per person £10.00 Single £10.00 Double	Open May-Sep	

Key to symbols is on back flap. Details of Classification and Grading are on page vi.

119

HUNTLY continued — Map 4 F9

Mrs Manson
Greenmount, 43 Gordon Street
AB5 5EQ
Tel. Huntly (0466) 2482
2 Single / 4 Dble/Twin / 1 Family — 2 Public Bath/Sh — B&B per person £8.00 Single £8.50 Double — Open Jan-Dec Dinner 1800

Mrs Stewart
Mains of Corse
AB5 6GS
Tel. Drumblade (046684) 249
2 Dble/Twin — 1 Public Bath/Sh — B&B per person £6.50 Double — Open Jan-Dec Dinner 1800

Mrs R M Thomson
Southview, Victoria Road
AB5 5AH
Tel. Huntly (0466) 2456
3 Dble/Twin / 1 Family — 1 Public Bath/Sh — B&B per person £7.00 Double — Open Jan-Dec Dinner 1700

INNERLEITHEN — Peeblesshire — Map 2 D6

Mrs A Thomson
The Grange, Buccleuch St
Tel. Innerleithen (0896) 830676
1 Dble/Twin / 1 Family — 1 Public Bath/Sh — B&B per person £7.50-£8.00 Double — Open May-Oct

INVERARAY — Argyll — Map 1 F3

Mrs Crawford
Brenchoille Farm
Tel. Furnace (04995) 662
1 Family — 1 Public Bath/Sh — B&B per person £7.50-£8.00 Double — Open Apr-Oct

Mrs Mchugash
Creagdhiu
2 Dble/Twin / 1 Family — 1 Private Bath/Sh / 1 Public Bath/Sh — B&B per person £8.50 Double — Open Apr-Oct

Mrs Mclaren
Old Rectory
Tel. Inveraray (0499) 2280
2 Dble/Twin / 2 Family — 1 Public Bath/Sh — B&B per person £8.00 Double — Open Apr-Oct

Mrs Semple
Killean House
Tel. Inveraray (0499) 2474
3 Dble/Twin — 2 Public Bath/Sh — B&B per person £7.50-£8.50 Double — Open Jan-Dec

INVERGARRY — Inverness-shire — Map 3 H11

Faichem Lodge Guest House
Faichem
Tel. Invergarry (08093) 314
3 Dble/Twin / 1 Family — 1 Public Bath/Sh — B&B per person £9.00-£10.00 Double — Open Mar-Nov Dinner 1900

Forest Lodge Guest House
South Laggan
PH34 4EA
Tel. Invergarry (08093) 219
COMMENDED
5 Dble/Twin / 2 Family — 2 Public Bath/Sh — B&B per person £8.00 Double — Open Mar-Nov Dinner 1930

Pleasantly situated beside main A82 tourist route. Beautiful views of surrounding mountains.

Lundie View Guest House
PH35 4HN
Tel. Invergarry (08093) 291
APPROVED
1 Single / 2 Dble/Twin / 3 Family — 2 Private Bath/Sh / 1 Public Bath/Sh — B&B per person £8.00 Single £8.00 Double — Open Jan-Dec

Family run, all accommodation on ground level. Set in open countryside.

Miss Ellice
Taigh-an-Lianach,
Aberchalder Farm
Tel. Invergarry (08093) 287
1 Single / 1 Dble/Twin — 1 Public Bath/Sh — B&B per person £8.50-£9.00 Single £8.00-£8.50 Double — Open Apr-Dec

INVERGARRY continued	Map 3 H11					
Mrs J Grant Faichemard Farm PH35 4HS Tel. Invergarry (08093) 334		2 Dble/Twin 1 Family	1 Public Bath/Sh	B&B per person £8.00 Double	Open May-Sep Dinner 1830	
Mr & Mrs Mackenzie Rogers Tigh-na-car-Ruadh PH35 4HG Tel. Invergarry (08093) 359	Awaiting Inspection	1 Dble/Twin	1 Public Bath/Sh	B&B per person £7.25 Double	Open Jan-Dec Dinner 1930	

NORTH LAGGAN FARMHOUSE

By Spean Bridge, Inverness.   **Telephone 080 93 335**

Overlooking the Caledonian Canal and Loch Oich, set ½ mile off the A82, 2 miles south of Invergarry, amidst sheep farming country, North Laggan Farmhouse is a comfortably modernised croft, which retains much of its original character. Two comfortable bed/sittingrooms with TV, HC and tea-making facilities. Home-made bread and good food. Children and pets welcome. Individual attention guaranteed.

Mrs Waugh North Laggan Farmhouse PH34 4EB Tel. Invergarry (08093) 335	COMMENDED Listed	1 Dble/Twin 1 Family	1 Public Bath/Sh	B&B per person £8.00 Double	Open Apr-Oct Dinner 1900	
		Peaceful open countryside, superb views. Warm welcome, home-made bread. Hill walking, boat hire.				
Mr Wilson Argarry Farm, Faichem Tel. Invergarry (08093) 226		2 Dble/Twin 1 Family	2 Public Bath/Sh	B&B per person £9.00 Double	Open Jan-Dec Dinner 1800	
INVERGLOY, by Spean Bridge Inverness-shire Mrs D Bennet Riverside Tel. Invergloy (039784) 284	Map 3 H11	1 Dble/Twin 1 Family	1 Public Bath/Sh	B&B per person £8.00-£9.00 Double	Open Jan-Dec Dinner 1900	
INVERGORDON Ross-shire Newmore Country House Guest House Tel. Invergordon (0349) 853361	Map 4 B7 COMMENDED 👑👑👑	2 Dble/Twin 1 Family	3 Private Bath/Sh 2 Public Bath/Sh	B&B per person £17.00 Double	Open Jan-Dec Dinner 1930	
		Of architectural interest, built on site of castle ruin. Views of open farmland and Cromarty Firth.				
INVERKEITHING Fife Mrs J E Singal Nirvaana, Hope Street KY11 1LN Tel. Inverkeithing (0383) 413876	Map 2 C4	1 Single 2 Dble/Twin	1 Public Bath/Sh	B&B per person £8.50 Single £8.50 Double	Open Mar-Nov	
INVERNESS Aberfeldy Lodge Guest House 11 Southside Road IV2 3BG Tel. Inverness (0463) 231120	Map 4 B8 COMMENDED 👑👑👑	5 Dble/Twin 4 Family	5 Private Bath/Sh 2 Public Bath/Sh	B&B per person £10.00 Double	Open Jan-Dec Dinner 1800	
		Substantial detached house with large garden. Quiet area close to town centre and near rail station.				

INVERNESS continued	Map 4 B8					

Abermar Guest House
25 Fairfield Road
IV3 5QD
Tel. Inverness (0463)
239019

2 Single / 7 Dble/Twin / 2 Family — 5 Private Bath/Sh — B&B per person £8.00-£9.00 Single / £8.00-£9.00 Double — Open Jan-Dec

---

Ardnacoille Guest House
1a Annfield Road
IV2 3HP
Tel. Inverness (0463)
233451

COMMENDED

4 Dble/Twin / 2 Family — 2 Public Bath/Sh — B&B per person £9.50-£10.00 Double — Open Mar-Oct

Substantial victorian house with spacious rooms and large garden. Quiet residential area near centre.

Clachnaharry Guest House
41 Clachnaharry Road
IV3 6RA
Tel. Inverness (0463)
231432

5 Dble/Twin / 3 Family — 2 Public Bath/Sh — B&B per person £9.50-£11.50 Double — Open Apr-Oct / Dinner 1850

Craigside Guest House
4 Gordon Terrace
IV2 3HD
Tel. Inverness (0463)
231576

COMMENDED

5 Dble/Twin / 1 Family — 4 Private Bath/Sh / 1 Public Bath/Sh — B&B per person £11.00-£15.00 Double — Open Mar-Dec / Dinner 1900

Detached victorian house set in quiet elevated position. Views of castle, river and town from lounge.

Crownleigh Guest House
6 Midmills Road
IV2 3WX
Tel. Inverness (0463)
220316

2 Single / 2 Dble/Twin / 1 Family — 1 Public Bath/Sh — B&B per person £7.00-£9.00 Single / £8.00 Double — Open Jan-Dec

---

Culduthel Lodge Guest House
14 Culduthel Road
Tel. Inverness (0463)
240089

1 Single / 2 Dble/Twin / 2 Family — 1 Private Bath/Sh / 1 Public Bath/Sh — B&B per person £10.00-£12.00 Single / £9.00-£11.00 Double — Open Jan-Dec

---

Felstead Guest House
18 Ness Bank
IV2 4SF
Tel. Inverness (0463)
231634

1 Single / 5 Dble/Twin / 2 Family — 1 Public Bath/Sh — B&B per person £11.00 Single — Open May-Sep

---

The Firs Guest House
Dores Road
IV2 4QU
Tel. Inverness (0463)
225197

HIGHLY COMMENDED

1 Single / 4 Dble/Twin / 1 Family — 1 Public Bath/Sh — B&B per person £10.00-£12.00 Single / £10.00 Double — Open Jan-Dec

Stately 'B' listed house with grounds to river. Elegantly furnished and comfortable. Log fire.

Glen Fruin Guest House
50 Fairfield Road
IV3 5QW
Tel. Inverness (0463)
232984

1 Dble/Twin / 2 Family — 1 Public Bath/Sh — B&B per person £7.50-£8.00 Double — Open Jan-Dec

---

Gowanlea Guest House
27 Fairfield Road
IV3 5QD
Tel. Inverness (0463)
230127

1 Single / 2 Dble/Twin / 2 Family — 1 Private Bath/Sh — B&B per person £8.00-£10.00 Single / £8.00-£9.00 Double — Open Jan-Dec / Dinner 1800

Inverglen Guest House
7 Abertarff Road
IV2 3NW
Tel. Inverness (0463)
237610

COMMENDED

3 Dble/Twin / 1 Family — 4 Private Bath/Sh — B&B per person £9.00-£12.00 Double — Open Mar-Nov

Detached villa, quiet residential area. Refurbished and decorated throughout. Relaxing atmosphere.

VAT is shown at 15%: changes in this rate may affect prices. Prices shown are for guidance only. Please send SAE with each enquiry.

INVERNESS continued	Map 4 B8						
Leinster Lodge Guest House 27 Southside Road IV2 4XA Tel. Inverness (0463) 233311		APPROVED 👑 👑	1 Single 3 Dble/Twin 1 Family	2 Public Bath/Sh	B&B per person £9.00-£9.50 Single £9.00-£9.50 Double	Open Jan-Dec	
			Personally run 19C stone house in quiet residential area. Easy access to town centre and shops.				
Taymount Guest House 27 Crown Drive IV2 3QF Tel. Inverness (0463) 232741			2 Dble/Twin 1 Family	3 Public Bath/Sh	B&B per person £8.00-£9.50 Double	Open Jan-Dec Dinner 1800	
The Terraces Guest House 3 Victoria Terrace IV2 3QA Tel. Inverness (0463) 225535		COMMENDED 👑	1 Dble/Twin 1 Family		B&B per person £8.00 Double	Open Jan-Dec	
			Victorian, terraced house with views over town. Short walking distance to town centre and shops.				
Mrs C Baillie 1 Victoria Terrace IV2 3QA Tel. Inverness (0463) 237682			2 Dble/Twin 2 Family	4 Private Bath/Sh 1 Public Bath/Sh	B&B per person £9.00 Double	Open Jan-Dec	
Mrs Barr 48 Union Road IV2 3JY Tel. Inverness (0463) 235987			1 Single 1 Dble/Twin 1 Family	1 Public Bath/Sh	B&B per person £7.50-£8.50 Single £7.50-£8.50 Double	Open Jan-Dec Dinner 1830	
Mrs Boynton 12 Annfield Road IV2 3HX Tel. Inverness (0463) 233188			1 Dble/Twin 1 Family	2 Public Bath/Sh	B&B per person £7.50-£8.00 Double	Open Jan-Dec	
Mrs A Buchan 1 Cuthbert Road IV2 3RU Tel. Inverness (0463) 237924			3 Dble/Twin	2 Public Bath/Sh	B&B per person £6.00 Double	Open Jan-Dec	
Mrs Cantlay 5 Beaufort Road IV2 3NP Tel. Inverness (0463) 231298		Listed	1 Dble/Twin 1 Family		B&B per person £7.50-£8.50 Double	Open Jan-Dec	
Mrs Carson Cambeth Lodge, 49 Fairfield Rd IV3 5QP Tel. Inverness (0463) 231764			1 Single 1 Dble/Twin 2 Family	1 Public Bath/Sh	B&B per person £9.00-£10.00 Single £8.00-£8.50 Double	Open Jan-Dec Dinner 1800	
Mrs C A Clarke Inchberry House, Lentran IV3 6RJ Tel. Drumchardine (046383) 342			3 Dble/Twin 1 Family	2 Private Bath/Sh 1 Public Bath/Sh	B&B per person £8.50-£10.50 Double	Open Jan-Dec Dinner 1800	
Mrs I Donald 4 Muirfield Road IV2 4AY Tel. Inverness (0463) 235489		COMMENDED 👑 👑	2 Dble/Twin 1 Family	1 Public Bath/Sh	B&B per person £8.50-£9.00 Double	Open Jan-Dec Dinner 1800	
			Spacious, victorian house with large garden. Quiet area, close to town centre. Taste of Scotland.				

Key to symbols is on back flap. Details of Classification and Grading are on page vi.

123

INVERNESS continued	Map 4 B8						
Mrs J R Elmslie 7 Harris Road IV2 3LS Tel. Inverness (0463) 237059			2 Single 1 Dble/Twin	1 Public Bath/Sh	B&B per person £8.00 Single £7.50 Double	Open Apr-Oct	
Mrs P Ferguson Strath-Mhor, 3 Attadale Road IV3 5QH Tel. Inverness (0463) 232998			2 Dble/Twin 1 Family	2 Public Bath/Sh	B&B per person £8.00-£8.50 Double	Open Jan-Dec	
Mrs C M Fraser Borlum House, Scaniport Tel. Dores (046375) 306			2 Dble/Twin 2 Family	2 Public Bath/Sh	B&B per person £8.00-£8.50 Double	Open Jan-Dec Dinner 1800	
J M Fraser 8 Crown Street IV2 3AX Tel. Inverness (0463) 235874			1 Dble/Twin 1 Family		B&B per person £7.00-£8.00 Double	Open Apr-Oct	
Mrs L Fraser Edenview, 26 Ness Bank Tel. Inverness (0463) 234397			1 Dble/Twin 1 Family	2 Public Bath/Sh	B&B per person £9.00-£10.00 Double	Open Jan-Dec	
Mrs D Fraser 2 Old Edinburgh Road			3 Dble/Twin	1 Public Bath/Sh	B&B per person £8.50-£9.50 Double	Open Mar-Oct	
Mrs Geddes Sandale, 37 Midmills Road IV2 3NZ Tel. Inverness (0463) 235382		Awaiting Inspection	3 Dble/Twin	1 Public Bath/Sh	B&B per person £8.00 Double	Open Apr-Oct	
Mr & Mrs W G Gillespie Ness Bank House, 7 Ness Bank IV2 4SF Tel. Inverness (0463) 232939			1 Single 2 Dble/Twin 1 Family		B&B per person £10.00-£11.00 Single £10.00-£11.00 Double	Open Jan-Dec	
Mrs I Gillies Kildare, 2 Broadstone Park IV2 3LA Tel. Inverness (0463) 232179			1 Single 1 Family	1 Public Bath/Sh	B&B per person £8.50-£9.00 Double	Open Apr-Oct	
Mrs Gunn 97 Kenneth Street IV3 5QQ Tel. Inverness (0463) 234420			3 Dble/Twin	1 Public Bath/Sh	B&B per person £7.00-£8.00 Double	Open Apr-Oct	
Mrs A Hamilton 11 Southside Place IV2 3JF Tel. Inverness (0463) 231457			1 Family	1 Private Bath/Sh	B&B per person £7.50-£8.50 Double	Open Apr-Oct	
Mrs Joan Hendry Tamarue, 70A Ballifeary Road, IV3 5PF Tel. Inverness (0463) 239724		COMMENDED Listed	3 Dble/Twin	1 Public Bath/Sh	B&B per person £8.00-£8.50 Double	Open Apr-Oct	

Situated in quiet residential area, yet within easy reach of town centre and local amenities.

INVERNESS continued	Map 4 B8

"Drumbuie Cottage"

Nairnside Road, Westhill Inverness.   Tel. (0463) 791 591

Enjoy comfort and old world charm of 1740 Drumbuie Cottage, tastefully extended and modernised to offer excellent accommodation. Set amidst acres of farmland and panoramic views towards the Moray Firth and beyond. Excellent variety of good home cooking. En suite facilities available. Brochure available. Children's rates on request.

May and September DBB £98.00 per person per week.
June, July and August DBB £105.00 per person per week.

Name/Address	Grading	Rooms	Bathrooms	Price	Opening
Mrs G Hornby Drumbuie, Westhill IV1 2BX Tel. Inverness (0463) 791591	COMMENDED Listed	2 Dble/Twin 1 Family	2 Private Bath/Sh 1 Public Bath/Sh	B&B per person £7.00-£8.00 Double	Open Apr-Oct Dinner 1830
1740, family cottage of character; log fire. Views over Firth and farms. Near Culloden Battlefield.					
Mrs Johnstone 20 Crown Street Tel. Inverness (0463) 230448		2 Dble/Twin	2 Public Bath/Sh	B&B per person £7.50-£8.00 Double	Open Jan-Dec
Mrs G Lee Millwood, 36 Old Mill Road IV2 3HR Tel. Inverness (0463) 237254	COMMENDED Listed	3 Dble/Twin	2 Public Bath/Sh	B&B per person £8.50 Double	Open Jan-Dec
Family house with large garden, centrally situated in a residential area of the town.					
Mrs Neina Lister The Old Rectory, 9 Southside Road IV2 3BG Tel. Inverness (0463) 220969	COMMENDED	3 Dble/Twin 1 Family	1 Public Bath/Sh	B&B per person £9.00 Double	Open Jan-Dec Dinner 1800
Privately owned, former victorian manse with large garden. Residential area close to town centre.					
Miss E Lothian Ardgour, 83 Old Edinburgh Road Tel. Inverness (0463) 236972		1 Single 3 Dble/Twin	1 Public Bath/Sh	B&B per person £8.00-£8.50 Single £8.00-£8.50 Double	Open Jan-Dec Dinner 1900
Mrs A MacDonald 98 Kenneth Street IV3 5QG Tel. Inverness (0463) 235954		1 Single 1 Dble/Twin	1 Public Bath/Sh	B&B per person £7.00 Single £6.50-£7.50 Double	Open Apr-Oct
Mrs C MacKay Eildon, 29 Old Edinburgh Road IV2 3HJ Tel. Inverness (0463) 231969		2 Dble/Twin 1 Family	2 Public Bath/Sh	B&B per person £8.50 Double	Open Jan-Dec
Mrs MacKenzie 7 Broadstone Avenue IV2 3LE Tel. Inverness (0463) 225728		1 Single 2 Dble/Twin 1 Family	1 Public Bath/Sh	B&B per person £7.50-£8.50 Single £7.50-£8.50 Double	Open Jan-Dec
Mrs A Mackenzie 5 Crown Circus Tel. Inverness (0463) 224222		2 Dble/Twin 1 Family	2 Public Bath/Sh	B&B per person £8.00 Double	Open Jan-Dec

INVERNESS continued	Map 4 B8		Rooms	Bath	B&B	Opening	Facilities
Mrs M MacLean 15 Damfield Road IV2 3LP Tel. Inverness (0463) 231141			1 Single 1 Dble/Twin 1 Family	1 Public Bath/Sh	B&B per person £8.00 Single £8.00 Double	Open Jan-Dec	
Mrs M MacLennan 21 Planefield Road Tel. Inverness (0463) 230337			1 Dble/Twin	1 Private Bath/Sh	B&B per person £8.50-£10.00 Double	Open Apr-Oct	
Mrs C M MacLeod 42 Island Bank Road IV2 4QT Tel. Inverness (0463) 224692			2 Dble/Twin 1 Family	1 Public Bath/Sh	B&B per person £8.00-£9.50 Double	Open Jan-Dec Dinner 1730	
Mrs MacTaggart 1 Ross Avenue IV3 5QJ Tel. Inverness (0463) 236356			3 Dble/Twin 1 Family	1 Public Bath/Sh	B&B per person £7.50-£8.00 Double	Open Jan-Dec	
Mrs Mackenzie The Whins, 114 Kenneth Street IV3 5QG Tel. Inverness (0463) 236215			2 Dble/Twin	1 Public Bath/Sh	B&B per person £7.00-£8.00 Double	Open Apr-Oct	
Mrs Mackintosh Ardentorrie House, 2 Gordon Terrace IV2 3HD Tel. Inverness (0463) 230090		Awaiting Inspection	1 Dble/Twin 2 Family	3 Private Bath/Sh 2 Public Bath/Sh	B&B per person £10.00-£11.50 Double	Open Apr-Oct	
Mrs A Maclean 101 Kenneth Street IV3 5QG Tel. Inverness (0463) 237224			4 Dble/Twin 2 Family	2 Public Bath/Sh	B&B per person £7.50 Double	Open Feb-Oct	
Mrs Robina A Maclean 42 Fairfield Road IV3 5QD Tel. Inverness (0463) 240240			1 Single 1 Dble/Twin 1 Family	2 Public Bath/Sh	B&B per person £7.50-£8.50 Single	Open Jan-Dec	
Mrs McCuish 50 Argyle Street IV2 3BB Tel. Inverness (0463) 235150			1 Dble/Twin 1 Family	1 Public Bath/Sh	B&B per person £6.50-£7.00 Double	Open Apr-Oct	
Mrs McCuish Ardmay, 5 Drumblair Crescent IV2 4RG Tel. Inverness (0463) 231104			2 Dble/Twin	2 Public Bath/Sh	B&B per person £8.00-£8.50 Double	Open May-Sep Dinner 1750	
Mrs C McInnes 39 Fairfield Road IV3 5QD Tel. Inverness (0463) 236158			2 Dble/Twin 1 Family	1 Public Bath/Sh	B&B per person £8.00 Double	Open Jan-Dec	

VAT is shown at 15%: changes in this rate may affect prices. Prices shown are for guidance only. Please send SAE with each enquiry.

INVERNESS continued	Map 4 B8						
Mrs K McLeod 28 Ardconnel Terrace IV2 3AG Tel. Inverness (0463) 237405			1 Single 1 Dble/Twin 2 Family	2 Public Bath/Sh	B&B per person £8.50 Single £7.50 Double	Open Jan-Dec Dinner 1800	🛠 M ⬛ V 🍴 ⬛ TV 🚲 🐕 ✳ C
Mrs A McPhee 135 Culduthel Road Tel. Inverness (0463) 225822			1 Single 1 Dble/Twin 1 Family	1 Public Bath/Sh	B&B per person £6.00 Single £6.00 Double	Open Mar-Oct Dinner 1700	🛠 ⬛ ☕ ⬛ TV ✳ P C
Mrs C M Mirtle Aros, 5 Abertaff Road IV2 3NW Tel. Inverness (0463) 235674		COMMENDED 👑 👑	1 Single 2 Dble/Twin 2 Family	1 Public Bath/Sh	B&B per person £9.00-£10.00 Single £9.00-£10.00 Double	Open Mar-Nov	🛠 ⬛ V 🍴 ⬛ TV ⬛ 🐕 ✳ P C
			Detached victorian villa, many original features. In quiet residential area close to town centre.				
Mrs A Munro Rose Vale, 50 Culcabock Avenue Tel. Inverness (0463) 224730			1 Dble/Twin 1 Family	1 Public Bath/Sh	B&B per person £8.00 Double	Open Jan-Dec	🍴 ⬛ ☕ 🍴 ⬛ TV P C
Mrs Larkin 28A Old Edinburgh Road IV2 3HJ Tel. Inverness (0463) 240441			2 Dble/Twin		B&B per person £8.00-£9.00 Double	Open Jan-Dec	🍴 🍴 ⬛ TV P
Marjory O'Conner Bonnieview, Tower Brae, North Westhill IV1 2BP Tel. Inverness (0463) 792468			1 Single 2 Dble/Twin 1 Family	3 Private Bath/Sh 1 Public Bath/Sh	B&B per person £8.00 Single £8.00 Double	Open Jan-Dec Dinner 1800	🛠 ⬛ 🍴 V 🍴 ⬛ TV 🚲 ⬛ 🐕 ✂ 🐕 ✳ P C
Mrs Ross Melrose Villa, 35 Kenneth Street IV3 5DH Tel. Inverness (0463) 233745			1 Single 3 Dble/Twin 1 Family	1 Public Bath/Sh	B&B per person £8.50 Single £8.50 Double	Open Mar-Dec	M V 🍴 ⬛ TV ⬛ 🐕 🐕 C
Mrs S Smith 1 Dochfour Drive Tel. Inverness (0463) 230439			1 Dble/Twin 1 Family	1 Public Bath/Sh	B&B per person **£8.00 Double**	Open Apr-Oct	🛠 ⬛ TV P C
Mrs Stewart Crossroads Bungalow, 44 Culcabock Road IV2 3XQ Tel. Inverness (0463) 236649			3 Dble/Twin	2 Public Bath/Sh	B&B per person £7.50 Double	Open Jan-Nov	🛠 🍴 🍴 ⬛ TV ✂ ✳ P
Miss Storrar 11 Douglas Row IV1 1RE Tel. Inverness (0463) 233486			2 Dble/Twin 1 Family		B&B per person £8.50 Double	Open Feb-Dec Dinner 1800	🛠 🍴 V 🍴 ⬛ TV 🎯
Mrs Telford 5 Porterfield Road IV2 3HW Tel. Inverness (0463) 240436		Listed	1 Single 1 Dble/Twin 1 Family	1 Public Bath/Sh	B&B per person £8.00-£9.00 Single £7.50-£8.00 Double	Open Apr-Oct	🍴 ⬛ TV 🚲 ⬛ 🐕 P C

Location	Map	Grade	Accommodation	Bath	B&B	Open	Facilities
INVERURIE Aberdeenshire	Map 4 G9						
Mrs H Duncan East Blairdaff Farm, kemnay AB5 9LT Tel. Monymusk (04677) 339			1 Single 1 Dble/Twin 2 Family	2 Public Bath/Sh	B&B per person £8.00-£9.00 Single £8.00 Double	Open Jan-Dec Dinner 1800	
Mrs G Lee Glenburnie, Blackhall Road AB5 9JE Tel. Inverurie (0467) 23044			4 Dble/Twin	1 Public Bath/Sh	B&B per person £8.00 Double	Open Jan-Dec	
Mrs Wink 15 High Street AB5 9QA Tel. Inverurie (0467) 21142			2 Dble/Twin 1 Family	1 Public Bath/Sh	B&B per person £9.00 Double	Open Feb-Nov	
IONA, Isle of Argyll	Map 1 B3						
Mr R E Finlay Finlay, Ross Limited Tel. Iona (06817) 357/365			5 Dble/Twin 2 Family	2 Public Bath/Sh	B&B per person £6.50-£10.00 Double	Open Jan-Dec	
Miss J Watson Warden, Bishops House, Retreat House Tel. Iona (06817) 306			4 Single 5 Dble/Twin	2 Public Bath/Sh	B&B per person £9.50 Single £9.50 Double	Open Mar-Oct Dinner 1900	
IRVINE Ayrshire	Map 1 G7						
John & Morag Adrain Spinningdale, 76 Waterside Tel. Irvine (0294) 71385			2 Single 2 Dble/Twin 1 Family	1 Public Bath/Sh	B&B per person £8.00-£9.00 Single £15.00-£18.00 Double	Open Jan-Dec	
ISLE ORNSAY, Sleat Isle of Skye, Inverness-shire	Map 3 E10						
Old Post Office Guest House Tel. Isle Ornsay (04713) 201		COMMENDED Listed	6 Dble/Twin	2 Public Bath/Sh	B&B per person £8.00 Double	Open Apr-Oct	
			Modern bungalow with large attractive garden overlooking the Sound of Sleat.				
ISLE OF WHITHORN Wigtownshire	Map 1 H11						
Mrs D Clarke Hall House, 12 Main Street DG8 8LF Tel. Whithorn (09885) 533			4 Family	1 Public Bath/Sh	B&B per person £8.00 Single £8.00 Double	Open Mar-Oct Dinner 1830	
JEDBURGH Roxburghshire	Map 2 E7						
Kenmore Bank Guest House Oxnam Road Tel. Jedburgh (0835) 62369		COMMENDED 👑👑	4 Dble/Twin 2 Family	1 Public Bath/Sh	B&B per person £10.00 Double	Open Jan-Dec Dinner 1800	
			Family run, with views over river and town. Ideal for touring Border Country.				
The Spinney Guest House Langlee Tel. Jedburgh (0835) 63525		HIGHLY COMMENDED 👑👑	3 Dble/Twin	3 Private Bath/Sh	B&B per person £12.00-£13.00 Double	Open Apr-Oct	
			Attractive house recently modernised. Large pleasant garden. Hearty breakfasts with a wide choice.				

VAT is shown at 15%: changes in this rate may affect prices. Prices shown are for guidance only. Please send SAE with each enquiry.

	Map	Grade	Rooms	Bath	Prices	Open	
JEDBURGH continued	Map 2 E7						
Mrs M C Bathgate 64 Castlegate TD8 6BB Tel. Jedburgh (0835) 62466		COMMENDED Listed	3 Dble/Twin	1 Public Bath/Sh	B&B per person £8.00-£8.50 Double	Open Jan-Dec	(symbols)
Family home in terraced row. With mature and well kept garden. Views over Cheviot Hills.							
Mrs Clark Strowan, Oxnam Road Tel. Jedburgh (0835) 62248			4 Dble/Twin	1 Private Bath/Sh 1 Public Bath/Sh	B&B per person £10.00-£11.50 Double	Open Apr-Oct Dinner 1900	(symbols)
Mrs Elliot Akaso-Uram, 7 Queen Street Tel. Jedburgh (0835) 62482			2 Dble/Twin 1 Family	1 Public Bath/Sh	B&B per person £8.00-£8.50 Double	Open Jan-Dec	(symbols)
Mrs M Hume 62 Castlegate Tel. Jedburgh (0835) 62504		Awaiting Inspection	1 Dble/Twin 1 Family	2 Public Bath/Sh	B&B per person £8.00-£8.50 Double	Open Jan-Dec	(symbols)
Mrs H H Irvine Froylehurst, The Friars Tel. Jedburgh (0835) 62477		COMMENDED Listed	1 Single 2 Dble/Twin 1 Family	2 Public Bath/Sh	B&B per person £8.50-£9.50 Single £8.50-£9.50 Double	Open Apr-Oct	(symbols)
Detached victorian house with large garden. Spacious rooms. Overlooking town centre; 2 minutes walk.							
Mrs H Oliver 75 Castlegate Tel. Jedburgh (0835) 63353		Awaiting Inspection	2 Dble/Twin	2 Public Bath/Sh	B&B per person £8.50 Double	Open Jan-Dec	(symbols)
Mrs M E Owens 30 High Street Tel. Jedburgh (0835) 62604			1 Single 2 Dble/Twin 3 Family	2 Public Bath/Sh	B&B per person £8.50-£10.00 Single £8.50-£10.00 Double	Open Jan-Dec Dinner 2100	(symbols)
Mrs A Richardson 124 Bongate TD8 6DY Tel. Jedburgh (0835) 62480		APPROVED (crown)	1 Dble/Twin 1 Family		B&B per person £8.25-£8.50 Double	Open Jan-Dec Dinner 1800	(symbols)
Upper flat of house in housing estate near town centre. Local tourist attractions walking distance.							
Mrs Till Mayfield, Sharplaw Road Tel. Jedburgh (0835) 63696		COMMENDED (crown)	1 Single 1 Dble/Twin 1 Family	1 Public Bath/Sh	B&B per person £8.50 Single £8.50 Double	Open Apr-Oct Dinner 1830	(symbols)
Detached country home with views over town. Central for touring Border Country. Home produce.							
Mr K Tomkowicz Normanie Friars Tel. Jedburgh (0835) 63382		Awaiting Inspection	3 Dble/Twin	2 Public Bath/Sh	B&B per person £8.50 Double	Open Apr-Nov	(symbols)
Mrs R Walker Strathmore, 67 Castlegate Tel. Jedburgh (0835) 62728		Listed	3 Dble/Twin	1 Public Bath/Sh	B&B per person £8.00 Double	Open Apr-Oct Dinner 1850	(symbols)
Mrs C Watson Glendouglas Lodge Farm Tel. Jedburgh (0835) 63802			1 Dble/Twin 1 Family		B&B per person £10.00 Double	Open Jan-Dec Dinner 1600	(symbols)
JOHN O'GROATS Caithness Caber-feidh Guest House KW1 4YR Tel. John O'Groats (095581) 219	Map 4 E2		4 Single 3 Dble/Twin 5 Family	2 Public Bath/Sh	B&B per person £7.50-£8.50 Single £6.50-£7.50 Double	Open Jan-Dec Dinner 1730	(symbols)

Key to symbols is on back flap. Details of Classification and Grading are on page vi.

JOHN O'GROATS – KEITH

	Map	Inspection	Rooms	Bath	B&B	Open	Facilities
JOHN O'GROATS continued Mrs M S Green Haven Gore KW1 4YL Tel. John O'Groats (095581) 314	Map 4 E2		2 Dble/Twin 2 Family	1 Public Bath/Sh	B&B per person £6.50-£7.00 Double	Open Jan-Dec Dinner 1830	
JOHNSTONE Renfrewshire Mrs J Robertson Lilybank, Brewery Street Tel. Johnstone (0505) 20271	Map 1 H5		1 Single 3 Dble/Twin 1 Family		B&B per person £7.00-£7.50 Single £7.00-£7.50 Double	Open Jan-Dec Dinner 1800	
KEITH Banffshire Mrs Barbara Allan Barlane, 66 Fife Street AB5 3EG Tel. Keith (05422) 2651	Map 4 E8		3 Dble/Twin	1 Public Bath/Sh	B&B per person £7.50 Double	Open Jan-Dec	
Mrs Elizabeth Bain Saughwells Farm AB5 3RJ Tel. Fochabers (0343) 820409			3 Dble/Twin	1 Public Bath/Sh	B&B per person £6.50-£7.00 Double	Open Jan-Dec Dinner 1700	
Mrs Dorothy F Balgowan An Teallach, 29 Station Road AB5 3BU Tel. Keith (05422) 2734/7594			1 Dble/Twin 2 Family	1 Public Bath/Sh	B&B per person £6.50-£7.00 Double	Open May-Sep Dinner 1700	
Mrs Elma M Burgess Lochiel, 68 Fife Street AB5 3EG Tel. Keith (05422) 2608			3 Dble/Twin	1 Public Bath/Sh	B&B per person £7.50 Double	Open Jan-Dec	
Mr W R Cameron Braelyon, 107 Regent Street AB5 3ED Tel. Keith (05422) 2268			2 Dble/Twin	1 Public Bath/Sh	B&B per person £5.00-£5.50 Double	Open Jan-Dec	
Mrs M Gow Glenalves, 7 Land Street AB5 3AU Tel. Keith (05422) 7512		Awaiting Inspection	2 Dble/Twin	1 Public Bath/Sh	B&B per person £8.00-£8.50 Double	Open Apr-Oct	
Mrs Jean Jackson The Haughs AB5 3QN Tel. Keith (05422) 2238		COMMENDED 👑👑	3 Dble/Twin 1 Family	2 Public Bath/Sh	B&B per person £7.75-£8.50 Double	Open May-Oct Dinner 1800	
			Traditional farmhouse on 220 acre farm near town, just off main road. On Whisky Trail. Local sports.				
Mrs Elizabeth C Leith Montgrew Farm AB5 3LE Tel. Keith (05422) 2852		COMMENDED Listed	3 Dble/Twin 1 Family	1 Public Bath/Sh	B&B per person £8.00 Double	Open May-Sep Dinner 1830	
			Traditional stone built farmhouse on 211 acre mixed arable farm with beef cattle. 1ml(2km) from town.				
Mrs Carol Mackie 134 Land Street AB5 3DH Tel. Keith (05422) 7878			2 Dble/Twin	1 Public Bath/Sh	B&B per person £7.50 Double	Open May-Sep	
Mrs Gladys Murphy Tarnash House AB5 3PB Tel. Keith (05422) 2728		COMMENDED 👑👑	3 Dble/Twin 1 Family	1 Public Bath/Sh	B&B per person £8.00 Double	Open May-Oct	
			Victorian farmhouse on 100 acre arable farm. Cattle, pet donkeys and large ornamental garden.				

VAT is shown at 15%: changes in this rate may affect prices. Prices shown are for guidance only. Please send SAE with each enquiry.

KEITH continued Mrs Gillian Shand Levante, 3 Balloch Road AB5 3HU Tel. Keith (05422) 2578	Map 4 E8 Awaiting Inspection	3 Dble/Twin 1 Family	1 Private Bath/Sh 1 Public Bath/Sh	B&B per person £7.50 Double	Open May-Oct	
KELSO Roxburghshire Bellevue Guest House Bowmont Street Tel. Kelso (0573) 24588	Map 2 F6 COMMENDED 👑👑	3 Single 3 Dble/Twin 2 Family	2 Private Bath/Sh 2 Public Bath/Sh	B&B per person £9.00 Single £9.00-£11.00 Double	Open Mar-Oct Dinner 1830	

Victorian stone house with Adam fireplace. Quiet area. Real home cooking with fresh produce.

RAC Listed   # Maxmill Park   STB 👑

Kelso, Scottish Borders   **Telephone: 0573 24468**

Open all year. Luxury accommodation set in its own secluded garden. Twin, double and family bedrooms. Vanity basin, shaver point, centrally heated throughout, plenty hot water, all towels, some private shower-rooms. Suitable for disabled person. Evening cup of tea served 9pm, home baking, colour TV. Full Scottish breakfast served. Ideal touring centre. Evening meals readily available in town.

Details: Mrs P. Halley.

Maxmill Park Guest House Maxmill Park Tel. Kelso (0573) 24468	APPROVED 👑	3 Single 4 Dble/Twin 3 Family	6 Private Bath/Sh 2 Public Bath/Sh	B&B per person £10.00-£11.00 Single £10.00-£11.00 Double	Open Jan-Dec	

In own grounds close to town centre. B&B accommodation provided in self contained apartments.

Mrs L S Hurst Lochside Tel. Yetholm (057382) 349	Listed	1 Single 2 Dble/Twin	1 Public Bath/Sh	B&B per person £8.50 Single £8.50 Double	Open Apr-Sep	
Mrs G Wark Ivy Neuk, 62 Horsemarket Tel. Kelso (0573) 24428		1 Single 2 Dble/Twin	1 Public Bath/Sh	B&B per person £9.00 Single £9.00 Double	Open Jan-Dec	
KEMNAY Aberdeenshire Mrs G Adam Boatleys Farm AB5 9NA Tel. Kemnay (0467) 42533	Map 4 G10	3 Dble/Twin	2 Public Bath/Sh	B&B per person £9.00 Double	Open Jan-Dec Dinner 1800	
KENMORE, by Shieldaig Ross-shire Mrs M A Cameron Post Office House IV54 8XH Tel. Shieldaig (05205) 219	Map 3 E8	2 Dble/Twin 1 Family	2 Public Bath/Sh	B&B per person £8.00 Double	Open Apr-Oct Dinner 1900	
KENNETHMONT, by Huntly Aberdeenshire Mrs Grant Earlsfield AB5 6YQ Tel. Kennethmont (04643) 207	Map 4 E9	1 Dble/Twin 1 Family	1 Public Bath/Sh	B&B per person £7.50-£8.00 Double	Open Jan-Dec Dinner 1900	

Key to symbols is on back flap. Details of Classification and Grading are on page vi.

KENNETHMONT, by Huntly continued Major & Mrs D G Wells Craighall AB5 4QN Tel. Kennethmont (04643) 215	Map 4 E9		1 Single 1 Dble/Twin 1 Family	2 Private Bath/Sh 2 Public Bath/Sh	B&B per person £10.00 Single £10.00 Double	Open Jan-Nov Dinner 1800	
KENSALEYRE, by Portree Isle of Skye, Inverness-shire Corran Guest House Eyre Tel. Skeabost Bridge (047032) 311	Map 3 D8		1 Single 2 Dble/Twin 3 Family	2 Public Bath/Sh	B&B per person £18.00 Double	Open Jan-Dec Dinner 1900	
KEOSE GLEBE Lewis, Western Isles Mrs Morrison Handa, 18 Keose Glebe	Map 3 C5		1 Dble/Twin 1 Family	1 Public Bath/Sh	B&B per person £8.00-£9.00 Double	Open Jan-Dec Dinner 1900	
KILBARCHAN, by Johnstone Renfrewshire Ashburn Guest House Milliken Park Road Tel. Kilbarchan (05057) 5477	Map 1 H5	Listed	1 Single 1 Dble/Twin 4 Family	2 Public Bath/Sh	B&B per person £10.00-£12.00 Single £9.00-£11.00 Double	Open Jan-Dec Dinner 1800	
Mrs Douglas Gladstone Farm Tel. Kilbarchan (05057) 2579			2 Dble/Twin	1 Public Bath/Sh	B&B per person £8.00 Single £8.00 Double	Open Jan-Dec Dinner 1800	
Mrs Ruby Paterson Meikle Burntshields Farm Tel. Kilbarchan (05057) 2642			2 Dble/Twin	1 Public Bath/Sh	B&B per person £8.00 Double	Open Jan-Nov	
KILBRIDE, by Broadford Isle of Skye, Inverness-shire Mrs Larkman Ashbank Tel. Broadford (04712) 424	Map 3 E10		2 Single 2 Dble/Twin 2 Family	1 Public Bath/Sh	B&B per person £8.50-£9.00 Single £8.50-£9.00 Double	Open Mar-Oct	
KILCHRENAN, by Taynuilt Argyll Jean A Gordon Braeside Tel. Kilchrenan (08663) 273	Map 1 F2		4 Dble/Twin	1 Public Bath/Sh	B&B per person £8.00-£10.00 Double	Open Apr-Oct Dinner 1900	
KILDRUMMY, by Alford Aberdeenshire Mrs L Allan Malt Croft AB3 8QY Tel. Kildrummy (03365) 338	Map 4 E10		1 Dble/Twin 1 Family	1 Public Bath/Sh	B&B per person £7.00 Double	Open Jan-Dec Dinner 1700	

Name / Address	Map Ref	Grading	Rooms	Bath	Terms	Open	Symbols
KILLIECRANKIE Perthshire	Map 4 C12						
Garry Guest House PH16 5LW Tel. Pitlochry (0796) 3219			1 Single 3 Dble/Twin 1 Family	1 Private Bath/Sh 1 Public Bath/Sh	B&B per person £10.00 Single £9.50 Double	Open Apr-Oct	
Mrs Henderson Old Faskally House PH16 5LR Tel. Pitlochry (0796) 3414			3 Dble/Twin	1 Private Bath/Sh 2 Public Bath/Sh	B&B per person £8.50 Single £8.50 Double	Open Jan-Dec Dinner 1830	
Mrs Sanderson Druimuan PH16 5LG Tel. Pitlochry (0796) 3214			1 Dble/Twin 1 Family	2 Private Bath/Sh	B&B per person £9.00-£11.00 Double	Open Jan-Dec	
KILLIN Perthshire	Map 1 H2						
Craigbuie Guest House Main Street FK21 8UH Tel. Killin (05672) 439			5 Dble/Twin 2 Family		B&B per person £8.00 Double	Open Apr-Oct Dinner 1900	
Fairview House Guest House Main Street FK21 8UT Tel. Killin (05672) 667		COMMENDED 👑👑	1 Single 3 Dble/Twin 1 Family	1 Public Bath/Sh	B&B per person £7.50-£8.50 Single £7.50-£8.50 Double	Open Jan-Dec Dinner 1930	
Family run, in centre of village. Near west side of Loch Tay.							
Invertay House Guest House FK21 8TN Tel. Killin (05672) 492			1 Single 3 Dble/Twin 2 Family		B&B per person £8.00 Single £8.00 Double	Open Jan-Dec Dinner 1900	
Ms Lois Dommersnes Shieling Restaurant FK21 8TX Tel. Killin (05672) 334		APPROVED Listed	2 Single 2 Dble/Twin	1 Public Bath/Sh	B&B per person £7.50 Single £7.50 Double	Open Apr-Oct Dinner 1600	
Woodland setting on outskirt of popular village. Washbasins in rooms. Golf, fishing, walking locally.							
Mr & Mrs L Mudd Falls O'Dochart Cottage FK21 8SW Tel. Killin (05672) 363		COMMENDED Listed	1 Single 2 Dble/Twin 1 Family	1 Public Bath/Sh	B&B per person £7.50 Single £7.50 Double	Open Jan-Dec Dinner 1900	
Situated adjacent to the attractive Falls of Dochart. Easy walking distance to shops.							
KILMARNOCK Ayrshire	Map 1 H7						
Busbiehill Guest House Knockentiber KA2 0DJ Tel. Kilmarnock (0563) 32985			2 Single 8 Dble/Twin	2 Private Bath/Sh 6 Public Bath/Sh	B&B per person £6.00-£8.50 Single £6.00-£7.50 Double	Open Jan-Dec Dinner 1800	
Mrs D Bird 3 Dundonald Road Tel. Kilmarnock (0563) 39010			1 Single 4 Dble/Twin 2 Family	1 Private Bath/Sh 3 Public Bath/Sh	B&B per person £8.00-£10.00 Single £8.00-£10.00 Double	Open Jan-Dec	
Mr & Mrs W R Bruce Blenheim, 69 London Road Tel. Kilmarnock (0563) 26386		👑👑	2 Dble/Twin 1 Family	1 Private Bath/Sh 1 Public Bath/Sh	B&B per person £9.50-£10.00 Double	Open Jan-Nov	
Mrs A Grant 177 Dundonald Road Tel. Kilmarnock (0563) 22733		Awaiting Inspection	3 Dble/Twin	1 Public Bath/Sh	B&B per person £9.00-£18.00 Double	Open May-Sep	

Key to symbols is on back flap. Details of Classification and Grading are on page vi.

133

	Map		Rooms	Bath	B&B	Open	
KILMARNOCK continued	Map 1 H7						
Mrs C Hannah, 61 Irvine Road, Tel. Kilmarnock (0563) 28392			2 Dble/Twin	2 Public Bath/Sh	B&B per person £8.50–£9.50 Double	Open Jan-Dec	
Mrs Hill, 2A Beech Avenue, Tel. Kilmarnock (0563) 23970/20959			1 Dble/Twin 1 Family	1 Public Bath/Sh	B&B per person £9.00–£10.00 Double	Open Jan-Dec	
KILMARTIN, by Lochgilphead Argyll	Map 1 E4						
Mrs Gordon, Ri-Cruin, Tel. Kilmartin (05465) 231			2 Dble/Twin 1 Family	1 Public Bath/Sh	B&B per person £8.00–£8.50 Double	Open Apr-Oct	
KILMORE, by Oban Argyll	Map 1 E2						
Mrs P L Baber, Glenfeochan, Tel. Kilmore (063177) 273			3 Dble/Twin	3 Private Bath/Sh	B&B per person £25.00–£45.00 Double Dinner 2000	Open Jan-Dec	
KILMORY Isle of Arran	Map 1 F7						
Mrs Adamson, Rosebank, Corriecravie, Tel. Sliddery (077087) 228		COMMENDED ♛♛	1 Single 2 Dble/Twin 1 Family	1 Public Bath/Sh	B&B per person £7.50 Single £7.50 Double	Open Jan-Dec Dinner 1800	
Traditional family farmhouse with views over sea to Mull of Kintyre. Home cooking, log fires.							
Mr & Mrs N C McLean, Torlin Villa, Tel. Sliddery (077087) 240		♛♛	1 Single 2 Dble/Twin 1 Family	1 Public Bath/Sh	B&B per person £8.00 Single £8.00 Double	Open Jan-Dec Dinner 1800	
KILMUIR Isle of Skye, Inverness-shire	Map 3 D8						
Mr & Mrs R Phelps, Kilmuir House, Tel. Uig (047042) 262			2 Dble/Twin 1 Family	2 Public Bath/Sh	B&B per person £7.50–£9.00 Double	Open Jan-Dec Dinner 1900	
KINCRAIG Inverness-shire	Map 4 B10						
Grampian View Guest House, Tel. Kincraig (05404) 383			1 Single 3 Dble/Twin 1 Family	1 Public Bath/Sh	B&B per person £10.00 Single £10.00 Double	Open Jan-Dec	
Insh House Guest House, PH21 1NU, Tel. Kincraig (05404) 377			2 Single 2 Dble/Twin 1 Family	2 Public Bath/Sh	B&B per person £9.00 Single £9.00 Double	Open Jan-Dec Dinner 1900	
March House Guest House, PH21 1NA, Tel. Kincraig (05404) 388		COMMENDED ♛	5 Dble/Twin 1 Family	5 Private Bath/Sh 1 Public Bath/Sh	B&B per person £9.00–£10.50 Double Dinner 1900	Open Dec-Oct	
Modern, purpose built. Set in beautiful Glenfeshie with excellent views of surrounding hills							
Mrs J Love, Birchfield, Tel. Kincraig (05404) 239			1 Single 1 Dble/Twin 1 Family	2 Public Bath/Sh	B&B per person £7.00–£7.50 Single £7.00–£7.50 Double	Open Jan-Dec Dinner 1830	

VAT is shown at 15%: changes in this rate may affect prices. Prices shown are for guidance only. Please send SAE with each enquiry.

KINCRAIG continued Mr G Reid Caber An Feidh Tel. Kincraig (05404) 300	Map 4 B10		2 Dble/Twin 1 Family	1 Public Bath/Sh	B&B per person £7.50-£8.50 Double	Open Jan-Dec Dinner 1830	▢V ▢ ▢TV ✀ ⌕ ✻ ▢P ⌂ ⅟ ▢C
KING EDWARD **Banffshire** Mrs R Elrick Blackton Farm AB4 3NJ Tel. King Edward (08885) 205	Map 4 F8	COMMENDED 👑 👑	1 Single 3 Dble/Twin 1 Family	1 Public Bath/Sh	B&B per person £8.00 Single	Open May-Oct Dinner 1800	♞ ⌕ ☞ ▢V ⌖ ⒉ ▢TV ✀ ▢ ⌑ ✁ ⌕ ⅋ ▢P ▢C ⌸ ⅟
			Farmhouse on 120 acre farm in quiet countryside. Local activities include golf, fishing and walks.				
KINGHORN **Fife** Mrs Ritchie 66 Pettycur Road KY3 9RL Tel. Kinghorn (0592) 890090	Map 2 D4	Awaiting Inspection	1 Dble/Twin 1 Family	1 Public Bath/Sh	B&B per person £8.50-£10.00 Double	Open Jan-Nov	♞ ⌕ ⬜ ⌖ ☞ ⒉ ▢TV ✀ ▢ ⌑ ✻ ▢P ⌂ ⅟ ⅟ ▢C
Mrs Wasik Carlin, 68 Pettycur Road KY3 9RW Tel. Kinghorn (0592) 890393			2 Dble/Twin 1 Family	1 Public Bath/Sh	B&B per person £8.00 Double	Open Mar-Nov Dinner 1800	⌖ ☞ ▢V ⒉ ⌖ ▢TV ▢ ⌑ ⌂ ▢C ⌸
KINGUSSIE **Inverness-shire** Benula Guest House Acres Road Tel. Kingussie (05402) 775	Map 4 B11		4 Dble/Twin	1 Public Bath/Sh	B&B per person £8.00 Double	Open Jan-Dec Dinner 1830	♞ ▢V ⒉ ⌖ ▢TV ✀ ▢ ⌑ ⅟ ✻ ⅋ ▢P ⌂ ⅟ ▢C ▢T
Sonnhalde Guest House East Terrace PH21 1JS Tel. Kingussie (05402) 266			1 Single 4 Dble/Twin 2 Family	2 Public Bath/Sh	B&B per person £8.50-£9.00 Single £8.50-£9.00 Double	Open Jan-Oct	♞ ⌖ ⌕ ▢V ⒉ ⌖ ▢TV ✀ ▢ ⅟ ✻ ▢P ⌂ ⅟ ⅟ ▢C ▢T
Tirveyne Guest House West Terrace Tel. Kingussie (05402) 667		APPROVED 👑 👑	2 Single 3 Dble/Twin 3 Family	2 Public Bath/Sh	B&B per person £8.00-£9.00 Single £8.00-£9.00 Double	Open Jan-Dec Dinner 1800	♞ ⌕ ⌖ ▢V ▢Y ⒉ ⌖ ▢TV ✄ ✻ ▢P ⌂ ⅟ ▢C
			Family run in own grounds above village. Panoramic views of Spey Valley and Cairngorm Mountains.				
Mrs Cunningham Cornerways, Newtonmore Road PH21 1HE Tel. Kingussie (05402) 446		Awaiting Inspection	4 Dble/Twin	1 Private Bath/Sh 1 Public Bath/Sh	B&B per person £7.50-£8.50 Double	Open Apr-Oct	♞ ▢V ⒉ ⌖ ▢TV ⅟ ✄ ▢P ⌂ ⅟ ▢C
Mrs J Filshie Arden House, Newtonmore Road PH21 1HE Tel. Kingussie (05402) 369			1 Single 2 Dble/Twin 2 Family	2 Public Bath/Sh	B&B per person £9.00-£10.00 Single £8.50-£9.50 Double	Open Jan-Dec	♞ ⬜ ⌖ ⒉ ⌖ ▢TV ✀ ▢ ⌂ ✻ ▢P ⌂ ▢C
Mrs S Gibson Gynack Villa, High Street Tel. Kingussie (05402) 223			1 Dble/Twin 2 Family	2 Public Bath/Sh	B&B per person £7.50 Double	Open Jan-Dec	☞ ⒉ ⌖ ▢TV ▢ ⅟ ⅋ ▢£ ▢P ⌂ ⅟ ⅟ ▢C
Mrs A Gibson Brae Rannoch, Gynack Road Tel. Kingussie (05402) 675			3 Dble/Twin	1 Private Bath/Sh 1 Public Bath/Sh	B&B per person £7.50-£8.00 Double	Open Jan-Dec Dinner 1800	▢V ⌖ ⒉ ⌖ ▢TV ✀ ▢ ⅟ ⌑ ⅋ ▢£ ▢P ⅟ ▢C

Key to symbols is on back flap. Details of Classification and Grading are on page vi.

135

KINGUSSIE continued — Map 4 B11

Name	Grade	Rooms	Bath	Prices	Open	Facilities
Mrs E MacDonald, Deveron House, 85 High Street, Tel. Kingussie (05402) 343		1 Single, 1 Dble/Twin, 1 Family	1 Public Bath/Sh	B&B per person £7.00 Single £7.00 Double	Open Jan-Dec Dinner 1830	
Mrs A Melvin, The Hermitage, Spey Street, Tel. Kingussie (05402) 501	COMMENDED ♛♛	1 Single, 3 Dble/Twin, 1 Family	1 Public Bath/Sh	B&B per person £9.00 Single £8.50 Double	Open Jan-Dec Dinner 1830	
	19th century town house built of local stone. In residential area close to village centre.					
Mrs K Morris, Tomliadh, Gynack Road, Tel. Kingussie (05402) 579		2 Family	1 Public Bath/Sh	B&B per person £7.00 Double	Open Jan-Dec Dinner 1800	
Mrs D T Smith, Ardvonie, Ardvonie Road, Tel. Kingussie (05402) 362	♛	2 Dble/Twin, 1 Family	1 Public Bath/Sh	B&B per person £7.00-£8.00 Double	Open Apr-Oct	
Mrs Thackrey, Tighvonie, West Terrace, Tel. Kingussie (05402) 263		1 Dble/Twin, 1 Family	1 Public Bath/Sh	B&B per person £7.50 Double	Open Jan-Dec Dinner 1830	

KINLOCH RANNOCH, Perthshire — Map 2 A1

Name	Grade	Rooms	Bath	Prices	Open	Facilities
Mrs Steffen, Cuilmore Cottage, PH16 5QB, Tel. Kinloch Rannoch (08822) 218	COMMENDED Listed	1 Single, 1 Dble/Twin	1 Public Bath/Sh	B&B per person £6.50 Single £6.50 Double	Open Jan-Dec Dinner 1700	
	Stone cottage close to Kinloch Rannoch, fresh produce, home cooking. Boat and bicycle available.					

KINLOCHBERVIE, Sutherland — Map 3 G3

Name	Grade	Rooms	Bath	Prices	Open	Facilities
Mr & Mrs Gregory, Garbet Rooms, IV27 4RP, Tel. Kinlochbervie (097182) 271 275		1 Single, 5 Dble/Twin	6 Private Bath/Sh, 4 Public Bath/Sh	B&B per person £15.00 Single £10.00 Double	Open Jan-Dec Dinner 1800	
Mrs E Marshall, North Fleet Cottage, Sheigra, Tel. Kinlochbervie (097182) 328		2 Dble/Twin	1 Public Bath/Sh	B&B per person £7.50 Double	Open Apr-Nov Dinner 1930	

KINLOCHLEVEN, Argyll — Map 1 F1

Name	Grade	Rooms	Bath	Prices	Open	Facilities
Mr P Bush, Mamore Lodge, PA40 4QW, Tel. Kinlochleven (08554) 213		5 Family	5 Private Bath/Sh	B&B per person £6.50-£8.50 Double	Open Jan-Dec Dinner 1700	

(See advert p. 137)

KINNEFF, Kincardineshire — Map 4 G12

Name	Grade	Rooms	Bath	Prices	Open	Facilities
Corbieknowe Guest House, DD10 0TB, Tel. Catterline (05695) 341	COMMENDED ♛♛	1 Single, 2 Dble/Twin, 3 Family	2 Public Bath/Sh	B&B per person £10.00 Single £9.50 Double	Open Jan-Dec Dinner 1800	
	Family run. On A92 road, 6 miles (9km) south of Stonehaven.					

KINROSS — Map 2 C3

Name	Grade	Rooms	Bath	Prices	Open	Facilities
Mrs Barnes, Phileuan, 36 The Muirs, KY13 7AU, Tel. Kinross (0577) 63502		1 Dble/Twin, 2 Family	1 Public Bath/Sh	B&B per person £9.00 Double	Open Jan-Dec	

VAT is shown at 15%: changes in this rate may affect prices. Prices shown are for guidance only. Please send SAE with each enquiry.

Mamore Holiday Lodge

KINLOCHLEVEN · ARGYLL · PA40 4QN
Telephone: (085 54) 213

MAMORE is an ideal centre for ramblers and birdwatchers alike, close to to the **WEST HIGHLAND WAY WALK.**

The new lodge, built around the turn of the century high on the hillside above Kinlochleven, commands magnificent views in all directions. To the south and west over Loch Leven are the mountains of Glencoe and Appin, and to the north and east lie the Blackwater Reservoir and the Mamores themselves.

The wild grandeur of the estate, virtually unchanged for centuries, extends to some 45,000 acres, rising from sea level to eight lofty peaks, all over 3,000 feet. Miles of stalking tracks and zigzagging pony paths give access to the natural habitat of an abundance of wildlife, including red deer, roe deer, eagles and a large variety of birds.

There are trout in the hill lochans, mackerel in the sea loch and salmon in the rivers Leven and Coe.

	Map	Award	Accommodation	Bathrooms	Terms	Opening
KINROSS continued Mrs C Cochrane 126 High Street KY13 7DA Tel. Kinross (0577) 62498	Map 2 C3		1 Single 3 Dble/Twin 2 Family	1 Public Bath/Sh	B&B per person £10.00-£12.00 Single £9.00-£10.00 Double	Open Jan-Dec Dinner 1800
Mrs Mary Riddell 37 Muirs Tel. Kinross (0577) 62226			3 Dble/Twin	2 Public Bath/Sh	B&B per person £9.00 Double	Open Apr-Sep
KIPPEN Stirlingshire I & H McGregor Delphi, 35 Oakwood Tel. Kippen (078687) 419	Map 2 A4	COMMENDED 👑👑	2 Dble/Twin	1 Public Bath/Sh	B&B per person £6.50-£7.50 Double	Open Jan-Dec Dinner 1900
In picturesque village of central Scotland. Home cooking. Good walking area. Opposite tennis court.						
KIPPFORD Kirkcudbrightshire Orchardknowes Guest House Orchardknowes Tel. Kippford (055662) 639	Map 2 B10		1 Single 2 Dble/Twin 3 Family	2 Public Bath/Sh	B&B per person £10.00 Single £10.00 Double	Open Jan-Dec Dinner 1930
Mrs J B Beckitt Milnbrae Tel. Kippford (055662) 605			2 Dble/Twin		B&B per person £7.00 Double	Open Apr-Oct Dinner 1900
Mrs D Wray Kipp Lodge Tel. Kippford (055662) 212		COMMENDED Listed	1 Dble/Twin 1 Family	1 Public Bath/Sh	B&B per person £8.00-£8.50 Double	Open Apr-Oct
Victorian listed building. Former octagonal lodge. Rural setting near village. Sailing centre nearby.						
KIRKBEAN, by Dumfries Dumfriesshire Cavens Guest House Tel. Kirkbean (038788) 234	Map 2 B10		5 Dble/Twin 1 Family	6 Private Bath/Sh	B&B per person £15.00 Double	Open Jan-Dec Dinner 1845
KIRKCALDY Fife Townsend Cottage Guest House 30 Townsend Place Tel. Kirkcaldy (0592) 262713	Map 2 D4		1 Dble/Twin 2 Family	1 Public Bath/Sh	B&B per person £9.00-£10.00 Double	Open Jan-Dec Dinner 1800
Mrs Linda Duffy Invertiel House, 21 Pratt Street Tel. Kirkcaldy (0592) 264849		COMMENDED 👑	1 Single 1 Dble/Twin 1 Family	1 Public Bath/Sh	B&B per person £9.00-£10.00 Single £8.50-£9.00 Double	Open Jan-Dec Dinner 1800
Detached victorian house with original plasterwork. Own garden. Convenient for town centre.						
Mrs Elizabeth Duncan Bennochy Bank, 26 Carlyle Road Tel. Kirkcaldy (0592) 200733		👑👑	2 Dble/Twin 1 Family	2 Public Bath/Sh	B&B per person £8.50 Double	Open Jan-Dec
Mrs Simpson Abbeville, 34 Hopetoun Pl, Newliston Est. KY2 6TY Tel. Kirkcaldy (0592) 266866			1 Dble/Twin 1 Family	2 Public Bath/Sh	B&B per person £8.50-£9.00 Double	Open Jan-Dec

VAT is shown at 15%: changes in this rate may affect prices. Prices shown are for guidance only. Please send SAE with each enquiry.

KIRKCALDY continued Mrs Watson Anchorage, 13 Adamson Avenue KY2 5EH Tel. Kirkcaldy (0592) 269399	Map 2 D4		2 Dble/Twin	1 Public Bath/Sh	B&B per person £8.00-£10.00 Double	Open Jan-Dec	▣ ▢ ▰ ▦ ◣ ⤵ C
KIRKCOWAN Wigtownshire Mrs G Oliver Kirkland House, Beechgrove Tel. Kirkcowan (067183) 236	Map 1 G10		3 Dble/Twin 1 Family	2 Public Bath/Sh	B&B per person £8.00-£9.00 Double	Open Apr-Oct	▢ ▦ TV ⚡ ◣ ⤵ P C
KIRKCUDBRIGHT Anchorlee Guest House 95 St Mary's Street Tel. Kirkcudbright (0557) 30793	Map 2 A11	HIGHLY COMMENDED ♕ ♕	2 Dble/Twin 1 Family	1 Public Bath/Sh	B&B per person £9.00-£10.50 Double	Open Jan-Dec Dinner 1830	⚞ ▰ ◲ ▦ TV ❋ P C
			Elegant, detached stone house. Large walled garden and sun verandah. Situated on edge of town.				
Castle Guest House 16 Castle Street Tel. Kirkcudbright (0557) 30204		APPROVED ♕ ♕	4 Dble/Twin 1 Family	1 Private Bath/Sh 1 Public Bath/Sh	B&B per person £8.50-£9.00 Double	Open Feb-Nov Dinner 1800	⚞ ◳ V ◲ ◲ ▦ TV ⚡ ◣ ⤵ ☂ P △ C ▦
			Family run. Close to Kirkcudbright Castle and town centre amenities.				
Mrs H Caygill Marks Farm Tel. Kirkcudbright (0557) 30854		COMMENDED ♕ ♕	3 Dble/Twin	1 Public Bath/Sh	B&B per person £10.50 Double	Open Jan-Dec Dinner 1800	⚞ ▰ V ▦ TV ☂ ❋ P △ ⛏
			16C stone built farmhouse with large garden. Excellent views over peaceful countryside. Home cooking.				
Mrs E Fisher Beaconsfield, Bridge Street Tel. Kirkcudbright (0557) 30488		♕	2 Dble/Twin 1 Family	1 Public Bath/Sh	B&B per person £8.00 Double	Open Jan-Dec	⚞ ◲ ◲ TV P C
Mrs K McIlwraith Parkview, 22 Millburn Street DG6 4EA Tel. Kirkcudbright (0557) 30056		Awaiting Inspection	2 Dble/Twin 1 Family	2 Public Bath/Sh	B&B per person £7.50 Double	Open Jan-Dec Dinner 1700	⚞ V ◲ ▦ TV ⚡ ◣ ⤵ ☂ ❋ P △ C ▦
Mrs Proctor Grange Farm House Tel. Kirkcudbright (0557) 30552		HIGHLY COMMENDED ♕	3 Dble/Twin	1 Public Bath/Sh	B&B per person £10.50 Double	Open Jan-Dec Dinner 1900	V ▦ ⤵ ⚄ ❋ P
			Quiet situation with superb views over bay. Home cooked fresh food a speciality. Request no smoking.				
KIRKFIELD BANK, by Lanark Lanarkshire Mrs M Rayworth Mousemill House, Mousemill Road Tel. Lanark (0555) 61273	Map 2 B6		1 Single 1 Family	1 Public Bath/Sh	B&B per person £13.00 Single £9.00 Double	Open Apr-Oct	◲ ▰ ▦ TV ⚡ ◣ ⤵ ☂ ❋ △ C
KIRKHILL, by Inverness Inverness-shire Mrs Munro Wester Moniack Farm IV5 7PQ Tel. Drumchardine (046383) 237	Map 4 A8	COMMENDED Listed	1 Dble/Twin 1 Family	1 Public Bath/Sh	B&B per person £7.50-£8.00 Double	Open Jan-Dec Dinner 1830	⚞ V ◲ ◲ ▦ TV ☂ ❋ P C ⛏
			Well sited for touring Highlands, 10 mins drive Inverness. Peaceful setting. Family atmosphere.				

Key to symbols is on back flap. Details of Classification and Grading are on page vi.

139

KIRKMICHAEL Perthshire Mr & Mrs Mills Ardlebrig PH10 7NY Tel. Strathardle (025081) 350	Map 2 C1		1 Single 1 Dble/Twin 1 Family	1 Public Bath/Sh	B&B per person £7.50-£8.00 Single £7.50-£8.00 Double	Open Jan-Dec Dinner 1800	
KIRKMICHAEL, Maybole Ayrshire Mrs M Mcfarlane Dalvennan Farm KA19 7LB Tel. Patna (0292) 531237	Map 1 G8		1 Dble/Twin 1 Family	1 Public Bath/Sh	B&B per person £7.50-£8.00 Double	Open Jan-Dec Dinner 2000	
Mr & Mrs Ravenscroft Anvil Cottage, 27 Patna Road KA19 7PJ Tel. Kirkmichael (06555) 281			2 Dble/Twin	1 Public Bath/Sh	B&B per person £7.00-£8.00 Double	Open Jan-Dec	
KIRKMUIRHILL Lanarkshire I H McInally Dykehead Farm, Boghead Tel. Lesmahagow (0555) 892226	Map 2 A6		1 Dble/Twin 1 Family	1 Public Bath/Sh	B&B per person £8.00 Double	Open Jan-Dec	
KIRKPATRICK DURHAM, **Castle Douglas** Kirkcudbrightshire Mrs M Mathie Kirkland Tel. Kirkpatrick Durham (055665) 274	Map 2 B10		1 Dble/Twin 1 Family	1 Public Bath/Sh	B&B per person £7.50-£8.00 Double	Open Mar-Oct Dinner 1800	
KIRKPATRICK FLEMING Dumfriesshire Mrs F M Irving Gillshaw View, Chapelknowe DG14 0YD Tel. Kirkpatrick Fleming (04618) 673	Map 2 D10		1 Dble/Twin 1 Family	1 Public Bath/Sh	B&B per person £8.00-£8.50 Double	Open Jan-Dec Dinner 1800	
KIRKWALL Orkney Bellavista Guest House Carness Road Tel. Kirkwall (0856) 2306	Map 5 B11	COMMENDED	1 Single 7 Dble/Twin	1 Public Bath/Sh	B&B per person £9.00 Single £9.00 Double	Open Nov-Sep Dinner 1830	
Family run, attractive and comfortable. Evening meal and picnic lunch available. 1 mile from town.							
Mrs M Bain 6 Frasers Close KW15 1DT Tel. Kirkwall (0856) 2862			1 Single 3 Dble/Twin	1 Private Bath/Sh 3 Public Bath/Sh	B&B per person £6.50 Single £6.50 Double	Open Jan-Dec	
Mrs Cooper Miada, 1 Papdale Drive, Berstane Rd Tel. Kirkwall (0856) 3599			2 Dble/Twin 1 Family	2 Public Bath/Sh	B&B per person £7.50 Double	Open Jan-Dec Dinner 1800	
Mrs M Flett Briarlea, 10 Dundas Crescent Tel. Kirkwall (0856) 2747		COMMENDED Listed	2 Single 1 Dble/Twin	1 Public Bath/Sh	B&B per person £7.50 Single £7.50 Double	Open Jan-Dec	
19C stone detached villa with large walled garden. Access at all times. Short walk to town centre.							

VAT is shown at 15%: changes in this rate may affect prices. Prices shown are for guidance only. Please send SAE with each enquiry.

	Map	Grade	Rooms	Bath	B&B	Open	Symbols
KIRKWALL continued Mrs J Forsyth 21 Willowburn Road Tel. Kirkwall (0856) 4020	Map 5 B11		1 Single 2 Dble/Twin	1 Public Bath/Sh	B&B per person £7.00 Single £7.00 Double	Open Jan-Dec	
Mrs I Gray Bilmaris, Glaitness Road Tel. Kirkwall (0856) 4515		Listed	3 Dble/Twin 2 Family	1 Public Bath/Sh	B&B per person £7.00 Double	Open Jan-Dec	
Mrs M Hourie Heathfield Farmhouse, St Ola KW15 1TR Tel. Kirkwall (0856) 2378			1 Single 2 Dble/Twin 1 Family	1 Public Bath/Sh	B&B per person £7.00 Single £7.00 Double	Open Jan-Dec	
Mrs Elizabeth Lea 6 Old Scapa Road Tel. Kirkwall (0856) 4260		COMMENDED 👑👑	3 Dble/Twin	1 Public Bath/Sh	B&B per person £6.00-£7.50 Double	Open Jan-Dec	
Family home on quiet road. Near St Magnus Cathedral and town centre. Breakfast served in bedrooms.							
Mrs M Leask Brantwood, Holm Branch Road Tel. Kirkwall (0856) 3309			2 Dble/Twin	1 Public Bath/Sh	B&B per person £6.50 Double	Open Apr-Oct Dinner 1730	
Mainlands 76 Victoria Street Tel. Kirkwall (0856) 2041			2 Single 2 Dble/Twin 1 Family	1 Public Bath/Sh	B&B per person £7.00-£7.50 Single £7.00-£7.50 Double	Open Jan-Dec	
Mrs Mills Sycamore, Berstane Road Tel. Kirkwall (0856) 2586			2 Dble/Twin	1 Public Bath/Sh	B&B per person £7.00 Double	Open May-Oct	
Mrs Shearer 36 Craigie Crescent Tel. Kirkwall (0856) 3638			1 Single 1 Dble/Twin	1 Public Bath/Sh	B&B per person £7.00 Single £7.00 Double	Open Jan-Dec Dinner 1800	
Mrs P Sutherland Papdale Mill, Mill Street Tel. Kirkwall (0856) 5399			2 Dble/Twin 2 Family	1 Private Bath/Sh 1 Public Bath/Sh	B&B per person £8.00-£9.00 Double	Open Jan-Dec	
Mrs Thornton The Manse, Palace Road Tel. Kirkwall (0856) 4761			3 Dble/Twin	1 Public Bath/Sh	B&B per person £6.50-£7.00 Double	Open Jan-Dec	
KIRRIEMUIR Angus Mrs Dryburgh Broadmuir, Kingoldrum Tel. Kingoldrum (057581) 230	Map 2 D1		2 Dble/Twin	1 Public Bath/Sh	B&B per person £7.50 Double	Open Jan-Dec Dinner 1700	
Mrs B Ewart Middlefield House, Knowehead Tel. Kirriemuir (0575) 72924			1 Single 2 Dble/Twin	2 Private Bath/Sh 1 Public Bath/Sh	B&B per person £7.00 Single £7.00 Double	Open Jan-Dec	
Mrs J Lindsay Crepto, Kinnordy Place Tel. Kirriemuir (0575) 72746			1 Single 2 Dble/Twin	1 Public Bath/Sh	B&B per person £8.50 Single £8.50 Double	Open Jan-Dec	
Mrs C Murray St Colms, Glengate Tel. Kirriemuir (0575) 72210		COMMENDED Listed	2 Family	1 Public Bath/Sh	B&B per person £7.00-£7.50 Double	Open Apr-Oct Dinner 1900	
Edwardian red sandstone house with garden. Residential area near town centre and leisure park.							

Key to symbols is on back flap. Details of Classification and Grading are on page vi.

141

KIRTLEBRIDGE, by Lockerbie Dumfriesshire	Map 2 D10		

KIRTLE HOUSE
Kirtlebridge, Nr. Lockerbie, Dumfriesshire
Tel: 046 15 221 — Mrs B. J. Crouch

Kirtlebridge is a tiny Hamlet set amid farmland, yet only ¼ mile from the A74 main route in Scotland. The situation is ideal for exploring this beautiful unspoilt area of Scotland. With visitors' lounge, full central heating, first class food and personal service, Kirtle House extends a warm welcome.
Reductions for children and for bookings of 7 days or more.

Mrs B Crouch Kirtle House Tel. Kirtlebridge (04615) 221			2 Dble/Twin 2 Family	1 Public Bath/Sh	B&B per person £8.00 Double	Open Jan-Dec Dinner 1900	

KYLE OF LOCHALSH Ross-shire	Map 3 F10						
The Retreat Guest House Main Street IV40 8BY Tel. Kyle (0599) 4308		COMMENDED ♛ ♛	2 Single 9 Dble/Twin 2 Family	4 Public Bath/Sh	B&B per person £8.00-£10.00 Single £8.00-£10.00 Double	Open Jan-Dec Dinner 1845	
			Friendly, family run, in centre of village. Easy access to ferry, good touring base for West Coast.				
Mr & Mrs N Beaton Glenrowan, Erbusaig Tel. Kyle (0599) 4596			4 Dble/Twin		B&B per person £8.00 Double	Open Jan-Dec Dinner 1800	
Mrs I Finlayson Sunnybank, Main Street IV40 8DA Tel. Kyle (0599) 4265			3 Dble/Twin	1 Public Bath/Sh	B&B per person £7.50-£8.50 Double	Open Jan-Dec	
Mrs C Matheson 13 Lochalsh Road IV40 8BP Tel. Kyle (0599) 4297			2 Dble/Twin	1 Public Bath/Sh	B&B per person £7.50 Double	Open Jan-Dec	

KYLEAKIN Isle of Skye, Inverness-shire	Map 3 E10						
Mrs F Gillies Ceol-na-Mara, South Obbe Tel. Kyle (0599) 4443			1 Dble/Twin 3 Family	1 Public Bath/Sh	B&B per person £8.00-£10.00 Double	Open Jan-Dec Dinner 1800	
Mrs MacLeod Ardmhor		APPROVED Listed	1 Dble/Twin 2 Family	1 Public Bath/Sh	B&B per person £7.50-£8.00 Double	Open Apr-Oct Dinner 1900	
			Detached bungalow with garden, overlooks sea to Kyle. Washbasins in bedrooms, lounge with sea view.				

KYLESKU Sutherland	Map 3 G4						
Mrs F J MacAulay Linne Mhuirich, Unapool IV27 4HW Tel. Kylestrome (097183) 227		COMMENDED ♛ ♛	1 Single 2 Dble/Twin 1 Family	2 Public Bath/Sh	B&B per person £8.00 Single £8.00 Double	Open May-Oct Dinner 1900	
			Friendly farmhouse on working croft. Local produce seafood and home baking. View over hill and loch.				

VAT is shown at 15%: changes in this rate may affect prices. Prices shown are for guidance only. Please send SAE with each enquiry.

LADYBANK **Fife** Mrs Algie Briarmont, 42 Church Street Tel. Ladybank (0337) 30359	Map 2 D3		1 Single 3 Dble/Twin	1 Public Bath/Sh	B&B per person £8.50-£9.50 Single £8.50-£9.50 Double	Open Jan-Dec Dinner 1800	
Mrs M Pretswell 1 Melville Road Tel. Ladybank (0337) 30118			3 Dble/Twin	1 Public Bath/Sh	B&B per person £7.00 Double	Open Jan-Dec Dinner 2000	
LAIRG **Sutherland** Mrs B Coghill Croft House, Station Road IV27 4DH Tel. Lairg (0549) 2398	Map 4 A6		2 Dble/Twin 1 Family	1 Public Bath/Sh	B&B per person £7.00 Double	Open Apr-Oct Dinner 1800	
Mrs S Hayhurst Builnatobrach Farm IV27 4DB Tel. Lairg (0549) 2018			1 Single 3 Dble/Twin	1 Public Bath/Sh	B&B per person £8.00 Single £8.00 Double	Open Jan-Dec Dinner 1800	
Mrs M Macleod 3 Main Street IV27 4DB Tel. Lairg (0549) 2149			1 Dble/Twin 1 Family	1 Public Bath/Sh	B&B per person £7.00 Double	Open Apr-Oct	
Mrs B M Paterson Strathwin IV27 4AZ Tel. Lairg (0549) 2487			1 Dble/Twin 1 Family	1 Public Bath/Sh	B&B per person £7.00 Double	Open Jun-Sep	
LAMLASH **Isle of Arran** Mrs H Driver Glenscorrodale Farm, Ross Rd Tel. Sliddery (077087) 241	Map 1 F7		2 Single 2 Dble/Twin 1 Family	2 Public Bath/Sh	B&B per person £8.50-£10.00 Single £8.00-£9.50 Double	Open Apr-Oct Dinner 1730	
LANARK Mrs M Bennie Cygnet Bank, Hyndford Bridge Tel. Lanark (0555) 2903	Map 2 B6		2 Dble/Twin 1 Family	1 Public Bath/Sh	B&B per person £8.00 Double	Open Jan-Dec	
Mrs A P Findlater Jerviswood Mains Farm Tel. Lanark (0555) 3987		Awaiting Inspection	2 Dble/Twin 1 Family	2 Public Bath/Sh	B&B per person £8.50 Double	Open Jan-Dec	
Mrs J Forrest New House Farm, Ravenstruther Tel. Carstairs (0555) 870228			1 Dble/Twin 3 Family		B&B per person £8.00 Double	Open Apr-Oct	

| LANARK continued | Map 2 B6 | | |

EASTERTOWN FARM

Sandilands, Lanark ML11 9TX.   Douglas Water (055 588) 236

The accommodation at this working sheep farm, situated in lovely countryside near Lanark and 2½ miles from A74 Glasgow-Carlisle road, is available all year round. Home baking and home grown produce in plenty. Corehouse Nature Reserve, Falls of Clyde, New Lanark and other places of historic interest are nearby. Fishing, golf and riding arranged, many lovely walks all around.

Mrs J Tennant Eastertown Farm, Sandilands ML11 9TX Tel. Douglas Water (055588) 236	COMMENDED ♛ ♛	1 Single 3 Dble/Twin 1 Family	3 Public Bath/Sh	B&B per person £9.00 Single £9.00 Double	Open Jan-Dec Dinner ✦800
		Traditional stone built farmhouse on working farm. Home produce includes meat , vegetables, baking.			
LANGBANK Renfrewshire Mrs Royden East Morningside Tel. Langbank (047554) 219	Map 1 H5	2 Single 3 Dble/Twin	2 Public Bath/Sh	B&B per person £7.50-£8.00 Single £7.50-£8.00 Double	Open Jan-Nov
LANGHOLM Dumfriesshire Mrs Alderson Ewes School House Tel. Ewes (05417) 261	Map 2 D9	2 Dble/Twin 1 Family	1 Public Bath/Sh	B&B per person £8.00-£8.50 Double	Open Apr-Nov
Mrs S Geddes Esk Brae Tel. Langholm (0541) 80377		2 Dble/Twin	1 Public Bath/Sh	B&B per person £6.00-£7.00 Double	Open Apr-Oct
Mr W Riding Whiteshiels Tel. Langholm (0541) 80494		1 Dble/Twin 1 Family	1 Public Bath/Sh	B&B per person £7.50-£8.00 Double	Open Jan-Dec Dinner 1800
LARBERT Stirlingshire Mrs S Taylor Wester Carmuirs Farm FK5 3NW Tel. Bonnybridge (0324) 812459	Map 2 B4	2 Dble/Twin	1 Public Bath/Sh	B&B per person £9.00 Double	Open May-Sep
LARGS Ayrshire Avondale Guest House 8 Aubery Crescent KA30 8PR Tel. Largs (0475) 672773	Map 1 G6	4 Dble/Twin 2 Family	2 Public Bath/Sh	B&B per person £7.50-£8.50 Double	Open Apr-Sep Dinner 1730
Crawfordlea Guest House 12 Charles Street KA30 8HJ Tel. Largs (0475) 675825		1 Single 3 Dble/Twin	1 Public Bath/Sh	B&B per person £8.00-£8.50 Single £8.00-£8.50 Double	Open Oct-Sep Dinner 1800
Elmore Guest House 14 Glenburn Crescent KA30 8PB Tel. Largs (0475) 672835		3 Dble/Twin 1 Family	1 Public Bath/Sh	B&B per person £7.50 Double	Open Jan-Nov Dinner 1730

LARGS continued	Map 1 G6						
Lea-Mar Guest House 20 Douglas Street KA30 8PS Tel. Largs (0475) 672447	COMMENDED Listed	5 Dble/Twin 1 Family		B&B per person £8.50-£9.00 Double	Open Feb-Nov Dinner 1800		
		Detached bungalow in quiet area, yet close to town. 100 yards from beach.					
Ledard Guest House 94 Brisbane Road KA30 8NN Tel. Largs (0475) 675800	Listed	3 Dble/Twin	1 Public Bath/Sh	B&B per person £7.50-£8.00 Double	Open May-Sep		
Lilac Holm Guest House 14 Noddleburn Road KA30 8PY Tel. Largs (0475) 672020	Awaiting Inspection	2 Single 5 Dble/Twin 1 Family	2 Public Bath/Sh	B&B per person £9.00-£9.50 Single £8.50-£9.00 Double	Open Jan-Dec Dinner 1800		
Netherbank Guest House 9 Routenburn Road KA30 8QA Tel. Largs (0475) 672185		2 Single 7 Dble/Twin 3 Family	1 Public Bath/Sh	B&B per person £8.00 Single £7.50 Double	Open Jan-Dec Dinner 1830		
Tigh-na-Ligh Guest House 104 Brisbane Road KA30 8NN Tel. Largs (0475) 673975	APPROVED ♔♔	4 Dble/Twin 2 Family	1 Private Bath/Sh 1 Public Bath/Sh	B&B per person £8.50-£9.00 Double	Open Jan-Dec Dinner 1730		
		Red sandstone house in quiet residential area, close to all amenities and for touring Firth of Clyde.					

Whin Park Guest House

16 Douglas Street, Largs, Ayrshire KA30 8PS
Telephone: 0475 673437

"Whin Park" is an excellent base for those wishing to explore the Islands of the Clyde and West Central Scotland. All rooms have tea/coffee-making facilities and are complemented by a comfortable lounge and dining room. We can offer 3 and 7 night holidays including half board, National Trust Pass, entry to Kelburn Country Centre and Sea World at Irvine, from £45 per person for 3 nights.

Phone or write Mrs J. Henderson for brochure.

Whin-Park Guest House 16 Douglas Street Tel. Largs (0475) 673437	COMMENDED ♔♔	4 Dble/Twin 1 Family	1 Public Bath/Sh	B&B per person £9.00 Double	Open Apr-Oct Dinner 1800		
		Comfortable rooms and relaxing atmosphere, near seafront. Emphasis on good food.					
Mrs Adams Jacmar, 24 Charles Street Tel. Largs (0475) 675779		1 Single 1 Dble/Twin	1 Public Bath/Sh	B&B per person £8.00 Single £7.50 Double	Open Apr-Oct Dinner 1800		
Mrs Allan Rosalan, 56 Brisbane Road Tel. Largs (0475) 672024		1 Single 2 Dble/Twin	1 Public Bath/Sh	B&B per person £8.00 Double	Open Jan-Dec Dinner 1800		
Mrs D W Bateman Kedron, 11a Brisbane Street KA30 8QW Tel. Largs (0475) 675283		1 Single 3 Dble/Twin	1 Public Bath/Sh	B&B per person £7.50 Single £7.50 Double	Open Apr-Sep Dinner 1830		
Mrs H Cranston Laigh Middleton, Brisbane Glen Tel. Largs (0475) 673275		1 Dble/Twin	2 Public Bath/Sh	B&B per person £7.00-£7.50 Double	Open Jan-Dec		
Mrs Elliot Roan-Mar, 76 Brisbane Road Tel. Largs (0475) 672897		2 Single 2 Dble/Twin	1 Public Bath/Sh	B&B per person £8.00 Single £8.00 Double	Open Jan-Dec Dinner 1800		

LARGS continued — Map 1 G8

Mrs J Hughes
Casmara, 7 Bankhouse Avenue
KA30 9PG
Tel. Largs (0475) 673900
Listed
1 Dble/Twin, 1 Family
1 Public Bath/Sh
B&B per person £7.50-£8.50 Double
Open Jan-Dec

Mrs Pattinson
Riversdale, 22 Barr Crescent
Tel. Largs (0475) 673057
2 Dble/Twin, 1 Family
1 Public Bath/Sh
B&B per person £7.50-£8.00 Double
Open Apr-Oct, Dinner 1800

LASSWADE — Midlothian — Map 2 D5

Mrs Jennifer Carpenter
Dunesk House
Tel. 031 663 8388
1 Single, 3 Dble/Twin
1 Private Bath/Sh, 1 Public Bath/Sh
B&B per person £20.00 Single, £20.00 Double
Open Jun-Sep

Mrs Ciupik
Eskvale, Polton Bank
Tel. 031 663 9600
1 Dble/Twin, 2 Family
2 Private Bath/Sh, 1 Public Bath/Sh
B&B per person £9.00 Double
Open Jan-Dec

Mrs D O'Brien
Droman House
Tel. 031 663 9239
3 Dble/Twin
2 Public Bath/Sh
B&B per person £8.50 Double
Open Jan-Dec

Mrs J Winkler
Ord, 23 Polton Bank
EH18 1JR
Tel. 031 663 1250
Listed
1 Single, 1 Dble/Twin, 1 Family
1 Private Bath/Sh, 1 Public Bath/Sh
B&B per person £10.00 Single, £10.00-£9.00 Double
Open Jun-Sep

LATHERON — Caithness — Map 4 D4

Mrs C Sinclair
Glenview, Upper Latheron Farm
Tel. Latheron (05934) 224
1 Single, 2 Dble/Twin, 1 Family
1 Public Bath/Sh
B&B per person £7.00-£8.00 Single, £6.00-£8.00 Double
Open May-Oct

LAUDER — Berwickshire — Map 2 E6

Ms Beth Tocher
Pyatfield
TD2 6SH
Tel. Lauder (05782) 270
1 Single, 1 Dble/Twin
1 Public Bath/Sh
B&B per person £8.50-£9.00 Single, £8.50-£9.00 Double
Open May-Oct, Dinner 1900

LAURENCEKIRK — Kincardineshire — Map 4 G12

Mrs M Anderson
Ringwood, Fordoun
AB3 1JS
Tel. Auchenblae (05612) 313
COMMENDED
3 Dble/Twin, 1 Family
1 Public Bath/Sh
B&B per person £16.00 Double
Open Apr-Oct

Country home on small croft, attractive garden. Views of coast and hills to rear. Good touring base.

LAURIESTON, Castle Douglas — Kirkcudbrightshire — Map 2 A10

Mrs Margaret Gordon
Craig of Balmaghie Farm
DG7 2NA
Tel. Laurieston (06445) 287
COMMENDED
1 Dble/Twin, 1 Family
1 Public Bath/Sh
B&B per person £7.00-£8.00 Double
Open Apr-Oct, Dinner 1800

In peaceful rural setting on working farm, 8 miles (13 km) from Castle Douglas and shops.

VAT is shown at 15%; changes in this rate may affect prices. Prices shown are for guidance only. Please send SAE with each enquiry.

LERWICK Shetland	**Map 5** G4						
Glen Orchy Guest House 20 Knab Road Tel. Lerwick (0595) 2031		**APPROVED** Listed	1 Single 4 Dble/Twin 1 Family	2 Public Bath/Sh	B&B per person £11.00 Single £9.00 Double	Open Jan-Dec Dinner 1800	
Detached stone building in quiet residential area. Former manse.							
Solheim Guest House 34 King Harald Street ZE1 0EQ Tel. Lerwick (0595) 3613			1 Single 2 Dble/Twin	1 Public Bath/Sh	B&B per person £10.00-£13.00 Single £9.00-£11.00 Double	Open Jan-Dec	
Mrs D Anderson Seafield Tel. Lerwick (0595) 3853			2 Dble/Twin	1 Public Bath/Sh	B&B per person £9.00-£10.00 Double	Open Jan-Dec Dinner 1700-	
Mrs I Nicolson Cee Ae, 133 North Road Tel. Lerwick (0595) 3362		**COMMENDED** Listed	2 Dble/Twin 1 Family		B&B per person £8.00 Double	Open Jan-Dec	
Detached house convenient for ferry terminal. Overlooks Bressay Sound.							
Mrs I M Pearse 93 King Harald Street Tel. Lerwick (0595) 5386			1 Dble/Twin	1 Private Bath/Sh	B&B per person £8.00-£10.00 Double	Open Apr-Oct Dinner 1830	
Mrs L K Tulloch 9 Helendale Drive Tel. Lerwick (0595) 4508		**COMMENDED** Listed	2 Single 1 Dble/Twin	2 Public Bath/Sh	B&B per person £7.00-£7.30 Single £7.00-£7.30 Double	Open Jan-Dec	
Quiet residential area convenient to leisure and sports centre. View over Clichimin Broch.							
Mrs M Tulloch 50 St Olaf Street Tel. Lerwick (0595) 2257			2 Dble/Twin	2 Public Bath/Sh	B&B per person £8.00-£10.00 Double	Open Jan-Dec	
LESMAHAGOW Lanarkshire	**Map 2** A6						
Mrs V Jones Abbeynethan, 1 Abbeygreen Tel. Lesmahagow (0555) 894020			1 Dble/Twin 1 Family	1 Public Bath/Sh	B&B per person £9.00 Double	Open Jan-Dec	
Mrs R H Muirhead Auldton Farm Tel. Lesmahagow (0555) 892310			2 Dble/Twin 1 Family	1 Public Bath/Sh	B&B per person £8.00 Double	Open Apr-Oct	
Mrs Neville Moatyett Farm Tel. Lesmahagow (0555) 893301			1 Dble/Twin 1 Family	1 Public Bath/Sh	B&B per person £8.00 Double	Open Jan-Dec	
Mrs Ritchie 330 New Trows Road Tel. Lesmahagow (0555) 893618			2 Dble/Twin 1 Family	1 Public Bath/Sh	B&B per person £6.00-£7.00 Double	Open Jan-Dec Dinner 1700	
LESWALT, by Stranraer Wigtownshire	**Map 1** F10						
Mrs E Oldfield Challoch Farm Tel. Leswalt (077687) 253			2 Dble/Twin 1 Family	2 Public Bath/Sh	B&B per person £7.50 Double	Open Mar-Nov	

Key to symbols is on back flap. Details of Classification and Grading are on page vi.

LEVERBURGH
Harris, Western Isles — Map 3 B7

Mrs M F MacCuish
Clachan Cottage
Tel. Leverburgh (085982)
352

2 Dble/Twin   1 Public Bath/Sh   B&B per person £6.00-£6.50 Double   Open Jan-Dec, Dinner 1800

LINICLATE
Isle of Benbecula, Western Isles — Map 3 A9

Inchyra Guest House
27 Liniclate
PA88 5PY
Tel. Benbecula (0870) 2176

COMMENDED

1 Single, 4 Dble/Twin, 1 Family   4 Private Bath/Sh, 1 Public Bath/Sh   B&B per person £10.00-£11.50 Single £10.00-£11.50 Double   Open Jan-Dec, Dinner 1800

Family run, on working farm. On main Lochmaddy to Lochboisdale road, 6 miles (10km) from airport.

Mrs Robertson
9 Liniclate
Tel. Benbecula (0870) 2532

1 Single, 2 Dble/Twin   1 Public Bath/Sh   B&B per person £9.00-£10.00 Single £8.00-£9.00 Double   Open Jan-Nov, Dinner 1800

Mrs M M Shepherd
Heisker
Tel. Benbecula (0870) 2235

1 Single, 4 Dble/Twin, 1 Family   1 Private Bath/Sh, 3 Public Bath/Sh   B&B per person £10.50-£11.00 Single £10.00-£10.50 Double   Open Jan-Dec, Dinner 1830

LINICRO, by Portree
Isle of Skye, Inverness-shire — Map 3 D8

Mrs C Macdonald
Creagan-Ban
Tel. Uig (047042) 286

1 Single, 1 Dble/Twin, 1 Family   1 Public Bath/Sh   B&B per person £8.00-£8.50 Single   Open Apr-Oct, Dinner 1800

LINLITHGOW
West Lothian — Map 2 B5

The Cedars Guest House
High Street
Tel. Linlithgow (0506)
845952

1 Single, 2 Dble/Twin, 1 Family   1 Public Bath/Sh   B&B per person £10.00-£15.00 Single £9.00-£11.00 Double   Open Jan-Dec

---

Mrs M Doyle
51 Braehead Terrace
Tel. Linlithgow (0506)
844915

2 Dble/Twin   1 Public Bath/Sh   B&B per person £8.50-£9.00 Double   Open Jan-Dec

---

WOODCOCKDALE FARM

LANARK ROAD, LINLITHGOW. Tel: 0506 842088

A pleasant visit and homely atmosphere with farmhouse fare and personal attention awaits you at Woodcockdale which has a traditional four-poster bed. Restful view from windows. 20 minutes by train to Edinburgh and easy access to all central tourist attractions: Loch Lomond, Trossachs, Glasgow Life, Borders and Forth Valley.

Mrs W Erskine
Woodcockdale Farm, Lanark Road
EH49 6QE
Tel. Linlithgow (0506)
842088

COMMENDED
Listed

3 Dble/Twin, 1 Family   1 Public Bath/Sh   B&B per person £9.00 Double   Open Jan-Dec

Modern, on working dairy and sheep farm. Superb views over village towards Ochil Hills.

Mrs M Findlay
43 Clarendon Crescent
Tel. Linlithgow (0506)
842574

1 Single, 2 Dble/Twin   1 Public Bath/Sh   B&B per person £7.50 Single £7.50 Double   Open Jan-Dec, Dinner 1800

VAT is shown at 15%: changes in this rate may affect prices. Prices shown are for guidance only. Please send SAE with each enquiry.

LINLITHGOW continued Mrs A Hay Belsyde Farm, Lanark Road EH49 6QE Tel. Linlithgow (0506) 842098	**Map 2** B5	**COMMENDED** 👑 👑	1 Single 2 Dble/Twin 2 Family	1 Public Bath/Sh	B&B per person £8.50 Single £8.50 Double	Open Feb-Nov Dinner 1900
			Late 18C, on 100 acre sheep and cattle farm beside Union Canal. Views over Forth Estuary and Ochils.			
Mrs Jack Learigg, 21 Mannerston Tel. Philipstoun (0506) 834888			1 Dble/Twin 1 Family	1 Public Bath/Sh	B&B per person £8.50 Double	Open Jan-Dec
Mrs E Mooney 137 Baron's Hill Avenue Tel. Linlithgow (0506) 843903			1 Single 1 Dble/Twin	1 Public Bath/Sh	B&B per person £6.50-£7.50 Single £6.50-£7.50 Double	Open Apr-Oct
Mrs J Robb St Annes, St Ninians Road EH49 7BN Tel. Linlithgow (0506) 842509			1 Single 2 Dble/Twin 1 Family	1 Public Bath/Sh	B&B per person £8.50-£9.00 Single £8.50-£9.00 Double	Open Jan-Dec
Mrs Sprot 11 Jock's Hill Cresent Tel. Linlithgow (0506) 842866			1 Dble/Twin 1 Family	1 Public Bath/Sh	B&B per person £8.50-£10.50 Double	Open Jan-Dec
LINLITHGOW BRIDGE West Lothian Mrs Thomas 23 Main Street Tel. Linlithgow (0506) 843075	**Map 2** B5		1 Dble/Twin 1 Family	1 Private Bath/Sh 1 Public Bath/Sh	B&B per person £8.50-£9.00 Double	Open Jan-Dec Dinner 1800
LISMORE, Isle of Argyll Isle of Lismore Guest House PA34 5UL Tel. Lismore (063176) 207	**Map 1** E2		1 Single 4 Dble/Twin 1 Family	3 Public Bath/Sh	B&B per person £9.00 Single £9.00 Double	Open Jan-Dec Dinner 1900
LOCHBOISDALE S Uist, Western Isles The Grianaig Guest House Garryhallie Tel. Lochboisdale (08784) 406	**Map 3** A10	**COMMENDED** 👑 👑 👑	6 Dble/Twin 1 Family	3 Private Bath/Sh 2 Public Bath/Sh	B&B per person £11.00-£13.00 Double	Open Jan-Dec Dinner 1900
			Modern bungalow on road to Lochmaddy. Near golf course, sandy beaches. Ferry terminal 4 miles (6km).			
Mrs M MacDonald Lochside Cottage, 27 Lochboisdale Tel. Lochboisdale (08784) 472			3 Dble/Twin	1 Public Bath/Sh	B&B per person £6.50-£8.50 Double	Open Jan-Dec
Mrs Mary Ann MacLellan Bayview Tel. Lochboisdale (08784) 329			2 Dble/Twin	1 Public Bath/Sh	B&B per person £8.00 Double	Open May-Oct Dinner 1900
Mrs A MacLennan Riverside Tel. Lochboisdale (08784) 250			2 Dble/Twin	1 Public Bath/Sh	B&B per person £7.50 Double	Open Jan-Dec

LOCHBOISDALE continued Mrs C MacLeod Innis Ghorm, 422 Lochboisdale Tel. Lochboisdale (08784) 232	**Map 3** A10		2 Dble/Twin	1 Public Bath/Sh	B&B per person £8.00 Double	Open Jan-Dec Dinner 1800	🐟 Ⓥ ♿ 🅿 ▥ ⊞ ⚡ 🅿
LOCHCARRON Ross-shire Mrs Flora Catto The Creagan Tel. Lochcarron (05202) 430	**Map 3** F9 Listed		1 Dble/Twin 1 Family	1 Public Bath/Sh	B&B per person £7.50 Double	Open Apr-Oct Dinner 1900	🐟 ♿ 🅿 ▥ ⊞ 🐕 🅿 △ Ⓒ
Mrs E Mackay Strathdle, Croft Road Tel. Lochcarron (05202) 301		**COMMENDED** 👑 👑	1 Dble/Twin 1 Family	1 Public Bath/Sh	B&B per person £7.50 Double	Open Apr-Oct	🐟 ♿ 🅿 ▥ ⊞ 🔌 ⅟ 🐕 ❄ ✂ Ⓒ **Modern, comfortable house with garden. On hillside overlooking village and loch. Superb views.**
Mrs S L Macleod Tigh-na-Ault, Hillside IV54 8YQ Tel. Lochcarron (05202) 416		Listed	2 Dble/Twin	1 Public Bath/Sh	B&B per person £7.50 Double	Open Apr-Sep Dinner 1900	🐟 ♿ 🍴 Ⓥ 🅿 ▥ ⊞ 🐕 ❄ ✂ 🅿 △
Mr Pillinger Glaisbheinn IV54 8YB Tel. Lochcarron (05202) 367		**COMMENDED** 👑 👑	3 Dble/Twin	1 Public Bath/Sh	B&B per person £7.00-£7.50 Double	Open May-Sep	🐟 🍴 ▥ ⊞ ⚡ 🅿 🔌 ⅟ 🅿 **Comfortable house overlooking loch. Traditionally furnished, full central heating. TV on request.**
LOCHGILPHEAD Argyll Mrs Campbell 3 Cossack Street Tel. Lochgilphead (0546) 2573	**Map 1** F4		2 Dble/Twin		B&B per person £7.00 Double	Open Jan-Dec	🐕 Ⓒ
LOCHINVER, Lairg Sutherland Mrs Campbell Tigh Lios IV27 4JY Tel. Lochinver (05714) 316	**Map 3** G5		3 Dble/Twin	1 Public Bath/Sh	B&B per person £15.00-£17.00 Double	Open Apr-Oct	🅿 ⊞ ⚡ 🔌 ⅟ Ⓒ
Mrs S J MacLeod Rose Cottage, 74 Baddidarroch IV27 4LP Tel. Lochinver (05714) 457			1 Dble/Twin	1 Public Bath/Sh	B&B per person £8.50 Double	Open Jan-Dec	🔔 🅿 ▥ ⊞ ⚡ 🅿 🔌 ❄ 🅿 △ 🍴
Mrs K J Macleod Glenview, 37 Strathan IV27 4LR Tel. Lochinver (05714) 324			1 Single 2 Dble/Twin 1 Family	1 Public Bath/Sh	B&B per person £8.00-£9.00 Single £8.00 Double	Open Apr-Oct	♿ 🅿 ▥ ⊞ 🅿
Mrs J Matheson Polcraig Tel. Lochinver (05714) 429			2 Dble/Twin 2 Family	2 Public Bath/Sh	B&B per person £8.00-£11.00 Double	Open Jan-Dec	🐟 ♿ 🅿 ▥ ⊞ ⚡ 🅿 🔌 🅿 △ Ⓒ 🛏
Mr & Mrs McBain Ardglass IV27 4LI Tel. Lochinver (05714) 257		**COMMENDED** 👑 👑	1 Single 5 Dble/Twin 2 Family	1 Public Bath/Sh	B&B per person £8.00-£10.00 Single £8.00-£10.00 Double	Open Mar-Nov	🐟 ♿ Ⓥ 🅿 ▥ ⊞ ⚡ 🅿 🔌 ⅟ 🐕 ❄ 🅿 △ Ⓒ **Commanding position above fishing harbour. Superb mountain views. Balcony garden**

VAT is shown at 15%: changes in this rate may affect prices. Prices shown are for guidance only. Please send SAE with each enquiry.

LOCHLUICHART, by Garve Ross-shire Mrs Niblett Railway Cottages Tel. Garve (09974) 264	Map 3 H8	COMMENDED ♔	2 Dble/Twin	2 Public Bath/Sh	B&B per person £7.50-£8.00 Double	Open May-Sep Dinner 1800	(symbols)

Request stop on the beautiful Kyle railway line is nearby. Homely atmosphere, peaceful countryside.

LOCHS Lewis, Western Isles Mrs Jean Smith Penamber, 55 Balallan Tel. Garrabost (0851) 83351	Map 3 C5		2 Dble/Twin 1 Family	2 Public Bath/Sh	B&B per person £6.50-£7.50 Double	Open Apr-Oct Dinner 1800	(symbols)
LOCKERBIE Dumfriesshire Rosehill Guest House Carlisle Road Tel. Lockerbie (05762) 2378	Map 2 C9		1 Single 2 Dble/Twin 2 Family	1 Public Bath/Sh	B&B per person £8.50 Single £8.50 Double	Open Jan-Dec	(symbols)

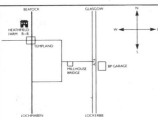

HEATHFIELD FARM
TEMPLAND, LOCKERBIE TEL. 05764 488

Ideal family accommodation in this tastefully modernised farmhouse enjoying full central heating on our 206-acre dairy farm. Situated 2 miles north of Templand on the B7020 Lochmaben to Moffat Road only a short distance from the A74. It's ideal for an overnight stay. Lovely walks with an abundance of wildlife. Golf, fishing and pony trekking close by. Traditional farmhouse cooking a speciality. **B&B £7, BB&EM £12.**

Mrs J M MacDougal Heathfield Farm, Templand Tel. Johnstone Bridge (05764) 488			2 Dble/Twin 1 Family	1 Public Bath/Sh	B&B per person £7.00 Double	Open Mar-Oct Dinner 1830	(symbols)
Barbara J J Roxburgh Newton House, Boreland DG11 2LL Tel. Boreland (05766) 269		COMMENDED ♔♔	2 Dble/Twin 1 Family	2 Private Bath/Sh 1 Public Bath/Sh	B&B per person £8.00-£9.50 Double	Open Apr-Oct Dinner 1800	(symbols)

Modern house with spacious rooms in quiet rural surroundings.

Mrs M Vaughan Braehead, Heck Tel. Lochmaben (038781) 444		Listed	1 Dble/Twin 2 Family	1 Public Bath/Sh	B&B per person £7.50-£8.50 Double	Open Jan-Dec Dinner 1700	(symbols)
LONGFORMACUS Berwickshire Mrs M Amos Eildon Cottage Tel. Longformacus (03617) 230	Map 2 F5	Awaiting Inspection	1 Dble/Twin 1 Family	1 Public Bath/Sh	B&B per person £8.00-£8.50 Double	Open Jan-Dec	(symbols)
LONGNIDDRY East Lothian Mrs A Playfair Ballencrieff Farm EH32 0PJ Tel. Aberlady (08757) 362	Map 2 D5	Listed	3 Dble/Twin	2 Public Bath/Sh	B&B per person £7.50-£10.00 Double	Open Mar-Nov	(symbols)

Key to symbols is on back flap. Details of Classification and Grading are on page vi.

151

LOSSIEMOUTH Moray	Map 4 D7						
Mrs M Jean D Cox Mormond, Prospect Terrace IV31 6JS Tel. Lossiemouth (034381) 3143			1 Single 2 Dble/Twin 1 Family	1 Public Bath/Sh	B&B per person £8.00 Single £8.00 Double	Open Apr-Oct	
Mrs Catherine A Greig Dunnideich, 38 Elgin Road IV31 6HG Tel. Lossiemouth (034381) 3520			3 Dble/Twin		B&B per person £7.50-£8.00 Double	Open Jan-Dec	
Mrs Frances Reddy Lossiemouth House, 33 Clifton Road IV31 6DP Tel. Lossiemouth (034381) 3397			1 Single 2 Dble/Twin 1 Family	1 Public Bath/Sh	B&B per person £8.00-£8.50 Single £8.00-£8.50 Double	Open Jan-Dec Dinner 1800	
LOWER CABRACH, Huntly Banffshire	Map 4 E9						
Mrs M McGinley Inverharroch Farm AB5 4EU Tel. Cabrach (046689) 260			3 Dble/Twin 1 Family	1 Public Bath/Sh	B&B per person £7.00 Double	Open Apr-Oct	
LOWER LARGO Fife	Map 2 D3						
Mrs M Elliot Mersing, 30 Bourtree Brae KY8 6HX Tel. Lundin Links (0333) 320375			3 Dble/Twin	1 Private Bath/Sh 1 Public Bath/Sh	B&B per person £8.50-£9.00 Double	Open Jan-Dec Dinner 1800	
LUIB Isle of Skye	Map 3 E10						
Mrs Carol Joan Lamond Lindisfarne Tel. Broadford (04712) 564			4 Dble/Twin	1 Public Bath/Sh	B&B per person £7.00-£8.00 Double	Open Apr-Oct Dinner 1800	
LUING, Isle of Argyll	Map 1 E3						
Mrs M A Morris Jones Cullipool House Tel. Luing (08524) 215			2 Dble/Twin	1 Public Bath/Sh	B&B per person £7.00-£7.50 Double	Open Jan-Dec	
LUMSDEN, by Huntly Aberdeenshire	Map 4 E10						
Mrs E Petrie Chapelton Farm AB5 4JL Tel. Lumsden (04648) 740		COMMENDED	1 Dble/Twin 2 Family	1 Public Bath/Sh	B&B per person £7.00 Double	Open Jan-Dec Dinner 1800	

30 acre sheep and cattle croft. Home baking a speciality. Local golf, hillwalking and ski slopes.

VAT is shown at 15%: changes in this rate may affect prices. Prices shown are for guidance only. Please send SAE with each enquiry.

LUNCARTY, Perth Perthshire	Map 2 C2					
Mrs A Grant Pebble Mill PH1 3ES Tel. Stanley (073882) 8268		2 Dble/Twin	2 Private Bath/Sh 1 Public Bath/Sh	B&B per person £10.00 Double	Open Apr-Oct	
Mrs Haddow Ordie House PH1 4PR Tel. Stanley (073882) 471		2 Dble/Twin 1 Family	1 Public Bath/Sh	B&B per person £8.00-£8.50 Double	Open May-Sep	
LUNDIN LINKS Fife	Map 2 D3					
Mrs K Foster Harvey House, 7 Golf Road Tel. Lundin Links (0333) 320670		2 Dble/Twin	2 Public Bath/Sh	B&B per person £12.50 Double	Open Apr-Oct	
LYBSTER Caithness	Map 4 D4					
Mrs K B McIvor Hollytree Cottage, Parkside Tel. Lybster (05932) 376		3 Dble/Twin	1 Public Bath/Sh	B&B per person £7.00-£7.50 Double	Open Apr-Oct Dinner 1800	
MACHRIE Isle of Arran	Map 1 E7					
Mrs Smith Ashlar Farm Tel. Machrie (077084) 246		2 Dble/Twin 2 Family	1 Public Bath/Sh	B&B per person £8.00 Double	Open Apr-Sep Dinner 1800	
MAIDENS Ayrshire	Map 1 G8					
Mrs Gibson Anchorage, 12 Bainshill Drive Tel. Turnberry (06553) 244		2 Family	1 Public Bath/Sh	B&B per person £7.00 Double	Open Apr-Oct	
MAINSRIDDLE Dumfriesshire	Map 2 B10					
Mrs L Sykes Hall House Tel. Southwick (038778) 638		2 Dble/Twin 1 Family	2 Public Bath/Sh	B&B per person £7.75 Single £7.75 Double	Open Jan-Dec Dinner 1900	
MALLAIG Inverness-shire	Map 3 E11					
The Anchorage Guest House Tel. Mallaig (0687) 2454		4 Dble/Twin 2 Family	2 Public Bath/Sh	B&B per person £8.00-£9.00 Double	Open Jan-Dec Dinner 1900	
Mabel Crocket Cruachan, Coteachan Hill Tel. Mallaig (0687) 2422		2 Family	1 Private Bath/Sh 1 Public Bath/Sh	B&B per person £8.00-£9.00 Double	Open May-Sep	
Mrs Henderson The Moorings, East Bay Tel. Mallaig (0687) 2225		1 Single 2 Dble/Twin 1 Family	1 Public Bath/Sh	B&B per person £8.00-£10.00 Single £7.50-£10.00 Double	Open Jan-Dec	
Mrs C King Seaview Tel. Mallaig (0687) 2059		3 Dble/Twin	1 Public Bath/Sh	B&B per person £7.50-£8.50 Double	Open Jan-Dec	

Key to symbols is on back flap. Details of Classification and Grading are on page vi.

MALLAIG continued C MacPherson Hillside Tel. Mallaig (0687) 2253	Map 3 E11		5 Dble/Twin 1 Family	1 Public Bath/Sh	B&B per person £7.00 Double	Open Apr-Oct	⌂ symbols
MARYBANK, by Muir of Ord **Ross-shire** Mrs J S Bell Birchgrove, Arcan IV6 7UL Tel. Urray (09973) 245	Map 4 A8		1 Dble/Twin 1 Family	1 Public Bath/Sh	B&B per person £7.50-£8.00 Double	Open Apr-Oct Dinner 1900	symbols
Mrs R Macleod Easter Balloon Farm IV6 7UW Tel. Urray (09973) 211		Listed	1 Single 2 Dble/Twin 2 Family	2 Public Bath/Sh	B&B per person £7.50 Single £7.50 Double	Open Apr-Oct Dinner 1900	symbols
MAUCHLINE **Ayrshire** Mrs M Dishington Eildon, 15A Cumnock Road Tel. Mauchline (0290) 50098	Map 1 H7		2 Dble/Twin	1 Public Bath/Sh	B&B per person £9.00 Double	Open Apr-Sep Dinner 1800	symbols
Mrs M MacMillan Knowehead Tel. Mauchline (0290) 50566			1 Single 2 Dble/Twin	3 Public Bath/Sh	B&B per person £8.50 Double	Open Jan-Dec	symbols
Mrs Riding Crosshands House, Crosshands Tel. Mauchline (0290) 50828			3 Dble/Twin	1 Public Bath/Sh	B&B per person £8.50 Double	Open Apr-Oct	symbols
Mrs Janet B Walker Lizburn, Sorn Road Tel. Mauchline (0290) 50401/50695		Listed	2 Dble/Twin	1 Public Bath/Sh	B&B per person £8.00-£9.50 Double	Open Jan-Dec Dinner 1700	symbols
Mrs P de Sylva Rottenrow Farm, Crosshands Tel. Mauchline (0290) 52240			2 Single 3 Dble/Twin 2 Family	2 Public Bath/Sh	B&B per person £10.50-£13.00 Single £10.00-£12.50 Double	Open Jan-Dec Dinner 1800	symbols
MAYBOLE **Ayrshire** Mrs Sheena Sheehan Bennan Straiton Farm Stud KA19 7NB Tel. Straiton (06557) 229	Map 1 G8		3 Dble/Twin	1 Public Bath/Sh	B&B per person £7.50 Double	Open Apr-Oct	symbols
Mrs A Whiteford Chapelton Farm KA19 7LR Tel. Kirkmichael (Ayrshire) (06555) 273		♛ ♛	1 Dble/Twin 1 Family	1 Public Bath/Sh	B&B per person £8.00-£8.50 Double	Open Apr-Oct Dinner 1800	symbols
MEIGLE **Perthshire** Scottish National Camps Association Belmont Outdoor Centre PH12 8TQ Tel. Meigle (08284) 275	Map 2 D1		24 Single	6 Public Bath/Sh	B&B per person £6.33-£7.13 Single	Open Mar-Oct Dinner 1700	symbols

VAT is shown at 15%. changes in this rate may affect prices. Prices shown are for guidance only. Please send SAE with each enquiry.

MEIGLE continued Mrs H Turner The Old Manse, Ardler Tel. Meigle (08284) 234	Map 2 D1		2 Dble/Twin	1 Public Bath/Sh	B&B per person £7.50-£7.75 Double	Open Jan-Dec Dinner 1900

MELROSE **Roxburghshire** Mrs G Graham Craigard, Huntly Avenue Tel. Melrose (089682) 2041	Map 2 E6	APPROVED Listed	2 Dble/Twin	1 Public Bath/Sh	B&B per person £8.00-£8.50 Double	Open Mar-Oct
Modern bungalow in quiet part of town, yet only 5 minutes walk from town centre and Abbey.						
Mrs S Graham Dunfermline House, Buccleuch St Tel. Melrose (089682) 2148		Awaiting Inspection	3 Dble/Twin	1 Private Bath/Sh 1 Public Bath/Sh	B&B per person £8.00-£9.50 Double	Open Jan-Dec Dinner 1800
Mrs J Kilshaw Dinglesyde, Newlyn Road Tel. Melrose (089682) 3113		Listed	2 Dble/Twin	1 Public Bath/Sh	B&B per person £9.00-£10.00 Double	Open Mar-Oct Dinner 1800
Mrs Betty Lockie Little Fordel, Abbey Street Tel. Melrose (089682) 2206		Listed	2 Dble/Twin 1 Family		B&B per person £7.50-£8.00 Double	Open Jan-Dec
Mrs Meldrum 12 Quarrydene PD6 9SZ Tel. Melrose (089682) 2324			2 Dble/Twin	1 Public Bath/Sh	B&B per person £7.50-£8.00 Double	Open Jan-Dec
Mrs Schofield Torwood Lodge, High Cross Avenue Tel. Melrose (089682) 2220		Awaiting Inspection	1 Dble/Twin 1 Family	1 Public Bath/Sh	B&B per person £9.00-£10.00 Double	Open Apr-Nov
Mrs S Sugden Collingwood, Waverley Road Tel. Melrose (089682) 2670			2 Dble/Twin 1 Family	2 Public Bath/Sh	B&B per person £9.00-£10.00 Double	Open Mar-Oct Dinner 1830

MELVICH **Sutherland** Mrs J Campbell The Shieling KW14 7YJ Tel. Melvich (06413) 256	Map 4 B3	Awaiting Inspection	3 Dble/Twin 2 Family	1 Public Bath/Sh	B&B per person £8.00 Double	Open Apr-Sep Dinner 1800
Mrs J E C Ritchie Tigh-na-Clash, 81 Melvich KW14 7YJ Tel. Melvich (06413) 262		COMMENDED ♛ ♛	2 Single 3 Dble/Twin 1 Family	2 Public Bath/Sh	B&B per person £8.50 Single £8.50 Double	Open Apr-Oct Dinner 1700
Family run, overlooking the sea and River Halladale. Pub and restaurant nearby.						

METHIL **Fife** Miss Kay Glen Glentara, 207 High Street Tel. Leven (0333) 25277	Map 2 D3		3 Dble/Twin	1 Public Bath/Sh	B&B per person £9.00-£10.00 Double	Open Jan-Dec Dinner 1830

MEY, by Thurso Caithness	Map 4 D2						
Mrs Geddes Island View, East Mey Tel. Barrock (084785) 254		1 Dble/Twin 1 Family	2 Public Bath/Sh	B&B per person £7.00-£7.50 Double	Open Apr-Oct	
Mrs M Mackay Creag-na-Mara Tel. Barrock (084785) 710		2 Dble/Twin	1 Public Bath/Sh	B&B per person £6.00-£7.00 Double	Open Apr-Oct	

GLENEARN
East Mey, Thurso, Caithness KW14 8XL   084 785 608
Here is true Scottish hospitality with value for money by a homely peat fire. House overlooks Castle of Mey with a panoramic view of Orkney Islands and Dunnet Head with its lighthouse and natural bird sanctuary. Beaches and coastal walk nearby. Seven minutes to John o' Groats where ferry crosses daily to Orkney Isles.

Three bedrooms, all with central heating, electric blankets and duck down quilts. Ample washbasin and toilet facilities, bathroom and separate shower.
S.A.E. please for terms.

Mrs Morrison Glenearn, East Mey KW14 8XL Tel. Barrock (084785) 608		2 Dble/Twin 1 Family	1 Public Bath/Sh	B&B per person £7.00-£7.50 Double	Open Apr-Oct Dinner 1800	
MILNGAVIE, Glasgow	Map 1 H5						
Barloch Guest House 82 Strathblane Road G62 8DH Tel. 041 956 1432	Listed	5 Dble/Twin		B&B per person £10.00 Double	Open Jan-Dec	
Mrs E J Chapman Arnish, 14 Blane Drive G62 8HG Tel. 041 956 1767		2 Dble/Twin	1 Public Bath/Sh	B&B per person £8.00 Double	Open Jan-Dec	
MINTLAW, by Peterhead Aberdeenshire	Map 4 H8						
Mr Alan, Shallong House Longhill Farm, New Leeds Tel. Lonmay (0346) 32564		2 Dble/Twin	1 Public Bath/Sh	B&B per person £6.00 Double	Open Jan-Dec Dinner 1600	
Mrs C M Clark Ivydene AB4 8EB Tel. Mintlaw (0771) 23118	APPROVED Listed	1 Single 1 Dble/Twin 1 Family	1 Public Bath/Sh	B&B per person £6.50 Single £6.50 Double	Open Jan-Dec Dinner 1800	
		Cottage style house with roses. Opposite Arden Country Park, 10 mile /16 km from Peterhead.				

VAT is shown at 15%: changes in this rate may affect prices. Prices shown are for guidance only. Please send SAE with each enquiry.

MOCHRUM, by Port William Wigtownshire Mrs M McMuldroch Jacob's Ladder Tel. Mochrum (098886) 227	**Map 1** H11		3 Family	2 Public Bath/Sh	B&B per person £7.50-£8.00 Double	Open Jan-Dec Dinner 1800	🔣
MOFFAT Dumfriesshire Barnhill Springs Country Guest House Tel. Moffat (0683) 20580	**Map 2** C8	**APPROVED** 👑👑	5 Dble/Twin 1 Family	2 Public Bath/Sh	B&B per person £9.50-£10.50 Double	Open Jan-Dec Dinner 1830	🔣
			Early victorian ideally situated for walking Southern Upland Way. Access from A74 south, slip road.				

Cabana Guest House

BALLPLAY ROAD, MOFFAT Tel: 0683 20400

Best Bed and Breakfast in the World Listed. Quietly situated on the eastern side of Moffat, with views of the Moffat Hills. Private parking, excellent food and accommodation with every modern convenience offering a high standard of personal service. An ideal stopover centre to and from the Highlands or touring the Lowlands.
Bed and Breakfast £9. Dinner, Bed and Breakfast from £14.

Cabana Guest House Ballplay Road DG10 9JX Tel. Moffat (0683) 20400	**Awaiting Inspection**	1 Single 3 Dble/Twin	2 Public Bath/Sh	B&B per person £9.50-£10.50 Single £9.50-£10.00 Double	Open Jan-Dec Dinner 1830	🔣
Greenbank Guest House Well Road DG10 9BT Tel. Moffat (0683) 20074	**Awaiting Inspection**	2 Dble/Twin 2 Family	1 Private Bath/Sh 1 Public Bath/Sh	B&B per person £7.00-£8.50 Double	Open Jan-Nov Dinner 1830	🔣
Hartfell Guest House Hartfell Crescent DG10 9AL Tel. Moffat (0683) 20153	**APPROVED** 👑👑	2 Single 4 Dble/Twin 3 Family	2 Public Bath/Sh	B&B per person £9.50-£10.00 Single £9.50-£10.00 Double	Open Mar-Dec Dinner 1830	🔣
		Family run, in rural setting, yet only 400 yards from town centre. Large, well maintained garden.				
Rockhill Guest House 14 Beech Grove DG10 9RS Tel. Moffat (0683) 20283	**COMMENDED** 👑	2 Single 5 Dble/Twin 3 Family	2 Public Bath/Sh	B&B per person £8.50-£9.00 Single £8.50-£9.00 Double	Open Mar-Oct Dinner 1830	🔣
		Victorian house overlooking bowling green and park. Quiet area close to centre. Open view to hills.				

AA Listed ## "Del-Robin" STB 👑👑
(formerly "ROBIN-HILL")
Beechgrove, Moffat DG10 9RS. Tel. E. Baty (0683) 20050
Residential, 5 minutes from town. All rooms with showers, two en-suite. Tea/coffee-making facilities, parking in own ground, C.H., electric blankets, non-smoking areas. large patio to rear with uninterrupted view of surrounding hills, quietly situated, fire certificate held. Completely redecorated throughout. "Del-Robin", third house on left past tennis courts.

Mrs Baty Del-Robin, Beechgrove Tel. Moffat (0683) 20050	**COMMENDED** 👑👑	2 Single 4 Dble/Twin 2 Family	8 Private Bath/Sh 2 Public Bath/Sh	B&B per person £9.50-£10.00 Single £10.00 Double	Open Apr-Oct	🔣
		Family run and comfortable. Quiet situation and open views. Local mill shops nearby.				

MOFFAT continued	Map 2 C8	

Seamore House TEL: 0683 20404
ACADEMY ROAD · MOFFAT

Seamore House is a small guest house situated near the town centre, convenient for shops and restaurants, offering the tourist every comfort and personal attention.

An ideal centre for hill walking, golf, fishing and sightseeing in the surrounding area.

Mrs Carroll Seamore House, Academy Road Tel. Moffat (0683) 20404			1 Single 4 Dble/Twin 2 Family	2 Public Bath/Sh	B&B per person £7.00 Single £7.00 Double	Open Apr-Oct
K E Draper Kirkland House, Well Road Tel. Moffat (0683) 20138			3 Dble/Twin	1 Public Bath/Sh	B&B per person £8.50 Double	Open Jan-Dec Dinner 1800
Mrs Durno St Nicolas, Ballplay Road DG10 9JU Tel. Moffat (0683) 20274			3 Dble/Twin	2 Private Bath/Sh	B&B per person £8.50-£9.00 Double	Open May-Oct Dinner 1830
Mrs Gourlay Fernhill, Grange Road Tel. Moffat (0683) 20077			3 Dble/Twin	1 Private Bath/Sh 1 Public Bath/Sh	B&B per person £9.50 Double	Open May-Sep
Mrs A C Hall The Lodge, Sidmount Avenue DG10 9BS Tel. Moffat (0683) 20440			2 Single 2 Dble/Twin 1 Family	1 Private Bath/Sh 1 Public Bath/Sh	B&B per person £7.50-£8.00 Single £7.50-£8.00 Double	Open Jan-Dec Dinner 1900
Mrs D Halliwell The Schoolhouse, Roundstonefoot DG10 9LG Tel. Moffat (0683) 20950			1 Single 1 Dble/Twin 1 Family	2 Public Bath/Sh	B&B per person £7.00-£9.00 Single £7.00-£8.00 Double	Open Jan-Dec
Mrs E Little Marvig, Academy Road Tel. Moffat (0683) 20628			1 Single 5 Dble/Twin 1 Family	2 Public Bath/Sh	B&B per person £8.00 Single £8.00 Double	Open Apr-Oct
Mrs J McKenzie Hidden Corner, Beattock Road Tel. Moffat (0683) 20243			2 Dble/Twin 1 Family	1 Public Bath/Sh	B&B per person £8.00-£9.00 Double	Open Apr-Oct
Mrs Sheila Murray Marchbank, Beechgrove Tel. Moffat (0683) 21001			3 Dble/Twin	1 Public Bath/Sh	B&B per person £9.00-£10.00 Double	Open Apr-Sep Dinner 1900
Mr & Mrs Stevenson Warrender House, Haywood Road Tel. Moffat (0683) 20320			2 Dble/Twin 1 Family	2 Private Bath/Sh 1 Public Bath/Sh	B&B per person £8.50 Double	Open Jan-Dec Dinner 1830

| MOFFAT continued | Map 2 C8 | | | | | | |

"ANNAVAH" GUEST HOUSE
23 Beechgrove, Moffat.   Tel: (0683) 20550

A most attractive, deceptively spacious town house, belying its cottage-like appearance, offering bed, breakfast and evening meal in twin, double and twin and nursery (en suite) accommodation. Vanity units and tea/coffee facilities in all rooms. Central heating, parking, colour TV in residents' lounge. Five minutes walk from town centre, adjacent bowling, tennis and pleasant walks. Dogs welcome

Name / Address	Grading	Rooms	Bath	B&B	Open	Symbols
Mrs P Pirie Annavah, 23 Beechgrove DG10 9RS Tel. Moffat (0683) 20550		2 Dble/Twin 1 Family	1 Public Bath/Sh	B&B per person £9.00 Double	Open Jan-Dec Dinner 1800	
Mrs Margaret Struthers Wykeham Lodge, Old Well Road Tel. Moffat (0683) 20188		1 Single 2 Dble/Twin	1 Public Bath/Sh	B&B per person £8.00 Single £8.00 Double	Open Apr-Oct	
Mrs G T Walker Springbank, Beechgrove DG10 9RS Tel. Moffat (0683) 20070	Awaiting Inspection	3 Dble/Twin	2 Public Bath/Sh	B&B per person £7.50-£8.00 Double	Open Apr-Oct	
Mrs B C Williams Corehead Farm, Annanwater Tel. Moffat (0683) 20182	Awaiting Inspection	2 Dble/Twin 1 Family	1 Public Bath/Sh	B&B per person £8.50 Double	Open Jan-Dec Dinner 1830	
MONIAIVE Dumfriesshire	Map 2 A9					
Mrs Alison Boon Bainoon, High Street Tel. Moniaive (08482) 266		1 Single 1 Family	1 Public Bath/Sh	B&B per person £7.00 Single £7.00 Double	Open Jan-Nov	
MONTROSE Angus	Map 2 E1					
Cranes Meadow Guest House 28 The Mall Tel. Montrose (0674) 72296		1 Single 2 Dble/Twin 2 Family	2 Public Bath/Sh	B&B per person £10.00 Single £8.00 Double	Open Jan-Dec	
The Limes Guest House 15 King Street Tel. Montrose (0674) 72399	COMMENDED	2 Single 7 Dble/Twin 2 Family	6 Private Bath/Sh 1 Public Bath/Sh	B&B per person £13.00 Single £10.00 Double	Open Jan-Dec Dinner 1800	
Family run. Centrally situated in quiet, residential part of town.						
Linksgate Guest House 11 Dorward Road Tel. Montrose (0674) 72273		1 Single 4 Dble/Twin 4 Family	2 Private Bath/Sh 2 Public Bath/Sh	B&B per person £10.00 Single £10.00 Double	Open Jan-Dec Dinner 1800	
Mrs Barron Bonavista, 18 Palmerston Street Tel. Montrose (0674) 73402		2 Dble/Twin	1 Public Bath/Sh	B&B per person £7.50 Double	Open Mar-Oct	
Mrs E Duncan Myrus, 29 Bents Road Tel. Montrose (0674) 73491		1 Single 2 Dble/Twin	1 Public Bath/Sh	B&B per person £8.00-£8.50 Single £8.00-£8.50 Double	Open Apr-Oct	

Key to symbols is on back flap. Details of Classification and Grading are on page vi.

159

MONTROSE continued Mrs A Ruxton Muirshade of Gallery Farm DD10 9JU Tel. Northwaterbridge (067484) 209	Map 2 E1		1 Dble/Twin 1 Family	1 Public Bath/Sh	B&B per person £7.50 Double	Open Apr-Oct Dinner 1800	
MONYMUSK **Aberdeenshire** Mrs C Sibbald Rothens AB3 7JA Tel. Monymusk (04677) 426	Map 4 F10		1 Dble/Twin 1 Family		B&B per person £10.00 Double	Open Jan-Dec Dinner 1830	
MORAR, by Mallaig **Inverness-shire** Glengorm Guest House PH40 4PA Tel. Mallaig (0687) 2165	Map 3 E11	COMMENDED 👑 👑	3 Dble/Twin	1 Public Bath/Sh	B&B per person £8.00 Double	Open Apr-Sep Dinner 1800	
Modern, in quiet situation overlooking Morar estuary and famous Silver Sands.							
Mrs C MacLean Sunset Tel. Mallaig (0687) 2259			4 Dble/Twin	1 Public Bath/Sh	B&B per person £8.00-£9.00 Double	Open Apr-Sep Dinner 1730	
Mr T MacLean Invermorar House Tel. Mallaig (0687) 2274			1 Single 1 Dble/Twin 1 Family	1 Public Bath/Sh	B&B per person £10.00-£11.00 Single	Open Apr-Sep	
Miss Macdonald Kinsadel PH40 4PA Tel. Mallaig (0687) 2198			2 Dble/Twin 1 Family	1 Public Bath/Sh	B&B per person £7.50-£8.50 Double	Open Apr-Oct Dinner 1900	
MORNESS, Rogart **Sutherland** Mrs J Corbett Benview IV28 3XG Tel. Rogart (04084) 222	Map 4 B5		2 Single 3 Dble/Twin 1 Family	1 Private Bath/Sh 1 Public Bath/Sh	B&B per person £8.00 Single £7.50 Double	Open May-Oct Dinner 1800	
MOSSDALE, New **Galloway** **Kirkcudbrightshire** Mrs Eular Garry House DG7 2NF Tel. Laurieston (06445) 253	Map 2 A9		2 Dble/Twin 1 Family	1 Public Bath/Sh	B&B per person £8.50 Double	Open Jan-Dec Dinner 1900	
MOTHERWELL **Lanarkshire** Easdale Guest House 10 Nigel St, off Hamilton Rd Tel. Motherwell (0698) 67312	Map 2 A5	COMMENDED 👑 👑	2 Single 1 Dble/Twin 1 Family		B&B per person £10.00-£12.50 Single £9.00-£10.00 Double	Open Jan-Dec Dinner 1730	
Chalet-bungalow style building in quiet residential area. Two minutes drive from M74.							
Strathclyde Guest House 90 Hamilton Road Tel. Motherwell (0698) 64076/63691			2 Single 4 Dble/Twin 2 Family	1 Public Bath/Sh	B&B per person £8.50 Single £8.00 Double	Open Jan-Dec Dinner 1700	

	Map		Rooms	Bath	B&B	Open	Symbols
MOTHERWELL continued Mrs J Kerr 97 Hamilton Road Tel. Motherwell (0698) 62400	Map 2 A5		1 Single 3 Dble/Twin	1 Public Bath/Sh	B&B per person £8.50 Single £8.50 Double	Open Jan-Dec Dinner 1800	V ⚲ 🍴 🛏 TV P C
MUASDALE, by Tayinloan **Argyll** Mrs MacMillan Seafield Tel. Glenbarr (05832) 240	Map 1 D6		2 Dble/Twin 1 Family	1 Public Bath/Sh	B&B per person £7.00 Double	Open Mar-Oct Dinner 1800	⚲ 🍴 🛏 TV 🐕 ❄ C
MUIR OF FOWLIS, by **Alford** **Aberdeenshire** Mrs D Robertson Bridgeton Farm AB3 8NT Tel. Muir of Fowlis (03364) 272	Map 4 F10		1 Dble/Twin 2 Family	1 Public Bath/Sh	B&B per person £6.50 Double	Open Jan-Dec Dinner 1900	V 🍴 TV 🛏 🐕 ❄ P C T
MUIR OF ORD **Ross-shire** Mrs A B G Fraser Gilchrist Farm Tel. Muir of Ord (0463) 870243	Map 4 A8	COMMENDED Listed	2 Dble/Twin Working farmhouse with home cooking and baking. Attractive garden setting. Ideal Highlands tour base.	1 Public Bath/Sh	B&B per person £6.50-£12.50 Double	Open Apr-Oct Dinner 1800	🍴 TV 🛏 🐕 C
Mrs C MacKenzie Dungrianach, Corry Road IV6 7TN Tel. Muir of Ord (0463) 870316			2 Dble/Twin		B&B per person £6.50 Double	Open Jun-Aug Dinner 1830	⚲ 🍴 🛏 TV 🛏 P C
Mrs E Tuach Corrievannie IV6 7TN Tel. Muir of Ord (0463) 870534		COMMENDED Listed	2 Dble/Twin 1 Family On working croft with open views. Home cooking. Good walking area.	1 Public Bath/Sh	B&B per person £6.50-£7.00 Double	Open May-Sep Dinner 1900	⚲ 🛏 TV P C
Mrs E Urquhart Vulcan Cottage, Main Street Tel. Muir-of-Ord (0463) 870462		COMMENDED 👑👑	4 Dble/Twin Former smiddy with large lawned garden. In good decorative order, lounge, TV. Tea/coffee in evening.	2 Public Bath/Sh	B&B per person £8.00 Double	Open Jan-Dec	🍴 🛏 TV 🐕 ❄ C
MUNLOCHY **Ross-shire** Mrs Anne E Sigrist Leopold House Tel. Munlochy (046381) 450	Map 4 A8	COMMENDED Listed	2 Dble/Twin 1 Family In quiet village, adjacent to beaches and golf courses. Central for touring.	1 Private Bath/Sh 1 Public Bath/Sh	B&B per person £7.50 Double	Open Jan-Dec	🍴 TV 🐕 P C
MUSSELBURGH **East Lothian** Craigesk Guest House 10 Albert Terrace EH21 7LR Tel. 031 665 3344/3170	Map 2 D5		1 Single 2 Dble/Twin 2 Family	1 Public Bath/Sh	B&B per person £8.00 Single £8.00 Double	Open Jan-Dec	🛁 🍴 V 🛏 TV 🐕 ❄ P C
Mrs J M Aitken 18 Woodside Gardens EH21 7LJ Tel. 031 665 3170/3344			1 Single 1 Dble/Twin 1 Family	1 Public Bath/Sh	B&B per person £8.00 Single £8.00 Double	Open Jan-Dec	🛁 🍴 V 🛏 TV 🐕 ❄ P C

MUSSELBURGH continued — Map 2 D5

Mrs P Bell Smeaton House, Carberry Rd, Inveresk Tel. 031 665 2940	1 Single 2 Dble/Twin	1 Public Bath/Sh	B&B per person £8.50 Single £8.50 Double	Open Apr-Oct
Mrs Burton 4a Victoria Terrace Tel. 031 665 4802	2 Family	1 Public Bath/Sh	B&B per person £7.50-£8.00 Double	Open Jan-Dec
Mrs Caven 19 Bridge Street Tel. 031 665 6560	2 Dble/Twin 1 Family	1 Public Bath/Sh	B&B per person £7.50 Double	Open May-Sep
Mrs J R M Dewar Glenesk, 6 Delta Place, Inveresk Tel. 031 665 3217	3 Dble/Twin	3 Private Bath/Sh	B&B per person £9.50-£11.00 Double	Open May-Sep
Mrs C Douglas 5 Craighall Terrace Tel. 031 665 4294	1 Dble/Twin 1 Family	1 Public Bath/Sh	B&B per person £7.00 Double	Open Jun-Sep
Mrs Livitt 3a Victoria Terrace Tel. 031 665 2509	2 Dble/Twin 1 Family	1 Private Bath/Sh 1 Public Bath/Sh	B&B per person £8.00 Double	Open Jan-Dec
Mr D F Mather 14 Eskside West	2 Single 2 Dble/Twin	1 Public Bath/Sh	B&B per person £10.00-£12.00 Single £9.00-£11.00 Double	Open Apr-Oct
Mrs J H Millar 3 Beulah Tel. 031 665 2317	1 Single 1 Dble/Twin 1 Family	1 Public Bath/Sh	B&B per person £7.00-£8.00 Single £7.00-£8.00 Double	Open Jan-Dec
Mrs Ross Lochnagar, 12 Hope Place EH21 7QD Tel. 031 665 2029	1 Dble/Twin 3 Family	1 Public Bath/Sh	B&B per person £8.50 Double	Open Jan-Dec
Mrs Tait Fairways, 21 Linkfield Road Tel. 031 665 5050	1 Dble/Twin 2 Family	1 Private Bath/Sh	B&B per person £8.50 Double	Open Jan-Dec

NAIRN — Map 4 C8

Name / Address	Rating	Rooms	Bath	Price	Open
Bruach Guest House 35 Seabank Road Tel. Nairn (0667) 54194	COMMENDED	2 Single 2 Dble/Twin 3 Family	3 Private Bath/Sh 2 Public Bath/Sh	B&B per person £10.50 Single £10.00 Double	Open Jan-Dec Dinner 1900

Detached; victorian, in quiet area. Seafront 200 yards. Town centre 400 yards.

| Orcadia Guest House
2 Castle Lane
IV12 4DA
Tel. Nairn (0667) 52350 | | 2 Single
4 Family | 2 Public Bath/Sh | B&B per person
£8.00-£8.50 Single
£8.00-£8.50 Double | Open Jan-Dec
Dinner 1900 |

| Sunny Brae Guest House
Marine Road
IV12 4EA
Tel. Nairn (0667) 52309 | COMMENDED | 3 Single
6 Dble/Twin
1 Family | 4 Public Bath/Sh | B&B per person
£13.00-£15.00 Single
£13.00-£15.00 Double | Open Apr-Oct
Dinner 1900 |

Under personal supervision of the owners. Purpose-built, with splendid views across Moray Firth.

VAT is shown at 15%; changes in this rate may affect prices. Prices shown are for guidance only. Please send SAE with each enquiry.

NAIRN continued A & P Duff Kingsteps, Lochloy Road Tel. Nairn (0667) 52033	Map 4 C8		2 Dble/Twin 1 Family	2 Public Bath/Sh	B&B per person £8.00 Double	Open Jan-Dec Dinner 1800	
Mrs Ewan Durham House, 4 Academy Street IV1 1JT Tel. Nairn (0667) 52345			1 Single 1 Dble/Twin 1 Family	1 Public Bath/Sh	B&B per person £8.50 Single £8.00 Double	Open Apr-Oct	
Mrs E E Mills An Dhachaidh, 6 Wellington Road IV12 4RE Tel. Nairn (0667) 53339		Awaiting Inspection	2 Dble/Twin 2 Family	1 Public Bath/Sh	B&B per person £7.50-£8.00 Double	Open Jan-Dec Dinner 1830	
NEILSTON, Barrhead Renfrewshire Mrs Myra Wilson Capellie Farm G78 3AG Tel. 041 881 6546	Map 1 H6	Listed	1 Dble/Twin 2 Family	1 Public Bath/Sh	B&B per person £7.00-£8.50 Double	Open Jan-Dec Dinner 1900	
NESS Lewis, Western Isles Mrs MacLeod 26 Lionel Tel. Port-of-Ness (085181) 496	Map 3 D3		2 Dble/Twin 1 Family	1 Public Bath/Sh	B&B per person **£7.50 Double**	Open Jan-Dec Dinner 1800	
Miss C I MacLeod 12 Fivepenny Tel. Port-of-Ness (085181) 240			1 Single 1 Dble/Twin 1 Family	1 Public Bath/Sh	B&B per person £7.50 Single £7.50 Double	Open Jan-Dec Dinner 2200	
NETHERLEY, by Stonehaven Kincardineshire Mrs M Anderson The Bungalow, Brucewell Farm AB3 2RB Tel. Newtonhill (0569) 30495	Map 4 G11		1 Dble/Twin 1 Family	1 Public Bath/Sh	B&B per person £5.50-£6.00 Double	Open Jan-Dec Dinner 1700	
NETHYBRIDGE Inverness-shire Mrs Anderson Tigh-na-Drochit PH25 3DW Tel. Nethybridge (047982) 666	Map 4 C10		3 Dble/Twin	1 Public Bath/Sh	B&B per person £7.50 Single £7.50 Double	Open Jan-Dec Dinner 1800	
Mr & Mrs T R Dunn Duacklodge PH25 3DB Tel. Nethybridge (047982) 284			3 Family	1 Public Bath/Sh	B&B per person £7.50-£8.50 Double	Open Jan-Dec Dinner 1830	
James & Hilda Thomson Kimberley Holiday Homes PH25 3ED Tel. Nethybridge (047982) 255			2 Single 2 Dble/Twin	1 Private Bath/Sh 2 Public Bath/Sh	B&B per person £7.00 Single £7.00 Double	Open Apr-Mar Dinner 1900	

NEW GALLOWAY Kirkcudbrightshire Mr McPhee The Smithy Restaurant & Craft Shop Tel. New Galloway (06442) 269	Map 2 A9		2 Dble/Twin	1 Public Bath/Sh	B&B per person £9.00 Double	Open Mar-Oct Dinner 1200	V ⚲ TV 🐕 🏠 P C
NEW LUCE Wigtownshire Mrs M Johnston Galdenoch Farm Tel. New Luce (05816) 283	Map 1 G10		2 Dble/Twin	1 Public Bath/Sh	B&B per person £6.50 Double	Open Apr-Oct Dinner 1800	V ⚲ TV 🐕 🏠 P ⛰ C 🪀 🐾
NEWBURGH Fife Mrs J Morgan Homehill, Grange of Lindores Tel. Newburgh (0337) 40742	Map 2 C3		2 Dble/Twin	1 Public Bath/Sh	B&B per person £8.50 Double	Open Jan-Dec Dinner 1830	⚲ ▥ TV P
NEWCASTLETON Roxburghshire Mrs M Jones Forest Lodge, Kershopefoot TD9 0TJ Tel. Liddesdale (054121) 392	Map 2 E9	COMMENDED Listed	1 Dble/Twin 1 Family **Forest setting with superb views to Border hills. Large garden. Garden furniture for picnics.**	1 Public Bath/Sh	B&B per person £8.00-£10.00 Double	Open Jan-Nov	☕ ▥ ❊ P C
NEWPORT-ON-TAY Fife Mrs K Hepworth 1 Linden Avenue DD6 8DU Tel. Newport-on-Tay (0382) 542423	Map 2 D2		1 Dble/Twin 1 Family	1 Public Bath/Sh	B&B per person £8.00 Double	Open Jan-Dec Dinner 1800	V ⚲ ▥ TV ✕ 🏠 ✂ C
NEWTON STEWART Wigtownshire Duncree Guest House King Street Tel. Newton Stewart (0671) 2001	Map 1 H10		1 Single 2 Dble/Twin 3 Family	2 Public Bath/Sh	B&B per person £9.00 Single £9.00 Double	Open Jan-Dec Dinner 1830	🚶 M ⚲ V ♕ ⚲ TV ✕ 🐕 ❊ 🖴 P ✂ ⛰ C 🪀 🏘
Flower Bank Guest House Minnigaff Tel. Newton Stewart (0671) 2629			3 Dble/Twin 2 Family	1 Public Bath/Sh	B&B per person £8.00 Double	Open Jan-Dec Dinner 1900	🚶 V ⚲ ▥ TV ✕ 🏠 ✂ 🐕 ❊ ✂ P C 🏘
Glen Cree Guest House 6 Albert Street Tel. Newton Stewart (0671) 3317			4 Dble/Twin 1 Family		B&B per person £8.00-£9.00 Double	Open Jan-Dec Dinner 1800	🚶 ☕ V ⚲ ⚲ ▥ TV ✕ ✂ 🐕 ✂ C
Mrs M Hewitson Auchenlock Farm Tel. Newton Stewart (0671) 2035		APPROVED 👑👑	3 Dble/Twin **Turreted former shooting lodge on farm with cattle and sheep. Set within Glentrool National Park.**	1 Public Bath/Sh	B&B per person £9.00 Double	Open Apr-Oct Dinner 1800	🚶 ☕ ⚲ ▥ TV ❊ P C 🏘 🐾
Mrs M Mccormack Arran-Emm, Corsbie Road Tel. Newton Stewart (0671) 2157			6 Dble/Twin	2 Public Bath/Sh	B&B per person £8.50 Double	Open Apr-Oct Dinner 1800	V ⚲ ▥ TV 🏠 ✂ 🐕 ❊ P C

VAT is shown at 15%; changes in this rate may affect prices. Prices shown are for guidance only. Please send SAE with each enquiry.

NEWTON STEWART continued Mrs E Mcknight Cullach Farm Tel. Newton Stewart (0671) 2603	Map 1 H10		2 Dble/Twin 1 Family	1 Public Bath/Sh	B&B per person £8.00-£8.50 Double	Open Apr-Oct Dinner 1800
Mrs F Oxley Skaith Farm Tel. Newton Stewart (0671) 2774			2 Dble/Twin	1 Public Bath/Sh	B&B per person £8.00-£8.50 Double	Open Apr-Oct Dinner 1800
Miss K Wallace Kiloran, 6 Auchendoon Road Tel. Newton Stewart (0671) 2818		Awaiting Inspection	2 Dble/Twin	1 Public Bath/Sh	B&B per person £8.50-£9.50 Double	Open Apr-Oct
NEWTONMORE Inverness-shire Alder Lodge Guest House Glen Road PH20 1EA Tel. Newtonmore (05403) 376	Map 4 B11		2 Single 5 Dble/Twin	2 Public Bath/Sh	B&B per person £9.00 Single £9.00 Double	Open Jan-Dec Dinner 1900

Coig Na Shee

FORT WILLIAM ROAD, NEWTONMORE, INVERNESS-SHIRE
Telephone: 05403 216

Delightful Spey Valley Guest House set in extensive grounds on peaceful outskirts of village. Home-made bread, soups, pâtés. Personal service. Central heating. Log fire in lounge. Ideal centre for touring.

Coig Na Shee Guest House Fort William Road PH20 1DG Tel. Newtonmore (05403) 216			1 Single 4 Dble/Twin 1 Family	2 Public Bath/Sh	B&B per person £11.50-£12.50 Single £11.50-£12.50 Double	Open Feb-Nov Dinner 1900
Glen Quoich Guest House Glen Road Tel. Newtonmore (05403) 461		Awaiting Inspection	2 Single 1 Dble/Twin 3 Family	2 Public Bath/Sh	B&B per person £9.90 Single £9.90 Double	Open Jan-Dec Dinner 1900

Spey Valley Lodge

Station Road, Newtonmore, Inverness-shire, Scotland. Tel. (05403) 398

Open all year. Situated in its own half acre grounds. Magnificent views. Personally supervised by owners. French, Italian, English spoken. Six bedrooms, each H&C water, central heating, television. Facilities include tea/coffee making. Two shower rooms.

Newtonmore, Spey Valley, offer numerous variety of sports including winter skiing. Beautiful sightseeing. Tariff per person per night £8 B&B. Double or twin £16. D, B&B per person £14. Supplement £3 festive season.

Spey Valley Lodge Guest House Station Road PH20 1AR Tel. Newtonmore (05403) 398		2 Single 1 Dble/Twin 3 Family		B&B per person £7.00-£8.00 Single £7.00-£8.00 Double	Open Mar-Oct Dinner 1800

NEWTONMORE continued	Map 4 B11					
Mrs Blackburn Craigellachie House Tel. Newtonmore (05403) 264			3 Dble/Twin 1 Family	1 Public Bath/Sh	B&B per person £7.50-£8.00 Double	Open Jan-Dec
Valerie Tonkin Eagle View, Perth Road Tel. Newtonmore (05403) 675			1 Single 2 Dble/Twin		B&B per person £7.50 Single £7.50 Double	Open Jan-Dec
NORTH BERWICK East Lothian	Map 2 E4					
Cragside Guest House Marine Parade Tel. North Berwick (0620) 2879		APPROVED ♕	1 Single 4 Dble/Twin 1 Family	1 Public Bath/Sh	B&B per person £10.00 Single £10.00 Double	Open Jan-Dec Dinner 1800
			Overlooking beaches and Firth of Forth. Friendly atmosphere.			
Rockend Guest House 17 Marine Parade Tel. North Berwick (0620) 3970		COMMENDED ♕ ♕	1 Single 3 Dble/Twin 1 Family	1 Private Bath/Sh 2 Public Bath/Sh	B&B per person £12.50-£14.00 Single £11.00-£12.00 Double	Open Jan-Dec Dinner 1900-
			Personally supervised victorian house in superb situation. Safe beach, tennis courts, putting green.			
The Wing Guest House Marine Parade Tel. North Berwick (0620) 4168			3 Dble/Twin 1 Family	1 Public Bath/Sh	B&B per person £7.00-£9.50 Double	Open Jan-Dec Dinner 1800
Mrs May Barbour Windygates, Windygates Road Tel. North Berwick (0620) 2936			2 Single 2 Dble/Twin	2 Public Bath/Sh	B&B per person £8.50 Single £8.50-£9.50 Double	Open Apr-Oct
Mrs I Brown 14 Marine Parade EH39 4LD Tel. North Berwick (0620) 2063			1 Single 2 Dble/Twin	1 Public Bath/Sh	B&B per person £8.00-£9.00 Single £8.00-£9.00 Double	Open Jan-Dec Dinner 1830
Mrs Byrne Skeochwood, 29 St Andrew Street Tel. North Berwick (0620) 2704			1 Dble/Twin 1 Family		B&B per person £8.50 Double	Open Apr-Oct
Miss R Capaldi Redan, 7 Hamilton Road Tel. North Berwick (0620) 2533			1 Dble/Twin 1 Family		B&B per person £8.00-£8.50 Double	Open May-Sep
Miss C Capaldi Tantallon House, 2 West Bay Rd Tel. North Berwick (0620) 2259			1 Single 1 Dble/Twin 1 Family	1 Private Bath/Sh	B&B per person £7.00-£8.50 Single £13.50-£16.00 Double	Open Jun-Sep
Mrs K Hardie Abbotscroft, Tantallon Road Tel. North Berwick (0620) 3887			1 Single 2 Dble/Twin		B&B per person £8.00-£8.50 Single £8.00-£8.50 Double	Open May-Sep Dinner 1900
Mrs R Lumsden 26 Dundas Avenue Tel. North Berwick (0620) 2651		Listed	2 Dble/Twin	1 Public Bath/Sh	B&B per person £9.00-£10.00 Double	Open Apr-Sep

NORTH BERWICK continued	Map 2 E4						
Mrs Patey Lochiel, 19 Dundas Avenue Tel. North Berwick (0620) 2947			2 Dble/Twin	2 Private Bath/Sh	B&B per person £8.00-£9.00 Double	Open Jun-Sep	
Mrs C Rae 2 The Quadrant Tel. North Berwick (0620) 3835			3 Dble/Twin	3 Public Bath/Sh	B&B per person £8.50-£9.50 Double	Open Apr-Oct Dinner 1830	
Mrs Moira Ralph Craigmore, 13 Westgate Tel. North Berwick (0620) 2782			2 Dble/Twin	1 Public Bath/Sh	B&B per person £12.00-£13.50 Double	Open Jan-Dec Dinner 1830	
Mrs Joyce Strachan Fairways, 17 Beach Road Tel. North Berwick (0620) 2241			2 Dble/Twin 1 Family	1 Private Bath/Sh 1 Public Bath/Sh	B&B per person £9.00 Double	Open Jan-Dec Dinner 1830	
NORTH BOISDALE S Uist, Western Isles	Map 3 A10						
Mrs M Steele 340 North Boisdale Tel. Lochboisdale (08784) 243			1 Single 2 Dble/Twin	1 Public Bath/Sh	B&B per person £7.00-£7.50 Single £7.00 Double	Open Apr-Oct Dinner 1800	
NORTH CONNEL Argyll	Map 1 E2						
Mrs J Law The Shore Tel. Connel (063171) 652			2 Family	2 Public Bath/Sh	B&B per person £7.50-£9.00 Double	Open Jan-Dec Dinner 1830	
NORTH LOCHEYNORT S Uist, Western Isles	Map 3 A10						
Mrs A MacDonald 8 North Locheynort, Bornish Tel. Bornish (08785) 379			1 Single 2 Dble/Twin	1 Public Bath/Sh	B&B per person £7.50 Single £7.50 Double	Open May-Oct Dinner 1800	
NORTHBAY Isle of Barra, Western Isles	Map 3 A11						
Northbay Guest House Tel. Northbay (08715) 255			1 Single 2 Dble/Twin 1 Family	1 Private Bath/Sh 1 Public Bath/Sh	B&B per person £8.00 Single £8.00 Double	Open Apr-Oct Dinner 1800	
Mrs Macleod Oiteag Na Mara, Bruernish PA80 5UY Tel. Northbay (08715) 384		**COMMENDED** Listed	1 Single 2 Dble/Twin	2 Public Bath/Sh	B&B per person £8.00 Single £8.00 Double	Open Jan-Dec Dinner 1700	
Modern bungalow, in peaceful setting overlooking sea. 3 miles (5km) from Barra Airport.							
Mrs C MacPherson Aros Cottage, Bolnabodach Tel. Northbay (08715) 355			3 Dble/Twin	1 Public Bath/Sh	B&B per person £8.50-£9.50 Double	Open Jan-Dec Dinner 1800	
OBAN Argyll	Map 1 E2						
Ardblair Guest House Dalriach Road PA34 5JB Tel. Oban (0631) 62668			3 Single 15 Dble/Twin 4 Family	8 Public Bath/Sh	B&B per person £6.50-£8.00 Single	Open May-Sep Dinner 1830	

Key to symbols is on back flap. Details of Classification and Grading are on page vi.

167

OBAN continued	Map 1 E2						
Armadale Guest House Dunollie Road PA34 5PH Tel. Oban (0631) 62981		Awaiting Inspection	3 Single 3 Dble/Twin 1 Family	2 Public Bath/Sn	B&B per person £7.50-£9.00 Single £7.50-£9.00 Double	Open Apr-Nov Dinner 1830	
Beechgrove Guest House Croft Road PA34 5JL Tel. Oban (0631) 66111		COMMENDED ♕♕	3 Dble/Twin 1 Family	2 Public Bath/Sh	B&B per person £8.00-£9.00 Double	Open Jan-Dec Dinner 1830	
			Family run. Short walk from harbour and shops. Views of Oban Bay and Sound of Kerrera.				
Braehead Guest House Albert Road Tel. Oban (0631) 63341			5 Dble/Twin 1 Family		B&B per person £8.00-£9.00 Double	Open Jan-Dec Dinner 1830	
Elmbank Guest House Croft Road Tel. Oban (0631) 62545		Listed	1 Single 4 Dble/Twin 2 Family	1 Public Bath/Sh	B&B per person £9.00-£10.00 Single £9.00-£10.00 Double	Open Jan-Dec Dinner 1830	
Glenbervie Guest House Dalriach Road Tel. Oban (0631) 64770			2 Single 4 Dble/Twin 2 Family	1 Public Bath/Sh	B&B per person £9.00-£10.00 Single £9.00-£10.00 Double	Open Jan-Dec Dinner 1830	
Glenroy Guest House Rockfield Road PA34 5DQ Tel. Oban (0631) 62585			1 Single 6 Dble/Twin 2 Family	2 Private Bath/Sh 3 Public Bath/Sh	B&B per person £8.50-£10.00 Double	Open Jan-Dec Dinner 1800	
Harbour View Guest House Shore Street Tel. Oban (0631) 63462			1 Dble/Twin 4 Family	2 Public Bath/Sh	B&B per person £7.50-£8.50 Double	Open Jan-Dec	
Invercloy Guest House Ardconnel Terrace Tel. Oban (0631) 62058		APPROVED Listed	4 Dble/Twin 3 Family	1 Public Bath/Sh	B&B per person £7.00-£9.50 Double	Open Jan-Dec Dinner 1830	
			Victorian house, high above town. Overlooks Oban Bay with views to Hills of Mull.				
Rahoy Lodge Guest House Gallanach Road Tel. Oban (0631) 62301		COMMENDED ♕	2 Dble/Twin 5 Family	1 Public Bath/Sh	B&B per person £7.50-£10.00 Double	Open Feb-Nov Dinner 1830	
			Family run on waterfront of Oban Bay. Open view to Sound of Kerrera and Isle of Mull. Home cooking.				
Sand Villa Guest House Breadalbane Street Tel. Oban (0631) 62803			9 Dble/Twin 6 Family	2 Public Bath/Sh	B&B per person £7.00-£9.00 Double	Open Jan-Dec Dinner 1800	
Sgeir Mhaol Guest House Soroba Road Tel. Oban (0631) 62650			3 Dble/Twin 3 Family	2 Public Bath/Sh	B&B per person £8.50-£10.00 Double	Open Jan-Dec Dinner 1830	
Westmount Guest House Dalriach Road Tel. Oban (0631) 62884			3 Dble/Twin 5 Family	1 Public Bath/Sh	B&B per person £8.50 Double	Open Apr-Sep	
Mrs Billimore Tyree, Glenshellach Road Tel. Oban (0631) 64944			2 Dble/Twin 2 Family	1 Public Bath/Sh	B&B per person £7.50-£8.50 Double	Open Jan-Dec Dinner 1800	
Mrs K Clark 5 High Street Tel. Oban (0631) 62475			1 Single 2 Dble/Twin 1 Family	3 Private Bath/Sh 1 Public Bath/Sh	B&B per person £7.50-£8.50 Single £7.00-£8.00 Double	Open Jan-Dec	
Mrs Crawford Cnoc Aluinn, Mossfield Drive Tel. Oban (0631) 63703			2 Dble/Twin	1 Public Bath/Sh	B&B per person £7.00 Double	Open May-Sep	

VAT is shown at 15%: changes in this rate may affect prices. Prices shown are for guidance only. Please send SAE with each enquiry.

OBAN continued	Map 1 E2						
Ann Edwards Rhumor, Drummore Road Tel. Oban (0631) 63544	COMMENDED ☻	2 Single 2 Dble/Twin	1 Public Bath/Sh	B&B per person £8.50-£9.00 Single £8.00-£8.50 Double	Open Mar-Oct	♿ 🖥 🛏 🍴
		Stone built, in quiet area on edge of town. Can collect from station or ferry. Picnic lunches.				
J & D Ledwidge Drumriggend, 22 Drummore Road Tel. Oban (0631) 63330	☻	1 Dble/Twin 1 Family	1 Public Bath/Sh	B&B per person £7.50-£8.00 Double	Open Apr-Oct Dinner 1800	
Mrs C Logan Antrim, Soroba Road Tel. Oban (0631) 63239		6 Dble/Twin 4 Family	1 Public Bath/Sh	B&B per person £9.50 Double	Open Jan-Dec	
Mrs MacCalman Duncarden, Rowan Road PA34 5TQ Tel. Oban (0631) 64947	Listed	3 Dble/Twin	1 Public Bath/Sh	B&B per person £8.50-£9.00 Double	Open Apr-Sep	
Mrs B MacColl Glengorm, Dunollie Road Tel. Oban (0631) 65361	Awaiting Inspection	1 Single 3 Dble/Twin 1 Family	2 Public Bath/Sh	B&B per person £7.50-£8.00 Single £7.50-£8.00 Double	Open Apr-Oct	

"DON-MUIR"
PULPIT HILL, OBAN   Tel: 0631 64536
Situated in a quiet residential area, three-quarters of the way up Pulpit Hill.
Tea/coffee-making facilities, colour TV, H&C in all bedrooms, central heating throughout.
Residents' Lounge, garden and parking.
☻ ☻ **Commended**

Mrs M J MacDonald Don-Muir, Pulpit Hill Tel. Oban (0631) 64536	COMMENDED ☻ ☻	3 Dble/Twin	2 Public Bath/Sh	B&B per person £7.50-£8.00 Double	Open Jan-Dec	
		Quiet residential area, in elevated position on Pulpit Hill. Close to public transport terminals.				
Mrs A MacDonald 1 Albany Street Tel. Oban (0631) 62946		2 Dble/Twin	1 Public Bath/Sh	B&B per person £8.00 Double	Open Jan-Dec Dinner 1800	
Mrs L MacGillvray Homefarm, Barcaldine Tel. Ledaig (063171) 253		2 Dble/Twin 1 Family	1 Public Bath/Sh	B&B per person £7.50-£8.00 Double	Open May-Sep	
Mrs E M MacLean Lorne View, Ardconnel Road Tel. Oban (0631) 65500	COMMENDED ☻	3 Dble/Twin	3 Private Bath/Sh 1 Public Bath/Sh	B&B per person £8.50-£9.00 Double	Open Apr-Oct Dinner 1815	
		Quiet location overlooking Oban Bay. Near local sports amenities and town centre.				
Mrs N May Lynwood, Longsdale Road Tel. Oban (0631) 62949		2 Single 2 Dble/Twin		B&B per person £7.50-£8.00 Single £7.50-£8.00 Double	Open Apr-Oct	
Mrs McIver Loudon, Dalriach Road PA34 5EQ Tel. Oban (0631) 63298	☻ ☻	2 Single 3 Dble/Twin	1 Public Bath/Sh	B&B per person £7.00 Single £7.00 Double	Open Jan-Dec Dinner 1815	

Key to symbols is on back flap. Details of Classification and Grading are on page vi.

169

OBAN continued — Map 1 E2

Name & Address	Grading	Rooms	Bath	Terms	Opening
Mrs C McQuade, Ard Struan, Croft Road, Tel. Oban (0631) 63689	Awaiting Inspection	3 Dble/Twin	1 Public Bath/Sh	B&B per person £7.50-£8.00 Double	Open Mar-Sep Dinner 1800
Mr J Nisbet, Claremont Villa, Craigard Road, PA34 5NP, Tel. Oban (0631) 63124	♕	3 Dble/Twin 1 Family	1 Private Bath/Sh 1 Public Bath/Sh	B&B per person £7.50-£8.50 Double	Open Jan-Dec
Mrs Petrie, Willowdene, Glencruitten Road, Tel. Oban (0631) 64601		1 Single 3 Dble/Twin 1 Family	1 Public Bath/Sh	B&B per person £7.50 Single £7.50 Double	Open Apr-Oct

---

"Dungrianach" ♕ ♕ HIGHLY COMMENDED

PULPIT HILL, OBAN.   TELEPHONE: 0631 62840

"Dungrianach" (Gaelic—the sunny house on the hill) sits in its own grounds right above the yacht moorings, with unsurpassed views of sea and islands. Visitors are coming to a family home where they are welcomed into a friendly informal atmosphere. Each bedroom has private shower, w.c. and w.h.b.

Bed and Breakfast from £10, dinner from £4

Name & Address	Grading	Rooms	Bath	Terms	Opening
Mrs Robertson, Dungrianach, Pulpit Hill, Tel. Oban (0631) 62840	HIGHLY COMMENDED ♕ ♕	3 Dble/Twin	3 Private Bath/Sh 1 Public Bath/Sh	B&B per person £8.50-£10.00 Double	Open Apr-Sep Dinner 1830
		Secluded, in 4 acres of wooded garden on top of Pulpit Hill. Magnificent views over bay and islands.			
Mrs M J Skeels, North Cuan Croft, Cuan Ferry, PA34 4RB, Tel. Balvicar (08523) 367		2 Dble/Twin		B&B per person £8.50-£9.50 Double	Open Apr-Oct Dinner 1830-
Mrs Smyth, Kinlochan, Ardconnel Road, Tel. Oban (0631) 64277		1 Single 2 Dble/Twin	1 Public Bath/Sh	B&B per person £8.00-£9.00 Single £7.50-£8.50 Double	Open May-Sep Dinner 1830-
Mrs J Steel, Whinbank, Rowan Road, Tel. Oban (0631) 64307		1 Family	1 Public Bath/Sh	B&B per person £8.00-£9.00 Double	Open Jul-Aug Dinner 1800-
Mrs Stephenson, Island View, Ganavan Sands, Tel. Oban (0631) 64362		3 Dble/Twin	2 Public Bath/Sh	B&B per person £7.50-£8.00 Double	Open Jan-Dec
Mrs M Tindall, 8 Dalrigh, Dunollie Road, Tel. Oban (0631) 64167	COMMENDED Listed	1 Dble/Twin 1 Family	1 Public Bath/Sh	B&B per person £7.50-£8.00 Double	Open May-Sep
		Semi-detached house, centrally situated close to promenade, harbour and town centre.			
Mrs Walker, Greencourt, Benvoulin Road, Tel. Oban (0631) 62497		1 Single 2 Dble/Twin	1 Public Bath/Sh	B&B per person £7.50-£8.00 Single £7.50-£8.00 Double	Open May-Oct Dinner 1830
Mr Woodman, Cologin Homes Ltd, Lerags, Tel. Oban (0631) 64501	COMMENDED Listed	20 Dble/Twin	20 Private Bath/Sh 20 Public Bath/Sh	B&B per person £7.50-£9.00 Double	Open Jan-Dec Dinner 1700
		On peaceful, private site, 3 miles/5 km from Oban. Informal atmosphere in bar, food all day.			

VAT is shown at 15%; changes in this rate may affect prices. Prices shown are for guidance only. Please send SAE with each enquiry.

Location	Map	Classification	Accommodation	Bathrooms	B&B Rates	Opening
OLDMELDRUM Aberdeenshire Mrs J Hidalgo Cromlet Hill, South Road AB5 0AB Tel. Oldmeldrum (06512) 2315	Map 4 G9	Listed	2 Single 1 Dble/Twin	1 Public Bath/Sh	B&B per person £9.00 Single £8.00 Double	Open Jan-Dec
ONICH Inverness-shire Camus Guest House Tel. Onich (08553) 200	Map 1 F1		2 Single 3 Dble/Twin 1 Family	2 Private Bath/Sh 2 Public Bath/Sh	B&B per person £10.00 Single £9.00 Double	Open Apr-Oct Dinner 1830
Mrs M Maclean Janika, Bunree Tel. Onich (08553) 359			4 Dble/Twin	1 Public Bath/Sh	B&B per person £8.00 Double	Open Apr-Oct
Mrs J Mclean Forester's Bungalow, Inchree PH33 6SE Tel. Onich (08553) 285			2 Dble/Twin 1 Family	1 Public Bath/Sh	B&B per person £7.50 Double	Open Apr-Oct Dinner 1900
Mr & Mrs I Rae Lismore House Tel. Onich (08553) 344		COMMENDED Listed	2 Dble/Twin 1 Family	1 Public Bath/Sh	B&B per person £8.00-£9.50 Double	Open Jan-Oct
Modern detached villa in quiet setting. Beautiful, open views over Loch Linnhe and Glencoe Hills.						
Mrs S Williamson Sandala, Inchree Tel. Onich (08553) 330			3 Dble/Twin	1 Public Bath/Sh	B&B per person £8.00 Double	Open Jan-Dec
ORBOST, by Dunvegan Isle of Skye, Inverness-shire Mrs MacDonald Orbost Farm Tel. Dunvegan (047022) 225	Map 3 C9		1 Dble/Twin 1 Family	1 Public Bath/Sh	B&B per person £7.00-£7.50 Double	Open Apr-Oct
ORD Isle of Skye, Inverness-shire Mrs B La Trobe Fiordhem Tel. Tarykavaig (04715) 226	Map 3 E10		1 Single 3 Dble/Twin	1 Public Bath/Sh	B&B per person £9.50-£10.00 Single £9.50-£10.00 Double	Open Jan-Dec Dinner 1830
ORMICLATE S Uist, Western Isles Mrs C Macphee 7 Ormiclate Tel. Bornish (08785) 373	Map 3 A10	Listed	2 Dble/Twin 1 Family	1 Public Bath/Sh	B&B per person £7.00 Double	Open Jan-Dec Dinner 1830
ORPHIR Orkney Mrs Bostock Newhouse KW16 3HD Tel. Orphir (085681) 313	Map 5 B11		1 Dble/Twin	1 Public Bath/Sh	B&B per person £7.00 Double	Open Jan-Dec Dinner 1900
OUT SKERRIES Shetland Mrs K Johnson Rocklea, East Isle Tel. Out Skerries (08065) 228	Map 5 H3		2 Dble/Twin	1 Public Bath/Sh	B&B per person £7.00-£7.50 Double	Open Jan-Dec Dinner 2000

Key to symbols is on back flap. Details of Classification and Grading are on page vi.

Location	Map Ref		Rooms	Bath	B&B	Open	Facilities
PAISLEY Renfrewshire	Map 1 H5						
Adelphi Guest House 91 New Sneddon Street PA3 2GD Tel. 041 889 2642			2 Single 4 Dble/Twin 2 Family	4 Public Bath/Sh	B&B per person £10.00 Single £9.00 Double	Open Jan-Dec	
Ardgowan Guest House 92 Renfrew Road Tel. 041 889 4763 Telex 777647			1 Single 3 Dble/Twin 3 Family	2 Public Bath/Sh	B&B per person £12.50-£15.00 Single £9.00-£10.00 Double	Open Jan-Nov	
Clabern Guest House 88 Renfrew Road PA3 4BJ Tel. 041 889 6194			1 Dble/Twin 2 Family	1 Public Bath/Sh	B&B per person £12.50 Double	Open Jan-Dec	
Colinslee Guest House 163 Neilston Road PA2 6QW Tel. 041 884 2317			1 Single 3 Dble/Twin	1 Public Bath/Sh	B&B per person £10.00 Single £10.00 Double	Open Jan-Dec	
Mrs McDonald 12 Greenlaw Drive Tel. 041 889 5359			3 Single 1 Dble/Twin 3 Family	3 Public Bath/Sh	B&B per person £9.00-£10.00 Single £9.00 Double	Open Jan-Dec	
Mrs Thomson Bent Farm, Gleniffer Braes Tel. Brediland (050581) 4858			1 Single 3 Dble/Twin 1 Family	1 Public Bath/Sh	B&B per person £10.00-£12.00 Single £10.00-£12.00 Double	Open Jan-Dec Dinner 1730	
PAPA WESTRAY Orkney	Map 5 C9	COMMENDED 👑 👑	4 Dble/Twin	4 Private Bath/Sh	B&B per person £10.00-£12.00 Double	Open Jan-Dec Dinner 1800	
Papay Community Co-operative Ltd Beltane House Tel. Papa Westray (08574) 267/238			Attractive conversion from terraced cottages. All rooms with shower. Island of history and birdlife.				
PATHHEAD Midlothian	Map 2 D5						
Mrs F B Ward 194 Main Street Tel. Ford (0875) 320366			1 Single 1 Dble/Twin 1 Family	1 Public Bath/Sh	B&B per person £8.00 Single £8.00 Double	Open Mar-Nov	
PEAT INN Fife	Map 2 D3						
Mrs A C Fraser Kirkton of Radernie Tel. Peat Inn (033484) 316			3 Dble/Twin	1 Public Bath/Sh	B&B per person £9.00-£10.00 Double	Open May-Oct	
Mrs Mary Grant Greigston Farm KY15 5LF Tel. Peat Inn (033484) 284			1 Dble/Twin 1 Family	2 Public Bath/Sh	B&B per person £9.50 Double	Open Apr-Oct Dinner 1700	
Mrs Anne Hardy South Bowhill Farm Tel. Peat Inn (033484) 346			1 Single 2 Dble/Twin	1 Public Bath/Sh	B&B per person £9.00 Single £9.00 Double	Open Jan-Dec Dinner 1900	
PEEBLES	Map 2 C6						
Mrs T Arnott 9 East Gate EH45 8AD			1 Dble/Twin	1 Public Bath/Sh	B&B per person £8.00-£9.00 Double	Open Apr-Oct Dinner 1930	

VAT is shown at 15%; changes in this rate may affect prices. Prices shown are for guidance only. Please send SAE with each enquiry.

PEEBLES continued	Map 2 C6						
Mrs M Chandler St Mary's, 98 Neidpath Road Tel. Peebles (0721) 20823	Awaiting Inspection		1 Single 2 Dble/Twin	1 Public Bath/Sh	B&B per person £8.00 Single £8.00 Double	Open Jan-Dec	
Mr & Mrs C De Freitas Lindores, Old Town EH45 8JE Tel. Peebles (0721) 20441	♔		2 Dble/Twin 3 Family	1 Public Bath/Sh	B&B per person £8.50-£9.00 Double	Open Jan-Dec	
Mrs M Dennison Brookside, Eshiels Tel. Peebles (0721) 21178			1 Single 2 Dble/Twin	1 Public Bath/Sh	B&B per person £8.00-£9.00 Single £8.00-£9.00 Double	Open Apr-Dec Dinner 1830	
Mrs M Hamilton Margarth, 3 Dukeshaugh Tel. Peebles (0721) 20426	♔		2 Dble/Twin		B&B per person £7.50-£8.00 Double	Open Apr-Oct	
Mrs Haydock Winkston Farmhouse Tel. Peebles (0721) 21264			3 Dble/Twin	1 Public Bath/Sh	B&B per person £8.25-£9.00 Double	Open Apr-Oct	
Mrs Mitchell 1 Rosetta Road Tel. Peebles (0721) 21232			2 Family	1 Public Bath/Sh	B&B per person £8.50 Double	Open Feb-Nov	
Mrs Morrison 9 Witchwood Crescent Tel. Peebles (0721) 21206	COMMENDED Listed		1 Single 1 Dble/Twin	1 Public Bath/Sh	B&B per person £8.50-£9.00 Single £8.00-£8.50 Double	Open Apr-Oct	
			Quiet, comfortable modern house in pleasant surroundings. Homely atmosphere.				
Mrs Muir Whitestone House, Innerleithen Road Tel. Peebles (0721) 20337	COMMENDED ♔		3 Dble/Twin 2 Family	2 Public Bath/Sh	B&B per person £8.50-£9.00 Double	Open Jan-Dec	
			Attractive victorian house, personally run. On main A72 with fine views to parkland and hills.				
Mrs O'Hara Rowanbrae, Northgate Tel. Peebles (0721) 21630			2 Dble/Twin	1 Public Bath/Sh	B&B per person £8.00 Double	Open Apr-Oct	
Mrs J K Phillips Drumore, Venlaw High Road Tel. Peebles (0721) 20336	♔ ♔		1 Single 2 Dble/Twin	1 Public Bath/Sh	B&B per person £8.50-£9.50 Single £8.50-£9.50 Double	Open Apr-Oct Dinner 1900	
Mrs H Ross Winterchimes, 39 Dukehaugh EH45 9DN Tel. Peebles (0721) 21258	Listed		1 Single 2 Dble/Twin	1 Public Bath/Sh	B&B per person £7.50-£8.00 Single £7.50-£8.00 Double	Open Jan-Dec	
Mrs A Sked 21 Kirkland Street EH45 8EU Tel. Peebles (0721) 20525			2 Dble/Twin	1 Public Bath/Sh	B&B per person £7.50-£8.00 Double	Open Jan-Dec	
Mrs R Smith Chapel Hill Farm Tel. Peebles (0721) 20188			2 Dble/Twin 1 Family	1 Public Bath/Sh	B&B per person £8.00 Double	Open May-Sep	
Mrs Morag Wilson Tomory, 105 Northgate Tel. Peebles (0721) 21909	COMMENDED ♔ ♔		1 Dble/Twin 2 Family	1 Public Bath/Sh	B&B per person £7.50 Double	Open Apr-Oct	
			19 c whinstone semi villa. Near to shops and bus station. Park, fishing, golf, swimming locally.				

PENICUIK Midlothian	Map 2 C5		

Silverburn Steading
SILVERBURN · PENICUIK · MIDLOTHIAN EH26 9LJ
Telephone: (0968) 78420

A converted farm steading of charm and character in a rural setting at the foot of the Pentland Hills, 10 miles SW of Edinburgh on the edge of the Scottish Borders. Conveniently located on the A702, it is an ideal base for Edinburgh and the South of Scotland. Excellent accommodation, good food and a warm welcome.

Bed and Breakfast £9. Dinner, Bed and Breakfast £15. Mrs Joan Taylor.

Mr & Mrs Taylor The Steading, Silverburn Tel. Penicuik (0968) 78420			1 Single 2 Dble/Twin	1 Private Bath/Sh 1 Public Bath/Sh	B&B per person £8.00-£9.00 Single £8.00-£9.00 Double	Open Jan-Dec Dinner 1900	
PENIFILER, by Portree Isle of Skye, Inverness-shire Mrs Mackenzie 2 Heatherfield Tel. Portree (0478) 2820	Map 3 D9		2 Dble/Twin	1 Public Bath/Sh	B&B per person £7.50 Double	Open Apr-Oct	
PENINVER, by Campbeltown Argyll Mrs Graham Fairwinds Tel. Campbeltown (0586) 52240	Map 1 E7		2 Dble/Twin 1 Family	1 Public Bath/Sh	B&B per person £6.50-£7.00 Double	Open Apr-Oct Dinner 1700	
Mrs Semple Ballochgair Farm			4 Dble/Twin	2 Public Bath/Sh	B&B per person £7.00-£7.50 Double	Open Apr-Oct Dinner 1800	
PERTH Clark Kimberley Guest House 57-59 Dunkeld Road PH1 5RP Tel. Perth (0738) 37406	Map 2 C2		2 Single 4 Dble/Twin 3 Family	2 Public Bath/Sh	B&B per person £10.00 Single £8.00-£9.00 Double	Open Jan-Dec	
Clunie Guest House 12 Pitcullen Crescent PH2 7HT Tel. Perth (0738) 23625		COMMENDED 👑👑👑	1 Single 5 Dble/Twin 1 Family	7 Private Bath/Sh 2 Public Bath/Sh	B&B per person £10.00 Single £10.00 Double	Open Jan-Dec Dinner 1800	
			Personally run in residential part of town. Easy access to town centre, on main bus route.				
The Darroch Guest House 9 Pitcullen Crescent PH2 7HT Tel. Perth (0738) 36893		COMMENDED 👑👑	2 Single 2 Dble/Twin 2 Family	3 Private Bath/Sh 2 Public Bath/Sh	B&B per person £9.00-£10.00 Single £9.00-£10.00 Double	Open Jan-Dec Dinner 1800	
			Personally run. Conveniently situated on main A94 tourist route. All rooms double glazed.				
The Gables Guest House 24-26 Dunkeld Road PH1 5RW Tel. Perth (0738) 24717			2 Single 3 Dble/Twin 4 Family	2 Public Bath/Sh	B&B per person £10.00 Single £8.50 Double	Open Jan-Dec Dinner 1900	
Iona Guest House 2 Pitcullen Crescent PH2 7HT Tel. Perth (0738) 27261		COMMENDED 👑👑	2 Single 2 Dble/Twin 2 Family	2 Public Bath/Sh	B&B per person £9.50-£12.00 Single £9.50-£11.00 Double	Open Jan-Dec	
			In residential area, 10 minutes from town centre. Double glazed front bedrooms.				

VAT is shown at 15%: changes in this rate may affect prices. Prices shown are for guidance only. Please send SAE with each enquiry.

PERTH continued	Map 2 C2					
Kinnoull Guest House 5 Pitcullen Crescent PH2 7HT Tel. Perth (0738) 34165			3 Dble/Twin 1 Family	4 Private Bath/Sh	B&B per person £9.00-£10.00 Double	Open Jan-Dec Dinner 1800

Pitcullen Guest House
17 Pitcullen Crescent, Perth PH2 7HT.
Telephone: (0738) 26506/28265

Attractive Guest House, situated in residential district, only minutes away from city centre. The house has central heating throughout, all bedrooms have hot and cold water, shaving points and tea/coffee making facilities. Comfortable lounge with TV. Evening meals. Private parking facilities, AA & RAC listed. Brochure from Mrs. J. Grainger.

Name/Address	Grading	Rooms	Bath	B&B	Open
Pitcullen Guest House 17 Pitcullen Crescent PH2 7HT Tel. Perth (0738) 26506/28265		1 Single 3 Dble/Twin 1 Family	1 Public Bath/Sh	B&B per person £9.00-£12.50 Single £9.00-£10.00 Double	Open Jan-Dec Dinner 1800
Rowanbank Guest House 3 Pitcullen Crescent PH2 7HT Tel. Perth (0738) 21421		1 Dble/Twin 3 Family	2 Public Bath/Sh	B&B per person £8.50-£9.00 Double	Open Jan-Dec Dinner 1800
Struan Guest House 7 Strathview Terrace PH2 7HY Tel. Perth (0738) 37687		1 Single 2 Dble/Twin 1 Family	2 Private Bath/Sh 1 Public Bath/Sh	B&B per person £8.50-£10.00 Single £8.50 Double	Open Jan-Dec Dinner 1800
Tatra Guest House 1 Pitcullen Crescent PH2 7HT Tel. Perth (0738) 25951	COMMENDED	1 Single 2 Dble/Twin 1 Family	1 Public Bath/Sh	B&B per person £10.00 Single £9.00 Double	Open Jan-Dec Dinner 1800
Personally run, conveniently situated on main A94 tourist route. Within easy reach of town centre.					
Tigh Mhorag Guest House 69 Dunkeld Road PH1 5RP Tel. Perth (0738) 22902		2 Single 3 Dble/Twin 1 Family	1 Public Bath/Sh	B&B per person £10.00 Single £16.00 Double	Open Mar-Oct Dinner 1800
Mrs C Booth Bellview, 38 Hay Street PH1 5HS Tel. Perth (0738) 38375		2 Dble/Twin 1 Family	1 Public Bath/Sh	B&B per person £7.50-£8.00 Double	Open Jan-Nov Dinner 1700
Mrs C Brown Dunallan, 10 Pitcullen Crescent PH2 7TH Tel. Perth (0738) 22551	COMMENDED	2 Single 2 Dble/Twin	1 Private Bath/Sh 2 Public Bath/Sh	B&B per person £9.00-£9.50 Single £9.00-£10.00 Double	Open Jan-Dec Dinner 1800
Family run. Convenient location on A94 tourist route, within easy reach of town centre.					
Mrs J Davidson Fernlea, 37 Needless Road PH2 0LE Tel. Perth (0738) 27766		1 Single 1 Family	1 Public Bath/Sh	B&B per person £8.00-£8.50 Single £8.00-£8.50 Double	Open Jan-Dec Dinner 1700
Mrs E M Ferguson Rosebank, 53 Dunkeld Road PH1 5RP Tel. Perth (0738) 21737		2 Dble/Twin 1 Family	1 Public Bath/Sh	B&B per person £8.00 Double	Open Mar-Nov

Key to symbols is on back flap. Details of Classification and Grading are on page vi.

175

PERTH continued	Map 2 C2						
Mrs J Glennie 54 Glasgow Road PH2 0PB Tel. Perth (0738) 26723			1 Single 1 Dble/Twin 1 Family	2 Public Bath/Sh	B&B per person £8.50 Single £8.00 Double	Open Apr-Oct Dinner 1700	
Mr & Mrs Haggart Abbotsford, 23 James Street PH2 8LX Tel. Perth (0738) 35219		COMMENDED Listed	1 Single 2 Dble/Twin 3 Family	6 Private Bath/Sh	B&B per person £9.00 Single £8.50 Double	Open Jan-Dec Dinner 1800	
			Victorian terraced house in residential area. Private shower and colour tv in all bedrooms.				
Mrs A Hughes 57 Wilson Street PH2 0EY Tel. Perth (0738) 23608			1 Single 1 Dble/Twin 1 Family	1 Public Bath/Sh	B&B per person £8.00 Single £8.00 Double	Open Jan-Dec	
Mrs E P Lanni Lochiel House, 13 Pitcullen Crescent PH2 7HT Tel. Perth (0738) 33183		HIGHLY COMMENDED 👑👑	3 Dble/Twin	2 Public Bath/Sh	B&B per person £10.00 Double	Open Mar-Dec	
			Semi detached victorian house. Near town centre and Scone Palace.				
Mrs MacDiarmid Bellamar, 6 Pitcullen Crescent PH2 7HT Tel. Perth (0738) 27179			1 Single 3 Dble/Twin 1 Family	2 Public Bath/Sh	B&B per person £9.00-£9.50 Single £8.50-£9.00 Double	Open Jan-Dec Dinner 1800	
Mrs Bridget McCole Saddlebank, 8 Murray Crescent PH2 0HU Tel. Perth (0738) 28600			3 Dble/Twin	1 Public Bath/Sh	B&B per person £7.00-£8.00 Double	Open Jan-Dec Dinner 2100	
Mrs K McMahon Richmond House, 50 Glasgow Road PH2 0PB Tel. Perth (0738) 27548			1 Single 1 Dble/Twin 1 Family	2 Public Bath/Sh	B&B per person £8.50-£9.50 Single £8.00-£9.00 Double	Open Jan-Dec	
Mrs Carol Mcgrath Old Manse, Pitcullen Crescent PH1 7HT Tel. Perth (0738) 29187			1 Dble/Twin 2 Family	1 Public Bath/Sh	B&B per person £8.00-£8.50 Double	Open Jan-Dec Dinner 1830	
Mrs F Myles Garth, 92 Dundee Road PH2 7BA Tel. Perth (0738) 22368			3 Dble/Twin	1 Public Bath/Sh	B&B per person £8.00-£9.00 Double	Open Jan-Dec	
Mrs Ellen O'Donnell Avon Villa, 28 Abbot Street PH2 0EE Tel. Perth (0738) 27484			2 Dble/Twin 1 Family	1 Public Bath/Sh	B&B per person £7.50 Double	Open Jan-Dec Dinner 1700	
Mrs Oates 86 Glasgow Road PH2 0PG Tel. Perth (0738) 26827			2 Single 2 Dble/Twin	2 Public Bath/Sh	B&B per person £7.50 Single £7.50 Double	Open Jan-Dec	
Mrs E J Ross Almond Villa, 81 Glasgow Road PH2 0PQ Tel. Perth (0738) 26756			2 Dble/Twin 1 Family	1 Private Bath/Sh 1 Public Bath/Sh	B&B per person £8.00-£9.00 Double	Open Jan-Dec	

VAT is shown at 15%: changes in this rate may affect prices. Prices shown are for guidance only. Please send SAE with each enquiry.

PERTH continued Mrs R Stewart Parkview, 22 Marshall Place Tel. Perth (0738) 20297	Map 2 C2		1 Single 3 Dble/Twin 2 Family	1 Public Bath/Sh	B&B per person £8.00-£10.00 Single £8.00-£10.00 Double	Open Jan-Dec	🖥 📟 🐕 P C
Mrs J Todd Craighall House, 98 Dundee Road PH2 7BA Tel. Perth (0738) 22627			1 Single 2 Dble/Twin	1 Public Bath/Sh	B&B per person £8.00-£8.50 Single £9.00-£9.50 Double	Open Feb-Nov	🏃 🖥 📟 TV 🍴 🐕 P C
Mrs J Wilson 21 Marshall Place PH2 8AG Tel. Perth (0738) 28482			2 Single 2 Dble/Twin 2 Family	2 Public Bath/Sh	B&B per person £9.00 Single £8.00 Double	Open Jan-Dec Dinner 1900	V 📟 TV 🍴 🐕 P C
Mrs Angela Young Inchview, 25 Marshall Place PH2 8AG Tel. Perth (0738) 29610			1 Single 4 Dble/Twin 2 Family	2 Public Bath/Sh	B&B per person £10.00 Single £8.00-£9.00 Double	Open Jan-Dec Dinner 1730	🖥 V 🐕 TV 🐕 £ P C
PETERHEAD Aberdeenshire Carrick Guest House 16 Merchant Street AB4 6DU Tel. Peterhead (0779) 70610	Map 4 H8	Awaiting Inspection	2 Single 3 Dble/Twin 2 Family	2 Public Bath/Sh	B&B per person £7.50-£8.00 Single £7.50-£8.00 Double	Open Jan-Dec Dinner 1700	🖥 V 📟 TV 🐕 P C
Mrs Cook Clach View, Deer Road East, Maud AB4 8NQ Tel. Maud (07714) 302			2 Dble/Twin	1 Public Bath/Sh	B&B per person £7.00 Double	Open Jan-Dec Dinner 1700	TV P C
Mrs Macguire 113 Queen Street Tel. Peterhead (0779) 77166			1 Single 2 Dble/Twin 1 Family	2 Public Bath/Sh	B&B per person £10.00 Single £8.00 Double	Open Jan-Dec Dinner 1800	V 📟 TV C
Mrs Milne Greenridge, 4 South Road Tel. Peterhead (0779) 73072			1 Single 5 Family	2 Public Bath/Sh	B&B per person £9.00 Single £7.50 Double	Open Jan-Dec	📟 TV P C
PITLOCHRY Perthshire Atholl Bank Guest House 20 East Moulin Road PH16 5HY Tel. Pitlochry (0796) 2753	Map 2 B1		1 Single 2 Dble/Twin 2 Family	1 Public Bath/Sh	B&B per person £8.00-£9.00 Single £8.00-£9.00 Double	Open Jan-Dec Dinner 1800	V 📟 TV 🐕 ❄ P C

Key to symbols is on back flap. Details of Classification and Grading are on page vi.

| PITLOCHRY continued | Map 2 B1 | |

Carra-Beag Guest House

16 TOBERARGAN ROAD, PITLOCHRY
Telephone: 0796 2835

Centrally situated with commanding views and ample parking. H&C, shaving points, electric blankets, colour TV and tea/coffee-making facilities in all bedrooms. Some bedrooms with private facilities. Lounge, Patio and Putting Green. Child reductions. Dinner, Bed and Breakfast. Table licence.

For colour brochure and tariff contact the proprietor, Archie McGhie.

| Carra Beag Guest House 16 Toberargan Road PH16 5HQ Tel. Pitlochry (0796) 2835 | COMMENDED 👑 👑 👑 | 2 Single 5 Dble/Twin 3 Family | 4 Private Bath/Sh 1 Public Bath/Sh | B&B per person £9.75-£11.00 Single £9.75-£11.00 Double | Open Jan-Dec Dinner 1800 | |
| | | Family run, late 19C villa. Large south facing garden; soft fruit in season, putting green, tables. | | | | |

| Craigmore Guest House 27 West Moulin Road PH16 5EF Tel. Pitlochry (0796) 2123 | COMMENDED 👑 👑 | 2 Single 10 Dble/Twin 3 Family | 8 Private Bath/Sh 1 Public Bath/Sh | B&B per person £10.00-£12.50 Single £10.00-£12.50 Double | Open Mar-Nov Dinner 1830 | |
| | | Peacefully situated in large garden above town. Magnificent views from the dining room. | | | | |

Craigroyston House

LOWER OAKFIELD, PITLOCHRY
Telephone: 0796 2053

A Victorian Country House centrally situated in own grounds with direct access from garden to the town centre.

The spacious and comfortable rooms all have wash-hand basins, colour television, central heating, tea/coffee facilities.
Ample shower/bathrooms. Residents' lounge, dining room with separate tables. Pets welcome. Family rooms available. Car park.

The house is open all day for resident guests. For an enjoyable long or short stay in a friendly atmosphere contact Mrs Gretta Maxwell.

Bed and Breakfast from £8.50 per person.

| Craigroyston Guest House 2 Lower Oakfield PH16 5HQ Tel. Pitlochry (0796) 2053 | COMMENDED 👑 👑 | 1 Single 4 Dble/Twin 2 Family | 2 Public Bath/Sh | B&B per person £8.50-£9.50 Single £8.50-£9.50 Double | Open Apr-Oct | |
| | | Family run, victorian villa. Southfacing to wooded hills. Large terraced garden. Near town centre. | | | | |

PITLOCHRY continued | Map 2 B1

Derrybeg Guest House
18 Lower Oakfield, Pitlochry. Tel. 0796 2070

DERRYBEG is set in a quiet location only a few minutes' walk from the town centre, enjoying magnificent views of the Vale of Atholl. The resident proprietors, Tom and Lorraine Wallace, ensure only the finest hospitality, comfort, and good home cooking.
- Open all year for bed and breakfast OR dinner, bed and breakfast. Unlicensed, but guests welcome to supply own table wine.
- Full central heating throughout.
- Colour television, tea/coffee facilities, shaver points, and H&C in all bedrooms.
- Three bedrooms with private facilities.
- Comfortable lounge and dining room.
- Food Hygiene Excellent Award.
- Ample parking in the grounds.
- Leisure activities can easily be arranged, i.e. theatre bookings, golf, fishing, pony-trekking, etc.

Colour brochure/tariff and details of weekly reductions available on request.

Name	Grading	Rooms	Bath	B&B	Open	
Derrybeg Guest House, 18 Lower Oakfield, PH16 5DS, Tel. Pitlochry (0796) 2070	COMMENDED	2 Single, 6 Dble/Twin, 1 Family	3 Private Bath/Sh, 2 Public Bath/Sh	B&B per person £8.50-£10.50 Single £8.50-£10.50 Double	Open Jan-Dec Dinner 1830	
		Privately owned, large south facing garden. Quiet, but central location, overlooking Tummel Valley.				
Duntrune Guest House, 22 East Moulin Road, PH16 5HY, Tel. Pitlochry (0796) 2172	COMMENDED	2 Single, 4 Dble/Twin, 1 Family	5 Private Bath/Sh, 1 Public Bath/Sh	B&B per person £9.50-£10.50 Single £10.50-£11.50 Double	Open Apr-Oct	
		Stone built house in quiet residential area overlooking town. Large garden, excellent views.				
Macdonald's Guest House, 140-144 Atholl Road, PH16 5AG, Tel. Pitlochry (0796) 2170		2 Dble/Twin, 2 Family	1 Public Bath/Sh	B&B per person £7.50-£8.50 Double	Open Apr-Oct Dinner 1800	
Mansewood Guest House, 11 Nursing Home Brae, PH16 5HP, Tel. Pitlochry (0796) 2366	Awaiting Inspection	1 Single, 6 Dble/Twin, 1 Family	2 Public Bath/Sh	B&B per person £9.00 Single £9.00 Double	Open Apr-Oct	
The Moorings Guest House, Lower Oakfield, Tel. Pitlochry (0796) 3014	HIGHLY COMMENDED	3 Dble/Twin	2 Private Bath/Sh, 1 Public Bath/Sh	B&B per person £11.00-£16.00 Double	Open Apr-Oct Dinner 1830	
		Spacious and tastefully refurbished house with sun balcony and garden. In quiet residential area. **(See advert on outside back flap)**				
Tir Aluinn Guest House, 10 Higher Oakfield, PH16 5HT, Tel. Pitlochry (0796) 2231		2 Dble/Twin, 2 Family	1 Public Bath/Sh	B&B per person £8.00-£8.50 Double	Open Apr-Oct	

Key to symbols is on back flap. Details of Classification and Grading are on page vi.

PITLOCHRY continued	Map 2 B1					
Atholl Baptist Centre Atholl Road PH16 5BX Tel. Pitlochry (0796) 3044			2 Single 9 Dble/Twin 2 Family		B&B per person £8.50 Single £8.50 Double	Open Jan-Dec Dinner 1830-
YMCA Bonskeid House PH16 5NP Tel. Pitlochry (0796) 3208			5 Single 25 Dble/Twin 15 Family	12 Public Bath/Sh	B&B per person £8.05 Single £8.05 Double	Open Feb-Nov Dinner 1830
Miss W M Alexander Milwaukee, Lettoch Road PH16 5AZ Tel. Pitlochry (0796) 2811			1 Single 2 Dble/Twin	1 Public Bath/Sh	B&B per person £7.00 Single £7.00 Double	Open Apr-Oct
Mrs Beattie Cresta, 15 Lettoch Terrace PH16 5BA Tel. Pitlochry (0796) 2204			1 Dble/Twin 1 Family	1 Public Bath/Sh	B&B per person £8.00 Double	Open May-Sep
Mrs C A Bell Silver Howe, Perth Road PH16 5LY Tel. Pitlochry (0796) 2181		COMMENDED ♛	4 Dble/Twin	1 Public Bath/Sh	B&B per person £8.00 Double	Open Apr-Oct
			Detached, modern bungalow on town outskirts. Large, southfacing garden; open outlook to Tummel Valley.			
Mrs Y Chadwick Whinrigg, Aldour, Perth Road, PH16 5LY Tel. Pitlochry (0796) 2330			3 Dble/Twin	2 Public Bath/Sh	B&B per person £8.50 Double	Open Apr-Oct
Mrs Cochrane Kishorn, 5 Lettoch Terrace PH16 5BA Tel. Pitlochry (0796) 2152			4 Dble/Twin	1 Public Bath/Sh	B&B per person £8.50-£9.00 Double	Open Apr-Oct
Mrs Easton Inzievar, Lettoch Terr PH16 5BA Tel. Pitlochry (0796) 2539			3 Dble/Twin	1 Public Bath/Sh	B&B per person £7.60 Double	Open Mar-Oct
Mrs Gordon Rosehill, 47 Atholl Road PH16 5BX Tel. Pitlochry (0796) 2958			2 Dble/Twin 3 Family	1 Public Bath/Sh	B&B per person £8.50 Double	Open Apr-Oct
Mrs Hawkes Grove Cottage, 10 Lower Oakfield PH16 5DS Tel. Pitlochry (0796) 2374			1 Dble/Twin 3 Family	1 Private Bath/Sh 1 Public Bath/Sh	B&B per person £8.00-£8.50 Double	Open Jan-Dec Dinner 1700
Mrs Howman Auchnahyle, Tomcroy Terrace PH16 5JA Tel. Pitlochry (0796) 2318		♛ ♛	3 Dble/Twin	1 Private Bath/Sh 1 Public Bath/Sh	B&B per person £9.25-£10.25 Double	Open Apr-Sep Dinner 1900-
Mrs M MacNicoll Morag Cottage, 163 Atholl Road Tel. Pitlochry (0796) 2973			1 Dble/Twin 1 Family	1 Public Bath/Sh	B&B per person £7.50-£8.00 Double	Open Jan-Dec
Mrs Maclellan Cruachan, 14 Lower Oakfield PH16 5DS Tel. Pitlochry (0796) 2030			2 Dble/Twin	1 Public Bath/Sh	B&B per person £8.50 Double	Open Jan-Dec

PITLOCHRY continued	Map 2 B1						
Mrs Marion McDonald Santramara, 26 Lettoch Terrace PH16 5BA Tel. Pitlochry (0796) 3226		Awaiting Inspection	1 Family	1 Public Bath/Sh	B&B per person £7.25-£7.50 Double	Open Jan-Dec	🖥 V 🖻 📺 ⚡ 🛏 🐾 P C
Mrs Miller Dunreen, 8 Lettoch Terrace PH16 5BA Tel. Pitlochry (0796) 2974			2 Dble/Twin	1 Public Bath/Sh	B&B per person £7.50 Double	Open Mar-Oct	🚜 🖿 🐕 P
Mrs N Panton Panmure, 52 Bonnethill Road PH16 5ED Tel. Pitlochry (0796) 2857			2 Dble/Twin	1 Public Bath/Sh	B&B per person £8.00 Double	Open May-Oct	🚜 🖿 P
Mrs Rainger The Laurels, Park Terrace PH16 5AY Tel. Pitlochry (0796) 3298			1 Single 2 Dble/Twin 1 Family	1 Public Bath/Sh	B&B per person £7.00-£7.50 Single £7.00-£7.50 Double	Open Apr-Oct	🔌 V 🖻 🖿 📺 ⚡ 🐕 🛏 C
Mrs Sands Annslea, 164 Atholl Road PH16 5AR Tel. Pitlochry (0796) 2430			5 Dble/Twin	1 Private Bath/Sh 2 Public Bath/Sh	B&B per person £10.00-£11.50 Double	Open Apr-Oct	🚜 🔌 🖿 📺 P C
Mrs Kathleen Scott Landscape, Larchwood Road PH16 5AS Tel. Pitlochry (0796) 2765			2 Dble/Twin 1 Family	1 Public Bath/Sh	B&B per person £8.00 Double	Open Jan-Dec	🚜 M 🖻 🖿 📺 ⚡ ❄ P ⚠ C

DUNDARAVE HOUSE

Situated in one of the most enviable areas of Pitlochry, in its own grounds of approx. ½ acre. Dundarave offers the tourist of the nineteen-eighties every comfort and amenity required.
- All rooms, colour TV and tea/coffee making facilities.
- All double/twin bedded rooms with private bathroom.
- Fully heated.
- Residents lounge—open all day.

For your overnight stay or longer please contact your hosts:
Mr and Mrs E. M. Shuttleworth,
for full particulars.

STRATHVIEW TERRACE, PITLOCHRY
👑 👑 👑 Tel. (0796) 3109 COMMENDED

Mr & Mrs E M Shuttleworth Dundarave House, Strathview Terrace PH16 5AT Tel. Pitlochry (0796) 3109		COMMENDED 👑 👑 👑	2 Single 4 Dble/Twin 1 Family	5 Private Bath/Sh 2 Public Bath/Sh	B&B per person £14.00 Single £14.00 Double	Open Apr-Oct	🚜 🖥 🔌 ▬ V 🖻 🖿 📺 ⚡ 🖻 🐕 ❄ P T 🎰
			19c well furnished house overlooks town, Tummel Valley & Sonab Hills. Fine Scottish breakfasts.				
Mr & Mrs G Simpson Croft-na-Coille, 25 Toberargan Road PH16 5HG Tel. Pitlochry (0796) 2034			1 Single 4 Dble/Twin	1 Private Bath/Sh 1 Public Bath/Sh	B&B per person £8.80 Single £8.80 Double	Open Mar-Oct	🚜 🔌 🖿 📺 ❄ ✂ P

Key to symbols is on back flap. Details of Classification and Grading are on page vi.

Name & Address	Map Ref	Grade	Rooms	Bath	B&B	Opening	Facilities
PITLOCHRY continued Mrs Y Stewart, Elnagar, 2 Knockard Road, Tel. Pitlochry (0796) 2871	Map 2 B1		2 Dble/Twin	1 Public Bath/Sh	B&B per person £8.00 Double	Open Apr-Oct	
Mrs Swales, Ashbank, 14 Tomcroy Terrace, PH16 5JA, Tel. Pitlochry (0796) 2711			1 Single, 2 Dble/Twin, 1 Family	1 Public Bath/Sh	B&B per person £8.50 Single £8.50 Double	Open Jan-Dec Dinner 1800	
Mrs Vickers, Lonaig, Lettoch Terrace, Tel. Pitlochry (0796) 2422			2 Dble/Twin	1 Public Bath/Sh	B&B per person £7.00-£7.50 Double	Open May-Oct Dinner 1830	
PITTENWEEM Fife, Neil & Tricia Anderson, Welch House, 27 Viewforth Place, KY10 2PZ, Tel. Anstruther (0333) 311225	Map 2 E3		1 Single, 2 Dble/Twin, 1 Family	2 Public Bath/Sh	B&B per person £8.00-£10.00 Single £8.00-£10.00 Double	Open Jan-Dec Dinner 1730	
Mr & Mrs Andrew Hay, St John's, 29 Viewforth Place, Tel. Anstruther (0333) 311405			1 Family	1 Public Bath/Sh	B&B per person £8.00 Double	Open Apr-Sep	
PLOCKTON Ross-shire, Mrs J McKenzie, 32 Harbour Street, IV52 8TN, Tel. Plockton (059984) 306	Map 3 F9		1 Single, 1 Dble/Twin, 1 Family	1 Public Bath/Sh	B&B per person £7.50-£8.50 Single £7.50-£8.50 Double	Open Jan-Nov	
Mrs B Townend, Achnahenich Farm, IV52 8TY, Tel. Plockton (059984) 238		Listed	2 Dble/Twin, 1 Family	1 Public Bath/Sh	B&B per person £7.00-£8.00 Double	Open Apr-Oct Dinner 1800	
POLMONT Stirlingshire, Mrs L Browning, 61 Lawers Crescent, Tel. Falkirk (0324) 712065	Map 2 B4		2 Dble/Twin	1 Public Bath/Sh	B&B per person £7.00-£8.00 Double	Open Jan-Dec Dinner 1900	
POOLEWE Ross-shire, Mrs K Macdonald, Benlair, Near Cove, IV22 2LS, Tel. Poolewe (044586) 354	Map 3 F7	COMMENDED Listed	1 Dble/Twin, 1 Family	1 Public Bath/Sh	B&B per person £8.50 Double	Open Apr-Oct Dinner 1800	
Family run, in tranquil setting with superb views. Near Cove village and very close to sandy beach.							
Mrs P Scullin, Tigh-na-Moine, Tel. Poolewe (044586) 242		Awaiting Inspection	3 Dble/Twin		B&B per person £7.50 Double	Open Apr-Oct Dinner 1800	
PORT ASKAIG Isle of Islay, Argyll, Mrs Macmillan, Meadowbank, Keills	Map 1 C5		3 Dble/Twin	1 Public Bath/Sh	B&B per person £6.00-£7.50 Double	Open Jan-Dec Dinner 1730	

VAT is shown at 15%; changes in this rate may affect prices. Prices shown are for guidance only. Please send SAE with each enquiry.

| PORT ELLEN
Isle of Islay, Argyll

Mrs J Hastie
The Grange
Tel. Port Ellen (0496) 2035 | Map 1
C6 | | 1 Single
1 Dble/Twin
1 Family | 2 Public Bath/Sh | B&B per person
£8.00 Single
£8.00 Double | Open Apr-Oct
Dinner 1830 | 🛏️ ▥ 📺 🛥️ 🐕
❄️ C ♞ |

The Trout Fly Restaurant

8 Charlotte Street, Port Ellen, Isle of Islay
Telephone: 0496 2204

On the lovely island of Islay, in the garden of the Trout Fly Restaurant, is the stone-built, pine-lined chalet comprising twin beds, colour TV, toilet and wash-hand basin. With plenty of storage space for bicycles, it is an ideal touring centre. Also accommodation in main house (2 doubles with shower and wash-hand basin + 1 single).

Large menu which includes produce of the islands.

Mrs Hedley The Trout Fly Restaurant, 8 Charlotte St Tel. Port Ellen (0496) 2204	COMMENDED Listed	1 Single 3 Dble/Twin	1 Private Bath/Sh 1 Public Bath/Sh	B&B per person £7.50-£8.50 Single £8.50-£10.50 Double	Open Jan-Dec Dinner 1800	🛏️ V 🛏️ 🛏️ ▥ 📺 🛥️ 🍴 £ P △
		Situated in main street with enclosed garden to rear. Near ferry terminal, 3 miles/5km from golf.				
Pat & John Kent Tighcargaman Tel. Port Ellen (0496) 2345		2 Dble/Twin 1 Family	2 Public Bath/Sh	B&B per person £9.50-£10.50 Double	Open Jan-Dec Dinner 1900	🛏️ ▥ 🐕 ❄️ P △ C
PORT OF MENTEITH Perthshire Mrs Norma Erskine Inchie Farm FK8 3JZ Tel. Port-of-Menteith (08775) 233	Map 1 H3	2 Dble/Twin	1 Public Bath/Sh	B&B per person £8.00-£10.00 Single £8.00-£10.00 Double	Open May-Sep Dinner 1800	🛏️ 🍴 🐕 ❄️ P C 🏇
Mrs More Castle Rednock Farm FK8 3LD Tel. Port-of-Menteith (08775) 276		2 Dble/Twin 1 Family	1 Public Bath/Sh	B&B per person £8.00 Double	Open May-Sep	🛏️ 📺 🍴 ❄️ P C 🏇
PORTNACON, by Durness Sutherland Port-na-Con Guest House Loch Eriboll IV27 4UN Tel. Durness (097181) 367	Map 3 H3 👑 👑	2 Dble/Twin 2 Family	2 Public Bath/Sh	B&B per person £7.50 Double	Open Feb-Nov Dinner 1900	♣ V 🛏️ 🍷 🛏️ ▥ 🍴 🍴 🍽️ 🐕 ❄️ 🎿 P △ C 🎏
PORTNALONG Isle of Skye, Inverness-shire Mrs Nicolson Donann, 7 Fernilea Tel. Portnalong (047872) 275	Map 3 D9	2 Dble/Twin 1 Family	1 Public Bath/Sh	B&B per person £7.50 Double	Open Mar-Oct	🛏️ 🛏️ ▥ 📺 C
PORTPATRICK Wigtownshire Broomknowe Guest House School Brae Tel. Portpatrick (077681) 365	Map 1 F11 COMMENDED 👑 👑	2 Dble/Twin 1 Family	1 Public Bath/Sh	B&B per person £8.50-£9.00 Double	Open Jan-Dec Dinner 1830·	♣ ▭ 🛏️ 🍷 V 🛏️ ▥ 📺 🍴 🐕 ❄️ P 🎿 C
		Modern bungalow in quiet residential area overlooking village and sea beyond				

Key to symbols is on back flap. Details of Classification and Grading are on page vi.

183

	Map	Rating	Rooms	Bathrooms	B&B	Opening	Facilities
PORTPATRICK continued	Map 1 F11						
Mr & Mrs W Murray Campbell Monadail, 9 Dunskey Street Tel. Portpatrick (077681) 442			2 Dble/Twin 1 Family	1 Public Bath/Sh	B&B per person £8.50-£9.00 Double	Open Jan-Dec Dinner 1830	
Mrs D Pearce Bendochy, Heugh Road Tel. Portpatrick (077681) 318			3 Dble/Twin	1 Public Bath/Sh	B&B per person £8.50 Double	Open Apr-Oct Dinner 1800-	
Mrs Y Shuttleworth Glenview Tel. Portpatrick (077681) 349			2 Dble/Twin	1 Public Bath/Sh	B&B per person £8.35-£8.75 Double	Open Apr-Oct	
PORTREE Isle of Skye, Inverness-shire	Map 3 D9						
Almondbank Guest House Viewfield Road IV51 9EU Tel. Portree (0478) 2696			2 Dble/Twin 2 Family	2 Public Bath/Sh	B&B per person £9.50 Double	Open Apr-Oct Dinner 1800	
Dunalasdair Guest House Sluggans Tel. Portree (0478) 2893			4 Dble/Twin 1 Family	2 Public Bath/Sh	B&B per person £9.00-£10.00 Double	Open Jan-Dec Dinner 1830	
Greenacres Guest House Viewfield Road Tel. Portree (0478) 2605			6 Dble/Twin 4 Family	2 Public Bath/Sh	B&B per person £9.00-£9.50 Double	Open Mar-Oct	
Woodside Guest House Homefarm Road Tel. Portree (0478) 2598		COMMENDED ♛ ♛	5 Dble/Twin 2 Family	1 Public Bath/Sh	B&B per person £9.75-£11.25 Double	Open Jan-Dec Dinner 1900	
Modern, purpose built. Residential area close to village centre, bus station and local swimming pool.							
Mrs C Anderson 18 Viewfield Square Tel. Portree (0478) 2503			1 Single 1 Family	1 Public Bath/Sh	B&B per person £6.50-£7.00 Single £6.50-£7.00 Double	Open Jan-Dec	
Mrs Mary Gillies Ross Villa, 18 Kitson Crescent Tel. Portree (0478) 2709			2 Dble/Twin	1 Public Bath/Sh	B&B per person £6.50-£7.00 Double	Open Apr-Sep	
Mrs M J Gilmour Myrtle Bank, Achachork Tel. Portree (0478) 2597		♛	2 Dble/Twin 1 Family	1 Public Bath/Sh	B&B per person £8.00 Double	Open Apr-Oct	
Mrs C Graham Cairnmor, Viewfield Road Tel. Portree (0478) 2637			3 Dble/Twin	1 Public Bath/Sh	B&B per person £8.50-£9.50 Double	Open Jan-Dec	
Mrs C MacDougall Tor na Gillean, Viewfield Road Tel. Portree (0478) 2206			1 Single 3 Dble/Twin	2 Public Bath/Sh	B&B per person £9.00 Single £8.50 Double	Open Apr-Oct Dinner 1830	
Mrs MacFarlane Quiraing, Viewfield Road Tel. Portree (0478) 2870			4 Dble/Twin 2 Family	2 Private Bath/Sh 1 Public Bath/Sh	B&B per person £9.00-£11.00 Double	Open Jan-Dec	

VAT is shown at 15%: changes in this rate may affect prices. Prices shown are for guidance only. Please send SAE with each enquiry.

	Map		Rooms	Bathrooms	Terms	Opening	Facilities
PORTREE continued	Map 3 D9						
Mrs J Macdonald 10 Acachork, Staffin Road Tel. Portree (0478) 2213			1 Single 2 Dble/Twin 1 Family	2 Public Bath/Sh	B&B per person £8.00-£9.00 Single £8.00-£9.00 Double	Open Mar-Nov	
Mrs Morag Macdonald The Firs, Coolin Hills Estate Tel. Portree (0478) 2121			2 Dble/Twin	1 Public Bath/Sh	B&B per person £6.50 Double	Open Jan-Dec	
Mrs Macleod 6 Fisherfield, Viewfield Road Tel. Portree (0478) 2250			3 Dble/Twin 1 Family	1 Public Bath/Sh	B&B per person £8.50-£9.00 Double	Open Mar-Sep Dinner 1800	
Mrs M Matheson 8 Fraser Crescent Tel. Portree (0478) 2346			2 Dble/Twin	1 Public Bath/Sh	B&B per person £7.00 Double	Open Jan-Dec	
Mrs McPhie Balloch, Viewfield Road Tel. Portree (0478) 2093			3 Dble/Twin	1 Public Bath/Sh	B&B per person £8.00 Double	Open Mar-Oct	
Mrs E Morrison Wavecrest, Beaumont Crescent Tel. Portree (0478) 2066			2 Dble/Twin 2 Family	1 Public Bath/Sh	B&B per person £7.50-£8.50 Double	Open Apr-Oct	
Mrs C Murray Conusg, Coolin Hills Gardens Tel. Portree (0478) 2426			2 Single 2 Dble/Twin	1 Public Bath/Sh	B&B per person £8.50-£9.00 Single £8.50-£9.00 Double	Open Feb-Oct Dinner 1830	
Mrs P M Thorpe Jacamar, 5 Achachork Road Tel. Portree (0478) 2274			1 Dble/Twin 1 Family	1 Public Bath/Sh	B&B per person £7.00-£8.00 Double	Open Mar-Oct Dinner 1830	
PRESTONPANS East Lothian	Map 2 D5						
Mrs G Cunningham 23 Middleshot Square EH32 9RH Tel. Prestonpans (0875) 810617			2 Dble/Twin	1 Public Bath/Sh	B&B per person £8.00-£10.00 Double	Open Jan-Dec Dinner 1800	
PRESTWICK Ayrshire	Map 1 G7						
Mrs R Auld 66 Adamton Road KA9 2HD Tel. Prestwick (0292) 70399			1 Single 1 Dble/Twin 1 Family	2 Public Bath/Sh	B&B per person £7.50-£8.00 Single £7.50-£8.00 Double	Open Jan-Dec	
Mrs Bickerton 2 Duart Avenue KA9 1NA Tel. Prestwick (0292) 75287			3 Dble/Twin	1 Public Bath/Sh	B&B per person £8.00 Double	Open May-Sep	
Mrs Colgan Orianda, 13 Park Av, Central Esplanade KA9 1RG Tel. Prestwick (0292) 79523			1 Dble/Twin 1 Family	1 Public Bath/Sh	B&B per person £8.00 Double	Open May-Oct	
Mrs Crawford Lenniemore, 26 Burgh Road KA9 1QU Tel. Prestwick (0292) 76657			2 Dble/Twin	1 Public Bath/Sh	B&B per person £9.00-£9.50 Double	Open Apr-Oct	

Key to symbols is on back flap. Details of Classification and Grading are on page vi.

185

PRESTWICK continued	Map 1 G7						
Mrs Dawson Innishail, 1 Queens Terrace KA9 1AH Tel. Prestwick (0292) 78186	COMMENDED ♔♔	1 Single 1 Dble/Twin 1 Family	1 Public Bath/Sh	B&B per person £8.50 Single £8.50 Double	Open May-Sep Dinner 1800	
		Friendly, end terraced house within walking distance of beach, railway and town centre.				
Mr & Mrs J Galloway Hillview, 107 Ayr Road KA9 1TN Tel. Prestwick (0292) 70538		2 Dble/Twin 1 Family	1 Public Bath/Sh	B&B per person £9.00 Double	Open Jan-Dec Dinner 1900	
Mrs S Gracie Arran View, 9 St Ninians Road KA9 1SL Tel. Prestwick (0292) 77221		1 Single 2 Dble/Twin 2 Family	1 Public Bath/Sh	B&B per person £7.50-£8.50 Single £7.50-£8.00 Double	Open Jan-Dec	
Mrs Yvonne McInnes 25 Central Esplanade KA9 1RD Tel. Prestwick (0292) 78097		1 Single 2 Family	1 Public Bath/Sh	B&B per person £7.50-£8.00 Single £8.00-£8.50 Double	Open Apr-Oct	
Mrs Anne Murphy Westmount, 79 Ayr Road KA9 1TF Tel. Prestwick (0292) 74888	♔♔	1 Dble/Twin 1 Family	1 Public Bath/Sh	B&B per person £8.00-£9.00 Double	Open Jan-Dec	
Mrs Myles 6 The Crescent, Monkton Road KA9 1AP Tel. Prestwick (0292) 77366		1 Single 1 Dble/Twin 1 Family	1 Public Bath/Sh	B&B per person £8.50 Single £8.50 Double	Open Jan-Dec	
Mrs Prentice 12 Bridge Street KA9 1QY Tel. Prestwick (0292) 78521		3 Dble/Twin	2 Public Bath/Sh	B&B per person £9.00-£9.50 Double	Open Jan-Dec Dinner 1800	
Mrs D A Taylor Oakley, 17 Ayr Road KA9 1SX Tel. Prestwick (0292) 78556		2 Dble/Twin 1 Family	1 Public Bath/Sh	B&B per person £7.50-£8.00 Double	Open Mar-Oct	
Mrs M Young Balgownie, 115 Ayr Rd KA9 1TN Tel. Prestwick (0292) 77055		2 Dble/Twin 1 Family	2 Public Bath/Sh	B&B per person £8.00-£9.00 Double	Open Jan-Dec	
REDCASTLE, by Muir of Ord Ross-shire	Map 4 A8					
Mrs R T Macdonald Rosemount, Milton of Redcastle IV6 7SQ Tel. Muir of Ord (0463) 870213		2 Family	1 Public Bath/Sh	B&B per person £7.00 Double	Open May-Sep	
RHICONICH Sutherland	Map 3 G4					
Miss E Campbell Benview, Archrisgill West IV27 4RJ Tel. Kinlochbervie (097182) 242		1 Dble/Twin 1 Family	1 Private Bath/Sh 1 Public Bath/Sh	B&B per person £8.00 Double	Open Apr-Sep	

VAT is shown at 15%: changes in this rate may affect prices. Prices shown are for guidance only. Please send SAE with each enquiry.

RINGFORD Kirkcudbrightshire Mrs M Robertson Meiklewood Tel. Ringford (055722) 226	Map 2 A10	**COMMENDED** Listed	1 Single 2 Dble/Twin	2 Public Bath/Sh	B&B per person £7.50-£8.00 Single £7.00-£7.50 Double	Open Apr-Oct	🔌 ❄ 🅿 △ 🐾
			Working farm in rural setting. 4 miles (6km) from Castle Douglas, and on Euro Route to Stranraer.				
ROBERTON Lanarkshire Mrs C Craig Townfoot Tel. Lamington (08995) 655	Map 2 B7		2 Dble/Twin	1 Public Bath/Sh	B&B per person £7.50 Double	Open Jan-Dec	🛏 ▥ 📺 ➤ ❄ 🅿 C 🐾
ROCKCLIFFE, by Dalbeattie Kirkcudbrightshire	Map 2 B11						

"MALLAIG"
Barclay Road, Rockcliff, Dalbeattie
Telephone: Rockcliffe (340) 055 663
"MALLAIG" offers comfortable accommodation in private bungalow in quiet seaside village.
H&C in bedrooms. Ideal for touring, walking, golfing and fishing.
B & B from £7.50. Evening Meal (optional) £3.50.

Mrs Herries Mallaig, Barcloy Road DG5 4QJ Tel. Rockcliffe (055663) 340			2 Dble/Twin	1 Public Bath/Sh	B&B per person £7.50 Double	Open Apr-Oct Dinner 1800	🛏 ▥ 📺 ✂ ❄ 🅿
ROGART Sutherland Mrs A Nicolson Dalbhioran, 177 Muie IV28 3UB Tel. Rogart (04084) 345	Map 4 B6		1 Single 1 Dble/Twin 1 Family	1 Public Bath/Sh	B&B per person £7.00 Single £7.00 Double	Open May-Oct Dinner 1800	🛏 ▥ ⁄⁄ ➤ 🔌 🐕 🅿 C 🐾
ROSEMARKIE Ross-shire Mrs J Straw Springwells Cottage, Eathie Road Tel. Fortrose (0381) 20767	Map 4 B8		2 Family	1 Public Bath/Sh	B&B per person £6.50 Double	Open Jan-Dec Dinner 1800	▣ 🛏 V 🛏 ▥ ▥ 🐕 ❄ 🅿 C
ROTHESAY Isle of Bute Sunnyside Guest House 12 Argyle Place Tel. Rothesay (0700) 2351	Map 1 F5		1 Single 3 Dble/Twin 2 Family	1 Public Bath/Sh	B&B per person £7.50-£8.00 Single £7.50-£8.00 Double	Open Apr-Oct	🛏 M 🛏 ☕ V ▥ 📺 🐕 C T
Mrs Christine Hamilton Jones The Chimes, 20 Argyle Place PA20 0BA Tel. Rothesay (0700) 4216			2 Dble/Twin	1 Public Bath/Sh	B&B per person £7.50-£8.00 Double	Open Jan-Nov	🛏 V ▥ ▥ 📺 ➤ 🔌 C

Location	Map		Rooms	Bath	Price	Open	
ROTHIENORMAN, by Fyvie Aberdeenshire	Map 4 F9						
Mrs G Wilson Knowley Farm, Wartle AB5 9BR Tel. Rothienorman (065181) 275			2 Dble/Twin 1 Family	1 Public Bath/Sh	B&B per person £7.50-£8.50 Double	Open May-Oct	
ROUSAY Orkney	Map 5 B10						
Alastair & Elizabeth Findlay Fjalquoy Tel. Rousay (085682) 381			1 Single 1 Dble/Twin	1 Public Bath/Sh	B&B per person £8.50 Single £8.50 Double	Open Jan-Dec Dinner 1830-	
Mrs A Kovachich The Old Manse, Sourin Tel. Rousay (085682) 375			1 Single 2 Dble/Twin	1 Public Bath/Sh	B&B per person £7.00 Single £7.00 Double	Open Jan-Dec Dinner 1800	
ROY BRIDGE Inverness-shire	Map 3 H12	Listed					
Mrs Grieve Station House PH31 4AG Tel. Spean Bridge (039781) 285			2 Dble/Twin	1 Public Bath/Sh	B&B per person £7.50 Double	Open Apr-Oct Dinner 1830	
Mrs J Macfarlane Orosay, Inverroy Tel. Spean Bridge (039781) 318			1 Single 2 Dble/Twin	1 Public Bath/Sh	B&B per person £7.50 Single £7.50 Double	Open Apr-Oct Dinner 1830-	
SALEN Isle of Mull, Argyll	Map 1 D2						
Mrs I T Adam Cuilgown Tel. Aros (06803) 386			3 Dble/Twin	1 Public Bath/Sh	B&B per person £8.50 Double	Open Feb-Nov Dinner 1830-	
SALINE Fife	Map 2 B4						
Mrs J Cousar Lynn Farm Tel. New Oakley (0383) 852261			2 Dble/Twin		B&B per person £8.00-£9.00 Double	Open May-Oct	
SANDAY Orkney	Map 5 C10						
Belsair Guest House KW17 2BJ Tel. Sanday (08575) 206			3 Dble/Twin		B&B per person £7.00 Double	Open Jan-Dec Dinner 1700-	
SANDHEAD Wigtownshire	Map 1 F11						
Mrs M Rowan Mid Float Farm Tel. Sandhead (077683) 248			1 Single 1 Dble/Twin 2 Family	1 Public Bath/Sh	B&B per person £6.00 Single £6.00 Double	Open Apr-Oct Dinner 1700	
Mrs P G Wainwright Cairnlea, Main Street Tel. Sandhead (077683) 249			1 Single 2 Dble/Twin 1 Family	1 Public Bath/Sh	B&B per person £7.50 Single £7.50 Double	Open Jan-Dec Dinner 1800	

SANDILANDS, by Lanark Mrs J Lamb Hillhouse Farm Tel. Douglas Water (055588) 661	Map 2 B6		2 Dble/Twin	1 Public Bath/Sh	B&B per person £7.50 Double	Open Jan-Dec Dinner 1830-	▦ ▦ ▦ ▦ ▦ ▦ ▦ ▦ ▦ ▦ ▦
SANDWICK, by **Stromness** **Orkney** Keldroseed Guest House KW16 3HY Tel. Sandwick (Orkney) (085684) 628	Map 5 A11		3 Dble/Twin	1 Public Bath/Sh	B&B per person £12.00 Double	Open Jan-Dec Dinner 2000	▦ ▦ ▦ ▦ ▦ ▦ ▦ ▦ ▦ ▦ ▦ ▦ ▦ ▦
Mrs M Grieve Dencraigon Tel. Sandwick (Orkney) (085684) 647			2 Dble/Twin	1 Public Bath/Sh	B&B per person £7.00 Double	Open Apr-Oct	▦ ▦ ▦ ▦ ▦ ▦
Mrs Kirkpatrick Millburn Tel. Sandwick (085684) 656			3 Dble/Twin	2 Public Bath/Sh	B&B per person £6.50 Double	Open Apr-Oct Dinner 1800	▦ ▦ ▦ ▦ ▦ ▦ ▦ ▦ ▦ ▦
SANDYHILLS, by **Dalbeattie** **Kirkcudbrightshire** Mrs Smith Craigbittern Tel. Southwick (038778) 247	Map 2 B11	**COMMENDED** Listed	2 Dble/Twin 1 Family Granite built victorian house with large garden. Superb views over Solway Firth.	2 Public Bath/Sh	B&B per person £8.50-£9.50 Double	Open Jan-Dec Dinner 1900	▦ ▦ ▦ ▦ ▦ ▦ ▦ ▦ ▦
SANQUHAR **Dumfriesshire** Drumbringan Guest House 53 Castle Street Tel. Sanquhar (06592) 409	Map 2 A8	**COMMENDED** Listed	1 Single 2 Dble/Twin 2 Family Homely, georgian house on edge of ancient village. Picnic lunches available. H/C in bedrooms.	1 Public Bath/Sh	B&B per person £8.50 Single £8.50 Double	Open Jan-Dec Dinner 1800	▦ ▦ ▦ ▦ ▦ ▦ ▦ ▦ ▦ ▦ ▦ ▦ ▦ ▦ ▦
SCADABAY **Harris, Western Isles** Mrs I MacLeod Hillhead Tel. Drinishader (085981) 226	Map 3 C6		1 Single 1 Dble/Twin 2 Family	1 Public Bath/Sh	B&B per person £7.00-£7.50 Single £6.50-£7.00 Double	Open Apr-Oct Dinner 1900-2000	▦ ▦ ▦ ▦ ▦ ▦ ▦ ▦ ▦ ▦ ▦ ▦
SCALPAY, Isle of **Harris, Western Isles**	Map 3 C6						

Mr & Mrs R J Ford-Sagers Eilean Glas Lighthouse PA84 3YH Tel. Harris (0859) 84345			3 Dble/Twin	3 Private Bath/Sh	B&B per person £7.50 Double	Open Apr-Sep Dinner 1900-2200	▦ ▦ ▦ ▦ ▦ ▦ ▦ ▦ ▦ ▦ ▦ ▦ ▦ ▦ ▦ ▦ ▦ ▦

Key to symbols is on back flap. Details of Classification and Grading are on page vi.

189

	Map	Rating	Rooms	Bath	Price	Opening	Facilities
SCOTLANDWELL Kinross-shire Mrs Hodder The Grange Tel. Scotlandwell (059284) 220	Map 2 C3		3 Dble/Twin 1 Family	2 Private Bath/Sh	B&B per person £9.00-£13.00 Double	Open Jan-Dec Dinner 1800	
SCOURIE Sutherland Mrs H J Macdonald Minch View, Scouriemore IV27 4TG Tel. Scourie (0971) 2110	Map 3 G4		1 Single 4 Dble/Twin	2 Public Bath/Sh	B&B per person £10.00 Single £10.00 Double	Open Apr-Oct Dinner 1900	
Mrs M B Munro Tarbet IV27 4SS Tel. Scourie (0971) 2126			3 Dble/Twin	1 Public Bath/Sh	B&B per person £10.00 Double	Open Apr-Oct Dinner 1930	
SEAMILL Ayrshire Anne R R Wilkinson The Fort, 56 Ardrossan Road Tel. West Kilbride (0294) 822755	Map 1 G6		1 Dble/Twin	1 Public Bath/Sh	B&B per person £8.50 Double	Open Apr-Oct Dinner 1830	
SELKIRK Mrs S Hermiston 4 Castle Terrace Tel. Selkirk (0750) 20484	Map 2 E7	COMMENDED Listed	2 Dble/Twin	1 Public Bath/Sh	B&B per person £7.00-£7.50 Double	Open Apr-Sep	
Modern house in housing estate. Views of countryside to front. Convenient for town and touring.							
Mrs Lindores Dinsburn, 1 Shawpark Road Tel. Selkirk (0750) 20375			2 Dble/Twin 1 Family	1 Public Bath/Sh	B&B per person £8.50 Double	Open Jan-Dec Dinner 1800	
Mrs J F Mackenzie Ivybank, Hillside Terrace Tel. Selkirk (0750) 21270		COMMENDED Listed	2 Dble/Twin 1 Family	1 Public Bath/Sh	B&B per person £9.00 Double	Open Jan-Dec Dinner 1800	
Stone built house on town outskirts. Garden with seats to front, car park to rear. Home cooking.							
Mrs J C Mitchell Le Noyer, Ettrick Terrace Tel. Selkirk (0750) 20523		COMMENDED Listed	2 Dble/Twin	1 Public Bath/Sh	B&B per person £8.25 Single £8.25 Double	Open Apr-Sep Dinner 1800	
Modern house with excellent views of surrounding hills. Within walking distance of town centre.							
Mrs S M Todd 34 Hillside Terrace Tel. Selkirk (0750) 20792		COMMENDED Listed	3 Dble/Twin	2 Public Bath/Sh	B&B per person £8.50-£9.50 Double	Open Mar-Oct Dinner 1800	
Detached, victorian house set back from main Selkirk to Carlisle Road. Town centre about 500 yards.							
SHISKINE Isle of Arran Jan MacAlister Shedock Farm Tel. Shiskine (077086) 261	Map 1 E7		1 Single 1 Dble/Twin 2 Family	1 Public Bath/Sh	B&B per person £8.00 Single £8.00 Double	Open Apr-Oct Dinner 1800	

	Map		Rooms	Bath	B&B	Open	Symbols
SKEABOST, by Portree Isle of Skye, Inverness-shire Mrs Janice MacDonald Grianan, 8 Glenbernisdale Tel. Skeabost Bridge (047032) 387	Map 3 D9		1 Single 2 Dble/Twin	1 Public Bath/Sh	B&B per person £6.50-£7.00 Single £6.50-£7.00 Double	Open Jun-Sep Dinner 1800-	
SKELLISTER, South Nesting Shetland Mrs M A Blance Garth Tel. Skellister (059589) 206	Map 5 G4		3 Dble/Twin	1 Public Bath/Sh	B&B per person £7.50 Double	Open Jan-Dec Dinner 1900	
SKINIDIN, Dunvegan Isle of Skye, Inverness-shire Sarah Shurmer 13 Skinidin Tel. Dunvegan (047022) 380	Map 3 C9	Awaiting Inspection	2 Dble/Twin	2 Private Bath/Sh	B&B per person £8.00 Double	Open Jan-Dec	
SOUTH LOCHBOISDALE S Uist, Western Isles Mrs Flora MacInnes Sealladh Mara, 479 South Lochboisdale Tel. Lochboisdale (08784) 580	Map 3 A10		2 Dble/Twin	2 Public Bath/Sh	B&B per person £7.00 Double	Open May-Sep	
SOUTH QUEENSFERRY West Lothian Mrs W G Boggon The Banks Farm House, Hopetoun EH30 9SL Tel. 031 331 3878	Map 2 C5		3 Dble/Twin	1 Public Bath/Sh	B&B per person £8.50-£9.50 Double	Open Jan-Dec	
Ms N Smith St Mary's House, Kirkliston Rd EH3 9NY Tel. 031 331 2550			1 Single 2 Dble/Twin 1 Family	1 Public Bath/Sh	B&B per person £10.00 Single £10.00 Double	Open Jan-Dec	
SOUTH RONALDSAY Orkney Mrs Cogle Glendoran, South Parish Tel. St Margaret's Hope (085683) 410	Map 5 B12		1 Family	1 Public Bath/Sh	B&B per person £6.00 Single	Open Apr-Oct Dinner 1930	
SOUTHEND, by Campbeltown Argyll Mrs M Ronald Ormsary Farm Tel. Southend (058683) 665	Map 1 D8		1 Dble/Twin 1 Family	1 Public Bath/Sh	B&B per person £6.00-£7.00 Double	Open Jan-Dec Dinner 1800	
Mrs E Semple Low Cattadale Tel. Southend (058683) 205		**APPROVED** Listed	3 Dble/Twin	1 Public Bath/Sh	B&B per person £7.50 Double	Open Apr-Oct Dinner 1800	

Distinctive black and white farmhouse with pretty, colourful garden. Situated on Southend road.

| SPEAN BRIDGE
Inverness-shire | Map 3
H12 | | |

Coire Glas Guest House
SPEAN BRIDGE · INVERNESS-SHIRE
Telephone: 039 781 272

Family run established guest house situated on the outskirts of
Spean Bridge looking onto the hills of Ben Nevis range.
All rooms with H&C, heating, tea/coffee facilities and rooms with
toilet and shower. Good central area for touring Highlands. Near
bus and train.
3 and 7-day Bargain Breaks available.

| Coire Glas Guest House
PH34 4EU
Tel. Spean Bridge (039781)
272 | | 1 Single
12 Dble/Twin
1 Family | 5 Private Bath/Sh | B&B per person
£9.50 Single
£7.50 Double | Open Apr-Oct | |

Druimandarroch Guest House
SPEAN BRIDGE, INVERNESS-SHIRE PH34 4EU
Telephone: 039781 335

We would be pleased to welcome everyone including pets either
overnight or for our special priced 3/17/14- day packages.
Druimandarroch is ideally suited as a touring base. Our aim is for you to
have an enjoyable holiday. Senior citizen off-season holidays available.
Early booking discounts are available. Please take advantage of them.
Licensed. *"We look forward to welcoming you".*

| Druimandarroch Guest
House
PH34 4EU
Tel. Spean Bridge (039781)
335 | | 1 Single
3 Dble/Twin
3 Family | 2 Public Bath/Sh | B&B per person
£8.00 Single
£8.00 Double | Open Mar-Nov
Dinner 1900- | |

Inverour Guest House
SPEAN BRIDGE, INVERNESS-SHIRE. Tel: 039 781 218

Situated in the centre of the village, we offer a comfortable
homely atmosphere together with modern facilities. All
bedrooms have H&C, shaver points, heating and TV, some with
private facilities. Separate tables, guest lounge with log fire.
Private car park.
*Ideal centre for touring, fishing, climbing; everything available for
a relaxing holiday.* **S.A.E. for brochure, please.**

| Inverour Guest House
Tel. Spean Bridge (039781)
218 | APPROVED | 2 Single
4 Dble/Twin
1 Family | 2 Private Bath/Sh
2 Public Bath/Sh | B&B per person
£9.00 Single
£8.50 Double | Open Mar-Oct
Dinner 1900- | |

Comfortable, cosy atmosphere. Ideal centre for west coast touring.

VAT is shown at 15%: changes in this rate may affect prices. Prices shown are for guidance only. Please send SAE with each enquiry.

SPEAN BRIDGE continued	Map 3 H12

INVERGLOY HOUSE
SPEAN BRIDGE · INVERNESS-SHIRE · PH34 4DY
Tel. 0397-84-281. From early 1987: 039-781-681
100-year old coach house offering two twin-bedded rooms with wash-basins, one single, two bathrooms. Overlooking Loch Lochy in 50 acres of rhododendron woodland, 5 miles north of Spean Bridge on A82 to Inverness, signposted on left along wooded drive. Fishing from private beach, rowing boats, hard tennis court.
SAE for brochure.
Children over 8 years. B&B from £9.00. Evening meal on request £5.00

Mrs M Cairns Invergloy House, Invergloy Tel. Invergloy (039784) 281			1 Single 2 Dble/Twin	2 Public Bath/Sh	B&B per person £9.00-£10.00 Single £9.00-£10.00 Double	Open Jan-Dec Dinner 1915	
Mrs Duberley Curlevin, Altour Road Tel. Spean Bridge (039781) 385			2 Dble/Twin	1 Public Bath/Sh	B&B per person £6.00-£7.50 Double	Open Jan-Dec Dinner 1800	
Mrs P Fraser Allt-na-Sithean, South Laggan PH34 4EA Tel. Invergarry (08093) 311			2 Dble/Twin 1 Family	1 Public Bath/Sh	B&B per person £7.50 Double	Open May-Sep Dinner 1900	
SPITTALFIELD, by Murthly Perthshire Mrs M Campbell Easter Drumatherty Farmhouse PH1 4LE Tel. Caputh (073871) 243	Map 2 C2		1 Dble/Twin 2 Family	1 Public Bath/Sh	B&B per person £8.00 Double	Open Jan-Dec Dinner 1800-	
Mrs A W Smith Stralochy Farm PH1 4LQ Tel. Caputh (073871) 447			2 Dble/Twin	1 Public Bath/Sh	B&B per person £6.50-£7.50 Double	Open Apr-Oct Dinner 1830-	
ST ABBS Berwickshire Mrs S E Campbell Ebba Strand Tel. Coldingham (08907) 71329	Map 2 G5		1 Single 2 Dble/Twin 1 Family	2 Private Bath/Sh 1 Public Bath/Sh	B&B per person £7.00-£8.00 Single £8.00-£9.50 Double	Open Jan-Dec Dinner 1830	
ST ANDREWS Fife Albany Guest House 56 North Street Tel. St Andrews (0334) 77737	Map 2 E3	APPROVED 👑👑👑	2 Single 5 Dble/Twin 2 Family	3 Private Bath/Sh 3 Public Bath/Sh	B&B per person £9.00-£13.00 Single £9.00-£12.00 Double	Open Jan-Dec Dinner 1800-	
			Centrally situated opposite university. Close to castle, harbour, East Sands, shops and golf course.				
Ashleigh Guest House 37 St Marys Street Tel. St Andrews (0334) 75429			1 Single 5 Dble/Twin 2 Family	3 Public Bath/Sh	B&B per person £8.50-£13.00 Single £8.50-£10.00 Double	Open Jan-Dec	

ST ANDREWS continued	Map 2 E3		Rooms	Bath	Price	Open	Facilities
Aslar Guest House 120 North Street KY16 9AF Tel. St Andrews (0334) 73460	♛		1 Single 3 Dble/Twin 2 Family	2 Public Bath/Sh	B&B per person £10.00-£12.00 Single £10.00-£12.00 Double	Open May-Dec	
Cadzow Guest House 58 North Street KY16 9AH Tel. St Andrews (0334) 76933	APPROVED ♛ ♛		5 Dble/Twin 2 Family	1 Private Bath/Sh 2 Public Bath/Sh	B&B per person £8.50-£10.50 Double	Open Feb-Nov Dinner 1800	
	Privately owned victorian terraced house. Close to castle, cathedral, seafront and shops.						
Craigmore Guest House 3 Murray Park KY16 9AW Tel. St Andrews (0334) 72142			2 Dble/Twin 4 Family	1 Private Bath/Sh 2 Public Bath/Sh	B&B per person £7.50-£11.00 Double	Open Jan-Dec	
Number Ten Guest House 10 Hope Street KY16 9HJ Tel. St Andrews (0334) 74601	COMMENDED ♛ ♛		3 Single 4 Dble/Twin 3 Family	2 Private Bath/Sh 3 Public Bath/Sh	B&B per person £9.50-£12.50 Single £9.00-£11.00 Double	Open Jan-Nov Dinner 1800	
	Sandstone terrace with a neo-classical georgian facade. Close to town centre and the Old Course.						
Shandon Guest House 10 Murray Place KY16 9AP Tel. St Andrews (0334) 72412			2 Single 2 Dble/Twin 1 Family	1 Private Bath/Sh 2 Public Bath/Sh	B&B per person £9.00-£10.00 Single £8.50-£10.00 Double	Open Jan-Dec	
Shorecrest Guest House 23 Murray Park KY16 9AW Tel. St Andrews (0334) 75310			2 Single 6 Dble/Twin 4 Family	6 Private Bath/Sh 1 Public Bath/Sh	B&B per person £8.25-£16.00 Single £8.25-£16.00 Double	Open Jan-Dec Dinner 1800	
West Park Guest House 5 St Marys Place, Market Street Tel. St Andrews (0334) 75933	COMMENDED ♛ ♛ ♛		4 Dble/Twin 1 Family	4 Private Bath/Sh 2 Public Bath/Sh	B&B per person £10.50-£15.50 Double	Open Jan-Nov Dinner 1830	
	Beautiful georgian house retaining character in historic town. Gourmet restaurant dinners. Coffee shop.						
Univ of St Andrews David Russell Hall, Buchanan Gardens KY16 9AJ Tel. St Andrews (0334) 76161 Telex 76213			464 Single	60 Public Bath/Sh	B&B per person £11.50 Single £11.50 Double	Open Mar-Apr Jun-Sep Dinner 1800	
Mrs Clark Pipeland Farm Tel. St Andrews (0334) 72814			2 Dble/Twin	1 Public Bath/Sh	B&B per person £7.50-£8.00 Double	Open Apr-Oct	
Mrs A Duncan East Balrymonth Farm KY16 8PN Tel. St Andrews (0334) 73475			3 Dble/Twin	2 Public Bath/Sh	B&B per person £8.00-£9.00 Double	Open Jan-Dec Dinner 1830	
Mrs E Durie Eldream, 18 Lindsay Gardens Tel. St Andrews (0334) 76620	COMMENDED Listed		2 Dble/Twin	1 Public Bath/Sh	B&B per person £8.00-£9.00 Double	Open Apr-Oct	
	Modern, detached house in quiet residential area, close to town centre.						

VAT is shown at 15%: changes in this rate may affect prices. Prices shown are for guidance only. Please send SAE with each enquiry.

	Map 2 E3						
ST ANDREWS continued							
Mrs N Finnigan 72 Market Street KY16 9MU Tel. St Andrews (0334) 75156			4 Dble/Twin	1 Public Bath/Sh	B&B per person £10.00 Double	Open Mar-Oct	
Mr & Mrs M Frodsham Park Mill, Boarhills KY16 8PS Tel. Boarhills (033488) 254			1 Single 1 Dble/Twin 1 Family	1 Public Bath/Sh	B&B per person £10.00 Single £7.50-£8.00 Double	Open Jan-Dec Dinner 1830	
Mrs J Guest 31 Irvine Crescent KY16 8LG Tel. St Andrews (0334) 76401			1 Dble/Twin 1 Family	1 Public Bath/Sh	B&B per person £8.00-£9.00 Double	Open Apr-Oct	
Mrs J Jeffrey Tigh-na-Sithean, 25 Nelson Street Tel. St Andrews (0334) 75547		Awaiting Inspection	1 Single 2 Dble/Twin	1 Public Bath/Sh	B&B per person £8.50-£10.00 Single £7.50-£8.50 Double	Open Jan-Dec	
Mrs J P Joy 38 Chamberlain Street Tel. St Andrews (0334) 73749			1 Dble/Twin	1 Public Bath/Sh	B&B per person £7.50-£8.50 Double	Open Jan-Dec	
Mrs E Lawlor Aedel House, 12 Murray Place KY16 9AP Tel. St Andrews (0334) 72315			3 Dble/Twin	1 Public Bath/Sh	B&B per person £7.00-£9.50 Double	Open Jan-Dec	
Mrs J McIver 8 West Acres Tel. St Andrews (0334) 73281			1 Dble/Twin	1 Private Bath/Sh	B&B per person £11.00 Double	Open Apr-Oct	
Mrs Methven Ardmore, 1 Drumcarrow Road Tel. St Andrews (0334) 74574			2 Dble/Twin	1 Public Bath/Sh	B&B per person £8.00 Double	Open Jan-Dec	
Mr & Mrs A Pressegh St Nicholas Farmhouse Tel. St Andrews (0334) 73090			1 Dble/Twin 1 Family	1 Public Bath/Sh	B&B per person £8.50 Double	Open Jan-Dec Dinner 1800	
Mrs V Rhind Hazlehead, 16 Lindsay Gardens KY16 8XB Tel. St Andrews (0334) 75677		COMMENDED Listed	1 Dble/Twin 1 Family	1 Public Bath/Sh	B&B per person £8.25-£9.25 Double	Open Jan-Dec Dinner 1800	
			Modern detached villa in quiet residential area 1 mile (2km) from centre. Easy parking, home cooking.				
Mrs C Theobald Hilton House, 9 Melbourne Place KY16 9EY Tel. St Andrews (0334) 72332		Awaiting Inspection	3 Dble/Twin	1 Public Bath/Sh	B&B per person £8.50-£9.00 Double	Open Apr-Oct Dinner 1830	
Mrs H Watson Drumrack Farm Tel. Anstruther (0333) 310520			2 Single 1 Dble/Twin	1 Public Bath/Sh	B&B per person £8.00 Single £8.00 Double	Open Apr-Oct Dinner 2000	

	Map ref	Inspection	Rooms	Bath	Prices	Opening	Facilities
ST BOSWELLS Roxburghshire Mrs S Beighton Struan, Weirgate Way, Jenny Moore's Rd Tel. St Boswells (0835) 22711	Map 2 E7	Awaiting Inspection	2 Family	1 Private Bath/Sh 1 Public Bath/Sh	B&B per person £7.50 Double	Open Jan-Dec Dinner 1900	
Mrs N E Johnston Moorfield Tel. St Boswells (0835) 22310			2 Family	1 Public Bath/Sh	B&B per person £8.15 Double	Open Apr-Oct	
Mrs P Reilly Ashfield, Buccleuch Gardens Tel. St Boswells (0835) 22731		APPROVED	2 Dble/Twin 1 Family	1 Public Bath/Sh	B&B per person £7.50-£8.50 Double	Open Jan-Dec Dinner 1800	
			19c house on edge of village in conservation area. Ideal for touring Border towns.				
ST FILLANS Perthshire Mrs I S Ferguson Neish House Tel. St Fillans (076485) 238	Map 2 A2		4 Dble/Twin	1 Public Bath/Sh	B&B per person £9.50 Double	Open Apr-Oct	
Mrs Noakes Glengoynan Tel. St Fillans (076485) 316			1 Single 2 Dble/Twin	2 Public Bath/Sh	B&B per person £8.50 Single £8.00 Double	Open Apr-Oct	
STAFFIN Isle of Skye, Inverness-shire Mrs Jolly Alleanda, Glasphein Tel. Staffin (047062) 285	Map 3 D8		1 Dble/Twin 1 Family	1 Public Bath/Sh	B&B per person £7.50 Double	Open Mar-Oct Dinner 1900	
Mrs P MacDonald Keepers Cottage Tel. Staffin (047062) 217			2 Dble/Twin	1 Public Bath/Sh	B&B per person £7.50 Double	Open Apr-Oct	
Mrs Nicolson Graceland, 5 Clasphein Tel. Staffin (047062) 313			1 Single 2 Dble/Twin	2 Public Bath/Sh	B&B per person £7.50 Single £7.50 Double	Open Mar-Oct Dinner 1900	
STENNESS Orkney Mrs Kemp Upper Hobbister Tel. Finstown (085676) 296	Map 5 B11		3 Dble/Twin 1 Family	1 Public Bath/Sh	B&B per person £7.00 Double	Open Jan-Dec Dinner 1830	
Mrs Scott Upper Nist House Tel. Finstown (085676) 378			2 Dble/Twin 1 Family	1 Public Bath/Sh	B&B per person £6.00 Double	Open Apr-Oct	
STEWARTON Ayrshire Mrs Wallace Haysmuir Farm Tel. Torranyar (029485) 208	Map 1 H8		3 Dble/Twin	1 Public Bath/Sh	B&B per person £10.00 Double	Open May-Sep	
STIRLING Firgrove Guest House 13 Clifford Road FK8 2AQ Tel. Stirling (0786) 75805	Map 2 A4	Awaiting Inspection	2 Dble/Twin 3 Family	1 Private Bath/Sh 2 Public Bath/Sh	B&B per person £9.50-£10.00 Double	Open Apr-Oct	

VAT is shown at 15%: changes in this rate may affect prices. Prices shown are for guidance only. Please send SAE with each enquiry.

STIRLING continued	Map 2 A4						
Mia-Roo Guest House 37 Snowdon Place FK8 2JP Tel. Stirling (0786) 73979			2 Single 4 Dble/Twin 2 Family	1 Public Bath/Sh	B&B per person £11.00-£10.00 Single	Open Jan-Dec	🅼 ♨ Ⓥ ♩ 📺 ♨ 🐕 ❄ 🅿 Ⓒ ♿

University of Stirling

STIRLING FK9 4LA. Tel: (0786) 73171

The University's easily accessible, beautifully developed Campus, located by the centre point of Scotland, with good road and rail access from England and to the Highlands, Edinburgh and Glasgow, encourages the individual tourist and family to stay, to see and to enjoy a holiday.

Amenities include a small golf course, trout fishing, a shopping precinct and theatre/cinema. Self-cater, individual bed and breakfast and group stay bookings are all welcome in high summer.

University of Stirling FK9 4LA Tel. Stirling (0786) 73171 Ext.2039/2033 Telex 777759 STUNIV G Att. J.Riddy			1030 Single 50 Dble/Twin	105 Public Bath/Sh	B&B per person £12.50 Single £12.50 Double	Open Jun-Sep Dinner 1730-'	🏕 ♨ ☕ Ⓥ ♨ ♥ ♩ 🖥 ● 📺 ✗ 🍴 ❄ ✗ 🅿 🐕 ♨ ♿
Mrs J Allan 15 Albert Place FK8 2RE Tel. Stirling (0786) 75175			1 Dble/Twin 1 Family	1 Public Bath/Sh	B&B per person £10.00 Double	Open Apr-Oct	🏕 🍷 🖥 ♨ 🅿 Ⓒ
Mrs Ashbridge 27 Princes Street FK8 1HQ Tel. Stirling (0786) 75344			1 Single 3 Dble/Twin	1 Public Bath/Sh	B&B per person £8.50-£9.00 Single £8.50-£9.00 Double	Open Jan-Dec	Ⓥ ♩ 📺 🐕 Ⓒ
Mrs R S Bell Park View, 5 Balmoral Place FK8 2RD Tel. Stirling (0786) 61222	COMMENDED ♨ ♨		1 Single 2 Dble/Twin 1 Family	1 Private Bath/Sh 1 Public Bath/Sh	B&B per person £10.00 Single £10.00-£11.50 Double	Open Jan-Dec	♨ ♩ 🖥 📺 ♨ ❄ 🅿 Ⓒ ♿
			In peaceful situation near foot of Stirling Castle, Kings Park, golf course and town centre.				
Mrs E P Boon Alma House, Northend, Cambusbarron Tel. Stirling (0786) 61169			3 Dble/Twin	1 Public Bath/Sh	B&B per person £8.50-£9.00 Double	Open Jan-Nov Dinner 1800	🏕 ♩ 🖥 📺 ♨ 🐕 ❄ 🅿 Ⓒ
Mr & Mrs Chaffin 17 Princes Street FK8 1HQ Tel. Stirling (0786) 73064			1 Dble/Twin	1 Private Bath/Sh	B&B per person £9.50 Double	Open Jan-Dec Dinner 1800-900	♨ Ⓥ ♩ 🖥 📺 ✗ ♨ 🐕 🅿 Ⓒ ♿
Mrs J Colville 12 Argyll Avenue FK8 1UL Tel. Stirling (0786) 62632			1 Dble/Twin	1 Public Bath/Sh	B&B per person £8.00-£8.50 Double	Open Jan-Dec	🏕 ♩ 🖥 📺 ✗ ♨

STIRLING continued	Map 2 A4						
Mrs H S Dougall 14 Melville Terrace FK8 2NE Tel. Stirling (0786) 72847			1 Single 2 Dble/Twin	1 Public Bath/Sh	B&B per person £9.00-£10.00 Single £9.00-£10.00 Double	Open Apr-Oct	
Mrs S M Douglas Eiderslie, 3 Randolph Terr Tel. Stirling (0786) 62280			1 Single 2 Dble/Twin	1 Public Bath/Sh	B&B per person £8.00-£8.50 Single £8.00-£8.50 Double	Open Jan-Dec Dinner 1800	
Mrs R Johnson Shalom, 15 1/2 Manse Cresent FK7 9AJ Tel. Stirling (0786) 71092			1 Single 1 Dble/Twin	1 Public Bath/Sh	B&B per person £8.50 Single £8.50-£9.00 Double	Open Jan-Dec	
Mrs R Johnston Kings Park Farm FK8 3AA Tel. Stirling (0786) 74142			1 Dble/Twin 2 Family	1 Public Bath/Sh	B&B per person £9.50 Double	Open Apr-Oct	
Mrs L Laing Albany, 48 Park Place FK7 9JR Tel. Stirling (0786) 75145		Awaiting Inspection	2 Single 1 Dble/Twin 1 Family	1 Public Bath/Sh	B&B per person £8.00 Single £8.00 Double	Open Jan-Dec Dinner 1830	
Mrs I MacNair 26 Clarendon Place Tel. Stirling (0786) 72731			1 Dble/Twin 1 Family	1 Public Bath/Sh	B&B per person £7.50-£8.50 Double	Open Jan-Dec	
Mrs Marion MacPhee Sunnedene, 10 Causewayhead Road FK9 5EN Tel. Stirling (0786) 62310		COMMENDED ♛	3 Dble/Twin	1 Public Bath/Sh	B&B per person £9.00 Double	Open Apr-Oct	
			Traditional semi, conveniently situated for university on main A9. Double glazed front bedrooms.				
Mrs M McGloin 11 Argyll Avenue Tel. Stirling (0786) 74091			2 Dble/Twin	1 Public Bath/Sh	B&B per person £7.00-£8.00 Double	Open Apr-Oct Dinner 1800	
Mrs A McKenna 26 Queen Street Tel. Stirling (0786) 71043			1 Single 1 Dble/Twin 1 Family	2 Public Bath/Sh	B&B per person £8.00-£9.00 Single £8.00-£8.50 Double	Open Jan-Dec Dinner 1700	
Moira E McPhail 8 Pitt Terrace FK8 2EZ Tel. Stirling (0786) 72675			2 Dble/Twin 2 Family	2 Public Bath/Sh	B&B per person £8.00-£10.00 Double	Open Jan-Dec	
Mrs Mcintosh 28 Airthrey Road, Causewayhead FK9 5JS Tel. Stirling (0786) 61747			2 Family	2 Public Bath/Sh	B&B per person £8.00-£8.50 Double	Open Feb-Dec	
Mrs E Meehan 16 Victoria Place FK8 2QJ Tel. Stirling (0786) 62613		Awaiting Inspection	1 Dble/Twin 1 Family		B&B per person £8.50 Double	Open Apr-Oct	
Mrs J Preston Medway, 108 Causewayhead Road FK9 5HJ Tel. Stirling (0786) 72289			1 Dble/Twin 2 Family	2 Public Bath/Sh	B&B per person £8.50-£9.50 Double	Open Apr-Sep	

VAT is shown at 15%: changes in this rate may affect prices. Prices shown are for guidance only. Please send SAE with each enquiry.

	Map	Grade	Rooms	Bathrooms	Prices	Opening	Facilities
STIRLING continued Mrs M Rennie 67 Cedar Avenue FK8 2PJ Tel. Stirling (0786) 61007	Map 2 A4	APPROVED Listed	1 Dble/Twin	1 Private Bath/Sh	B&B per person £8.50 Double	Open Jun-Aug Dinner 1830	
In quiet cul de sac in residential area of town.							
W S Salmond Castlecroft, Ballengeich Road Tel. Stirling (0786) 74933		COMMENDED 👑👑👑	2 Dble/Twin 1 Family	3 Private Bath/Sh 1 Public Bath/Sh	B&B per person £12.50 Double	Open Jan-Dec Dinner 1900	
Situated close to Stirling Castle with comfortable, modern facilities and panoramic views.							
Mrs F Waddell 13 Victoria Place FK8 2QU Tel. Stirling (0786) 74193			1 Dble/Twin 1 Family	1 Public Bath/Sh	B&B per person £9.00 Double	Open Jan-Dec Dinner 1800	
Mrs Isobel Whitton 40 Spittal Street FK8 1DU Tel. Stirling (0786) 63231		Awaiting Inspection	1 Dble/Twin	1 Private Bath/Sh	B&B per person £7.50-£8.00 Double	Open Apr-Sep Dinner 1830	
STONEHAVEN Kincardineshire Mrs R Brown Culag, 7 Castle Street AB3 2LA Tel. Stonehaven (0569) 62508	Map 4 G11		3 Dble/Twin	1 Public Bath/Sh	B&B per person £7.50-£8.00 Double	Open Apr-Oct	
Mrs M Christie New Milldens, Netherley Road AB3 2PY Tel. Stonehaven (0569) 62084			1 Dble/Twin	1 Public Bath/Sh	B&B per person £8.50-£9.50 Double	Open Apr-Oct	
Mrs V Craib Car-Lyn-Vale, Rickarton AB3 2TD Tel. Stonehaven (0569) 62406		HIGHLY COMMENDED 👑👑	2 Dble/Twin 1 Family	2 Public Bath/Sh	B&B per person £10.00 Double	Open May-Sep	
Attractive house on 8 acre croft. Quiet situation, 5 miles (8km) from Stonehaven.							
Mrs J Murray 17 Carron Terrace AB3 2HX Tel. Stonehaven (0569) 64824			1 Single 1 Dble/Twin	1 Private Bath/Sh	B&B per person £6.00 Single £6.00 Double	Open Jan-Dec Dinner 1800	
Mrs C Pritchard 4 Urie Crescent AB3 2DY Tel. Stonehaven (0569) 62220			1 Single 2 Dble/Twin	1 Public Bath/Sh	B&B per person £7.00-£7.50 Single £7.00 Double	Open Jan-Dec	
Mrs J H Threipland Prospect House, 18 Carron Terrace AB3 2HX Tel. Stonehaven (0569) 62638		COMMENDED Listed	1 Single 2 Dble/Twin	2 Public Bath/Sh	B&B per person £9.00 Single £8.50 Double	Open Jan-Dec	
Detached victorian house with large garden. Antique furnishings. Quiet area close to town centre.							
STORNOWAY Lewis, Western Isles Hebridean Guest House Bayhead PA87 2DZ Tel. Stornoway (0851) 2268	Map 3 D4	Awaiting Inspection	4 Single 7 Dble/Twin	3 Public Bath/Sh	B&B per person £9.50-£10.50 Single £9.00-£10.00 Double	Open Jan-Dec Dinner 1830-2030	

Name / Address	Map		Rooms	Bath	Prices	Open / Dinner	Facilities
STORNOWAY continued	Map 3 D4						
Mrs Anne Chisholm 5 Sand Street PA87 2UE Tel. Stornoway (0851) 4658			3 Dble/Twin	1 Public Bath/Sh	B&B per person £7.50 Double	Open Jan-Dec Dinner 1800	[symbols]
Mrs Crichton 24 Perceval Road Tel. Stornoway (0851) 3584			3 Dble/Twin	2 Public Bath/Sh	B&B per person £7.50-£8.00 Double	Open Jan-Dec Dinner 1730	[symbols]
Mrs C Kilner 2 Plantation Road Tel. Stornoway (0851) 4272			2 Single 1 Dble/Twin	2 Public Bath/Sh	B&B per person £7.50-£8.00 Single £7.50-£8.00 Double	Open Jan-Dec Dinner 1830	[symbols]
Mrs A C Macleod Ravenswood, 12 Matheson Road Tel. Stornoway (0851) 2673			1 Single 1 Dble/Twin 1 Family	1 Public Bath/Sh	B&B per person £7.50-£8.00 Single £7.50-£8.00 Double	Open Jan-Dec	[symbols]
Mrs J Skinner Ardlonan, 29 Francis Street Tel. Stornoway (0851) 3482		**COMMENDED** 👑👑	4 Dble/Twin 1 Family	1 Public Bath/Sh	B&B per person £8.50 Single £8.50 Double	Open Jan-Dec	[symbols]
			Family, bed and breakfast house in quiet part of town. Near shops and ferry terminal.				
Mrs Smith 40 Goathill Road Tel. Stornoway (0851) 3681			1 Single 1 Dble/Twin	2 Public Bath/Sh	B&B per person £7.50-£8.00 Single £7.50-£8.00 Double	Open Jan-Dec	[symbols]
STRACHAN Kincardineshire	Map 4 F11						
Mrs D Fowlie Cairnview AB3 3NN Tel. Feughside (033045) 249			1 Dble/Twin	1 Public Bath/Sh	B&B per person £8.00 Double	Open Apr-Oct Dinner 1800	[symbols]
STRANRAER Wigtownshire	Map 1 F10						
Dunhaven Guest House 21 Agnew Crescent Tel. Stranraer (0776) 3118			2 Single 2 Dble/Twin 4 Family		B&B per person £9.00-£11.00 Single £9.00-£12.00 Double	Open Jan-Dec Dinner 1730	[symbols]
Harbour Guest House Market Street DG9 7RF Tel. Stranraer (0776) 4626		**COMMENDED** 👑👑	2 Single 1 Dble/Twin 2 Family	2 Public Bath/Sh	B&B per person £9.00-£10.00 Single £9.00-£10.00 Double	Open Jan-Dec Dinner 1700	[symbols]
			Ideally situated on harbour front. Convenient for ferry terminal and close to town centre.				
Lake View Guest House 19 Agnew Crescent Tel. Stranraer (0776) 3472			1 Single 3 Dble/Twin 1 Family	1 Public Bath/Sh	B&B per person £8.50-£9.50 Single £8.50-£9.00 Double	Open Jan-Dec Dinner 1700	[symbols]
Mrs C Howard 6 Birnam Place, Station Street Tel. Stranraer (0776) 2941			3 Dble/Twin 1 Family	2 Public Bath/Sh	B&B per person £8.00 Single £8.00 Double	Open Jan-Dec	[symbols]
Mrs F Hull Hartforth, 33 London Road Tel. Stranraer (0776) 4832			1 Single 2 Dble/Twin 1 Family	1 Public Bath/Sh	B&B per person £8.00-£9.00 Single £8.00-£9.00 Double	Open Jan-Dec	[symbols]

	Map	Grading	Rooms	Bathrooms	Prices	Opening	Facilities
STRANRAER continued Mrs Dawn Forbes-Mann 2 Birnam Place, Station Street Tel. Stranraer (0776) 5616	Map 1 F10		1 Single 2 Dble/Twin 2 Family	1 Public Bath/Sh	B&B per person £7.00 Single £7.00 Double	Open Jan-Dec Dinner 1700	(symbols)
Mrs M McCracken 6 Carleton Terrace Tel. Stranraer (0776) 3933			1 Single 3 Dble/Twin 1 Family	1 Public Bath/Sh	B&B per person £8.00-£8.50 Single £7.50-£8.00 Double	Open Jan-Dec	(symbols)
Mrs P Parker Low Balyett Farm, Cairnryan Road Tel. Stranraer (0776) 3395		COMMENDED Listed	1 Single 1 Dble/Twin 1 Family	1 Public Bath/Sh	B&B per person £8.00 Single £8.00 Double	Open Apr-Dec Dinner 1800	(symbols)
			Working farmhouse on edge of town, about 4 miles/ 6km from Cairnryan.				
Mrs M Spiers Fernlea, Lewis Street Tel. Stranraer (0776) 3037			2 Dble/Twin 1 Family	1 Public Bath/Sh	B&B per person £8.00-£8.50 Double	Open Jan-Dec	(symbols)
STRATHAVEN **Lanarkshire** Mrs Anne Marshall Windhill, Sandford ML10 6PN Tel. Strathaven (0357) 20821	Map 2 A6		3 Dble/Twin	1 Private Bath/Sh 2 Public Bath/Sh	B&B per person £8.00-£10.00 Double	Open Jan-Dec	(symbols)
Mrs A Stewart Avonside, 61 Townhead Street Tel. Strathaven (0357) 20725			1 Dble/Twin 1 Family		B&B per person £8.00 Double	Open Jan-Dec	(symbols)
Mrs Whitelaw Righead Farm, Udston Head Tel. Strathaven (0357) 20359			1 Dble/Twin 1 Family	1 Public Bath/Sh	B&B per person £8.50 Double	Open May-Oct	(symbols)
STRATHDON **Aberdeenshire** Mr & Mrs G M Hardie House of Newe Tel. Strathdon (09752) 247	Map 4 E10		1 Family	2 Public Bath/Sh	B&B per person £6.50-£8.50 Double	Open Jan-Dec Dinner 1900	(symbols)
Mrs E Ogg Buchaam Farm AB3 8TN Tel. Strathdon (09752) 238		Listed	1 Dble/Twin 1 Family	1 Public Bath/Sh	B&B per person £8.00 Double	Open May-Oct	(symbols)
STRATHMIGLO **Fife** J & J Brown Glentarkie Tel. Strathmiglo (03376) 212	Map 2 C3	Awaiting Inspection	1 Single 2 Family	1 Public Bath/Sh	B&B per person £12.00 Single £12.00 Double	Open Apr-Oct Dinner 1800-	(symbols)
STRATHPEFFER **Ross-shire** Mrs G P Cameron White Lodge Tel. Strathpeffer (0997) 21730	Map 4 A8		1 Single 1 Dble/Twin 1 Family	2 Public Bath/Sh	B&B per person £8.00-£9.00 Single £8.00-£9.00 Double	Open Apr-Oct	(symbols)

Key to symbols is on back flap. Details of Classification and Grading are on page vi.

201

	Map		Rooms	Bath	Prices	Open	
STRATHPEFFER continued	Map 4 A8						
Mrs M MacKenzie Francisville IV14 9AX Tel. Strathpeffer (0997) 21345			2 Family	1 Public Bath/Sh	B&B per person £8.00 Double	Open Apr-Oct	(symbols)
Mrs MacLean Linnmhor Tel. Strathpeffer (0997) 21528			2 Single 1 Dble/Twin 1 Family	1 Public Bath/Sh	B&B per person £9.00-£10.00 Single £8.00-£9.00 Double	Open May-Sep	(symbols)
Mrs D Mackintosh Red House Tel. Strathpeffer (0997) 21282			3 Dble/Twin	1 Public Bath/Sh	B&B per person £7.50 Double	Open Apr-Oct	(symbols)
Mrs I Murray Smithy Cottage, Blairninich Tel. Strathpeffer (0997) 21525			1 Dble/Twin 1 Family	1 Public Bath/Sh	B&B per person £7.50-£8.00 Double	Open Apr-Oct Dinner 1830	(symbols)
Mrs M Scott Craigvar, The Square Tel. Strathpeffer (0997) 21622		Awaiting Inspection	2 Single 1 Dble/Twin 1 Family	2 Private Bath/Sh 1 Public Bath/Sh	B&B per person £8.00-£9.00 Single £9.50-£11.50 Double	Open Apr-Oct	(symbols)
Mrs J Shaw Newton Villa IV14 9DH Tel. Strathpeffer (0997) 21248			3 Dble/Twin	1 Public Bath/Sh	B&B per person £9.00 Double	Open Jan-Dec Dinner 1830	(symbols)
Mrs M Tait Beechwood, Fodderty Tel. Strathpeffer (0997) 21387			2 Dble/Twin 1 Family	1 Public Bath/Sh	B&B per person £7.50-£8.00 Double	Open May-Oct Dinner 1830	(symbols)
STRATHYRE Perthshire Miss E Haydock & Mrs M Mylne Stroneslaney Farmhouse FK18 8NF Tel. Strathyre (08774) 676	Map 1 H3	COMMENDED ♕	2 Dble/Twin	1 Public Bath/Sh	B&B per person £8.00 Double	Open Jan-Dec Dinner 1830	(symbols)
18th century restored farmhouse in peaceful riverside setting. Trout fishing available.							
Mr & Mrs Reid Coire Buidhe FK18 8NA Tel. Strathyre (08774) 288			1 Single 4 Dble/Twin 3 Family	2 Public Bath/Sh	B&B per person £7.50 Single £7.50 Double	Open Jan-Dec Dinner 1900	(symbols)
STRAVITHIE, by St Andrews Fife Mr & Mrs J Chalmers Stravithie Country Estate Tel. Boarhills (033488) 251	Map 2 E3		8 Single 0 Dble/Twin	16 Private Bath/Sh	B&B per person £11.50-£16.50 Single £10.50-£16.50 Double	Open Apr-Oct	(symbols)
(See advert on p. 203)							
STRICHEN Aberdeenshire Mrs G Bremner 64 High Street Tel. Strichen (07715) 475	Map 4 H8		2 Dble/Twin 2 Family	1 Private Bath/Sh 1 Public Bath/Sh	B&B per person £7.50 Double	Open Jan-Dec Dinner 1700	(symbols)

VAT is shown at 15%; changes in this rate may affect prices. Prices shown are for guidance only. Please send SAE with each enquiry.

Establishment	Map Ref	Grade	Accommodation	Bath/Shower	Terms	Open / Meals
STRICHEN continued Mrs Mutch, Findon House, 36 High Street. Tel. Strichen (07715) 469	Map 4 H8		1 Single 1 Dble/Twin 1 Family	1 Public Bath/Sh	B&B per person £7.00-£7.20 Single £7.00-£7.20 Double	Open May-Oct Dinner 1700
STROMNESS Orkney Mrs A Brown, 10 North End. Tel. Stromness (0856) 850186	Map 5 A11		4 Dble/Twin		B&B per person £7.00 Double	Open Jan-Dec
Mrs D J Firth, Feawell Farm, KW16 3JU. Tel. Stromness (0856) 850443			1 Single 2 Dble/Twin 1 Family		B&B per person £7.50 Single £7.50 Double	Open Jan-Dec
Mrs C Hourston, 15 John Street. Tel. Stromness (0856) 850642			1 Single 2 Dble/Twin		B&B per person £7.50 Single £7.50 Double	Open Apr-Oct Dinner 1800
Mrs S Thomas, Stenigal. Tel. Stromness (0856) 850438			4 Dble/Twin	2 Public Bath/Sh	B&B per person £10.00 Double	Open May-Oct Dinner 1800-2100
STRUAN Isle of Skye, Inverness-shire Mrs Barnes, Aurora Crafts, 1-2 Ose. Tel. Struan (047072) 208	Map 3 C9		2 Dble/Twin	1 Public Bath/Sh	B&B per person £6.50 Double	Open Apr-Sep Dinner 1800
Mrs Moira Campbell, The Anchorage, 9 Ebost West. Tel. Struan (047072) 206			1 Dble/Twin 1 Family	1 Public Bath/Sh	B&B per person £7.00 Double	Open Jan-Dec
STRUY, by Beauly Inverness-shire Mauld Bridge Guest House. Tel. Struy (046376) 222	Map 3 H9		2 Dble/Twin 2 Family	4 Private Bath/Sh	B&B per person £10.00 Double	Open Apr-Nov Dinner 1930
SYMBISTER, Whalsay Shetland Lingaveg Guest House, Marrister. Tel. Symbister (08066) 489	Map 5 G3		2 Single 1 Dble/Twin 1 Family	1 Private Bath/Sh 1 Public Bath/Sh	B&B per person £10.50 Single £10.50 Double	Open Jan-Dec Dinner 1800
SYMINGTON Ayrshire Mrs M Lamont, Gorsehill, Corraith. Tel. Kilmarnock (0563) 830337	Map 2 B6	COMMENDED Listed	1 Dble/Twin 1 Family	1 Private Bath/Sh 1 Public Bath/Sh	B&B per person £7.00-£8.50 Double	Open Feb-Nov Dinner 1800-...

Attractive modern family home with rock garden. Peaceful setting surrounded by farmland.

SYMINGTON Lanarkshire	Map 2 B6	COMMENDED Listed	3 Dble/Twin 2 Family	1 Public Bath/Sh	B&B per person £8.20 Double	Open Jan-Dec Dinner 1800	⬧ V ⬧ 🛏 ▤ TV ⚡ 🛏 ⬧ 🐕 P C
Mrs Anderson Jara, West Side Lane Tel. Tinto (08993) 493/527			19c extended stone cottage with rural views. Dinner and packed lunches available.				
Mrs Goldsbrough The Old Manse Tel. Tinto (08993) 242			2 Family	2 Private Bath/Sh 1 Public Bath/Sh	B&B per person £8.50 Double	Open Apr-Sep	🛏 ⬧ ✂ 🐈 ✳ P C 🏤
Mrs M Howatson Eastfield of Wiston Farm Tel. Lamington (08995) 270			2 Dble/Twin 1 Family		B&B per person £8.50 Double	Open Jan-Dec Dinner 1700	V ⬧ 🛏 TV 🛏 🐈 C ⬧
TAIN Ross-shire	Map 4 B7		1 Single 2 Dble/Twin 2 Family	2 Public Bath/Sh	B&B per person £9.00-£10.00 Single £7.50-£8.00 Double	Open Jan-Dec Dinner 1830	⬧ V ⬧ 🛏 ▤ TV ⚡ 🛏 🐕 ✳ P C
Mrs Roberts Carringtons, Morangie Road Tel. Tain (0862) 2635		Listed					
TANGASDALE Isle of Barra, Western Isles	Map 3 A11		1 Single 4 Dble/Twin 1 Family	1 Public Bath/Sh	B&B per person £8.00 Single £8.00 Double	Open Apr-Oct	🐴 ⬧ 🛏 ▤ TV ⬧ P C ⬧
Mrs Clair MacNeil Tigh Chaisinn, 58 Tangasdale Tel. Castlebay (08714) 417							
TARBERT Argyll	Map 1 E3		1 Dble/Twin 2 Family	1 Public Bath/Sh	B&B per person £8.00-£8.50 Double	Open Jan-Dec	🐴 🛏 TV ⚡ 🛏 ⬧ 🐈 ⚠ ⬧ C
Mrs MacNab Knap House Tel. Tarbert (08802) 367							
Mrs Murray Atholl Villa, Lady Ileene Road Tel. Tarbert (08802) 746			3 Dble/Twin 2 Family	1 Public Bath/Sh	B&B per person £8.00 Double	Open Apr-Oct	🛏 ▤ TV ⚡ 🛏 ⬧ 🐈 P ⬧ C
Bob & Jean Pine Springside, Pier Road PA29 6UE Tel. Tarbert (08802) 413			3 Dble/Twin 1 Family	3 Public Bath/Sh	B&B per person £8.50-£9.00 Double	Open Jan-Dec	🐴 🛏 ▤ TV 🛏 ⬧ 🐈 ✳ 🍴 P ⚠ C
TARBERT Harris, Western Isles	Map 3 C6		1 Single 2 Family	1 Public Bath/Sh	B&B per person £11.00 Single £11.00 Double	Open Apr-Nov Dinner 1900	🐴 V 🛏 TV ⚡ 🐈 ⚠ C
Mrs C Macleod School View, Old Pier Road Tel. Harris (0859) 2481							
Mrs Morrison Dunard Tel. Harris (0859) 2340			1 Single 3 Dble/Twin	1 Public Bath/Sh	B&B per person £8.50 Single £8.50 Double	Open Jan-Dec Dinner 1900	🐴 ⬧ ⬧ 🛏 ▤ TV ⚡ 🛏 🐈 ✳ ⬧ P C
TARBET, Arrochar Dunbartonshire	Map 1 G3		1 Dble/Twin 2 Family	1 Public Bath/Sh	B&B per person £7.50-£8.50 Double	Open Jan-Dec Dinner 1800	V 🛏 ▤ TV 🐈 P C 🏤
Mrs E Fairfield Lochview Tel. Arrochar (03012) 200							
E Fraser Valtos Tel. Arrochar (03012) 373			3 Dble/Twin 1 Family	1 Private Bath/Sh 1 Public Bath/Sh	B&B per person £8.00-£10.00 Double	Open Mar-Dec	⬧ 🛏 ▤ TV ⚡ 🛏 ⬧ 🐈 P

TARBET, Arrochar continued — Map 1 G3

Annie S Logan
Ballyhennan, Toll House
Tel. Arrochar (03012) 203
1 Single / 2 Dble/Twin / 1 Family — 2 Public Bath/Sh
B&B per person £8.00 Single / £8.00 Double
Open Apr-Oct

Mrs M McDonald
Aye Servus, Tighloan
G83 7DD
Tel. Arrochar (03012) 491
2 Dble/Twin — 1 Public Bath/Sh
B&B per person £8.00 Double
Open Jan-Dec

Mrs A McMillan
4 Bemersyde Road
Tel. Arrochar (03012) 412
2 Dble/Twin
B&B per person £7.50-£8.00 Double
Open Apr-Sep

Mrs Allan Munro
27 Ballyhennan Crescent
G83 7DB
Tel. Arrochar (03012) 207
2 Dble/Twin / 1 Family — 1 Public Bath/Sh
B&B per person £7.00 Double
Open Apr-Oct

Mrs Reid
9 Ballyhennan Crescent
G83 7DB
Tel. Arrochar (03012) 351
2 Dble/Twin — 1 Public Bath/Sh
B&B per person £8.00-£8.50 Double
Open May-Oct

Mrs D Taylor
33 Ballyhennan Crescent
G83 8DA
Tel. Arrochar (03012) 213
2 Dble/Twin / 1 Family — 1 Public Bath/Sh
B&B per person £7.00-£7.50 Double
Open Jan-Dec

TARBOLTON, Ayrshire — Map 1 H7

Mrs Maurice Harrison
Scoutts Farm
Tel. Tarbolton (029254) 218
3 Dble/Twin / 1 Family — 1 Public Bath/Sh
B&B per person £9.50-£10.00 Double
Open Jan-Dec

TARLAND, Aberdeenshire — Map 4 E10

Mrs Anderson
Meadow Farm, Migvie
AB3 4XP
Tel. Tarland (033981) 333
2 Dble/Twin / 1 Family
B&B per person £5.00 Double
Open Apr-Oct / Dinner 1800

TARVIE, by Strathpeffer, Ross-shire — Map 4 A8

COMMENDED Listed

Mr & Mrs Frowley
Inchdrean
IV14 9EJ
Tel. Strathpeffer (0997) 21250
3 Dble/Twin — 1 Public Bath/Sh
B&B per person £5.00-£8.25 Double
Open Apr-Oct / Dinner 1800

Secluded but accessible modern lochside house. Superb views of surrounding hills.

TAYPORT, Fife — Map 2 D2

Mrs Paterson
51 Castle Street
Tel. Tayport (0382) 552581
2 Dble/Twin / 1 Family
B&B per person £7.00-£8.00 Double
Open Jan-Dec

THANKERTON, by Biggar, Lanarkshire — Map 2 B6

Mrs Isabella Orr
Heatherlea, by Tinto Tearoom
Tel. Tinto (08993) 631
1 Dble/Twin — 1 Public Bath/Sh
B&B per person £8.00 Double
Open Jan-Dec

			Accommodation	Bathrooms	B&B Rates	Opening	
THORNHILL Dumfriesshire Mrs Mackie Waterside Mains Tel. Thornhill (0848) 30405	Map 2 B9	COMMENDED Listed	1 Single 2 Dble/Twin 1 Family	1 Public Bath/Sh	B&B per person £8.50-£9.00 Single £8.50-£9.00 Double	Open Jan-Dec Dinner 1800	(symbols)
			Working farmhouse on banks of River Nith, about 2 miles/ 3km on A76 from village.				
Mrs Maxwell Druidhall Tel. Marrburn (08486) 271			2 Dble/Twin	2 Public Bath/Sh	B&B per person £7.00-£8.00 Double	Open Mar-Dec Dinner 1800	(symbols)
Miss M McKerrow Parkview, Closeburn DG3 5HT Tel. Thornhill (0848) 31239		Listed	1 Dble/Twin 1 Family	1 Public Bath/Sh	B&B per person £7.50-£8.00 Double	Open Apr-Nov Dinner 1800	(symbols)
THORNHILL Perthshire Mrs S Black The Braes Tel. Thornhill (078685) 267	Map 2 A4		1 Single 2 Dble/Twin 1 Family	2 Public Bath/Sh	B&B per person £9.00 Single £9.00 Double	Open Jan-Dec Dinner 1900	(symbols)
Mrs Brewster Wester Borland Farm FK8 3QL Tel. Thornhill (078685) 224			1 Single 2 Dble/Twin 1 Family	2 Public Bath/Sh	B&B per person £7.50-£8.00 Single £7.50-£8.00 Double	Open Apr-Oct Dinner 1800	(symbols)
Mrs Findlay Easter Tarr Farm FK8 3QL Tel. Thornhill (078685) 225			2 Dble/Twin 1 Family	1 Public Bath/Sh	B&B per person £7.50 Double	Open Apr-Oct Dinner 1830	(symbols)
THURSO Caithness	Map 4 C3						

Banniskirk House (Guest House)

This old Victorian mansion house delightfully set in 20 acres of wooded grounds is a haven of peace and quiet only 7 miles from Thurso and Orkney Ferry. Halkirk, Wick and John O'Groats easily reached. Guests enjoy choice of fine food and personal attention. Comfortable rooms with all amenities, Sea, River and Loch Fishing can be arranged.

OPEN—March to October

S.A.E. for brochure from:

BANNISKIRK HOUSE, BANNISKIRK (on A895)
By THURSO, CAITHNESS, KW12 6XA   Tel: 084 783 609

			Accommodation	Bathrooms	B&B Rates	Opening	
Banniskirk House Guest House KW12 6XA Tel. Halkirk (084783) 609			2 Single 4 Dble/Twin 2 Family	2 Public Bath/Sh	B&B per person £8.50 Single £8.50 Double	Open Apr-Oct Dinner 1830	(symbols)
Mrs J Anderson 3 Castle Street Tel. Thurso (0847) 63820		Listed	2 Dble/Twin 4 Family	1 Public Bath/Sh	B&B per person £7.00 Double	Open Jan-Dec	(symbols)

	Map 4 C3					
THURSO continued						
Mrs P Bremner 30 Olrig Street Tel. Thurso (0847) 65546		3 Dble/Twin	1 Public Bath/Sh	B&B per person £8.00 Double	Open Jan-Dec	
Mrs Bremner Stoneybank, Weydale Tel. Thurso (0847) 63880	COMMENDED ♛♛	3 Dble/Twin	1 Public Bath/Sh	B&B per person £7.00-£7.50 Double	Open Apr-Sep	
		Large detached bungalow with rural views, modern and comfortable. Good walking and birdlife locally.				
Mrs A K Cormack 1 Barrock Street Tel. Thurso (0847) 64148		2 Dble/Twin	1 Public Bath/Sh	B&B per person £7.50 Double	Open Jun-Sep	
Mrs M Fisher Carlingwark, 5 Mears Place Tel. Thurso (0847) 64124	COMMENDED Listed	1 Single 1 Dble/Twin	2 Public Bath/Sh	B&B per person £8.50 Single £8.00 Double	Open Jun-Sep	
		Modern detached bungalow with landscaped garden in quiet cul de sac. Comfortable family home.				
Mrs M J Henderson 3 Barrock Street Tel. Thurso (0847) 64008		1 Dble/Twin	1 Public Bath/Sh	B&B per person £7.50 Double	Open Apr-Sep	
Mrs MacKay 8 Pentland Crescent Tel. Thurso (0847) 63677	Listed	2 Dble/Twin 1 Family	1 Public Bath/Sh	B&B per person £8.00 Single £8.00 Double	Open May-Oct	
Mrs E Mackay 3 Pentland Crescent Tel. Thurso (0847) 62723		1 Dble/Twin 1 Family	1 Public Bath/Sh	B&B per person £8.00 Double	Open Mar-Nov	
Mrs Mcdonald Seaview Farm, Hill of Forss Tel. Thurso (0847) 62315	COMMENDED Listed	2 Dble/Twin 2 Family	1 Public Bath/Sh	B&B per person £7.00-£8.00 Double	Open Jan-Dec	
		On working farm; watch milking, butter making or walk around farm. Highland dance trophy display.				
Mrs Murray 1 Granville Crescent Tel. Thurso (0847) 62993		1 Single 1 Dble/Twin	1 Public Bath/Sh	B&B per person £8.00 Single £8.00 Double	Open Jan-Dec	
Mrs I Nicholas Cruachan, Duncans Hill Tel. Thurso (0847) 62754		3 Dble/Twin	2 Public Bath/Sh	B&B per person £7.50-£8.50 Double	Open Apr-Oct	
Mrs Sinclair 3 Hill Place Tel. Thurso (0847) 63900		2 Dble/Twin		B&B per person £9.00 Single £7.00 Double	Open Jan-Dec Dinner 1800	
Dorothy Thomson Annandale, 2 Rendel Govan Road KW14 7EP Tel. Thurso (0847) 63942		3 Dble/Twin	1 Public Bath/Sh	B&B per person £8.00-£8.50 Double	Open Apr-Sep	
TIGHNABRUAICH Argyll	Map 1 F5					
Mrs P C McLachlan Ferguslie, Seafront PA21 2BE Tel. Tighnabruaich (0700) 811414		2 Dble/Twin	1 Public Bath/Sh	B&B per person £8.00 Double	Open Apr-Oct Dinner 1800	

	Map	Grading	Rooms	Baths	B&B	Open	
TIGHNABRUAICH continued Mr & Mrs Morris Allt Beag PA21 2BE Tel. Tighnabruaich (0700) 811323	Map 1 F5		3 Dble/Twin	1 Public Bath/Sh	B&B per person £7.50 Double	Open Jan-Dec Dinner 1800-2100	V ⚲ ⌕ ▦ TV ⚡ ⌂ ⟊ ❋ P C
Mrs Wilson The Sheiling Tel. Tighnabruaich (0700) 811449			1 Dble/Twin 1 Family	1 Public Bath/Sh	B&B per person £7.50-£8.50 Double	Open Apr-Oct Dinner 1830	⟊ ☕ V ⌕ ▦ TV ⚡ ⌂ ❋ P ⚠ C
TOBERMORY Isle of Mull, Argyll Ach-Na-Craoibh Guest House Tel. Tobermory (0688) 2301	Map 1 C1		2 Dble/Twin 2 Family	3 Private Bath/Sh 2 Public Bath/Sh	B&B per person £6.50-£13.95 Double	Open Jan-Dec	⟊ M ▢ ⚲ ☕ V ⌕ ▦ ● TV ⚡ ⌂ ⟡ ⟊ ❋ ⚘ P ⚠ C ⟐ T ⌸ ⸙
Mrs Olive Brown Stronsaule PA75 6PR Tel. Tobermory (0688) 2381		COMMENDED Listed	1 Single 2 Dble/Twin	1 Public Bath/Sh	B&B per person £7.00-£8.00 Single £7.00-£8.00 Double	Open Apr-Oct	⚲ ⌕ TV ⟡ ❋ ⚘ C
			Attractive stone building with magnificent views over Tobermory Bay. Pleasant gardens.				
Mrs M Burgess Castlecroft Tel. Tobermory (0688) 2165			3 Dble/Twin	1 Public Bath/Sh	B&B per person £7.00-£8.50 Double	Open Jan-Dec Dinner 1830	⟊ ⚲ TV ⌂ P ⚠
Mrs E Cattanach 25 Breadalbane Street Tel. Tobermory (0688) 2402			1 Single 4 Dble/Twin 1 Family	1 Public Bath/Sh	B&B per person £7.00-£9.00 Single £7.00-£9.00 Double	Open Jan-Dec	⌕ ▦ TV ⟊ ⚘ P ⚠
Mrs Anne Harper 2 Victoria Street Tel. Tobermory (0688) 2263			2 Dble/Twin	1 Public Bath/Sh	B&B per person £6.00-£7.00 Double	Open Jan-Dec	☕ ⌕ ▦ TV ⟡ C
Mr Kirsop Failte, Main Street Tel. Tobermory (0688) 2107			2 Single 3 Dble/Twin 2 Family	2 Public Bath/Sh	B&B per person £8.50-£9.00 Single £8.50-£9.00 Double	Open Apr-Oct	⟊ ⌕ ▦ TV ⚡ ⟊ C
Mrs P Murphy Lone Cottage Tel. Tobermory (0688) 2461			2 Dble/Twin 1 Family	2 Public Bath/Sh	B&B per person £7.00 Double	Open Apr-Oct	⟊ ⚲ ⌕ ▦ TV ⟊ P C
TOLSTA CHAOLAIS Lewis, Western Isles Mrs A L Veals Rivington Tel. Callanish (08502) 332	Map 3 C4	COMMENDED Listed	2 Dble/Twin 1 Family	1 Public Bath/Sh	B&B per person £8.00 Double	Open Jan-Dec Dinner 1830	⌕ ▦ TV ⟊ P C ⟐
			Set in remote weaving village overlooking trout loch. Recreation room.				
TOMICH, by Beauly Inverness-shire Mrs E Munro Tomich House IV4 7AS Tel. Beauly (0463) 782225	Map 4 A9	HIGHLY COMMENDED 👑 👑	3 Dble/Twin	1 Public Bath/Sh	B&B per person £9.00 Double	Open Apr-Oct	⟊ ⌕ ▦ TV ⚡ ⌂ ⟡ ❋ P ⚠ ⌸
			Georgian mansion built 1805. Many original features. 8 acre grounds. Wide range of local activities.				

Key to symbols is on back flap. Details of Classification and Grading are on page vi.

209

TOMINTOUL, Ballindalloch Banffshire	Map 4 D10					
Argyle Guest House Main Street AB3 9EX Tel. Tomintoul (08074) 223		COMMENDED ♛	3 Dble/Twin 3 Family	1 Public Bath/Sh	B&B per person £9.00 Double	Open Jan-Oct Dinner 1900
			Traditional stone built house in centre of village. Pony trekking package. Convenient for ski centre.			
Mrs E Brown Conglass Hall, Main Street AB3 9EX Tel. Tomintoul (08074) 291			1 Single 4 Dble/Twin	1 Public Bath/Sh	B&B per person £7.50-£8.50 Single £7.50-£8.50 Double	Open Jan-Dec Dinner 1900-
Mrs Catherine Coutts Altachbeg, Braemar Road AB3 9ES Tel. Tomintoul (08074) 277			3 Family	1 Public Bath/Sh	B&B per person £7.00-£7.50 Double	Open Mar-Oct
TORLOISK, Ulva Ferry, Isle of Mull, Argyll	Map 1 C1					
Mr & Mrs Teare Keepers Cottage PA74 6NH Tel. Ulva Ferry (06885) 265			2 Dble/Twin	1 Public Bath/Sh	B&B per person £7.50-£8.50 Double	Open Jan-Dec Dinner 1900
TORPHINS Aberdeenshire	Map 4 F10					
Mrs E Shepherd Doorie Brae, 26 Beltie Road AB3 4JT Tel. Torphins (033982) 493			1 Dble/Twin	1 Public Bath/Sh	B&B per person £7.00 Double	Open Jan-Dec Dinner 1900
TORRIDON, Achnasheen Ross-shire	Map 3 F8					
Mrs June A Maclennan Riverside, Inveralligin Tel. Torridon (044587) 280		COMMENDED Listed	3 Dble/Twin	1 Public Bath/Sh	B&B per person £7.00 Double	Open Apr-Oct Dinner 1900-
			Converted croft house on edge of village. Overlooks Loch Torridon and mountains. Near nature reserve.			
Mrs B J Peacock Upper Diabaig Tel. Diabaig (044581) 227			1 Single 2 Dble/Twin	1 Public Bath/Sh	B&B per person £7.50 Single £7.50 Double	Open Mar-Oct Dinner 1830
Mrs I Ross Ben Bhraggie, Diabaig Tel. Diabaig (044581) 268		Listed	2 Dble/Twin	1 Public Bath/Sh	B&B per person £6.50 Double	Open Apr-Nov Dinner 1900
TORTHORWALD, by Dumfries Dumfriesshire	Map 2 C9					
Mrs Cranstoun Hemplands Farm Tel. Collin (038775) 225		COMMENDED Listed	2 Dble/Twin 1 Family	2 Public Bath/Sh	B&B per person £7.50 Double	Open May-Sep Dinner 1800
			On working farm, panoramic views over Solway Firth and Lakeland Hills. Yachting on nearby loch.			
Mr Ireson Smithy House Tel. Collin (038775) 518			5 Dble/Twin	3 Public Bath/Sh	B&B per person £7.00-£8.00 Double	Open Jan-Dec Dinner 1800

TRANENT East Lothian	Map 2 D5			

The Manor
Gladsmuir, Tranent, East Lothian.
Tel. 0875 52155

Charming Victorian Country House, 13 miles south of Edinburgh along A1 and 3 miles from the market town of Haddington. The Manor is quietly situated in 1½ acres of beautiful grounds with magnificent views of the Forth. Ideal base for touring with many places of historical interest nearby to explore, and a selection of golf courses, beaches, fishing and birdwatching areas a short drive away. Mr and Mrs Brian Smith have skilfully created a feeling of Victorian elegance and offer all the amenities associated with superior accommodation. A relaxing and comfortable holiday is assured. Non-smoking. Ample safe parking. Special golf tickets available. B & B rates, excellent restaurants nearby or EM on request.

			Rooms	Bath	Rates	Open	
The Manor Guest House Gladsmuir Tel. Longniddry (0875) 52155			1 Single 3 Dble/Twin 2 Family	1 Private Bath/Sh 1 Public Bath/Sh	B&B per person £12.00-£13.00 Single £12.00-£14.00 Double	Open Jan-Dec Dinner 1830	
Mrs Davenport Muirpark House, Haddington Road Tel. Tranent (0875) 611787			3 Dble/Twin	1 Public Bath/Sh	B&B per person £7.50-£8.00 Double	Open May-Sep	
Mrs R Harrison Rosebank House, 161 High Street Tel. Tranent (0875) 610967			2 Family	1 Public Bath/Sh	B&B per person £8.00 Double	Open Jan-Dec	
TROON Ayrshire	**Map 1** **G7**						
Mrs Gordon Braemar, 36 St Meddans Street Tel. Troon (0292) 313126			3 Dble/Twin	1 Public Bath/Sh	B&B per person £8.50 Single £7.50 Double	Open Jan-Dec	
Mrs Sheila Hamilton 30a South Beach KA10 6EF Tel. Troon (0292) 313270		Awaiting Inspection	3 Dble/Twin 1 Family	2 Public Bath/Sh	B&B per person £8.00 Single £8.50 Double	Open Apr-Oct	
Mrs A R Jamieson Knockmarloch, 57 St Meddans Street KA10 6NN Tel. Troon (0292) 312840			3 Dble/Twin	1 Public Bath/Sh	B&B per person £8.00 Double	Open Feb-Nov	
Mrs N Livingstone 31 Victoria Drive KA10 6JF Tel. Troon (0292) 311552			1 Single 3 Dble/Twin	2 Public Bath/Sh	B&B per person £9.00 Single £9.00 Double	Open Jan-Dec	
Mrs McDonald 55 Gailes Road, Barassie KA10 6TB Tel. Troon (0292) 311541			1 Single 2 Dble/Twin 1 Family	2 Public Bath/Sh	B&B per person £7.50-£8.00 Single £7.00-£7.50 Double	Open Jan-Dec	

TROON continued Mrs J Young Springfield, 16 Dallas Place KA10 6JE Tel. Troon (0292) 315495	Map 1 G7		2 Dble/Twin	1 Public Bath/Sh	B&B per person £9.00 Double	Open Jan-Dec	
TUMMEL BRIDGE Perthshire Mrs S McKenzie Bohally Tel. Tummel Bridge (08824) 253	Map 2 A1		1 Dble/Twin	1 Private Bath/Sh	B&B per person £10.00 Double	Open Apr-Oct	
TUNDERGARTH, by Lockerbie Dumfriesshire Mrs I D Woodburn Bankshill Tel. Bankshill (05767) 694	Map 2 C9		2 Dble/Twin	1 Public Bath/Sh	B&B per person £7.50 Double	Open Apr-Oct Dinner 1800	
TURRIFF Aberdeenshire Mrs Chalmers Midhill of Seggat, Auchterless Tel. Auchterless (08884) 361	Map 4 F8		1 Dble/Twin	1 Public Bath/Sh	B&B per person £10.00-£14.00 Double	Open Jan-Dec	
Mrs R Gracey Woodhead of Laithers AB5 8BT Tel. Auchterless (08884) 265		COMMENDED	2 Dble/Twin	1 Public Bath/Sh	B&B per person £8.50 Double	Open Jan-Dec Dinner 1800	
			19c house on 240 acre farm, quiet location. Golf, swimming, salmon fishing and shooting locally.				
TWEEDSMUIR Peeblesshire Menzion Farm Guest House ML12 6QR Tel. Tweedsmuir (08997) 247	Map 2 C7	COMMENDED	4 Dble/Twin 1 Family	1 Public Bath/Sh	B&B per person £12.00-£14.00 Double	Open Jan-Dec Dinner 1900	
			An old fashioned house with log fires, set among Tweedsmuir Hills, overlooking the River Tweed.				
TWYNHOLM Kirkcudbrightshire Mrs L Robson Glencroft DG6 4NU Tel. Twynholm (05576) 252	Map 2 A10	COMMENDED	1 Single 1 Dble/Twin 1 Family	1 Public Bath/Sh	B&B per person £7.50-£8.00 Single £7.50-£8.00 Double	Open Apr-Oct Dinner 1730	
			Victorian house standing in small garden overlooking fields. 5 mls(8 km) from Kirkcudbright.				
Mrs M Sloan Redfield Farm Tel. Twynholm (05576) 225			2 Family	1 Public Bath/Sh	B&B per person £7.50 Double	Open Apr-Oct Dinner 1730	
TYNDRUM, by Crianlarich Perthshire Mrs Coffield Dalkjell Tel. Tyndrum (08384) 285	Map 1 G2		1 Dble/Twin 2 Family	1 Public Bath/Sh	B&B per person £8.00-£8.50 Double	Open Jan-Dec Dinner 1900	

Location / Address	Map Ref	Grading	Accommodation	Bathrooms	Prices	Opening	Facilities
TYNINGHAME, by East Linton **East Lothian** Mrs G Norrie, Old Ale & Porter House EH42 1XL Tel. East Linton (0620) 860133	Map 2 E4	Listed	2 Dble/Twin	1 Public Bath/Sh	B&B per person £10.00 Single £10.00 Double	Open Jan-Dec Dinner 1830	(symbols)
UDDINGSTON **Lanarkshire** Northcote Guest House 2 Holmbrae Avenue G71 6AL Tel. Uddingston (0698) 813319	Map 2 A5	♛ ♛	1 Single 1 Dble/Twin 1 Family	1 Public Bath/Sh	B&B per person £8.00-£9.00 Single £8.00-£9.00 Double	Open Jan-Dec Dinner 1800	(symbols)
UIG **Isle of Skye, Inverness-shire** Mrs Devy Brae Holm, Pier Road Tel. Uig (047042) 396	Map 3 D8		2 Dble/Twin 2 Family	2 Public Bath/Sh	B&B per person £7.50 Double	Open Jan-Dec Dinner 1800	(symbols)
Mrs MacKinnon Harris Cottage Tel. Uig (047042) 268			3 Dble/Twin	2 Public Bath/Sh	B&B per person £8.50 Double	Open Apr-Sep Dinner 1830	(symbols)
Mrs N Maclean Learg, 9 Linicro Tel. Uig (047042) 353			2 Dble/Twin 1 Family	1 Public Bath/Sh	B&B per person £8.00 Double	Open Feb-Nov Dinner 1900	(symbols)
Mrs Macleod 11 Earlish Tel. Uig (047042) 319		Listed	3 Dble/Twin 1 Family	2 Public Bath/Sh	B&B per person £7.50 Double	Open Apr-Nov	(symbols)
UIG **Lewis, Western Isles** Mrs Jessie Buchanan 3 Carishader Tel. Timsgarry (08505) 252	Map 3 B5		2 Dble/Twin	1 Public Bath/Sh	B&B per person £7.00-£8.00 Double	Open Jan-Dec Dinner 1830	(symbols)
ULLAPOOL **Ross-shire** Mrs B A Birks Sunnybank Cottage Tel. Ullapool (0854) 2903	Map 3 G6		2 Family	1 Public Bath/Sh	B&B per person £8.50 Double	Open Apr-Sep	(symbols)
Mrs I Boa Ardale, Market Street IV26 2XE Tel. Ullapool (0854) 2220			2 Dble/Twin	1 Public Bath/Sh	B&B per person £8.50 Double	Open May-Oct	(symbols)
Mrs B Brinkler Old Bank House, Argyle Street IV26 2UB Tel. Ullapool (0854) 2166		Awaiting Inspection	1 Single 4 Dble/Twin	2 Public Bath/Sh	B&B per person £8.00 Single £8.00 Double	Open Jan-Dec	(symbols)
Mrs A Campbell Clisham, 56 Rhue IV26 2TJ Tel. Ullapool (0854) 2498		Listed	2 Family	1 Public Bath/Sh	B&B per person £7.50-£8.00 Double	Open May-Oct	(symbols)

ULLAPOOL continued Mrs P Farquhar Riverview, 2 Castle Terrace IV26 2XD Tel. Ullapool (0854) 2019	Map 3 G6		2 Dble/Twin 1 Family	1 Public Bath/Sh	B&B per person £7.50-£8.00 Double	Open Apr-Oct	🚰♨️🅿️
Mr & Mrs G Goudie Caber Feidh, Corry Heights, Braes Tel. Ullapool (0854) 2164		Awaiting Inspection	3 Dble/Twin	3 Private Bath/Sh	B&B per person £10.00-£11.25 Double	Open Apr-Oct	⬛❄️🅿️△
Mrs Griffiths Hillcrest, Corry Heights, Braes IV26 2SZ Tel. Ullapool (0854) 2188		Awaiting Inspection	1 Single 1 Dble/Twin	1 Public Bath/Sh	B&B per person £8.50-£9.00 Single £8.50-£9.00 Double	Open Apr-Sep	❄️🅿️
Mrs MacKenzie Green Pastures, Garve Road Tel. Ullapool (0854) 2008			4 Dble/Twin	2 Public Bath/Sh	B&B per person £8.50-£9.50 Double	Open May-Sep	❄️🅿️
Mrs Mackenzie Hill View, Moss Road Tel. Ullapool (0854) 2197			2 Dble/Twin	1 Public Bath/Sh	B&B per person £8.00 Double	Open Apr-Oct	🐕
Mrs K Stewart Rhue Tel. Ullapool (0854) 2435			1 Dble/Twin 1 Family	1 Public Bath/Sh	B&B per person £6.50-£7.00 Double	Open Apr-Oct	🐕❄️🅿️🅲
Mrs Urquhart Ardlair, Morefield IV26 2TH Tel. Ullapool (0854) 2087			1 Dble/Twin 2 Family	2 Public Bath/Sh	B&B per person £7.50-£8.00 Double	Open May-Oct	❄️🅿️🅲
UNST Shetland Mrs Irving Barns, New-gord, Uyeasound Tel. Uyeasound (095785) 249	Map 5 G1		1 Dble/Twin 1 Family	2 Public Bath/Sh	B&B per person £9.00 Double	Open Jan-Dec Dinner 1700-	❄️🅿️🅲🆃
VIDLIN, North Mainland Shetland Mrs B Ford Skeo Green, Lunning Tel. Vidlin (08067) 302	Map 5 G3		1 Dble/Twin	2 Public Bath/Sh	B&B per person £5.50-£6.80 Double	Open Jan-Dec Dinner 1700	❄️🅿️🅲
WALLS Shetland Mrs E Pole 6 Kirkidale Tel. Walls (059571) 358	Map 5 F4		1 Single 1 Dble/Twin	1 Public Bath/Sh	B&B per person £7.50 Single £7.50 Double	Open Jan-Dec Dinner 1800	❄️🅿️△🅲
WATERNISH Isle of Skye, Inverness-shire Mrs Greenhalgh Loch Bay Tearoom & Restaurant, Stein Tel. Waternish (047083) 235	Map 3 C8		1 Single 2 Family	1 Public Bath/Sh	B&B per person £8.50 Single £8.50 Double	Open Apr-Oct Dinner 1830	🅿️△🅲

VAT is shown at 15%; changes in this rate may affect prices. Prices shown are for guidance only. Please send SAE with each enquiry.

Location	Map	Grading	Rooms	Facilities	Rates	Opening	Symbols
WATTEN, by Wick **Caithness** Mrs D Roger Woodside House, Thurso Road Tel. Watten (095582) 254	Map 4 D3		1 Single 2 Dble/Twin	1 Public Bath/Sh	B&B per person £7.00-£8.00 Single £6.50-£7.50 Double	Open Jan-Dec	
WEST LINTON **Peeblesshire** Mrs Cottam Mountain Cross Tel. West Linton (0968) 60329	Map 2 C6		3 Dble/Twin	1 Public Bath/Sh	B&B per person £8.00 Double	Open May-Oct Dinner 1600-	
Mrs M Davidson Callands Farmhouse, Mountain Cross EH46 7DE Tel. Peebles (0721) 52268		Awaiting Inspection	1 Dble/Twin	1 Private Bath/Sh 1 Public Bath/Sh	B&B per person £8.00 Double	Open Apr-Oct	
WEST TARBERT **Harris, Western Isles** Mrs A Morrison Hillcrest Tel. Harris (0859) 2119	Map 3 B6		1 Dble/Twin 1 Family	1 Public Bath/Sh	B&B per person £7.00 Double	Open Apr-Sep Dinner 1900	
WESTRAY **Orkney** Mrs Costie Seafield	Map 5 B9		1 Dble/Twin 2 Family	3 Public Bath/Sh	B&B per person £8.00 Single £8.00 Double	Open Jan-Dec Dinner 1800	
WHITENESS, West **Mainland** **Shetland** Mrs B Bruce Kyendigaet ZE2 9LQ Tel. Weisdale (059572) 335	Map 5 F4	COMMENDED Listed	2 Single 1 Family	1 Public Bath/Sh	B&B per person £6.50-£8.00 Single £6.00-£7.00 Double	Open May-Aug	
			Detached house in quiet rural situation, with excellent views. Good bus service.				
WHITHORN **Wigtownshire** Mrs E Forsyth Baltier Tel. Garlieston (09886) 241	Map 1 H11	COMMENDED Listed	1 Dble/Twin 1 Family	3 Public Bath/Sh	B&B per person £8.50 Double	Open Jan-Nov Dinner 1830	
			Stone built dairy farm, own garden. High position gives fine views over surrounding countryside.				
WHITING BAY **Isle of Arran** Ferryway Private Guest House Kings Cross Tel. Whiting Bay (07707) 403	Map 1 F7		1 Single 2 Dble/Twin 1 Family	2 Public Bath/Sh	B&B per person £8.00-£8.50 Single £8.00-£8.50 Double	Open Jan-Dec Dinner 1800-	
Mrs MacGregor Balnabruaich, Ardlui Rd, Kings Cross Tel. Whiting Bay (07707) 453		COMMENDED	2 Dble/Twin	1 Public Bath/Sh	B&B per person £8.00-£8.50 Double	Open Apr-Sep	
			Warm welcome, quiet and relaxing. Large garden. Spectacular views over water to Holy Isle.				

Key to symbols is on back flap. Details of Classification and Grading are on page vi.

215

WICK Caithness	Map 4 E3					
County Guest House 101 High Street Tel. Wick (0955) 2911		1 Dble/Twin 5 Family	1 Public Bath/Sh	B&B per person £7.50 Double	Open Jan-Dec	
Harbour Guest House 6 Rose Street Tel. Wick (0955) 3276	APPROVED 👑 👑	1 Single 9 Dble/Twin	2 Public Bath/Sh	B&B per person £8.50 Single	Open Jan-Dec	
		Traditional stone cottages, now a listed building, about 200 yds from the harbour.				
Wellington Guest House 41-43 High Street Tel. Wick (0955) 3287		6 Dble/Twin		B&B per person £9.60 Double	Open May-Sep	
Mrs E Calder 9 Francis Street Tel. Wick (0955) 2136		1 Single 3 Family	2 Public Bath/Sh	B&B per person £8.00 Single £7.50 Double	Open Jan-Dec Dinner 1700	
Mrs Coghill Dunelm, 7 Sinclair Terrace Tel. Wick (0955) 2120	APPROVED Listed	1 Single 2 Family	2 Public Bath/Sh	B&B per person £8.00 Single £7.00-£7.50 Double	Open Jan-Dec	
		Stone terraced listed building, 5 minute walk from town centre and harbour. Spacious lounge.				
Mrs Cowie Maldon. Thurso Road Tel. Wick (0955) 2684		1 Single 1 Dble/Twin 1 Family	1 Public Bath/Sh	B&B per person £7.50 Single £7.00 Double	Open Jan-Dec	
Mrs S Gunn Papigoe Cottage. Papigoe KW1 4RD Tel. Wick (0955) 3363		1 Single 2 Dble/Twin	2 Public Bath/Sh	B&B per person £5.00-£5.50 Single £7.00-£7.50 Double	Open Jan-Dec Dinner 1900	
Mrs Millington 13 MacArthur Street Tel. Wick (0955) 5456	Awaiting Inspection	3 Dble/Twin	1 Public Bath/Sh	B&B per person £7.00 Double	Open Jan-Dec	

BILBSTER HOUSE
5 miles from Wick, phone Watten (095582) 212

An attractive country house situated in about 5 acres of garden and woodland. Dinner by prior arrangement (book before 5 p.m.).

Leave Wick on A882 (Wick-Watten-Thurso). After 5 miles see Line of Trees on Right and Signboard. Turn Right down Lane. Gates face you after 450 yards. (Bilbster House is shown on Ordnance Survey Map. Reference 282533.)

Mrs A Stewart Bilbster House Tel. Watten (095582) 212	COMMENDED 👑 👑	3 Dble/Twin	2 Public Bath/Sh	B&B per person £7.00 Double	Open Jan-Dec Dinner 1900	
		Dating from late 1700, listed country house in 5 acres. Traditionally furnished. Meals by arrangement.				
Mrs E Tait Rosebery Terrace, 82 Henrietta Street Tel. Wick (0955) 2531			1 Private Bath/Sh 1 Public Bath/Sh	B&B per person £7.00-£7.50 Double	Open Jan-Dec	
Mrs Weir Warrington, Thurso Road Tel. Wick (0955) 4138		1 Single 1 Dble/Twin		B&B per person £8.00 Single £7.50 Double	Open May-Sep	

VAT is shown at 15%. changes in this rate may affect prices. Prices shown are for guidance only. Please send SAE with each enquiry.

	Map	Grading	Rooms	Bathrooms	B&B	Opening	Facilities
WICK continued Mrs F White 7 West Park Tel. Wick (0955) 3162	Map 4 E3	COMMENDED Listed	2 Dble/Twin 1 Family	1 Public Bath/Sh	B&B per person £7.50 Double	Open Apr-Oct	
Family home in quiet cul de sac. Well furnished rooms, bedrooms with wash basins. Near train station.							
WIGTOWN Craigmount Guest House DG8 9EQ Tel. Wigtown (09884) 2291	Map 1 H10		1 Single 4 Dble/Twin	3 Public Bath/Sh	B&B per person £9.00 Single £9.00 Double	Open Jan-Dec Dinner 1900	
Mrs P Adams Clugston Farm Tel. Kirkcowan (067183) 338		Awaiting Inspection	3 Dble/Twin	1 Public Bath/Sh	B&B per person £7.50 Double	Open Apr-Oct Dinner 1800	
Mr & Mrs Boyd Sunnybrae DG8 9EQ Tel. Wigtown (09884) 3306			1 Single 1 Dble/Twin	1 Public Bath/Sh	B&B per person £7.00 Single £6.50 Double	Open Apr-Oct Dinner 1800	
WISTON Lanarkshire YMCA National Training Centre Wiston Lodge ML12 6HT Tel. Lamington (08995) 228	Map 2 B7		5 Dble/Twin 15 Family	1 Private Bath/Sh 4 Public Bath/Sh	B&B per person £7.25 Double	Open Jan-Dec Dinner 1700	
YELL Shetland Mrs A Anderson Parkhall, Mid-Yell Tel. Mid Yell (0957) 2358	Map 5 G2		1 Single 1 Dble/Twin 1 Family	1 Public Bath/Sh	B&B per person £8.00-£8.50 Single £8.00-£8.50 Double	Open Jan-Dec	
Mrs V Howe Ravensgio House, Ravensgio ZE2 9BN Tel. Mid Yell (0957) 2288			2 Single 2 Dble/Twin	1 Public Bath/Sh	B&B per person £8.00 Single £8.00 Double	Open Jan-Dec Dinner 1800	
YETHOLM Roxburghshire Bowmont Centre & Guest House Belford-on-Bowmont Tel. Yetholm (057382) 362 Telex 537174	Map 2 F7	APPROVED	2 Dble/Twin 1 Family	1 Public Bath/Sh	B&B per person £8.00 Double	Open Apr-Oct Dinner 1900	
Farmhouse accommodation offering country pursuits; pony trekking, walking. On 1350 acre hill farm.							
Mrs J Baston Grafton House Tel. Yetholm (057382) 515		Awaiting Inspection	1 Dble/Twin 1 Family	1 Private Bath/Sh 1 Public Bath/Sh	B&B per person £9.00 Double	Open Apr-Oct	
Mrs A Beveridge Sunnyside House Tel. Yetholm (057382) 529		Listed	2 Family	1 Public Bath/Sh	B&B per person £8.50-£9.00 Double	Open Apr-Oct	
Mrs A Freeland-Cook Cliftoncote Farm Tel. Yetholm (057382) 241		APPROVED Listed	2 Dble/Twin 1 Family	1 Public Bath/Sh	B&B per person £7.00-£8.00 Double	Open Apr-Oct Dinner 1800	
Stone built farmhouse dating in part from 18C. Peaceful location, set amidst rolling Border Country.							

Key to symbols is on back flap. Details of Classification and Grading are on page vi.

217

Glasgow Garden Festival '88

The Glasgow Garden Festival in 1988 guarantees to provide something for everyone. In addition to six themed parks, a varied and colourful programme of open air concerts, live displays and conferences will be staged from April-September.

FURTHER INFORMATION FOR DISABLED VISITORS

We are pleased to announce that from 1987, establishments in the accommodation guides displaying one of the three wheelchair access symbols, are now inspected under the Scottish Tourist Board's Classification and Grading Scheme. The three symbols indicate:

  Access for wheelchair users without assistance
Adequate parking or letting down area for visitor in wheelchair.
Clear, safe approach and entrance in wheelchair.
Access to reception and social area in wheelchair.
Public toilets fully suitable for all disabled use.
At least one bedroom on ground floor, or accessible by lift, with appropriate dimensions and facilities with suitable private bathroom for unattended visitor in wheelchair.

  A **Access for wheelchair users with assistance**
Parking, letting down and approach and entrance possible for the visitor in wheelchair with attendant help.
Access by permanent or portable ramps, or by lift, to reception and social areas.
Public toilets suitable for wheelchair use with attendant help.
At least one bedroom with appropriate dimensions and bathroom facilities, accessible by wheelchair user, or other disabled person, with attendant help.

  P **Access for ambulant disabled (other than wheelchair users)**
Parking, letting down, approach and entrance with safe steps or ramps, not too steep and preferably with hand rails.
Access to reception and social areas all accessible on same level, by lift or safe steps.
Public toilets suitable for walking, disabled visitor.
At least one bedroom suitable for visitor with walking disability with bathroom and toilet facility nearby.

Please use your discretion and telephone the establishments in advance if you require further information.

LOGEZ A l'ENSEIGNE DE L'HOSPITALITE ECOSSAISE

En Ecosse, nous pouvons désormais vous garantir le confort de centaines de logements prêts à vous accueillir.

Plus besoin de vous demander quel hôtel, quelle pension, quel "bed and breakfast" ou quel appartement de vacances vous conviendra le mieux.

Nous venons d'introduire un nouveau système de classification; facile à comprendre, il vous permettra de trouver en un coup d'oeil *exactement* ce que vous cherchez.

En quoi consiste cette *classification*?

La classification générale, qui va de "agréé" (en anglais "listed") à "cinq couronnes" est fondée sur le degré de confort de l'établissement. Ainsi par exemple la classification "agréé" garantit dans les hôtels, pensions et "bed and breakfast" que votre lit est d'une taille convenable (supérieure à un minimum réglementaire), qu'il y a de l'eau chaude et froide en temps voulu, que le petit déjeuner est compris dans le prix de la chambre et qu'elle est bien chauffée (selon la saison).

Dans les appartements de vacances, une couronne représente une unité dont la surface est supérieure à un minimum réglementaire: les vacanciers y disposeront d'au moins une chambre à coucher avec un grand lit ou des lits jumeaux, ils pourront y faire la cuisine et manger confortablement; il y aura également un réfrigérateur.

Bien entendu, plus de couronnes signifient plus de confort. Dans un établissement doté de cinq couronnes, vous trouverez de nombreux éléments supplémentaires destinés à rendre votre séjour encore plus confortable. Deux examples: dans les hôtels à cinq couronnes, *toutes* les chambres ont des salles de bain particulières; et les apartements de vacances à cinq couronnes sont équipés de tout le confort moderne, y compris un lave-vaisselle.

Toutes ces classifications ont été vérifiées par notre équipe d'experts indépendants.

LOGEZ A l'ENSEIGNE DE L'HOSPITALITE ECOSSAISE

Qu'est-ce que la *classification qualitative*?

La première classification ne porte que sur la nature de l'aménagement des logements, tandis que la *classification qualitative* a pour objet leur *qualité*. Les mentions "homologué", "recommandé" et "chaudement recommandé" (en anglais "approved", "commended" et "highly commended") sont fondées sur une évaluation indépendante de toute une série d'éléments, allant de l'apparence du bâtiment et du jardin à la qualité de l'ameublement, des installations et des revêtements de sol. La propreté est une condition indispensable; et nos experts savent également combien compte un accueil chaleureux et souriant.

Tout comme la classification générale, la classification qualitative est effectuée par une équipe d'experts de l'Office du tourisme écossais.
Vous trouverez des logement d'excellente qualité un peu partout en Ecosse, indépendamment des équipements disponibles: par exemple un "bed and breakfast agréé", avec un équipement minimum, mais d'excellente qualité, pourrait se voir décerner la mention "chaudement recommandé" alors qu'un appartement de vacances à cinq couronnes recevra la classification "homologué" si l'on estime moyenne la qualité de ses nombreux équipements.

Alors, comment ce nouveau système vous aide-t-il à préparer vos vacances?
C'est tout simple: il vous offre la garantie du confort fourni et de la qualité de l'accueil. Nous avons inspecté un grand nombre des établissements figurant dans cette brochure et cela est indiqué la liste à la rubrique correspondante. En choisissant un logement qui a fait l'objet d'une classification, ou même des deux classifications, vous avez la garantie qu'il a été examiné par des experts indépendants.
Ce système peut également vous aider si vous faites le tour d'une région et si vous réservez une chambre différente tous les jours. Tous les logements qui ont été examinés sont munis, près de l'entrée, d'un signe ovale bleu qui indique la mention obtenue dans la classification générale et qualitative. Et si vous vous adressez à un bureau de tourisme ("Tourist Information Centre"), vous y obtiendrez une liste des établissements de la région qui sont classés selon ce système. Cette liste contiendra d'ailleurs les établissements qui n'avaient pas encore été examinés au moment où la présente brochure était mise sous presse.
Quel que soit le genre de logement que vous cherchez, ce nouveau système de classification vous aidera à le trouver.
Veuillez noter que lorsque des logements de vacances comprennent plusieurs unités dont la classification générale et qualitative n'est pas uniforme, ils seront accompagnés ci-dessous de l'indication "jusqu'a" (en anglais "up to") et de la mention la plus élevée qu'ils aient obtenue. Il vous faudra vérifier au moment d'effectuer votre réservation la classification exacte de l'unité que vous allez réserver.

ÜBERNACHTEN SIE DORT, WO SIE DAS ZEICHEN FÜR ECHT SCHOTTISCHE GASTLICHKEIT SEHEN

Wir haben dafür gesorgt, daß Sie in Schottland in Hunderten von Hotels, Gästehäusern und Pensionen willkommen geheißen werden.

Jetzt brauchen Sie sich nicht mehr den Kopf darüber zu zerbrechen, welches Hotel, Gästehaus, welche Frühstückspension ("B & B = bed and breakfast) oder welche Unterkunft für Selbstversorger für Sie am geeignetsten ist.

Wir haben ein neues, leicht zu verstehendes Klassifizierungsund Bewertungssystem eingeführt; so können Sie nun auf einen Blick *genau* das finden, was Sie suchen.

Was bedeutet *Klassifizierung*?
Die Klassifizierungen, die von "Listed" (— keine Krone) bis zu fünf Kronen reichen, werden nach dem Angebot der zur Verfügung stehenden Einrichtungen vergeben. In Hotels, Gästehäusern und Frühstückspensionen garantiert Ihnen die Klassifizierung "Listed", daß z.B. Ihr Bett einer Mindestgröße entspricht, daß es zu angemessenen Zeiten warmes und kaltes Wasser gibt, daß ein Frühstück serviert wird, und daß je nach Jahreszeit geheizt wird.

Bei einer Unterkunft für Selbstversorger bedeutet eine Krone, daß die Wohneinheit einer Mindestgröße entspricht und mit mindestens einem Schlafzimmer mit zwei Einzelbetten oder einem Doppelbett und mit einer der Anzahl der Bewohner entsprechenden Eß- und Kochgelegenheit sowie mit einem Kühlschrank ausgestattet ist.

Mehr Kronen bedeutet natürlich mehr Komfort. Ein Haus mit fünf Kronen bietet Ihnen viele zusätzliche Einrichtungen für einen komfortablen Urlaub. Um nur zwei zu nennen: In einem Hotel mit fünf Kronen haben *alle* Zimmer ein angeschlossenes Badezimmer; Wohneinheiten für Selbstversorger mit fünf Kronen sind mit arbeitserleichternden Haushaltseinrichtungen, einschließlich einer Geschirrspülmaschine, ausgestattet.

Alle Klassifizierungen sind von einem vollausgebildeten Team unabhängiger Experten überprüft worden.

ÜBERNACHTEN SIE DORT, WO SIE DAS ZEICHEN FÜR ECHT SCHOTTISCHE GASTLICHKEIT SEHEN

Wie sieht es mit der *Bewertung* aus?

Die Klassifizierung bezieht sich also auf die Einrichtungen, während sich die *Bewertung* ausschließlich mit der *Qualität* dieser Einrichtungen befaßt. Die drei Bewertungen: "Approved" (befriedigend), "Commended" (empfehlenswert) und "Highly Commended" (sehr empfehlenswert) basieren auf eine unabhängige Beurteilung einer Vielzahl von Kriterien, die alles umfassen: vom Aussehen der Gebäude und der Gepflegtheit der Gärten bis hin zur Qualität der Einrichtung, der Installationen und der Fußbodenbeläge. Sauberkeit wird immer vorausgesetzt, und unsere Experten wissen natürlich auch, wie wichtig ein freundliches Lächeln ist.

Die Bewertung wird, wie die Klassifizierung, von dem Expertenteam der schottischen Fremdenverkehrsbehörde durchgeführt.

Sie können bei jeder Art von Unterkunft in Schottland ausgezeichnete Qualität finden, unabhängig davon, welche Einrichtungen angeboten werden: so würde z.B. eine Frühstückspension ohne Krone ("Listed") mit einem Minimum an Einrichtungen, die aber von ausgezeichneter Qualität wären, die Bewertung "Highly Commended" (sehr empfehlenswert) erhalten., während eine Wohneinheit mit fünf Kronen mit "Approved" (befriedigend) bewertet würde, wenn die Qualität ihrer zahlreichen Einrichtungen als durchschnittlich eingeschätzt würde.

Wie hilft Ihnen also dieses neue System bei der Planung Ihres Urlaubs?

Ganz einfach, es garantiert Ihnen sowohl die Einrichtungen als auch deren Qualität. Die von Experten geprüften Häuser wurden in dieser Broschüre gekennzeichnet. Wenn Sie also eine Unterkunft auswählen, die klassifiziert oder klassifiziert *und* bewertet wurde, dann können Sie sicher sein, daß das entsprechende Angebot unabhängig überprüft wurde.

Wenn Sie umherreisen und erst an Ort und Stelle eine Unterkunft buchen, kann Ihnen das neue System ebenfalls helfen. Am Eingang aller bereits geprüften Häuser finden Sie ein unverkennbares blaues, ovales Zeichen, das die Klassifizierung und Bewertung angibt. Und wenn Sie zu einem Fremdenverkehrsbüro gehen, können Sie nach einer Liste der dortigen diesem System angeschlossenen Hotels, Gästehäuser etc. fragen. Auf dieser Liste sind dann auch die Hotels etc. aufgeführt, die zu dem Zeitpunkt, als diese Broschüre in Druck ging, noch nicht geprüft worden waren.

Ganz gleich welche Art von Unterkunft Sie suchen, Sie können sicher sein, daß das neue Klassifizierungs- und Bewertungssystem Ihnen helfen wird, die geeignete Unterkunft zu finden.

Bitte beachten Sie, daß in dieser Broschüre bei der Unterkunft für Selbstversorger immer die höchste Bewertung mit "Up To" (bis zu) angegeben wird, wenn Wohneinheiten mit verschiedenen Klassifizierungen und Bewertungen angeboten werden. Bevor Sie buchen, sollten Sie noch nachfragen, welche Klassifizierung und Bewertung eine bestimmte Wohneinheit erhalten hat.

BRAESIDE GUEST HOUSE

**Kilmore, by Oban, Argyll
Tel: 0631 77 243**

BRAESIDE is a small, friendly Guest House situated in its own grounds with uninterrupted views of Loch Feochan, the Hills of Mullach Ban and Craigmhor, in the Village of Kilmore, 3 miles south of Oban on the A816.

Single, twin double and family rooms, some with private facilities, all on ground floor. H&C, tea and coffee makers, colour TV, central heating in all rooms. Private parking.

Prices from £8.50.

STRONLOSSIT HOTEL

ROY BRIDGE, INVERNESS-SHIRE. 0397 81 253

Stronlossit, situated amidst the most beautiful scenery in the West Highlands, offers comfortable accommodation, excellent cooking and a relaxed atmosphere.

All rooms have H/C water, colour TV and tea and coffee making facilities. Private bathrooms available.

Enjoy our Highland Ceilidhs and Dances held regularly during the Holiday Season. Pony trekking, golf and fishing by arrangement. The hotel features a separate most attractive restaurant offering Haute Cuisine and Traditional Scottish dishes. Lounge bar is open all day with bar snacks and bar meals service.

Situated 12 miles from Fort William and 59 miles from Inverness, Stronlossit is centrally situated for touring the West Highlands.

Guests booking minimum of 4 nights Dinner, B&B, offered a free afternoon tea or a free drink in our lounge bar.

For bookings and information contact: Maurice and Denise Vallely.

Taste of Scotland and Relais Routier Approved   STB Approved

·FREE·FACTORY·TOUR·

An Invitation
to see the art of Glassmaking
SCOTTISH CRYSTAL

Factory open seven days a week. Self-conducted
tours showing the manufacture of crystal.
Video on glassmaking and decoration.
Factory seconds shop open 9am–5pm Monday–
Saturday, 11am–5pm Sundays, (extended hours
during June – September)
Picnic Area. Children's Playground.
Muthill Road, Crieff, Perthshire,

Telephone Crieff (0764) 4004
for further information.

STUART
STRATHEARN

Scotland is beautiful

Litter Spoils It

 Issued by the Scottish Office

CLASSIFICATION AND GRADING OF ACCOMMODATION IN SCOTLAND

NEW FOR 1987

As you travel around Scotland this year, you will see signs that look like this 🏅. These denote the classification and grade of a particular establishment which has been checked out by our trained team of inspectors (see pages vi and vii for details). We hope this new scheme will be of benefit to you when booking accommodation and would welcome your views on it.

Q. Do you have any comments on the classification or grade of any establishment you stayed at?

A.

Thank you for your help.

Please return to:

Department of Verification and Grading
Scottish Tourist Board
23 Ravelston Terrace
Edinburgh EH4 3EU

BOOKS TO HELP YOU

SCOTLAND: WHERE TO STAY HOTELS AND GUEST HOUSES 1987
£4.40 inc p&p

2,000 places to stay in Scotland, ranging from luxury hotels to budget priced guest houses. Details of prices and facilities available. Location maps included. Completely revised each year. Now entries classified and graded. All full colour.

SCOTLAND: WHERE TO STAY BED AND BREAKFAST 1987
£2.80 inc p&p

Over 2,000 bed and breakfast establishments throughout Scotland offering inexpensive accommodation. The perfect way to enjoy a budget trip—and to meet the Scottish people in their own homes. Location maps included. Completely revised each year. Now entries classified and graded.

SCOTLAND: SELF CATERING ACCOMMODATION 1987
£4.50 inc p&p

Over 2,000 cottages, apartments, caravans and chalets—many in scenic areas—which can be rented. Details of prices and facilities available. Location maps included. Completely revised each year. Now entries classified and graded.

SCOTLAND: CAMPING AND CARAVAN PARKS 1987
£2.50 inc p&p

Nearly 400 parks detailed with prices, facilities available and other useful information. Location maps included. Completely revised each year. Entries now graded.

ENJOY SCOTLAND PACK
£5.70 inc p&p

A handy plastic wallet which contains the Scottish Tourist Board's **Touring Map of Scotland** (5 miles to inch) showing historic sites, gardens, museums, walks, beaches, etc together with **Scotland: 1001 Things to See**, which describes and locates these places with details of opening times and admission charges. Map completely revised this year.

SCOTLAND TOURING MAP
£2.70 inc p&p

As above, available separately. Completely revised this year.

SCOTLAND: 1001 THINGS TO SEE
£3.10 inc p&p

As above, available separately.

SCOTLAND: WALKS AND TRAILS
£1.90 inc p&p

A selection of walks over a wide variety of terrain, most of which do not require specialist equipment and are suitable for children.

SCOTLAND: HILLWALKING
£2.10 inc p&p

Detailed descriptions of over 60 more difficult walks and scrambles on hills in different parts of Scotland. Written by an expert.

POSTERS

A series of colourful posters is available, illustrating a wide range of Scotland's attractions for visitors. All posters are available on high quality paper, and the entire range is available with a plastic coating. This makes the posters much harder wearing—no more tears of folds—and gives them an attractive glossy sheen. They represent excellent value for money as a souvenir of Scotland.

Paper posters cost £2.50 inc p&p
Plastic coated cost £3.60 inc p&p

PLEASE ALLOW 21 DAYS FOR DELIVERY

ALL PRICES INCLUDE POSTAGE & PACKAGE

ORDER FORM OVER PAGE

PUBLICATIONS ORDER FORM

Please mark the publications you would like, cut out the complete page and send it with your cheque, postal order (made payable to the Scottish Tourist Board) or credit card details to: **The Scottish Tourist Board, PO Box 15, Edinburgh EH1 1UY.**
For free information/general enquiries only phone: 031-332 2433.

Scotland: Where to Stay Hotels and Guest Houses	**£4.40**	☐
Scotland: Where to Stay Bed and Breakfast	**£2.80**	☐
Scotland: Self-Catering Accommodation	**£4.50**	☐
Scotland: Camping and Caravan Parks	**£2.50**	☐
Enjoy Scotland Pack	**£5.70**	☐
Scotland: Touring Map	**£2.70**	☐
Scotland: 1001 Things to See	**£3.10**	☐
Scotland: Walks and Trails	**£1.90**	☐
Scotland: Hillwalking	**£2.10**	☐

	Plastic Coated £3.60	Paper £2.50
Posters		
Piper (24″ × 34″)	☐	
Edinburgh Castle (24″ × 34″)	☐	☐
Land o' Burns (27″ × 40″)	☐	☐
Isle of Skye (27″ × 40″)	☐	☐
Souvenir Wall Map of Scotland (24″ × 37″)	☐	☐
Highland Cattle (24″ × 34″)	☐	☐
Curling (24″ × 34″)	☐	☐
Scottish Post Boxes (24″ × 34″)	☐	☐
Five Sisters of Kintail (27″ × 40″)	☐	☐
Loch Eilt (24″ × 34″)	☐	☐

BLOCK CAPITALS PLEASE:

NAME (Mr/Mrs/Miss/Ms) _____

ADDRESS _____

_____

POST CODE _____ TELEPHONE NO. _____

SIGNATURE _____ DATE _____

TOTAL REMITTANCE ENCLOSED £ _____

PLEASE CHARGE MY *VISA/ACCESS ACCOUNT   (*delete as appropriate)

| Card No. | | | | | | | | | | | | | | Expiry Date | | | | |

To order BY PHONE ring 0 800 833 993 quoting the items you require and your credit card details.

Please tick for FREE BROCHURES:

Spring ☐   Summer ☐   Autumn ☐   Winter ☐   Ski Holidays ☐